PHILOSOPHY OF ANALOGY AND SYMBOLISM

THE PHILOSOPHY OF ANALOGY AND SYMBOLISM

TABLE A

THE TWELVE FUNDAMENTAL PROCESSES OF PSYCHOLOGY

See Chapter III

II	III	I	Columns / Tiers	
(2)	(3)	(1)	Colours Electrum.	I
(6)	(4)	(5)	Amber	II
(7) (Law)	(8) (Philosophy Ethics)	(9) (Religion)	Consciencious Mind. Purple	III
(11) Directive Association.	(12) Constructive Association. Effort.	(10) Equilibrative Association.	Conative Mind Blue.	IV
(13) Conception of Space	(15) Conception of State. Memory	(14) Conception of Time.	Subjective Mind. Green	V
(16) Individualistic Construction. Agreement.	(17) Hedonistic Construction.	(18) Impulsive Construction. Impulse.	Objective Mind. Yellow.	VI
(20) Immediate Presentation.	(21) Realism. Negation.	(19) Unit Concept.	Instinctive Mind Red.	VII
(24)	(22) (Subconscious Memory)	(23)	Preconscious Mind Brown.	VIII
(25)	(26)	(27)	Subconscious Mind. Grey	IX
(29)	(30)	(28)	Basic Mind. Black.	X

Contents: Wisdoms of East and West; Method of Analysis; Table of Symbolic Numbers; The Three Columns; Application of Principles to History; Astrology; Twelve Processes of the Mind; Logic; Speech; Mystical Philosophy; Creative Hierarchies; The Planets; Mathematics; Geology and Genesis; Speech; Music; Physiology, plus much more!

S.T. Cargill

ISBN 1-56459-586-2

Request our FREE CATALOG of over 1,000
Rare Esoteric Books
Unavailable Elsewhere

Alchemy, Ancient Wisdom, Astronomy, Baconian, Eastern-Thought, Egyptology, Esoteric, Freemasonry, Gnosticism, Hermetic, Magic, Metaphysics, Mysticism, Mystery Schools, Mythology, Occult, Philosophy, Psychology, Pyramids, Qabalah, Religions, Rosicrucian, Science, Spiritual, Symbolism, Tarot, Theosophy, *and many more!*

Kessinger Publishing Company
Montana, U.S.A.

THE PHILOSOPHY OF ANALOGY AND SYMBOLISM

It is a sottish presumption to disdain, and condemn that for false, which unto us seemeth to bear no show of likelihood or truth, which is an ordinary fault in those who persuade themselves to be of more sufficiency than the vulgar sort.

But reason hath taught me that so resolutely to condemn a thing for false and impossible is to assume unto himself the advantage to have the bounds and limits of God's will, and of the power of our common mother Nature tied to his sleeve; and that there is no greater folly in the world than to reduce them to the measure of our capacity and the bounds of our sufficiency.

If we term these things monsters and miracles to which our reason cannot attain, how many such do daily present themselves to our sight? Let us consider through what clouds and how blindfold we are led to the knowledge of most things that pass into our hands; verily we shall find it is rather custom than Science that removeth the strangeness of them from us, and that those things, were they newly presented to us, we should doubtless deem them as much, or more unlikely and incredible than any other.

Extract from *Essay XXVI* by MONTAIGNE

God formed things as they first arose according to forms and numbers. *Timæus*, PLATO.

The world is, through all its departments, a living arithmetic in its development, a realised geometry in its repose. W. ARCHER BUTLER.

CONTENTS

		PAGE
FOREWORD		7

Chapter

I	GENERAL PRINCIPLES	13

Differences between Wisdoms of East and West—Method of Analysis—Analogical Reasoning—Unwieldiness of Modern Knowledge—Difficulties of Presentation—Summary.

II	DESCRIPTION OF METHOD	23

Key Table of Symbolic Numbers—Influences of the Three Columns—The Tiers—12 Principles—Application of Principles to History—Involution and Evolution—Astrology—Summary of Method.

III	APPLICATION OF METHOD	52
	THE TWELVE FUNDAMENTAL PROCESSES OF THE MIND	55
IV	THE FUNDAMENTAL PROCESSES AND THE ANALYSIS OF LOGIC	68
	THE FUNDAMENTAL PROCESSES AND GRAMMATICAL PARTS OF SPEECH	80
V	THE TWELVE FUNDAMENTAL PRINCIPLES OF MYSTICISM	91
VI	MYSTICAL PHILOSOPHY. PRINCIPLES, HEAVENS AND CREATIVE HIERARCHIES	107

12 Principles—Mystical Experiences—Position of Humanity.

VII	THE FUNDAMENTAL PROCESSES AS ILLUSTRATED BY THE GRÆCO-LATIN GODS AND THE SOLAR SYSTEM	130
	THE OUTER PLANETS, THEIR DISTANCES AND NOMENCLATURE	145
VIII	THE PSYCHOLOGY OF MATHEMATICS	147
IX	THE ARTS AND THE FUNDAMENTAL PROCESSES OF THE MIND	159
X	GEOLOGY AND THE GENESIS STORY OF CREATION	173

The Strata—Creative Evolution of Animals—Creative Evolution of Plants—Creative Evolution of Man—The Story of Genesis—Theosophical Commentaries on Gen. i—The Great Pyramid.

XI	ANALYSIS OF STATIONARY ENGINES	192
XII	ANALYSIS OF SPEECH SOUNDS	201
	CLASSIFICATION OF MUSICAL INSTRUMENTS	208
XIII	HANDBOOK OF PHYSIOLOGY, 1950 (*Extracts*)	220
	THE GLANDULAR OR COLLOIDAL SYNDROME	233

LIST OF TABLES

Table		PAGE
A	THE TWELVE FUNDAMENTAL PROCESSES OF PSYCHOLOGY	239
B	ANALYSIS OF LOGIC	240
C	ANALYSIS OF GRAMMATICAL PARTS OF SPEECH	241
D	THE TWELVE FUNDAMENTAL PRINCIPLES OF MYSTICISM	242
E	THE TWELVE PRINCIPLES OF MYSTICAL PHILOSOPHY	243
F	THEOSOPHICAL PLANES AND WORLDS	244
G	HEAVENS AND HIERARCHIES	245
H	PHYSIOLOGICAL SYSTEMS	246
I	ARCHETYPAL PATTERN OF GRAND MAN. HUMAN SKELETON	247
J	GRÆCO-LATIN GODS. PLANETS AND ZODIACAL SIGNS	248
K	THE FIFTEEN BRANCHES OF MATHEMATICS	249
L	THIRTEEN ARTS	250
M	THE PHYSIOLOGICAL SENSES OF MAN	251
N	GEOLOGICAL PERIODS AND STRATA. EVOLUTIONARY	252
O	THE MAJOR GEOLOGICAL REVOLUTIONS	253
P	PRESENT COSMIC DAY. TWO PREPARATORY DAYS AND SEVEN CREATION DAYS	254
Q	CLASSIFICATION OF ANIMALS	255
R	CLASSIFICATION OF PLANTS	256
S	ANALYSIS OF STATIONARY ENGINES	257
T	PHILOLOGY. ANALYSIS OF SPEECH ORGANS	258
U	CLASSIFICATION OF CONSONANTS	259
V	CLASSIFICATION OF VOWELS	260
W	CLASSIFICATION OF MUSICAL INSTRUMENTS	261
X	CLASSIFICATION OF THE ORGANS OF THE ENCEPHALIC AND SPINAL SYSTEMS	262
Y	CORRESPONDENCE BETWEEN THE RUMINANTS AND THE GLANDS OF THE THYROID SYSTEM	263
Z	FRAMEWORK TABLE. SCHEME OF BRANCHES OF KNOWLEDGE	264

FOREWORD

It will hardly be questioned that the motive power behind all scientific investigation during the last few centuries in the Western World has been the rooted conviction that all natural laws must ultimately take their place as constituent elements of one comprehensive scheme of absolute knowledge. Though this belief has usually been but half-articulated it has proved itself to have been sufficiently deep-seated to stimulate men of philosophic minds to formulate ever-widening generalisations throughout the course of the progressive development of the inductive sciences. Within the last century this innate conviction has found expression in various evolutionary theories, designed not merely to explain the origin of the different forms of organic life existing in the world to-day or traceable in fossiliferous strata, but to prove that intellectual and even moral faculties have developed from purely physical functions of consciousness. Although attempts to explain the psychical in terms of the physical are foredoomed to failure yet the very assiduousness with which the search for chains of causation from the material to the immaterial has been prosecuted is evidence of the belief that the physical and metaphysical are cast in the same mould and are amenable to the same fundamental principles of classification.

It is needless to cite as witnesses the metaphysicians who have endeavoured intermittently from Pythagoras and Aristotle onwards to produce a comprehensive scheme of philosophy in which every kind of knowledge should find a niche. Whatever views we may hold as to the crudeness of their reasoning or the venturesomeness of their speculations, we cannot fail to perceive that their efforts were directed towards the same goal as that which the creators of the inductive sciences ever kept in view, the ultimate synthesis of all branches of human knowledge. In spite, however, of the prodigious amount of effort which has been expended in multiplying physical and metaphysical generalisations nothing has hitherto been produced which can establish a claim to be regarded as the philosophy behind philosophies or the science behind sciences.

The possibility of formulating a comprehensive theory of analogy and metaphor has occupied my attention for the past forty-five years, during which time I have made many attempts to tabulate various branches of knowledge in a simple *pro forma* with the object of making them throw light upon each other. It is only, however, within the last fifteen years that I succeeded in devising a *pro forma* which illustrated the fundamental principles on which all branches of knowledge were organisable. Such a *pro forma*, supposing it be capable of doing what I claim for it, must of necessity be archetypal in character, that is to say it constitutes a discovery rather than an invention.

Having settled the columns, tiers and compartments of the *pro forma*, I found that I had elaborated the principles of a philosophy the ramifications of which were endless, and the possibilities of which were incalculable. In more homely language the whole subject threatened to get out of hand because of its vastness. It is, in effect, a form of knowledge which is essentially unique of its kind, and must be treated accordingly. Since no human brain can, at the present time, hope to grasp its full potentialities, I have come to the conclusion that it is better for me to submit it to the judgment of others forthwith, than to spend what might prove to be years in attempting to present it in a form that will satisfy the requirements of the modern scientific mind in the matter of precision, copious references to accepted authorities, and so forth.

I feel somewhat in the position of an explorer who has discovered a hitherto unknown tract of territory, and who is faced with the problem as to whether he should go forward and attempt a complete survey of the country, study its inhabitants, flora and fauna, and prospect for mineral wealth, or whether he should make a general report upon the main features of the country, sufficiently clear and concise to convince the world that it exists in fact and not in his imagination, and then enlist the services of others to carry out in a reasonable period of time investigations which would entail many years of arduous toil for him to complete singlehanded. Under the circumstances the best and most practical policy to pursue is to outline the main features of the unexplored territory into which I have penetrated and attempt to establish a prima facie case, relying upon the public to show a sympathetic understanding of the formidable difficulties which confront anyone who essays the task of synthesising all branches of human knowledge.

The method of reasoning I have adopted is necessarily of the deductive and speculative kind. To deal with such a subject by cautious and tentative generalisations supported by constant appeals to experimentally-proved facts and the authorities for the same, as required by the approved rules of inductive reasoning, would not only necessitate a treatise running into many volumes, but would demand an encyclopædic knowledge of the results of modern scientific research such as no single individual could reasonably hope to attain in a lifetime.

The ideal mode of procedure to adopt would be to publish simultaneously with a deductive treatise, several volumes of experimental data, together with references to authorities supporting the accuracy of the same. I must, however, rest content with enunciating main principles on deductive lines in the hope that their symmetry and prima facie plausibility will arouse sufficient interest for them to be given a careful and searching investigation. It is unfortunately only too true that speculative reasoning is looked upon with a suspicious eye by modern science owing to its association in the past with rash generalisations and even headlong excursions into regions of pure fancy. Moreover, many people are liable to underestimate the debt owed by inductive reasoners to tentative hypotheses of a deductive nature, which they themselves formulated in the course of their investigations. Had they left records of the hypotheses which they tested and discarded before finally achieving success we should be surprised to find the extent to which they used their imaginative faculties. Newton who boasted "hypotheses *non fingo*" made wholesale use of them throughout his scientific career. Speculation to some extent or other is an essential item in the mental equipment of every explorer of nature's secrets. Without it the most patient investigations produce nothing but a barren array of disconnected facts.

Why is it, we may fairly ask ourselves, that speculative reasoning has acquired such a tainted reputation that even those who make free use of it try to cover up their tracks? No doubt it is firstly owing to the fact that inductive reasoning struggled into life as a protest against the shadowy and unsubstantial scientific hypotheses propounded by the ecclesiastical authorities of mediæval and post-mediæval times to be bound up essentially with revealed truth, and therefore to be supported at all cost by the anathematisation of those who questioned their validity. Secondly, it is owing to the danger that every intuitively-perceived generalisation has an inherent attractiveness of its own when first presented to the imagination, which furnishes to the unwary a wholly fallacious guarantee of its truth. The incautious speculator, when rejoicing in a newly-acquired treasure of this kind, turns to the inductive sciences, not to test the soundness of his theory, but to bolster it up at all costs by a judicious selection of all facts that seem to support it, and a no less studious ignoring of all those which contradict it. Thirdly, the deductive reasoner is apt to soar on eagles' wings into the region of vivid mental images, congratulating himself on his escape from the tedious and sluggish methods of the inductive reasoner, only to waste his brain power in philosophical aerobatics.

No doubt I shall be freely charged with falling into the very errors described above, but I claim that my method is one of systematic as opposed to haphazard deductive reasoning, and that it has resulted in the production of a self-contained and comprehensive scheme of classification and generalisation in which every form of knowledge finds a place reserved for it, and in which every section and department is correlated to its fellows by a nexus of interdependent philosophic principles.

At the present time the cult of the specialist is in general favour, but it may well be questioned whether the task of formulating a philosophy of wisdom and knowledge can ever be successfully achieved by anyone who is deeply involved in any particular branch of scientific investigation, or who is an enthusiastic believer in any particular school of scientific or philosophic teaching. By prolonged training along specified lines of thought one's mind becomes cast and set in a definite mould, and only regains plasticity with difficulty. And although mental detachment is more easily preserved in scientific research than in philosophy or religion, nevertheless anyone who, for a number of years, has interpreted all phenomena belonging to some special department of science in accordance with an officialised scheme of reasoning, will only emancipate himself with difficulty from the trammels to which he has submitted. There are, of course, cases in which the convert to some novel theory, whose faith in accepted dogmas has been undermined, will turn upon his former beliefs with a fury intensified by disillusionment, and will evince an unholy joy in rending them to fragments. In such a case the iconoclast usually fails to discriminate between the precious and the vile, and throws on the scrap-heap a great deal of what might profitably be retained. But the more common attitude is the conservative one, in virtue of which men are disposed to hesitate before embarking upon speculations involving a readjustment of habitual processes of investigation, natural inertia of mind being reinforced by sympathetic predilection for familiar paths of reasoning.

If we are to credit the teaching of oriental sages, the mind becomes as highly organised on its own plane by continuous thought along a particular line as the physical apparatus through whose convolutions it expresses itself, and it is no easier to adapt oneself quickly to radical and far-reaching modifications of customary mechanisms of thought than it is for an athlete who has specialised in one particular department of sport to become suddenly expert in another. Consequently the "all round" philosophic thinker, who seeks a middle way between conflicting and often irreconcilable theories, gains in freedom from preconceived ideas and acquired prejudices what he loses in systematic training and first-hand acquaintance with experimental facts. Moreover, such is the complexity of modern scientific teachings and beliefs, that no man can hope to speak with authority on them all, so that whoever sets himself to construct an all-embracing scheme of knowledge will have to pay attention to the criticisms of the specialist in each branch, however extensive his individual investigations may have been. It is high time that more heed was given to the synthesis of knowledge than is the fashion at present, otherwise the time will soon arrive when the tyranny of the specialist will be so firmly established and the differentiation of knowledge will have reached such a degree of ramification that all hopes of welding knowledge into one structure will have to be abandoned as impracticable.

This work is of the nature of an Organon, an instrument of thought, and it has had many predecessors, with or without the label in question. The weak point of most of these is that they lead you up to the transcendental empyrean and leave you there. The specific object of this Organon is to bring the reader down to earth as soon as the fundamental principles have been apprehended by him. An Organon is not something to be polished up and admired as a wonder in itself but something which should be made to do work and useful work at that. This particular one is designed to enable every form of knowledge to be classified archetypally. There is a mathematical word Combinatorial which is applied to a form of analysis which is complete of its kind and takes into account every possible element in the group to which it is applied. If an alleged archetypal analysis does not prove to be combinatorial then it does not merit the name archetypal. Logicians recognise the three modes of Explanatory Generalisation, of which the Classificatory is one, as of value, intrinsically and evidentially, because they may suggest the functioning of new laws given even if they cannot prove them. A perfectly symmetrical and exhaustive scheme of classification bears the stamp of its own soundness and utility upon it, apart from any logical justification. If tested out by the philosophical principles which it embodies it suggests countless new conceptions which would otherwise never present themselves to the mind. It may perhaps be considered that too much attention has been paid to the purely philosophic aspect of the subject-matter of this book but the demonstration has had to be made thoroughly in order to reduce to a minimum the risk of destructive criticism. Not that it would be fair to indulge in hostile criticism at this early stage for the value of the philosophy can only be accurately assessed in accordance with its capacity to accomplish what it claims to be able to, namely, to classify archetypally every form of knowledge hitherto explored by man. It should be given a chance to show its powers as a reagent on a reasonable number of forms before it is brought to judgment, especially in the sciences which require secondary and tertiary analyses as well as primary.

CHAPTER I

GENERAL PRINCIPLES

Differences between Wisdoms of East and West

The Philosophy of Analogy and Symbolism, as expounded in the following pages, should be regarded as a department of a still more comprehensive Philosophy of Wisdom and Knowledge and furthermore as the working mechanism by which the problems of the latter may be solved, analysed and explained. In thinking of the Philosophy of Wisdom and Knowledge we must put out of our minds all notions that the philosophers of the West are in advance of those of the East except in certain branches of analysis. Every generation is apt to imagine that it is far ahead of its predecessors in the matter of enlightenment, however much it may deplore its ignorance in those rare moments in which it exhibits the virtue of humility. Not only does time enter into the estimate which we form of our mental progress but space also, and taking the broadest division, the East and the West treat each other's theories with tolerant superiority and on occasions with openly-expressed contempt. It is impossible to approach the study of Wisdom and Knowledge in a parochial and sectional frame of mind. It must be freely conceded at the outset that every subject upon which millions of human beings have expended vast outputs of thought for innumerable generations must be worth sympathetic study, and any effort to discriminate unfairly in a spirit of sectarian conceit against one or other branch of knowledge, whether in time or space, can only serve to warp the judgment and narrow the outlook.

It is, needless to say, impracticable to try and formulate cut and dried definitions of what is to be understood by wisdom, philosophy, ethics, science, or any other of the subjects included in the Framework Table Z, which gives a bird's-eye view of the matter to be dealt with. For one thing human language does not admit the compression into a few stereotyped phrases of theories which require a hundred or more chapters to elucidate and, for another, rigid definitions adopted at an early stage of philosophic discussions are liable to cramp investigation and encourage adulation of the letter which killeth.

The phrase "Wisdom of the East" comes instinctively to the tip of the tongue when we contemplate the sum total of the lore which the minds of Asiatic sages have evolved. But it cannot be too strongly emphasised that the Wisdom of the East is inseparably bound up with religion of a kind which those learned in the Knowledge of the West are apt to ignore. To the eastern mind religion is a science which deals with the mode by which the Cosmos has been evolved and is now being governed and administered by vast hierarchies of spiritual beings.

"Theosophy" would be substituted for "religion," but for the fact that it is inapplicable to the religion of religions, the Hebrew Faith, and includes in its system many dogmas which orthodox Hebrews have always energetically repudiated. But the Hebrews are at one with all Semitic and East Aryan teachers of religion in regarding it as a science which is concerned with the relations between man and spiritual beings who control his actions to a very large degree. The Hebrews penetrate to the heart of the subject and say in effect "Religion is the science which lays down the conditions under which the Creator consents to co-operate with the creature." But they are primarily concerned with the personality and attributes of Jehovah and only in a secondary degree with the character of the hierarchies whom the Creator employs to effect His purpose. Theosophists, on the other hand, regarded God Himself as too remote to be approached in the manner which the Hebrews lay down as both necessary and practicable, and are far more occupied with understanding and defining the mode in which the hierarchical machinery operates, and the various stages by which the cosmos as we know it has been evolved out of chaos. Religion is therefore the science which teaches us the relationship of man to First Causes, or more accurately it is the practice of such relationships, Wisdom being the systematised knowledge acquired by man in the course of his relationships with first causes. It is impossible, of course, to draw a hard and fast line between theocratic government and ecclesiastical government, but the same may be said of all the "contents" of the various compartments. Wisdom is first and foremost a gift which enables rulers to govern in such a manner as to secure the ends and aims of government, and since no form of civilisation can exist without government, wisdom may fairly be regarded as the parent of all the elements of culture and civilisation, or if not the parent at least the guardian. The object of government is the benefit of the governed, and the modes in which the latter benefit by good government are too numerous to attempt to categorise. But unless government is organised on lines which enable the governed to progress, spiritually, morally, and physically, it becomes a strait-jacket and the reverse of a blessing. Consequently modern framers of constitutions pay particular attention to the organisation of the legislature and the basis of the franchise. The executive and judicial elements in the organisation are usually allowed legislative powers within certain defined limits, so that government is not brought to an entire standstill if the legislature ceases to function temporarily from overwork, but in human polities no legislature can afford to be inactive for long. Therefore, of the three kinds of political wisdom, legislative, executive and judicial, the first is the most important.

Divine government, if acknowledged at all, is regarded by the peoples of the West as a department of religion, and in so far as it is manifested in ecclesiastical organisations it may be considered as coming under that heading, but to many peoples of the East what we should call civil government is also regarded as partly theocratic, or as partaking of a sacrosanct character. The doctrine of the Divine right of kings, which so many of them interpreted as a divine right to misgovern or to govern inefficiently, was a remnant of the theocratic conception of government which found its highest expression in Europe in the Holy Roman Empire.

One of the chief means by which we estimate the wisdom of any particular age is the extent to which the rulers and leaders of the time stabilised political conditions to a point at which knowledge was able to progress and reap the rewards of its labours. Wisdom enables volition to be exercised in such a manner that intellect is free to exert its capabilities without let or hindrance. The height of folly is seen when ecclesiastical rulers such as those who held sway in Italy about three centuries ago, endeavoured to suppress the astronomical theories of Galileo on the ground that they were incompatible with what they conceived to be revealed truth. However much we may be disposed to exalt philosophy, art or science above politics, we must realise that in the absence of political wisdom all three are liable to become fossilised and perish. Wisdom is thus in a sense the guardian of all three. From this it follows that the term Philosophy of Wisdom is as comprehensive a heading as it would be possible to find of a scheme claiming to cover every possible field of human thought and activity.

Method of Analysis

The method by which I propose to analyse the organisation of the Pyramid of Wisdom is one which is unfamiliar to Western minds. It consists in the use of analogies, symbols and metaphors in a manner that constitutes a science of a novel kind, so that the former receive a philosophic value apart from their interest as elements of literary imagery. Hence the title "Philosophy of Analogy and Symbolism" constitutes an apt description of the processes to be worked out in the following chapters, the ultimate object of which is to elucidate the scheme of the analogical and symbolical relationships between all forms of knowledge.

Throughout the book the letterpress will be further explained by Tables which will exhibit in a standard *pro forma* the scheme of each science dealt with. Every analysis is of necessity carried out on the same lines which will be further defined when the construction of the Key Table is dealt with. It contains thirty compartments or spaces of which those from (10) to (21) inclusive will normally be used, those above and below being available for expansion upwards and downwards. Now it is evident that if we superpose, say, the primary Racial Table upon the Skeletal Table we should find that the contents of, say, the two compartments (13) should exhibit certain analogies. In this case (13) is the number of the Alpine Race in the Racial Table and of the upper backbone or dorsal vertebrae in the Skeletal Table, which suggests that we should be justified in inferring that the Alpine race is the backbone of the entire human species, in the sense that it produces institutions of a rigid, articulated and clearly defined nature.

Since the whole work depends upon the tables being so organised as to be capable of superposition in the afore-mentioned manner, subject to certain qualifications, the appropriateness of the title "Philosophy of Analogy and Symbolism" will be apparent. There is, needless to say, little that can be added about the nature and substance of formal logic that is not already familiar to educated people, whereas, on the other hand, the full implications of the Philosophy of Analogy have never been worked out before. Alexander Bain defined genius as the power of seeing analogies, and Professor William James said of the German philosopher Fechner that his great instrument for verifying the daylight view was analogy.[1] There was no limit to the number of analogies that Fechner was able to see, though he does not appear to have created a philosophy of them. But in the words of Professor James, "His most important conclusion is that the constitution of the world is identical throughout."

In order to get a vivid mental picture of the manner in which the philosophy of analogy interacts with the philosophy of wisdom, we need a model in three dimensions in the shape of a cylinder.

We have vertical columns and horizontal tiers in the tables which give a correct symbolic representation of the Philosophy of Analogy, except that the columns should be regarded more as the sides of a pyramid which converge to a point at the apex. It would not, however, be convenient to represent the columns in this manner in the tables for obvious reasons.

I spoke of superposing the tables one upon the other in order to get a picture of the workings of the Philosophy of Analogy, but inasmuch as the tables themselves are vertical, they should be regarded as being placed one behind the other, the most external and objective, such as those which deal with natural sciences, being nearest the reader, while the most internal and spiritual, such as the psychological tables, should be placed furthest away. Now suppose the tables to be folded round so as to make a cylinder, column I being brought adjacent to column II. The tables then resemble the layers of a cylindrical onion, and if we drop lines perpendicular to each compartment, so that all the 1's, 2's, 3's, etc., are strung on to their own perpendiculars, the latter become radii of the cylinder, and intersect at its axis. We thus preserve the conception of reasoning from the outward to the inward, which belongs to the very nature of parable, analogy and metaphor. The resulting model will then be a cylinder, which we can convert in imagination to a truncated cone, if we choose. Reasoning by columns will be inductive or deductive according as we pass from (30) to (1) or (1) to (30) of the Key Table. In reasoning by tiers only we do what the Western mind does habitually and without effort. In reasoning from outward to inward or the reverse along the radii of the cylinder, we do what the Eastern mind does instinctively and without effort. The conjunction of columns I and II, which is obtained by folding the tables backwards, has also symbolical significance, because everything

---

[1] *A Pluralistic Universe* (Lecture on Fechner).

in nature blends. Column III blends with I and II, and the two latter should not be regarded as vanishing laterally into nothingness, but as blending into each other.

ANALOGICAL REASONING

Reasoning by analogy is practised far more by most people than they are aware of. It appeals with special force to those who are artistic by nature, as well as to the uneducated. Christ taught the multitudes who listened to Him almost entirely by parables, and He employed these not merely to illustrate spiritual truths but to indicate spiritual processes. He would take, for instance, some natural process and say in effect to His hearers: "Observe the sequence of cause and effect in this natural process, and you will gain an insight into a corresponding sequence of cause and effect in the mystery kingdom which I am about to establish. For instance, there are tares which resemble wheat so closely that they cannot be distinguished with any certainty from each other until both are fully matured. So in my spiritual kingdom, the Church, there will be upholders of the faith and enemies of the faith whose true character will only be unfolded at the time of the end. Do not anticipate the work of judgment and separation before the time is ripe." If this advice had been taken to heart by the Church, a great deal of heresy-hunting would have been avoided. It would have been quite simple for Christ to have shown the futility of premature heresy-hunting by philosophic and psychological arguments of a strictly logical nature addressed to the intellect, as Paul would doubtless have done under similar circumstances. But He deliberately chose the parabolic method as more suitable to the mental immaturity of His hearers. Doubtless He also foresaw that His advice would be ignored by His followers however He chose to present it. The point of this excursion into the realm of the parable is to show that, if the parable leads to action, its dynamic value is equivalent to that of logical reasoning, and that is what really matters. Similarly if an orator is able to stimulate an audience to action by the use of felicitous metaphors, he can afford to ignore those who rail at logical flaws in his discourse.

We may get a clearer idea of the workings of the Philosophy by considering the analogy of a composite photograph.

The individual tables represent so many stages in the bringing of wisdom down from the snowy heights of esoteric mysticism to the realms of the palpable and objective. If we take a selection of tables and superpose them, we get composite photographs of the contents of whatever compartment we desire to examine. Each compartment will be found to be analogous, in regard to its relationship with its fellows in the same table, to those compartments of other tables which are intersected by the same radius. The outer compartments will be found to furnish an abundance of illuminating metaphors to describe the subject-matter and modes of activity of the inner compartments, so that symbol and antisymbol, type and antitype, the outward and visible form and the inward and invisible principle, will be correlated in a coherent and systematic manner. It should be continuously borne in mind that Eastern peoples greatly prefer analogical to logical reasoning, and that is why so much of their literature fails to appeal to Western minds, except for its poetic phraseology, for they reason radially with such agility that the Western mind totally fails to grasp what they are driving at and gives them up in despair as hopeless mystics. The Eastern mind is far more concerned with tracking principles, that is to say radii, outwards and inwards, and observing the points at which they intersect the various planes of knowledge, than in confining its energies to analysing any one department or table of knowledge. Similarly the Western mind concentrates on each department separately, and illustrates the contents of one by the other solely to express his meaning with vividness and clarity, and without any idea that strictly scientific use may be made of analogy.

During the greater part of this work I shall reason radially, and shall place less reliance on accurate verbal definition or on logical proofs than is usual in Western literature. The ground to be covered is so vast that I must perforce be somewhat elliptic in style and leave much to the common sense of the reader, but this deficiency will be compensated for by constant adherence to tabular analyses.

Needless to say, the mere fact of superposing one table upon another does not necessarily reveal the nature of the radii connecting compartments of the same number and indicate the process by which the inner compartment can be reached from the outer, or vice versa. Otherwise it would be enough to publish a series of tables without any explanatory letterpress. The whole purpose of the work is to train the mind to function in such a manner that the radii are easily followed up, but as the Western mind does not readily work along radii, a considerable degree of mental readjustment will be required before this is done spontaneously and with facility.

In presenting a prima facie case I cannot undertake to follow up the radii from, say, the plane of Energetics to that of Botany in detail. For one thing, the science of Energetics, as developed hitherto, does not lend itself readily to representation in tabular form, so that the starting points of the radii must of necessity be obscure under existing conditions. It is bound to be a case of *festina lente* in adjusting the mind to work along novel and untried paths, and there is no royal road to an encyclopædic knowledge of the mysteries of Nature.

There is one mode of reasoning which points with cogency to the universal applicability of the principles of systematic analogy on the lines which I have indicated, and that is connected with the undoubted fact that the various planes of knowledge shade into one another like the colours of the spectrum. If, therefore, each plane were organised on different principles we should expect sharp differences to manifest themselves between adjoining planes. We have, for instance, as the outer layer of the "cylinder" the plane of Energetics, which deals with statics, dynamics, physics, inorganic chemistry and electricity. Then we have the planes of Botany, Zoology, Physiology and innumerable others associated with them. In all these we find the same fundamental forces in action, though often metamorphosed so as to be recognisable with difficulty.

The Plant Kingdom makes use of the primary forces of the plane of Energetics to build up its characteristic forms, and the functions of the Animal Kingdom are for the most part adumbrated in a somewhat simpler fashion by those of the Plant Kingdom.

The physiology of the animal kingdom is substantially identical with that of man, who is nothing but a highly developed animal in so far as the functions of his body are concerned. And when we come to the study of Psychology, particularly in regard to what are known as the endocrine temperaments, that is temperamental abnormalities resulting from over- or under-active states of internally secreting glands, we begin to link up the body and the soul, while the study of the functions of the brain is concerned with the mind as much as with that of the grey matter. So closely are mind, feeling and other forms of consciousness united to the physical vehicles through which they operate, and so greatly do the sciences which deal with mind and matter tend to overlap, that the probabilities are overwhelmingly in favour of their being organisable on one general model.

Again, the development of language depends upon the fact that the laws of the mind are analogous in their modes of operation to those which regulate matter, otherwise it would be impossible to use words descriptive of natural processes or objects to symbolise mental concepts. There would be so much disharmony that language-builders would find themselves entangled at every point by contradictions. On the contrary, we are able to trace the growth of languages from mere vocabularies of names signifying material forms and processes to highly evolved speeches which are capable, like Sanscrit, Greek and German, of expressing the most subtle shades of philosophic meaning. But for the operation of the third great unity of method in conjunction with the other two unities, human speech would perforce remain rudimentary and onomatopoeic.

The reader is asked, therefore, to accept the following proposition provisionally, assuming that he has not already convinced himself of its truth, that the collected phenomena of the universe, from the most subtle and refined to the most objective and materialistic, from the most spiritual to the most gross, are capable of being classified on one archetypal system or model, which brings out the inner meaning and significance of such phenomena as no merely arbitrary schemes, differing for each separate department of knowledge, can possibly do. In other words, classification, so far from being merely dependent upon individual convenience and taste, is in itself the science of sciences.

It may perhaps be objected that no scheme of classification, however fundamentally sound and correct, can aspire to the title of a philosophy. This may be readily conceded, but it is a necessary antecedent to the creation of a universal philosophy, using the term not so much to describe logical processes of thought as to indicate methods of mental illumination, which bring out the inner meaning and significance of every branch of knowledge. Philosophy, in its widest signification, includes all mental processes by which the mysteries lurking behind the simplest phenomena are dragged from their lairs and compelled to give account of themselves. The most abstruse philosophical principles are often most easily grasped by an attentive contemplation of the commonplace and the seemingly obvious.

The object of that particular branch of philosophy which I call the "Philosophy of Analogy," is to make symbolism a precise and readily definable form of knowledge, with its own laws, axioms and postulates, instead of being as at present a mere matter of instinctive fancy or mystical perception. The philosophy of analogy is, of course, implicitly contained in human language, but in a subtle and elusive form. It is the purpose of this work to prove that analogous modes of activity on different planes or spheres have far more in common with each other than is commonly believed, and that analogies, which are ordinarily used simply for purposes of illustration and word painting, may be pushed very much further than is usually supposed, so that they have a positive scientific value and use. The dangers of pushing analogies too far is emphasised by most authorities on ratiocination, but if analogies cannot be pushed to the limit there is usually something faulty about them, the features which suggest the analogy being in such cases more apparent than real.

Western reasoners confine themselves to the analysis of each plane of knowledge on its merits, and when analogies are perceived between phenomena on two contiguous planes, they are simply used to emphasise or elucidate meaning, but in no way to prove the operation of similar laws. Eastern reasoners, on the other hand, assume the operation of such laws. For them a planet, such as Saturn, connotes a vast network of influences working according to law which interpenetrates every department of nature. All Eastern peoples, as already mentioned, tend to reason radially by the very nature of their mental constitution, and hence their languages are prolific of symbolism and imagery. The Eastern mind is for ever attempting to describe the "radial" principles which intersect the planes of knowledge, but gets lost in a maze of mysticism simply because it has never done sufficient inductive reasoning on each plane, considered independently, this being especially the case with the external physical planes.

When Western thinkers, such as the alchemists of the middle ages, commenced the systematic investigation of objective phenomena, they naturally inclined to the Eastern mode of viewing the universe, especially as the prestige of astrology stood very high in those times. Thus Mercury or Venus would conjure up before their minds a definite principle or mode of activity, an influence or motive force, which found expression on every plane of knowledge. What we rightly regard nowadays as proper methods of scientific investigation were almost entirely neglected.

Unwieldiness of Modern Knowledge

With the mental revolution usually described as the Renaissance, inductive methods of reasoning became more popular, but it was not until the philosophic activity of the eighteenth century and the industrial revolution of the early part of the nineteenth had made their mark on the world that inductive science began to make strides. From that time onwards science and industry have advanced hand in hand, industry supplying the demand for science that desire for social amelioration did for art during the Renaissance.

Now the progress of science has tended towards specialisation and differentiation rather than generalisation, and so vast is the material that has accrued as the result of observation, classification and experimental research, that no single individual, whatever his brain capacity, can hope to grasp the whole tree of knowledge, or even a single branch. A man is, indeed, fortunate if, during the course of a lifetime, he can become a recognised expert on a single twig. While brilliant generalisations are made and accepted from time to time, yet, on the whole, science and knowledge are becoming yearly more unwieldy and unmanageable. We have fallen to a large extent under the tyranny of the expert, who is apt to pour scorn upon generalisations attempted by anyone who is not also a recognised expert in the same line as himself. It lies within the province of the Philosophy of Analogy to counteract this unwieldiness and decentralisation before it reaches a stage when remedial measures will be impossible. The work of the "scientific symbolist" need in no way clash with that of the expert and specialist. The symbolist will undoubtedly require a fairly thick skin, but if he is honest and submits with good humour to be called a jack-of-all-trades and master of none, he will in due course find himself admitted to the ranks of orthodox explorers in the realms of science and knowledge, and recognised as an essential cog in the machine of research. The symbolist must take account of the psychological element in the situation, and realise that he cannot hope to establish himself as an important contributor to the sum total of human mental achievements without doing his share of hard work. Any premature posing as an expert in his own line will only engender antagonism among the experts and specialists who hold the field at present, and make them inclined to scoff at him as an amateur.

Difficulties of Presentation

The peculiar difficulties which have to be encountered in establishing a prima facie case for any such philosophic scheme as I have adumbrated, should be clearly recognised by the reader to start with. Using the term "table" to describe a "plane" of knowledge organised in accordance with the principles I have outlined, one is continually requiring to refer to completed but unproved tables in order to illustrate and prove one's theses in regard to the particular table under review. It is obviously impossible to complete more than one table at a time, so that the other tables used must be accepted provisionally by the reader as correct until they also have been analysed in detail. To attempt an exhaustive treatment of even a single plane in this work would swell the subject-matter to such dimensions that the cost of publication would be prohibitive. The only practicable way of handling such a novel and complex subject is to issue a series of commentaries on various sciences and branches of knowledge after the main philosophic principles have been fixed. For although generalisations on the lines I have sketched out are unconsciously used in everyday speech, particularly when illustrative analogies are made frequent use of, yet the scientific and systematic enunciation of the principles of symbolic exposition is both novel and complex.

In short, in undertaking pioneering work of this sort, I feel I can justly claim a certain amount of indulgence from the reader, and that I should not be called upon to reason according to the severely logical principles which admittedly cannot be dispensed with in dealing with the more exact of the inductive sciences.

Summary

The Philosophy of Analogy and Symbolism is essentially one which obtains results by tabulation. Correct classification of ideas is the prerequisite for clarity of thought. If a man can put down his ideas in tabular form he may not be deemed an infallible or even a reliable thinker on that account, but he will almost certainly be deemed a clear-headed thinker. The system here presented enables the headings of the most difficult subjects to be assessed as primary or secondary in importance, to be arranged in proper sequence, either involuntary or evolutionary. It will show up those which are redundant and indicate the nature of headings which cannot be omitted without impairing the structural equilibrium of the whole subject. Furthermore it enables the subject under analysis to be compared with numerous others which have been classified on similar principles with a view to extracting the utmost value from analogical resemblances and differences, which, in the absence of scientific treatment, can only be utilised in a haphazard fashion or in accordance with individual fancy. The system has enabled what is a virtually a new science to be created, that is the philosophy of national and racial characteristics which cannot fail to have a profound effect upon ethnological problems. It has also enabled a series of historical cycles to be recognised which throw light upon the future to an extent which only becomes realisable when the inevitability of the sequence of such cycles is appreciated.

CHAPTER II

DESCRIPTION OF METHOD

Key Table of Symbolic Numbers

THE table of symbolic numbers, I, is the key table to all the others, and must therefore be analysed in detail, as it contains implicitly all the principles which will be developed and applied throughout the book. First of all, it is clear that we must have some convenient symbols to describe the radial principles which intersect the compartments of the various tables and connect them to their respective partners. Such symbols should be as non-committal as possible and at the same time of the most highly generalised nature. Even the use of the signs of the Zodiac which, for the Eastern mind, represent abstract and cosmic principles, would unduly limit the scope of inquiry. Symbols should at the same time be significant, and not mere identification marks, such as letters of the alphabet. Numbers fulfil these conditions better than any other symbol, and have, therefore, been adopted.

At the same time I do not propose to enter at present into the question of occult numerology, and the reader is quite at liberty to regard the numbers as mere identification marks for the radii until such a time as he sees for himself that there is an actual philosophic significance in the numbers themselves. In other words, I might have sprinkled the numbers about haphazard without completely invalidating the general scheme, but, since numerals have to be employed, it is as well to utilise them in such a manner as to bring out their own inherent meaning.

The Tables are divided up into vertical columns and horizontal tiers and their intersections produce rectangular spaces which may be called compartments. The "contents" of any one compartment should be regarded as contributing to the integrated meaning of the radius which passes through it at right angles, that is to say, of the principles, characteristics, qualities, modes of activity and dynamic urges which are connected with the latter and which constitute its identifying mark or seal, to use a Gnostic term. The columns are three in number and their identifying Roman numerals have a definite symbolic value. It will be observed that the numbers of the three top compartments correspond with those of the columns. The influences of the columns should be regarded as extending from top to bottom of the Key Table, the upper regions being metaphysical and ethereal and the lower physical and materialistic. The tiers are also indicated by Roman numerals, and these likewise have a specific symbolic value. This is utilised in practice by expanding or contracting tables by converting compartments into tiers of the same numeration or vice versa. Another relationship of considerable significance is provided by numbers belonging to the same series. Every third number belongs to the same series as the first, that is to say (1), (4), (7), (10), (13), etc., belong to the same series. Every third series number is also an equivalent or harmonic number.

Equivalence in numeration is a very important principle and finds expression in the fact that the numerals in every tier are equivalent in symbolic value to those three tiers higher up or lower down. Thus (1) and (19) are equivalent to (10), (2) and (20) are equivalent to (11) and so on. Equivalent numbers may be called harmonics of each other. Any two compartments of equivalent numbers will be found to have contents which bear a marked resemblance to each other, making due allowance for the fact that the upper are refined in character and the lower relatively coarse. Equivalence in numeration may be recognised by the fact that the sum of the component digits is the same. The process of finding the lowest equivalent value of a number is called occult reduction. This reduction as applied to the past year 1945 gives us 19, 10 and 1, which is significant as pointing to the commencement of a New Era, for better or worse. The principle of harmonic numbers may also be extended to tiers, every fourth tier being a harmonic of 1, and so on downwards.

It will be evident from the foregoing that the term radius has a fairly precise meaning since each has its own number, there being 30 in all provided for in the existing scheme, though theoretically no limitation can be placed on the totality of radii. The integrated significance of a radius or number, say (10), is obtained by studying the meanings of (10) in a selected number of important tables ranging from the material to the metaphysical. The Egyptian Tarot Cards have preserved the symbolic meaning of the numbers (1) to (22) fairly accurately but the best information on the subject is given in a booklet called *Number, Name and Colour*, by O. Hashnu Hara. Thus we see that the contents of every compartment are subject to four influences, those of its radius, its column, its tier, and its series number. The last three correlate its contents with those of other compartments. If it be objected that the scheme here propounded is complicated it may be replied that if the scheme on which the phenomena of the cosmos is ordered were not complicated it would have been discovered long ago. The complexity is not, however, of such a character as to defy unravelling, but nicety of judgment is required in assessing the comparative value of the influences of radius, column, tier and series. The net result of organising all departments of knowledge on this basis is that a great deal of information is obtainable as to the relationship between phenomena belonging to one and the same plane, which cannot fail to be of great scientific value, to say nothing of the information obtainable by comparing analogous compartments belonging to the same radius. One is taken, so to speak, behind the scenes of nature, and enabled to observe her methods and processes of action in a manner that is quite impracticable by any other means. It becomes possible to penetrate right to the heart of every subject to which the scheme is applied with the minimum of trouble and delay, as will be evident as we proceed. When anyone sets out to learn a new language he does not expect to find the grammar and syntax so simple that he is able to master both in a few days or even weeks. In like manner the reader must be prepared to study the nature of the four influences if he seeks to penetrate to the heart of the Philosophy of Analogy. But there is no need for him to do this in order to understand a good deal about the Tables and he can learn much from their exhaustiveness and completeness and the light which they throw upon the structure of the sciences with which they deal, as, for instance, in Botany, Zoology, and Physiology. In fact, there are many tables in which the application of one or more of the four influences is obscure though enough evidence exists to prove their general soundness.

The key table, and all those tables which are constructed on the same principle, constitute a language in themselves, and speak an idiom of their own. One of the greatest difficulties in introducing a new philosophy or science is the fixation of a terminology which everyone shall be able to interpret in the sense desired by the introducer. This often entails considerable labour on the part of both author and reader, the latter being obliged to learn up what approximates almost to a foreign language. For instance, it took western theosophists several decades to agree upon the precise meaning to be attached to such a term as "etheric body." The analysis of knowledge in tabular form obviates to a large extent the creation of a new terminology, which in the present case would have to be very extensive. When taking words which already have a complex technical meaning, and putting them to new uses, the creator of a vocabulary has not merely the labour of defining the precise meaning which he attaches to each new word, but the reader has the labour of divesting his mind of many meanings which he has already attached to the word as the result of perusing other works in which it may have been employed.

It is evident that any scheme which claims to be applicable to human knowledge as a whole must be extremely elastic. The one mistake that must be avoided at all costs is to try to put knowledge into a straitwaistcoat, and to attempt to crystallise it out into a number of arbitrary definitions. In fact, any system which was not elastic would, *ipso facto*, stand self-condemned. Whatever its merits might be, it could never aspire to the title of archetypal. A very fair degree of elasticity in classification is obtainable by the methods already described, but the analysis of any one department of knowledge may be carried to any degree of minuteness required by the means of secondary, tertiary, or quaternary analyses. Examples of these will be found in the Zoological and Ethnological Tables.[1] For instance, a primary analysis of the animal kingdom of nature places the greater land mammals in compartment (10). A secondary analysis of the greater land mammals places the ruminants in compartment (13). And a tertiary analysis of the ruminants places the antelope in

[1] To be published in due course.

compartment (11). Which means that in assessing the characteristics of the antelope the influences of compartments (10), (13) and (11) have to be taken into account. All this sounds very formidable, but a great deal of the mental work entailed is done instinctively by zoologists, and it only sounds formidable because it is systematised and defined.

It is often convenient to make a semi-secondary analysis of a compartment, that is either into columns or tiers, without going to the length of dividing it up in nine sub-compartments. It will be readily appreciated that the terms primary or secondary analysis are relative and not absolute. For instance, the Ethnological Table gives a primary analysis of the human race, but if we construct a table in which all kinds of beings are represented, a primary analysis of the human race becomes a secondary in relationship to the more comprehensive classification. Secondary analyses may be superposed upon primary analyses in order to get composite effects, simply because they both consist of numbered compartments, and so a number (7), for instance, may always be placed perpendicularly over any other number (7), whatever be the degree of minuteness to which the analysis may be carried out, whether primary, secondary, or tertiary. To get a complete picture of the diagrammatic significance of a table, it should be regarded as being capable of folding round so that column II aligns itself with column I. As an alternative three tables of the same denominative number may be regarded as being placed side by side, and this would preserve the flatness of the tables. The purpose of this manipulation is to indicate that the columns shade into one another laterally, and this must be borne in mind especially when looking at the Table of Character Analysis, which will be published later on.

The Influences of the Three Columns

It is of paramount importance to get a clear conception of the influences of the three columns, and the only way to secure this is to observe the working of the influences in nature, beginning with the most palpable and external, and working gradually upwards towards the internal and universal. Let us start, therefore, by seeing how the columns manifest their activities in the energetics of the inorganic world, that is in mechanics, physics, chemistry, and electro-magnetism.

Every phenomenon of the world of energetics is due either to bound energy, free energy, or property energy, which operate in each of the three tiers of gravific energy, thermo-elastic energy, and electro-chemical energy. The influences of columns III, I, and II, are seen in bound, free, and property energy, respectively. I use the word "bound" here in a technical sense, and not as generally understood. It might, perhaps be better to coin some new word to describe this kind of energy, but the word "bound energy" describes so exactly what I wish to convey that I have no choice but to give it an arbitrary signification. Matter in this world is not inert. Every particle of matter tends to attract or bind itself to other particles by means of cohesive force. Now in the case of free energy we invariably postulate

DESCRIPTION OF METHOD

the existence of energy whenever we see force exerted, that is to say when it is clearly exerted by energy which is transferable and capable of doing work. Hence when we see matter exerting force of an attractive kind we are justified in inferring the existence of energy which is indissolubly bound up with matter, and which, for all we know, may actually be matter, so that there may possibly be no other kind of matter except bound energy. Matter or stuff is, however, too useful a conception to be readily discarded. It gives us a sense of stability which is too precious to be sacrificed.

Bound energy is divided into two kinds, which we may call attractive and cohesive. In the case of mechanics, using the word in its widest possible signification, attractive energy gives rise to the forces of gravitation or gravity. Both are one and the same force, except that we use the former term to describe pulls between heavenly bodies, and the latter to describe pulls between the earth, acting from its centre of gravity, and bodies on the surface of the earth. Both are due to the presence of bound gravific energy in matter manifesting as gravific force. Cohesion, unlike gravity, only operates at short distances. Mechanical cohesion causes particles of matter to adhere to one another.

Free energy is likewise divisible into potential and kinetic, in which forms it may be stored up by matter without doing work. We are usually able to get at a proportion of this free energy to make it work for us, but there is a great deal of it which is beyond our grasp. This does not, however, make it bound energy, because theoretically we ought to be able to get at it under suitable conditions, that is, by providing a fall of potential.

The most important form of free energy for the purposes of this exposition is anti-gravific energy, which should on no account be confused with gravific energy. If we lift a body through x feet, we put a certain amount of anti-gravific or free mechanical energy into it, which is measured by the product of the weight of the body and the distance through which we raise it. We can get nearly all this free energy back for useful work if we allow the same body to fall x feet. When it reaches the ground, however, we can get no further work out of it. If, however, we drop it down the shaft of a coal mine y feet deep, we can get more free energy out of it, measured by the product of the weight and y feet. To get this body back to the earth's surface we must put back into the body the same amount of free mechanical energy that it sacrificed as the result of its fall.

The trouble about identifying energy of property is not that it is so rare but that it is so common. Wherever there is property there is energy of property. And since every object in nature possesses many properties it must needs possess many kinds of specific energy. The quantity of specific energy of any particular kind that a body possesses determines its specific properties, that is to say, the specific equilibria which define these properties mathematically. Here we reach the fringe of a vast subject, which is almost virgin soil. Density, hardness, elasticity, solubility, state, colour, properties of the elements, electro-positiveness or electro-negativeness, are all examples of the operation of specific energies. We measure and define them by reference to standard equilibria provided by the interaction of specific and bound energies, from which we obtain our units of measurement.

There is doubtless a great deal in the foregoing which is new and controversial, but it is impossible to explain the modes by which the influences of the columns operate without covering a good deal of debatable ground. The whole subject will be examined fully in dealing with the analysis and tabulation of Energetics.

Comparing the three forms of energy with other triads, it is clear that free energy is dynamic in the full sense of the term, bound energy is static, and specific energy semi-dynamic. Matter is unquestionably static in its essence but it can appear to act dynamically when disrupted by an overplus of free energy as in the case of an earthquake or explosion. Specific energy can be transferred, otherwise the properties of matter would remain invariable under all conditions and change of state would be impossible, for the latter affects the cohesions between molecules.

In the case of the triad of time, space, and state it is obvious that static corresponds with state, for the former is an adjective formed from the latter. Space is clearly not as dynamic as time, for time flies but space stays where it is. If we think of a mountain torrent rushing down a gorge we have a picture of the movement of free energy along an electric conductor. Now if the torrent suddenly debouches on to a plain, spreads out and gets lost in sandy wastes, as do Abana and Pharpar, rivers of Damascus, then we have a picture of the dynamic being converted as it were into the semi-dynamic, for the water spreads and moves slowly forward over a wide area and when it soaks into the sand it becomes wholly static. We have a similar association with the three so-called dimensions of time, past, future, and present. What is past is finished and done with and plays its part in forming memories, which are fundamentally static. The future is the dimension which most clearly reveals the true nature of time which derives its supreme interest from the fact that it seems to be travelling to an unknown goal. Time is associated with life for most men look forward to living to a ripe old age. The present has the element of simultaneity which is characteristic of space. As regards the dimensions of space, matter or bound energy, enables free energy to be stored up as potential energy which in turn is associated with height in respect of matter, as seen in a water-tower which gives the needful head to a water-supply system. Length is invariably associated with time, for future, present, and past can be represented by one straight line running longitudinally and divided at one point which we think of as the present. Breadth may be thought of as lying horizontally across the time-line where it is bisected, and in this case it suggests simultaneity of events in time which brings us to the space condition. Many other triads of a similar nature can be cited, taking the order I, II, III, such as tensions, resolvents, and complexes in nervous conditions; passions, emotions, and desires in the classification of feelings; education, art, and religion in the cultural sphere. The mystical triads are numerous, the Three Great Logoi; Shiva, Vishnu, and Brahma; the attributes of the Logoi, Power, Wisdom, and Activity; Cardinal or Rajasic, Mutable or Sattvic, and Fixed or Tamasic; the Mental, the Motive, and the Vital, and so on. The Key Table shows progress from right to left or east to west, the assumption being that the observer stands facing north and writes as the Hebrews do. But it is, of course, legitimate to construct a Key Table on the assumption that the observer is facing south, in which case he reckons progress as from left to right and his script naturally runs in the same direction.

Certain difficulties have to be encountered in distributing the triads so as to agree item for item, for the influences of the columns are determined by the numbers (4), (5), and (6) in tier II and its lower harmonics. These are emphatically the numbers of State, Time, and Space but in some triads the other two tiers I and III make their own arrangements, so to speak, creating the complications which are the despair of every student of mystical philosophy. For instance, the identification of Tamas with (13), Rajas with (14), and Sattva with (15) does not preclude the identification of these with (10), (11) and (12) which belong to the same series. (10) corresponds with the point within the circle which sets forth Potentiality, a form of Tamas. (11) corresponds with the radius or radii, a form of Rajas. The obvious method of filling up the space within the circle to form a bi-dimensional surface is to vibrate the radii like a metronome but this is regarded as a vibration of Rajas, and instead the surface is created by the expansion of circles from the centre such as are formed when one throws a stone into a pond. This is called the 1st form of Sattva (12). To be logical the 2nd form of Sattva should be the expansion of globes from the central point but actually this form appears to be visualised as the revolution on its vertical axis of a vertical circular plane which thus produces a globe or sphere and merges into the Tamas of (13) by reason of the gyrostatic balance which it represents and which illustrates its essential nature. Another important triad is composed of Unity, Diversity, and Totality. Finally, we have the Three Gunas corresponding with (4), (5), or (6), or (13), (14), and (15); Sat, unification a centripetal force; Chit, mental activity; and Ananda, happiness and peace.

The symbolism of the three dimensions of space has always intrigued philosophers and Ouspensky has much to say on the subject in his *Tertium Organum*. He regards the line as corresponding with Sensation (Realism (21), the plane as corresponding with Perception (20), and the solid as corresponding with the Concept (19). But whatever be the validity of his conclusions as regards tier VII there is no question that the general influence of the columns as originating from (4), (5), and (6) is Col. I—Unidimensional, Col. II—Bidimensional, and Col. III—Tridimensional, on the assumption that the three co-ordinates of space are taken as lines, and not as planes in the original Cartesian sense. Whatever be the dimensions of abstract space there is no doubt that matter, mass, and the state of both are tridimensional and that we derive our conception of the material from the solid, which has three dimensions. There can be no question, however, that space as we sense it as a rule is bidimensional. For the eye, which is the chief sense organ by which we perceive spatial relationships, views its environment as a bidimensional panorama and the sky as the inside surface of an inverted bowl. When a man who has been blind from birth recovers his sight he sees his surroundings and the objects composing it as if they were on a dead flat plane without any stereoscopic effects. It is only by dint of practice that he learns to distinguish perspective effects and how to estimate the distance and solidity of objects which he perceives. The same applies to the arts of photography, cinematography, and the stage, all of which are visualised pictorially. Similarly we can only smell and touch the surfaces of solid objects and liquids. Time, on the other hand, is undimensional by common consent and concepts arise into consciousness in a determined time-sequence before they can be memorised. Hinton quite justifiably takes the time line, which is longitudinal, as the base dimension of a Cartesian plane and regards the vertical dimension as a symbol of eternity in time. But in that case we are justified in regarding the vertical dimension of the transverse line as representing the eternal now. We must also remember that although we think of leaving the past behind us, the archæologist thinks of it as beneath his feet and conceives of himself as standing on a flat plane which is moving vertically upwards, so that the debris of the past form successive strata. In this case the past can only include what has been and not also what might have been, as Ouspensky teaches.

A valuable and instructive work by E. L. Gardner, called *The Web of the Universe*, throws considerable light upon the tridimensional character of the central column III, which was numbered thus in order to bring out the nature of its influence, as were the other two columns. The following remarks should not, however, be regarded as an exposition of the views of the author, but rather as an application of his principles and a recognition of their value. If Table G is referred to it will be seen that the central column includes the 7th, 6th, and 2nd Heavens, all three of which have a formal and architectural character. The corresponding arts are architecture, mosaic, and sculpture which are represented by monuments and memorials of an enduring character (Table L). Now the tridimensional web is a columnar framework resembling the steel-girder framework of a concrete sky-scraper or the space-lattice of crystallography, and can be seen clairvoyantly in the Lower Mental Plane as composed of fine threads. These are affected by three modes of motion, a vortical which is characteristic of III, a vibrational which is characteristic of I, and a linear and ramifying which is characteristic of II. Mr. Gardner does not state specifically how high the web extends, but it serves to clarify one's mental picture if its upper and lower limits are marked by tiers IV and VII respectively. The vibrational force of column I is the basis of the rhythmic movements that control the brain functions, and appear in respiration and the peristaltic movements of the intestines (Table H). The linear and ramifying force of II is exemplified in the nerves of the cerebro-spinal system, the arteries and veins, and the lymphatics which all have a distributive character. The general form of the body is controlled or conditioned by the muscular-osseous system, the thyroid, and the liver, the third being chiefly concerned with growth. Mr. Gardner denies that there is any fourth dimension but says that the three dimensions can be and are viewed in the Mental and Astral Worlds in such a way as to produce the illusion of a fourth dimension. It is suggested that the dimension of breadth as viewed in these worlds creates a spatial illusion, for the panoramic sense of vision perceives all objects as on a vertical two-dimensional plane parallel to the dimension of breadth. The illusion of the fifth dimension in the region of universal consciousness, the Buddhic and the Nirvanic worlds, may be produced by the mode of viewing the dimensions of breadth and length, and the illusion of the sixth dimension in the region of cosmic consciousness, the two highest worlds of the Pleroma, may be produced by the mode of viewing the three dimensions of breadth, length, and height. These conceptions render superfluous brain-cracking efforts to imagine a fourth dimension in space and seeking to correlate it with a time dimension. Time and space are fundamental conditions of conscious existence which should no more be confused with each other than either should be confused with matter. The particular mode of viewing the dimension of breadth in the Mental and Astral Worlds, the spheres of racial, national, and tribal consciousness, may be understood as an enlarged stereoscopic effect. We do not view the world from a single point but from two points which are as far apart as the pupils of the eyes, and the impressions which we get through both organs are simultaneous. Let us imagine these points to be separated much further apart and we can then understand how the greatly increased stereoscopic vision of the Mental and Astral Worlds is obtained. It may be that the breadth line can be curved concavely so as to surround more effectively an object which it is desired to examine. Now if one views in imagination the dimension of length in the region of universal consciousness in such a manner as to be able to visualise points far ahead and far behind the point immediately opposite which represents the present, one can then see how prophetic time-consciousness is possible, for the cause which lies in the past, and the method of operation which lies in the present, and the effect which lies in the future can then be made to coalesce and the future can then be discerned up to a point with almost the same clarity as the present. If the dimension of height could be viewed in the region of cosmic consciousness on similar lines then we would be able to obtain a much clearer conception than we can possibly have at present of the spiritual state and the spiritual height or majesty of the Godhead. The condition in which the Godhead exists may be described as one of eternal state for there is no variableness with God neither shadow cast by turning, for He is the same, yesterday, to-day, and forever, the I AM THAT I WILL TO BE, though this would not impede HIM from progressing forward.

THE TIERS

The tiers are not so easy to classify as the columns in terms which are applicable to all sciences but there is an obvious descent from the ethereal and refined to the gross and materialistic in their arrangement. Since we shall normally adhere to a 12-compartment group in carrying out the analysis of most of the sciences, this means making use of four tiers, and there are good reasons for working from IV to VII inclusive, as this allows for expansion upwards and downwards. The four principles or modes in which matter subsists of etheric, airy, watery, and earthy correspond with these tiers, together with their psychological equivalents of will, imagination, reason, and affection, which are symbolised by the lion, the eagle, the man, and the ox of the Cherubim. The associated points of the compass are East, West, South, and North. The will and the imagination in this arrangement are subjective while the reason and the affections are objective. The corresponding colours are blue, green, yellow, and red which correlate tiers IV to VII with the visible spectrum. Tier III which corresponds to the three shades of red-blue, indigo, purple, and violet must also be placed in the visible spectrum. Psychologically the four tiers correspond to the spirit or will, the higher or spiritual mind which is imaginative; the lower or carnal mind, otherwise the animal soul which is practical and rational; and the etheric and physical bodies which are physical and are the seats of the instincts. But it must be clear from the very nature of the foregoing catalogue of tetrads that there are many sciences to which they cannot be applied. In the domain of the physical sciences we have a fourfold group of gravitation, thermo-luminosity, electro-chemistry, and wave-mechanics. It comes to this, therefore, that the contents of the tiers in each science must be arranged according to principles of commonsense in the first instance and then checked up against any philosophic tetrad that may be applicable.

There can be no better way of elucidating the philosophic nature of the tiers than by setting forth the Fundamental Principles recognised by thinkers of all times and first classified by Aristotle. If these are allotted to their correct tiers then we are able to predicate a good deal about them which could not be done by any other method. They include entities, processes, methods of limitation and expression, and canons and may be listed as follows: (10) Energy. (11) Conditioning. (12) Attribution. (13) Mensuration. (14) Motion. (15) Arrangement. (16) Adaptation. (17) Incorporation. (18) Expressiveness. (19) Impressiveness. (20) Finish. (21) Method.

TIER IV (10), ENERGY

It does not require much mental effort to find a term which covers energy in its three modes of manifestation, free, specific, and bound, since the word "energetics" is ready to hand and fulfils all needs.

Energetics implies the output of creative power, for we cannot conceive of the Cosmos having come into existence without the putting forth of prodigious amounts of energy by the Creator. According to the *Book of Genesis* the creation of the world proved such an exhausting task for God that He was glad to take a complete day's rest after six days of work, the day being a period of unspecified time.

(11) Conditioning

For the contents of Compartment (11) we need a word which generalises the conceptions of State, Time, and Space. The word "conditioning," which involves limitation and to some extent definition, is frequently applied to the restrictions imposed upon energy when it manifests itself in time and space, and since state is a cognate conception which is in a sense compounded of time and space with the conception of stereotyping superadded. The number (2) is connected with the bringing down of energy into a region in which its potentialities can be manifested and its inherent tendency towards differentiation permitted to express itself. The idea of reflection is involved to some extent, for energy, like the sun at night time, is invisible, but the moon reflects a portion of the sun's rays and assures of its existence during the night time when, in so far as our eyes are concerned, we can have no certainty that the sun has not disappeared for good and all. In the same manner the three primary conditions certify our senses of the existence of forms of energy which we could not otherwise perceive.

(12) Attribution

Once energy has become localised and crystallised so to speak by the condition action of state, time, and space, and become a species of ideational structure it becomes possible for us to apply to it the conceptions or attributes of Quiddity, Quality, and Quantity. These might be called Attributes of Valuation or Hyperbole, using the latter term in the Greek sense of excellence. Crystallised energy must be graded in order to be brought down still closer to our capacities of perception. Again we must be able to distinguish its essence from its accidence, its real nature from the forms which it assumes. Quality is something more than form, but it is a special attribute of form. Quality helps to determine value more than mere quantity, though, of course, two valuable things of the same kind are worth more than one. On the other hand, a hundred valuable things of the same kind may make them so common that they cease to have value. We shall find as we proceed that (3) is the number of refinement in the sense of purging. It contains the mystical idea of the Hebrew letter schin which denotes refining fire. It stands especially for all the troubles and sorrows of life by which men's characters are refined and their individualities brought into prominence so that their fellows may recognise them for what they really are, whether good or evil. Quality may be used for camouflage but not quiddity. A man may live many years enjoying a reputation which he does not deserve until some crisis arises which proves that he is unworthy of the respect of his fellows. Quantity is the link between the Hyperbolic and Mensurational Attributes. When it is said that value is intensive quantity this may involve reduction not increase of quantity, for ten men of courage are worth a hundred cowards. The Hyperbolic Attributes enable men to rise from low positions to exalted ones and act also in the reverse order by casting the mighty from their seats and sending the rich empty away. There is, however, another important function of Attributes and that is what grammarians call qualifying. They perform for substances in general what adjectives perform for nouns, that is to say they particularise and differentiate, enabling the science and art of classification to come into operation. Adverbs perform a similar service for verbs, and they may be classified roughly into adverbs of state, time, and space. In this sense state, time, and space qualify the energies which are, so to speak, discharged into the cosmos and compel them to become differentiated.

TIER V. (13) MENSURATION—NUMBERS

The last process which crystallised energy has to undergo in order to be apprehensible is measurement. Quantity initiates the process but can only carry it a certain distance. A hundred lumps of chalk do not convey any accurate conception of quantity for one lump may be bigger than a hundred. On the other hand, a hundred pounds of chalk or a hundred cubic feet of chalk must of necessity be a larger quantity than one pound or one cubic foot. The root significance of the number (4) is actualisation, definition, realisation, and separation. It includes receptacles such as a room which marks off the inside, measurable, say, as 10,000 cubic feet, from the outside which is infinite space. Measures are of three kinds, weights, rods, and receptacles. Those in common everyday use are the first and the third, but the second is used freely by those who deal in large quantities of goods, especially when they cannot be conveniently weighed or put into hollow measures of known capacity. In Physiology (4) is the number of the skin of man which limits the extent of his body in space and defines clearly what is inside him and what is outside. Put shortly, weight is an index of mass, dimensions of size, and capacity of aggregation and bulk. They are all interchangeable, for we can estimate the bulk of a substance if we know its density, and vessels of capacity can be subjected to measurement by tape so that their volume can be expressed in cubic feet or inches. With a number as a fourth mensurational device we can gain complete quantitative information regarding any material substance, and all four devices are used freely metaphorically to describe the definition of non-material things. If we say that a man has a gigantic brain we do not mean that it exceeds 1,600 c.c., but that its capacity is above the average. Mensuration is impossible without numbers and we cannot doubt that the instinct to measure brought about the wide use of numbers even though it did not originate them. Man probably learnt to count on his fingers and from the first he used thumb, hand, and forearm for measurement. If he found that a brick was two handbreadths long then 2 became an important index of measurement for the brick and a hand-breadth would represent one, otherwise a unit of measurement. The decimal system which is based on the ten fingers, is of very ancient origin.

(14) Motion

Motion is a fundamental conception which many philosophers would place higher on the list, but this would not be correct because crystallised energy must be fully defined before it can be subjected to the laws of motion, using the word definition to signify delimitation of boundary. Motion falls appropriately into the time column and the harmonic of special time compartment (5). Mensuration is an idea which is compatible with state, for we cannot know much about the state of anything unless it is defined, for it is by changes of measurements and numeration that we estimate changes of state. If the population of a country increases or decreases its state changes accordingly. Motion contains a space element as well as a time, for it is measured in feet per second or by similar units of time and space. Psychologically motion is bound up with life as mensuration is with form, and form precedes life. Few would dispute the order given in *Genesis* in which it is stated that God formed man of the dust of the earth and then breathed into his nostrils the breath of life. If an animal is still we cannot assume that it is dead, but if it moves we can be certain that it is alive. The accepted symbol of the Spirit of Life is the wind that bloweth where it listeth.

Motion is intimately associated with sound and tone in nature, just as Arrangement is associated with light and colour. We are, of course, familiar with the tonal arrangements which we call music as we are with the movements of colours which are depicted by colour photography in motion pictures. But in nature the connection of motion with sound has far-reaching consequences. Most animals either prey upon others or are themselves objects of prey and are quick to perceive all visible movements of potential enemies. Consequently, the predatory animal always seeks to approach its quarry without being seen, and if it proceeds up-wind it will not be scented. But sound, unlike smell, can and does move up-wind and many a hunting animal is detected by the noise which it makes in motion. This is especially the case at night when every sound is significant to the alert ears of an inadequately protected creature. The familiar moving objects in our present-day civilization, aircraft, trains, motor-cars, and steamships, all advertise their movements by the noise which they make. One of the most valuable devices for hunting submarines depends on the capacity of an artificial ear called a hydrophone to register the peculiar noise which the engines of a submarine make when submerged.

(15) Arrangement

Motion is a congenital disturber of the peace and when its activities manifest themselves all sorts of unexpected things happen. Although it operates in time, its effects become apparent in space. Consequently it becomes necessary to subject it to limitations other than its own laws. A motorist who drives dangerously is obeying the laws of mechanics, but he is breaking the law of the land. Furthermore there is a basic antagonism between crystallized energy as limited by measurement, which is virtually an aspect of state, and motion, the opposition being of the same kind as that which exists between conservatives and liberals or radicals. This antagonism is resolved and abated by the principle Arrangement in its threefold mode of application, orderly, formative, and regulative. These operate mainly in spatial environment in which animated bodies move and correct the state of chaos which would arise if motion were unrestricted in speed, direction, and momentum. The third element is important because a large object which moves fast is more dangerous than a small object moving at the same rate. Form affects speed in connection with the contouring of country, for vehicles move more slowly uphill for the same expenditure of fuel, and more quickly downhill. The size of vehicles is limited by law not only to safeguard small vehicles but to prevent danger to bridges, sticking in arches, and damage to the surface of roads. In the realm of psychology motion finds expression in the laws of life and arrangement in the law of environment. There is often a conflict between life as animating the isolated form and the environment in which it is placed. The living form fears that it may lose its individuality through being moulded by the laws of environment, and environment insists on its laws being obeyed in order to prevent the world from being thrown into confusion at the whim of the individual. If the life principle is unduly acquiescent, then it becomes time-serving and desirous of peace at any price. The conflict nearly always results in a certain amount of disequilibrium. Reference has already been made to the connection between arrangement and colour in nature. It is hardly possible to conceive what the world would be like without colour unless we compare it with the surface of the moon as seen through a high-powered telescope. Nature arranges her colour schemes with unrivalled artistry, and harmonises and blends them with a skill which no painter can equal.

Tier VI. (16) Adaptation

The purpose of adaptation is to adjust the conflict which is liable to arise between the moving body of crystallised energy and the surroundings in which it is compelled to move and function. Adaptation if not synonymous with balance is closely allied to it since there can be no successful adaptation without equilibration. Adaptation is frequently a matter of adjustment of rhythms which produce concord when they synchronise and discord when they do not. The principle of adaptation is well exemplified in the movements of the ballet dancer or interpretive dancer who gives the maximum expression to his vitality without infringing the mechanical laws of his environment. If he attempted to defy those laws he would instantly fall to the ground. The same is true of any professional acrobat or equilibrist. Proportion appears in dancing in the relations which the various phases of a dance bear to each other and also in the symmetry of form of the dancer himself. Structure is seen in the flexibility of the mechanism, i.e., of the skeletal framework of the dancer which is a highly dynamic instrument designed to enable him to execute complex movements after a rigorous training has been undergone.

The principle of adaptation is seen to a certain extent in Arrangement which enables a vitalised form to harmonise with its environment, but the operation of this principle tends to induce people to stay in surroundings which contribute to their comfort to a maximum extent, with the result that they become victims to Venusian luxuriousness and sensuousness, like many of the South Sea Islanders and the Europeans who "go native" in the Pacific islands. Adaptation is a martial principle which enables pioneers and nomads to accommodate themselves to novel and often rigorous conditions of existence. Physiologically the lymphatics assist in this process by regulating the heat of the body and manufacturing antitoxins to check the onslaughts of dangerous microbes. Adaptation plays a most important part in enabling the waste places of the earth to be overspread so that even the frozen North is able to attract and retain inhabitants. Of all animals the bear is the most adaptable since it is found thriving in both hot and cold climates.

It stands to reason that adaptable races should have a great advantage over non-adaptable races in conquering the world and for this reason Europeans have far outclassed Asiatics, Africans, and Aboriginal Americans in martial exploits. Of the Europeans Englishmen, Scotsmen, and Irishmen appear to be more liberally endowed with physical adaptability than any other people, with the exception of the Dutch.

(17) INCORPORATION

The principle of incorporation can only be studied to real advantage in the sphere of nation-building. Incorporation must be preceded by adaptation to be effective. First we must have equilibration, the development of the sense of balance of power between nations, then we must have the development of a sense of proportion as a prelude to constitution-building with special reference to the proportionate influence to be allowed to the classes and interests composing a nation. Finally we must have the sense of structure developed without which no skeleton framework of government can be produced, in order that in due course it may be covered with skin and flesh. In the history of European civilisation the initial work in the formulation of political theory was begun during the Italian Renaissance and many of its fundamental principles were laid down in the "Politics" of Machiavelli. Progress was made in the creation of a sense of proportion by following Greek models and in the creation of a sense of structure by following Roman models. It was not until the beginning of the nineteenth century that the real process of incorporation as we know began to be fully applied.

The first principle to be developed in Incorporation is Composition. In order to understand what this involves we may take the characteristic

Byzantine art of Mosaic as a guide. A nation consists of a number of localised units, races, religious bodies, provinces, cities, etc., and a number of varied interests or corporations as they are now called in Italy when organised, which like the pieces of glass or stone used for mosaic work have to be cemented together. The technical problem to be solved is as to what kind of cement to use. The experience of China and France who have been the pioneers in this class of work has conclusively demonstrated that the only lasting kind of cement that exists is ethical in character and may be called humanitarian idealism. The French began to do the work of modern incorporation at the close of the eighteenth century. The Revolution was begun under the watchwords of Liberty, Equality, and Fraternity, and the wholesale butchery which was carried out until Napoleon took a hand in the project of state-making, has caused cynics to wax merry whenever the slogan of Rousseau is mentioned. But for all that the best type of Frenchmen continued to assert that no civilisation could endure unless held together by humanitarian idealism and later on this belief took general hold on the peoples of Europe and the conception of the League of Nations was evolved which aimed at incorporating the various countries of Europe first and of the world afterwards in a world-mosaic of peoples, kindred, tongues, and nations. The grandiose project failed lamentably for the simple reasons that many of the components had not been properly incorporated as isolated units to start with and secondly because the international cement used was inferior in quality and too thinly applied. China has been engaged on the work of trying to solve the problems of incorporation for some 5,000 years with inconspicuous success, but at least she succeeded in producing a philosopher, Confucius, who discovered the necessary formula for a cement which would undoubtedly enable China to regenerate itself if it would only exploit the doctrine of its great Teacher.

The next principle to bring into operation in Incorporation is that of Pitch or Tension. Humanitarianism, if contemplated as a sole and self-sufficient remedy for the ills of mankind, inevitably produces a yearning for a flabby kind of pacificism. All the metaphorical muscles of the body politic lose their tone and the general appearance of the community becomes batrachian. The froglike qualities of interminable vociferousness and love of self-inflation emerge into view and all virile people react violently against the entire system of political altruism. The only possible mode of recovering the lost tension known to man in his present state of evolution is armament or rearmament. "If a strong man armed keepeth his palace his goods are in peace." Many of the nations of the world grew very wealthy under the slogan of political altruism which was too often used as a disguise for the most unblushing chicanery while those who lagged behind in the scramble for wealth and power grew envious of their more fortunate competitors. Every rich nation which neglected to arm itself soon discovered that it was at the mercy of any poor nation which accumulated weapons and munitions. We are now in the thick of the Pitch or Tension stage when there is hardly a nation in the world which can afford to do so which does not seek to string itself up to concert pitch to ensure self-protection. Needless to say the controversies waged between Humanitarians and Militarists are violent and unceasing and the former wax if anything more bellicose than the latter. Both sides appeal with confidence to the teachings of Christ as supporting their programmes. The conflict is an ever-recurrent one which has been waged from the days of the inception of the Chinese Empire in the East of Asia and of the Assyrian Empire in the West of Asia. Cumbrous and mollusc-like administrations of scholars bred in the maxims of Confucius but by no means averse to mingling them with less exalted maxims of their own, have been engaged in a ceaseless struggle with ambitious war-lords whose creed was that God was on the side of the big battalions. Reverting to our friend the frog, although this animal is commonly believed to be innocuous and pacific, yet in certain tropical countries armies of frogs wage ferocious warfare against each other leaving the fields of battle littered with myriads of corpses. At the time of writing the greater part of the civilised nations of the world are endeavouring to devise some sort of international authority to save themselves from being destroyed by political gangsterism and unless the principle Harmony prevails over that of war-mongering the peoples of the world will perish through self-extermination.

Remnants of harmony are to be seen in free nature, especially in the plant world, but for the most part animals and plants prey on each other precisely in the same manner as human beings. Harmony will seek to reconcile the discordant aims of pacifists and militarists and of capitalists and communists and no doubt will achieve a measure of success but ultimately human beings and especially children will be made flabby by over-indulgence and assiduous nursing on the part of sympathetic administrations.

(18) EXPRESSIVENESS

The Compositional or Group-formative influences of (17) result invariably in a sense of constriction arising in which man feels that he has sacrificed too much of his liberty to the group and seeks to reassert his freedom of action. He is satisfied with the progress of involution down to (16) but considers that the following stage (17) produces such glaring differences between the top-dog and the under-dog that it represents a retrograde process. This is substantially the Bolshevik creed to-day, in which there might be a progressive element if it could be divorced from the class-hatred, bloodthirstiness, and atheism, which seem at the present time to be inseparable from it. The first stage of Expressiveness is the manifestation of Intricacy, the scope and application of which is admirably seen in Biology and Physiology, which enable us to trace out the progressive growth of the most intricate and complex organisms. A fertilised animal germ cell seeks to express the essence of its being by growth into a fully-formed foetus, and then after an independent state of existence has been acquired through birth or hatching out, by growth to the highest state of physiological development possible to the species. This undoubted biological fact has caused a craze for encouraging unlimited self-expression in the upbringing of children and ignoring existence of the evil, perhaps through reluctance to trespass upon theological preserves, with the result that the conclusions drawn from it become completely invalidated. There is an appropriate physiological form corresponding to every germ cell, which when fully developed becomes capable of reproducing new forms. Thus Birth, Life, and Death are all forms of Expressiveness.

Ornament as already explained is intricacy as applied to form. There is no rigid standard by which we may distinguish what is ornamental from what is disfiguring. A savage chief may regard a pair of corsets as highly ornamental insignia of royalty. Here we have the principle of selectivity operating with especial vigour. Even in its own special sphere it is impossible to accord to Expressiveness full liberty of action, and it does not seek for such freedom for it knows well enough that in proportion as reproductiveness makes its activities apparent so good and evil come into prominence as opposing principles. We need not, in dealing with pure biology, attach a moral significance to the terms good and evil. When an organism multiplies there are certain to arise a number of individuals which do not fit into the group organisation. In addition to these, individuals from alien organisations seek hospitality and often prove to be about as useful as a wax moth in a beehive. Many people who worship expressiveness as a god because they imagine that it accords them perfect liberty to do what they like experience an unpleasant jar when they discover that it has laws of its own which are applied with iron rigidity, just as are those of Motion and Vitality. Self-expression is right and necessary in so far as every germ cell has a claim to develop according to the laws of its own being and ultimately assume a physiological form characteristic of its species, but self-expression, when carried to the point of being socially destructive has to be severely dealt with, and this is the function of police organisations. Even perpetual quarrelling without resort to violence becomes intolerable after a time and may need the intervention of the law. Criminal activities are more serious and are dealt with by a special department of law called the criminal code. Ornamentation in combination with Expressiveness may easily become a dangerous disease. It leads to a craving for embellishment and exaggeration and is specially prominent in forensic and political oratory. Popular orators are particularly addicted to it as florid speech attracts a certain type of mind. During the time when Expressiveness is tested out as a remedy for the evils of ill-judged philanthropy people will pin their faith to Law, and especially to Roman Law as the solvent of their woes. Let justice be done no matter what be the consequences to vested interests. It will be an age of judges and will doubtless deteriorate because justice will become a marketable commodity which may be purchased at any time by the highest bidder. When people have become sickened of judges they will turn to eloquent lawyers for salvation who by their persuasive eloquence will succeed in bamboozling judges, jurymen, and all those engaged in the dispensation of justice. Both virtues and vices will be magnified and caricatured out of all recognition and before long the world will begin to wonder if such a thing as truth exists. The exaggeration of vices invariably produces censoriousness and a total lack of a sense of proportion, for people rise in righteous indignation and howl for the blood of ordinary offenders who are depicted by their enemies as deserving the worst that can be meted out to them. Garrulousness and scandal-mongering are bound to receive a tremendous impetus under such conditions and the picturesque gossiper will always have a large circle of friends no matter how many reputations he trails in the mud. As will be seen when we come to Zoology, this will be an age in which no details will be too unsavoury for the human Mustelidae who will overrun the world.

Tone is a very useful word, especially when qualified by the adjectives healthy or unhealthy. It is applicable to groups of every grade from a culture of bacteria to a nation or race. A bacterial culture may be too young or too old to work properly, or it may be unhealthy through being improperly fed. The tone of a nation may become so bad that it becomes a nuisance to its neighbours and almost justify their attacking it. Such was the tone of the nations of Judah and Israel in the centuries immediately preceding their respective captivities. Judges, administrators, and police seldom succeed in arresting decadence of tone. They can weed out undesirables but when the national tone takes the downward path a time soon arrives when judges become corrupt, administrators inert, and police venal and despotic when nothing but a drastic purging by war, pestilence, or famine can restore the situation.

Tier VII. (19) Impressiveness

In following out the involution of principles one becomes increasingly dependent upon the phenomena of group organisations to illustrate one's meaning. As we have seen there is a perpetual oscillation in the involution of institutional groups between liberty and subordination. Human beings turn from one to the other as a restless sleeper turns from side to side, always seeking for a peace which never comes. When the running riot of liberty results in the general lowering of the group tone, as in the case already cited, people realise that very drastic remedies are required to save society from complete dissolution. Jupiter rules over the sphere of civil justice but if he goes to sleep so that injustice prevails then Saturn, the lord of criminal justice, is called upon to save society. In the case of the Jews their salvation was accomplished by the complete abrogation of their national independence and they found a peace under the heavy hands of Assyrian and Babylonian monarchs which they had long ceased to enjoy under their own rulers. Impressiveness in its aspect of accentuation is an involutionary development of weight as applied to group activities. The rhythms of national life proceed by Saturnian clockwork, the machinery of Kronos, but their nodal points are greatly accentuated which means that resistance to authority is visited by heavy punishment. The Law of Karma takes the place of the Law of Liberty and a man reaps quickly what he sows. If justice walks with leaden foot, at any rate when the foot is put down, the criminal is hardly recognisable afterwards.

Pose in its dynamic form of gesture serves the same purpose for the criminal lawyer that embellishment of oratory does for the civil lawyer. Both properly and fairly employed should enable judge and jury to perceive the case defended or attacked in its true proportions. Only too often exaggeration and gesture are put to precisely opposite uses. English people, who are accustomed to the staid procedure of their own law-courts, fail to appreciate the power of gesture to obtain convictions but numerous films depicting American procedure should serve to enlighten him, if he understands its inwardness. The man who understands how to reinforce an impressive manner with appropriate poses and gestures easily acquires influence over those of his fellows who are influenced by externals and lack the acumen to look beneath the surface.

The net result of the application of the heavy hand, reinforced if need be by the heavy foot, is to produce plasticity and malleability in those who feel their weight. The heavy metal lead is one of the most malleable, wherein lies a parable. There is a well-known kind of disciplinarianism commonly called iron which breaks people to shivers like a potter's vessel, and completely crushes the spirit out of them as the iron rod of the Inquisition did the Spanish nation for many centuries. But leaden discipline, though seemingly rigorous and oppressive, is often the only possible method of reducing a nation whose tone has been lowered to the state of plasticity in which it can be brought back to sanity. This was the effect of the Babylonish Captivity upon the Jews who were subsequently permitted by the Persians to return to their own land and rebuild the walls of Jerusalem. For some considerable time after the Restoration the Jews paid attention to the messages of their prophets with a deference they had never shown in the latter days of the Kings.

(20) FINISH

We must seek in the sphere of Mechanics to obtain the images needful to explain the components of Finish or Refinement. When a nation sets out to attain to Finish in the involution of its institutions it concentrates upon the complication of its political machinery, just as if it were bent on converting time into space and modelling its institutions on the clocks which measured time for it. All the civilised nations concentrated upon the devising of intricate political constitutions from the end of the eighth century B.C. and got them working with clockwork precision by the middle of the fourth. Then, largely as the result of the conquests of Alexander, the Greeks and Romans began to philosophise about their political machinery and to make it so intricate that ultimately it could not be worked. They made a hobby of constitutional law as a shop-window science. Every function had to be defined with precision, every crime had to be expiated by a punishment which was exactly fitted to it, every duty owed by the citizen to the state had to be explained to him in language which he could not fail to understand. The condition of affairs was in effect one of progressive regimentation, and since the Romans were more naturally adapted than the Greeks to respond to militarisation, they made the best of use of it and acquired a sense of discipline which enabled them to establish an empire reaching from Britain to the Euphrates. There is a great deal of similarity between the methods of Naziism in relation to the establishment of the totalitarian state and that of Romans in seeking to prepare themselves for world conquest. Not that the latter consciously set out to found an empire, on the contrary, they blundered into it much like the British, but they did seek to organise themselves on the Spartan model in order to overcome their troublesome neighbours, the Carthaginians, and once that had been accomplished the Greek states fell like ripe plums into their mouths. In all departments of human activities the Romans were clear thinkers as they were convincing talkers. They disdained the philosophic hair-splitting of the Greeks and concentrated upon a tireless pursuit of utilitarianism. They argued rightly that if a citizen did not have his duties explained to him in language which could admit of no misunderstanding he could not be held responsible for neglecting them, but if they were so explained then woe be to the defaulter. This is an inevitable feature of militarisation. Another and less desirable feature is the deification of the state which follows in the course of which efforts are made to deprive the individual of his right to follow his conscience. It was mainly because of this state-worship that Christianity was intermittently persecuted by the Roman Emperors, and not by any means the worst of them.

We see in the desolating civil wars which destroyed the Republic of Rome the inevitable outcome of over-militarisation, in which clear thinking and precise definition played no small a part, for the simple reason if a man is able to state his views simply and convincingly he becomes persuaded that he must of necessity be right and his military training predisposes him to back up words with action.

In Rome towards the end of the second century B.C. political differences became so acute that civil war supervened and thousands of needy adventurers who had become completely militarised in outlook and who vastly preferred fighting and plundering to honest toil flocked to the standards of the contestants. Every victory was followed by purges and proscriptions in which the aristocratic and business classes were mercilessly slaughtered till finally the Republic disappeared in a welter of blood and misery.

To sum up, the principles of Detail, Distinctness, and Clearness, are brought out more clearly in army organisation and military law than in any other institution or form of regulation. The efficiency of an army as a machine depends mainly upon the care and attention which is given to details. As regards distinctness "If the trumpet shall utter an uncertain sound, who shall prepare himself for battle?" Unless orders are given so distinctly that there is no possibility of their being misunderstood military operations are liable to end in chaos. Absolute clearness of vision both literally and metaphorically are essential prerequisites for an army commander. He must know what the enemy is doing in order to make his own plans and forestall those of the enemy. Hence the immense value attached to air reconnaissance, raiding, espionage, and other means of finding out what an enemy country is doing and thinking in time of war.

(21) METHOD

Method in the sense here used is allied to custom and habit and results in nations permitting their natural instincts of common sense and conceptions of mutual obligation to gain the upper hand and banish all military doctrinnairism and racial fanaticism. It is based on the belief that there is nothing undignified in service and that ambition is the root of all evil. In the case of Rome the Emperors made much of their desire to serve the state at the outset and renounced all self-seeking and desire to elevate themselves above their fellows, but unfortunately their outlook changed as they succeeded in making themselves virtually omnipotent by appropriating all magisterial offices of importance. There is nothing inimical to individuality in the notion and practice of service and it often happens that those who are animated by the laudable desire to help their fellows have very strong ideas how that help has to be given and flatly decline to be dictated to. It may sound paradoxical, but the more a man is in bondage to material laws and conditions the more chance there is of his developing real originality, the kind that pays and gets results instead of wasting itself on wild-cat schemes. For instance, it often happens that a young man who enters an old-established business is full of original ideas as to how he would improve it if he were the manager. But after a few years he appreciates the fact that most if not all of his early ideas would have speedily brought the business to bankruptcy and then having eliminated all the unworkable original ideas one fine day he thinks of one which will work and gets permission to put it into practice. Put shortly this means that real individuality cannot manifest its potentialities to the full except under a temporary state of subservience to laws, natural and economic.

Style is individuality clothed in form. The term is applied specially to architectural fashions, which are for the most part strongly individualised and easy to distinguish. It is highly selective since the possible modes of architectural structure and ornamentation are very numerous.

Appeal to the popular verdict is the foundation of democracy. Whatever the inventors, writers, artists, scientists, and engineers produce must be acceptable to the mass of the people if it is to enjoy permanent success. In the last resort government itself must rest on the consent of the governed, not because the people are theoretically the source of power but because practically they become ungovernable if misgoverned. Appeal is sympathetic understanding of the synthesis or manifold of the subconscious desires of humanity which cannot be browbeaten into subjection. If not allowed legitimate expression they become a storehouse of explosive energy which can reduce mighty empires to wreckage. Many causes of the decline and fall of the Roman Empire have been diagnosed, which was undoubtedly greatly weakened by the civil wars of rival emperors, but the chief of them were undoubtedly economic. The sources of information are fragmentary, but there seems no doubt that taxation was carried to a point which deprived the working classes of all incentive to work and made landowners indifferent as to whether their land was productive or otherwise. Governments which rule under the impression that the taxpayer is so public-spirited that he can be bled to any extent to finance the bureaucracies which oppress him sooner or later discover that they are labouring under the worst of delusions. A time will inevitably come when the milch-cow decides that if its own calves are made to starve for lack of milk there is no reason why it should produce milk at all. No revolution may break out but an economic rot will set in which undermines the fabric of the state so that it collapses by its own weight.

APPLICATION OF PRINCIPLES TO HISTORY

If we desire to review the fundamental principles in their historical application one must revert to the period immediately following the Assyrian Captivity of the Jews when the great empires of Assyria, Babylon, and Persia became a nursery of the political energies which were transferred by Alexander to the Greek kingdoms and then appropriated by Rome. All these centred in absolute and well-nigh irresponsible autocracy in so far as Egypt, Assyria, and Babylon were concerned. The mind of the Aryan has always manifested a philosophic bent, religious in the case of the Iranians and Brahmins, and secular in the case of the Greeks. The philosopher always seeks to bring imponderable energies within the regions of state, time, and space and examine their mode of manifestation under limiting conditions which compel the same energies to flow along ascertainable channels. The Greeks were the greatest of all political philosophers and Plato's *Republic* is still a text-book on the subject in spite of its aristocratic bias. The Romans, like the British, were more interested in character-building than in the education of the intellect, but, unlike the British, the method by which they sought to achieve their end was by rigorous discipline. They succeeded in producing many men, not a few of whom were emperors, who were outstanding examples of the success attainable by Roman disciplinarianism. Nearly all of them were either professed Stoics or sympathetically disposed towards that branch of philosophy. With the advent of the East Romans and Byzantines to prominence we reach a state in which the major energies of the government were devoted to what might be called the mensuration of administrative institutions, that is to say, the organisation of a large staff of civil servants whose duties were defined and prescribed to the last detail. As might have been anticipated it was not long before the man was swallowed up in the machine and the term Byzantine became synonymous with blind and irrational conservatism carried to the point of complete fossilisation. The well-nigh lifeless corpse of the Roman administrative system was however reanimated by the Barbarians who introduced the life principle into the institutional ensemble of Europe, retaining much that was of value in the system which they took over, and giving the nations of the West a new lease of vitality. Towards the close of the eleventh century the life principle of the Teuto-Slavonic races was brought under the limiting influences of design, form, and sequence, and as the outcome of this interplay of forces the Holy Roman Empire took shape and a social aristocracy arose which made a fetish of hereditary precedence, the craze taking deeper root in Austria than in any other country. With the advent of the Ranaissance the imperative need of adapting existing political and religious institutions to the expanding conscious of the nations became apparent and this was effected primarily by the monarchs of Europe appropriating and localising the functions of both emperor and pope. Furthermore, the colonising powers of the West began to overspread the face of the globe, which entailed not only physical adaptation to new climatic conditions but the freeing of constitutional principles from the shackles of the past, a process which has, however, been carried to a point which threatens to deprive them of all value. The present age in which we live, which we may date from the beginning of the nineteenth century, is one of Incorporation, as seen in the gigantic growth not only of the super-states like America but the consolidation of mighty empires like those of Britain and Russia into which a spirit of corporate patriotism has been infused. Incorporation nearly always involves the development of acquisitiveness which becomes belauded as an essential ingredient in patriotism. Appetite grows with the eating, as the French say. Those who have already acquired lebensraum refuse to permit their territories to be swamped by foreign aliens and those who have not got it are prepared to fight for it even though defeat may spell disaster as it has in the case of Germany. The advent of the limited liability company initiated the era of financial corporations which in the form of cartels have dominated world industries. The Germans made free use of these to control the output and distribution of all materials likely to be of service to them in the event of war. The projected Central World Organisation envisages the creation of a super-corporation. Hereditary estates are being converted into limited liability companies and miniature corporations are springing up everywhere, even among religious bodies under the name of trusteeships. There is a general movement on foot to bring about union among the Churches of Christendom which has borne fruit in the uniting of branches of the Wesleyan and Baptist communions, and of Presbyterian bodies in Scotland which remained outside the Established Church. Freemasonry, both Anglo-Saxon and Continental, constitute vast corporations, the latter having been largely responsible for engineering every revolution which has occurred in Europe since the French Revolution, with perhaps the exception of the Russian Revolution. The last-named upheaval resulted in every corporate body in Russia becoming absorbed into the state, which is now the only corporation that exercises any real power in the country. The Nazi Corporation has been, thank heaven, obliterated.

Involution and Evolution

Before proceeding with the classification of the various branches of knowledge it will be advisable to be clear as to the precise meaning of two terms, one of which is constantly on one's lips, namely, involution and evolution. We are accustomed to hear a great deal about the latter and to find it applied to the process by which all life progresses upwards from lower to higher forms and also to the development of institutions, languages, social customs, etc., which are in no way controlled by procreative functions; of the involutionary processes of Nature, on the other hand, we hear comparatively little, though they are equally important.

In all compartments of the (3) series the general impulse is upwards towards more highly evolved and complex forms of life, towards larger combinations of units, and towards functional activities performed on a more universal scale. The activities of the compartments of this series are synthetic, fruitful, multiplicatory, and feminine. The vital urge in compartments of the (2) series, on the other hand, is involutionary, the forcing down of spirit into matter in order to gather fresh experience, to exploit all the potentialities of matter, and to compel it to reveal its tendencies, whether for good or evil. In proportion as we proceed down the tiers from the higher to the lower we pass from the universal towards the particularistic, Involution is, therefore, analytical in character, and divides, disintegrates and separates, and illustrates all that is associated with maleness in nature.

If we trace out the history of political institutions of an executive and administrative character we shall find ourselves working from the higher to the lower tiers, whereas if we examine the trend of judicial institutions we shall find them progressing from the lower to the higher. Owing to the fact that both processes are in operation simultaneously, it is very easy to confound the two. Both result in simplification and complication, according to the point of view from which one regards them. For instance, in synthetic processes we group persons or objects together and to that extent make the resulting unit more complex. On the other hand, we give all the persons or objects a title describing the general characteristics of the whole group, and that is a process of simplification.

The natural home of the philosopher is in the clouds, which being already located in the atmosphere cannot ascend much higher. The natural habit of clouds is to condense into rain, i.e., differentiate into rain-drops and fall to earth, and the thoughts of philosophers gravitate earthwards in a similar manner. The zodiacal symbol of philosophy is Aquarius, the Water-carrier. The natural home of the scientist, on the other hand, is the earth, and he claims to be able to establish the truths which he discovers on certain foundations, building up his conclusions tier upon tier and minutely scrutinising each layer before he attempts to place another on top of it.

Those who work along involutionary lines favour the deductive method of reasoning, and those who work along evolutionary lines the inductive methods of reasoning. A very clear and concise description of the relations between the two methods will be found in chapter III of *Buckle's History of Civilisation*. The deductive reasoner starts by examining his ideas and the inductive reasoner his sensations. The former if he commences with the consideration of such a subject as space will inquire how the conception of space arises in the human mind, an idea which is "infinite and necessary" and which cannot owe its origin to the senses, because these can only supply information as to what is "finite and contingent." The latter starts by asserting that "we can have no idea of space until we have first had an idea of objects; and that the ideas of objects can only be the results of the sensations which these objects excite." The two schools of thought find themselves continually at variance as the result of their divergence of opinion over the fundamental processes of metaphysical inquiry. "The idealist asserts that our notions of cause, of time, of personal identity, and of substance, are universal and necessary; that they are simple; and that not being susceptible of analysis, they must be referred to the original constitution of the mind. On the other hand, the sensationalist, so far from recognising the simplicity of these ideas, considers them to be extremely complex, and looks upon their universality and necessity as merely the result of a frequent and intimate association. . . . The idealist is compelled to assert, that necessary truths and contingent truths have a different origin. The sensationalist is bound to affirm that they have the same origin. The further these two great schools advance, the more marked does their divergency become. They are at open war in every department of morals, of philosophy, and of art. The idealists say that all men have essentially the same notion of the good, the true, and the beautiful. The sensationalists affirm that there is no such standard, because ideas depend upon sensations, and because the sensations of men depend upon the changes in their bodies, and upon the external events by which their bodies are affected." As the result of contemplating the arid and unprofitable controversies which have arisen between the two schools of thought Buckle came to the conclusion that metaphysics could only be studied successfully by a comprehensive investigation of history.

In actual practice the two schools work more amicably together than a perusal of their standard works would lead us to believe. People whose characters belong to the (1) series, use both methods impartially according to the nature of the problem which they have to solve. And though people of the (2) series pin their faith on deduction as a guide to truth yet in practice they cannot move a step without making use of sensationalist machinery, and the same holds good, *mutatis mutandis*, of the people of the (3) series. The general influences of Columns II and III are involutionary and evolutionary respectively, while Column I favours both processes according to requirements.

The general trend of analytical science is evolutionary and of philosophy involutionary. Both should hold the balance between evolution and involution but at the present time science definitely favours the evolutionary method and is for ever working upwards in the effort to make fresh synthetic generalisations. Consequently we have witnessed a continuous tug-of-war between philosophers and scientists for some time past. Philosophy by persistent analysis and definition claims to tell us exactly what material things are in themselves, yet for all that the philosopher is for ever dinning into our ears that we can never know what things are in themselves. In so far as science is concerned he appears to demand absolute knowledge of the properties of material things before he is ready to concede any real knowledge. But absolute knowledge is unattainable in any branch of knowledge. Only God Himself has absolute knowledge of the works of creation. If we hand over any material substance to a first class scientist he will not only give us a catalogue of innumerable properties which serve to define its nature but will even enlighten us as to the constitution of the atoms of which it is composed giving us more or less accurate information as to the protons, neutrons, positrons, and negatrons of which it is composed with their orbits and distances from each other in space; yet the philosopher will calmly assure us that we can know nothing of things as they are in themselves, and get large numbers of people to believe him. Why? Because by depreciating the reliability of the information supplied by science he enhances, as he imagines, the reliability of the information which he supplies. He alone can tell us what reality is, so it seems. Furthermore he ignores the argument of consensus of opinion. He states that no two people can be sure that one senses blue in the same manner as the other. Possibly not in an absolute sense, but certainly so in a relative. If a draper advertises some rayon of a startling shade of blue, thousands of women will congregate to buy it; and all will agree that it is blue, though they may differ as to the extent to which it is startling.

All human brains agree that light of a certain wave frequency produces an optical sensation which they identify as one and the same for all practical purposes, and they call this sensation blue. No amount of philosophical mystification is going to alter that fact.

However, scientists have recently given a shrewd blow to philosophy, by taking up the theory of Relativity. Hitherto philosophers claimed that they alone were the judges of the qualitative difference between time and space, and that mathematicians and geometricians had no other function than to measure time and space. Mathematicians of the relativist school claim, however, that their science is fully competent to judge of qualitative as well as quantitative differences and, furthermore, that unless you are a mathematician you cannot possibly venture to convict them of error. They are to be the infallible prophets, it would seem, and unless philosophers sit at their feet and learn the mysteries of the tensor calculus they can have no certain knowledge as to what either time or space is, or any of the objects that exist in time and space. And so the merry game goes on, to the diversion of the onlooker who understands the inwardness of the various manœuvres for position.

Astrology

In view of the extent to which Astrology makes use of philosophic and abstract principles it is desirable to indicate the mode in which these can be harmonised with the archetypal scheme of the Key Table. These principles all relate to the classification of the signs of the zodiac in accordance with polar dualities, the triplicities, and the quadruples. The three Fiery signs, Leo, Aries, and Sagittarius belong to compartments (10), (14), and (18) of column I because fire is the symbol of free energy, since it is highly dynamic. The three Airy signs, Aquarius, Libra, and Gemini, which are semi-dynamic, belong to compartments (11), (15), and (16) of column II, and thus preserve the polarities of the Fiery and Airy signs in tiers IV, V, and VI. Since (4) is the number of fixation we place Taurus, the most tamasic of the signs, there and similarly Aries, the most cardinal and rajasic of the signs in (5). This is the number of Vitality and Aries is connected with birth and life. Scorpio, the polar opposite of Taurus, then falls naturally into compartment (12).

The basic pattern now begins to emerge for we have the four fixed signs, Leo, Aquarius, Scorpio, and Taurus in (1), (2), (3), and (4) which we may write down as (10), (11), (12), and (13) if we work between the tabular numbers of (10) and (21) instead of between (1) and (12). The above four signs correspond with the Lion, Eagle, Man, and Ox of the Cherubim. Theosophists erroneously assign the Man to Aquarius and the Eagle to Scorpio. But there are two "winged" decanates in Aquarius, Pegasus and Cygnus, and none in Scorpio. Also there are two "human" decanates in Scorpio, Ophiucus and Hercules. Aquila, the Eagle, belongs to Capricorn, which is the lower harmonic of Aquarius, and Sagitta, the Arrow, may be regarded as another winged sign. Virgo, the Virgin, is the lower harmonic of Scorpio, and the third member of the Cherubim might be called Man-Woman. There is one human decanate in Virgo, namely, Boōtes, and one semi-human, Centaurus, the Man-horse. Were it not for the principle of preserving the polarities we should look for a mutable sign for compartment (6), but Libra is the most mutable of the cardinal signs as is evident from its adaptability. Librans are all things to all men. It remains for us to fill up two polarities (17) and (21), and (19) and (20). Now Cancer is a cardinal sign and partakes of the authoritativeness of Leo, consequently it is placed in (19) and its polar opposite Capricorn is placed in (20). Pisces and Virgo are both mutable signs and, in accordance with the principle of grading water above earth, we place the Watery Pisces above the Earthy Virgo. We should get a more symmetrical arrangement as regards the quadruples of the Elements if we placed the Watery Cancer between Scorpio and

DESCRIPTION OF METHOD

Pisces, leaving the three earthy signs in tier VII, but this would upset the polarities. As it is we have the Mutable Signs forming a T-cross in the Table while the Cardinal Signs are at the four corners of a square. If now we inspect the signs of the Zodiac as set down in their circular arrangement we observe that Taurus, Gemini, Cancer, and Leo belong to the (1) series of numbers, Virgo, Libra, Scorpio, and Sagittarius to the (3) series, and Capricorn, Aquarius, Pisces, and Aries to the (2) series. Taurus was originally the first sign of the Zodiac. The arrangement as explained in the foregoing is set down in Table J at the end of chapter VII where it is compared with that of the planets taken in their natural order. The resulting correspondences obtained differ to some extent from those accepted by astrologers because of their traditional authority, but the new correspondences obtained by reverting to first principles can easily be justified by detailed analysis. It will, at any rate, be admitted that the orthodox scheme makes no allowance for the planets beyond Saturn.

Summary of Method

The reader may well come to the conclusion, after perusing all that has been said about the Method of Analysis, that the correct classification of any branch of knowledge involves so many complications that it is not worth the trouble of attempting. Undoubtedly the making of such a classification is not a simple matter and it is for this very reason that the writer has himself completed the work in nearly all departments of science, philosophy, mysticism, and religion. But a few words regarding the procedure adopted may serve to show that the task is worth attempting in the case of such branches or sub-branches of knowledge as have not been subjected to analysis. First of all one should get hold of a classification made by a recognised authority and list the headings, dividing the higher from the lower. We may take Physiology as an example. The nervous system is obviously higher than the assimilative and excretory while the respiratory and circulatory come in between. A study of comparative biology would confirm this. Below the alimentary system we may place the body coverings of skin and hair to make a fourth tier. The organs which confer stability and permanence of form should then be identified and grouped in the central column placing the muscles and bones in the top tier because of their intimate contact with the motor nerves. The thyroid and the liver will then follow in the other two central compartments. In column I we should place the organs which deal with energy or substances absorbed from without in bulk, which means that the brain, the lungs, and the alimentary canal are suitably arranged. Then in Col. II we have the organs which perform the tasks of the detailed distribution of energy and substances absorbed from without, that is the peripheral nerves, the circulatory system, and the lymphatics. In all cases a start should be made on common-sense lines and systems of classification already in existence should be studied and criticised. The higher and more abstruse characteristics of the tiers and the columns can be examined when common-sense methods fail to give good results or when it is desired to carry out an investigation of the subject on philosophical lines with a view to making it disclose its inner structure.

CHAPTER III

APPLICATION OF METHOD
See TABLE A.

THE FOUR CATEGORIES OF THOUGHT

THERE are four main categories of Thought, using the word category as synonymous with class, and not in a Kantian sense. They may be defined as Analogical, Logical, Psychological, and Grammatical, and are associable with East, South, West, and North, respectively.

(1) ANALOGICAL

The fundamental principle of thinking which manifests itself in the vast amount of literature, classified somewhat superciliously by Western thinkers as mystical, is reasoning by analogy, which as already mentioned, takes for granted as axiomatic that all things in heaven and earth are arranged in the same pattern. To the logician this mode of thinking does not appear as illogical so much as omissive, in that it proceeds from premises to conclusions by leaps, omitting steps which he regards as essential to rigorous proof. But nevertheless it is by means of analogical thinking that all language-building proceeds and words are coined which, though regarded with dismay by the linguistic purist, serve the purpose with which they were put into circulation. Unless the metaphysical were organised on the same grand pattern as the physical, or perhaps we should put it the other way about, no language-building of a natural, easy, spontaneous, and practical character would be possible at all. One has only to take a dictionary and pick out at random any word which is not merely a name for a physical act or thing to find out, by noting its derivation, that its metaphysical significance accords in one way or another with its primary and literal significance. Very few of the words we use are arbitrarily coined without bringing into operation some perception of analogy. But we must also recognise that, quite apart from any mode of reasoning about truth, the Eastern mystic claims to be able to verify it by excursions into higher regions, a process of reaching certainty upon metaphysical realities which the practical Westerner regards with suspicion and incredulity. There is some truth in the line of Kipling that "East is East and West is West and never the twain shall meet," for it is unlikely that the Wisdom of the East, whose primæval home was the monasteries of Tibet, India, and the Tarim Basin, would have reached the West but for the clearing houses established by the priestly colleges of Babylon and Egypt. Initiates from what was then regarded as the Far East forgathered with those from Egypt and perhaps even from Druidical Britain to discuss their problems and pool their experiences. Orpheus, the first Hellene who bridged the gulf between East and West, was an initiate of one of the Egyptian priesthoods and may have visited Babylon. Pythagoras, his spiritual disciple and expounder, who lived in the sixth century B.C., was initiated in Egypt and spent many years in Babylon, after which he returned and reorganised the Delphic priesthood, purifying and re-establishing the Orphic Mysteries. Then he organised his famous school of initiates at Crotona in South Italy and earned for himself the title of the founder of Greek Philosophy. Plato unquestionably owed much to him, and some of his followers migrated later on to Alexandria and fused his philosophy with the Egyptian Hermetic, creating what came to be known as the Neo-Platonic school. Aristotle and the Greek philosophers who succeeded him were more scientifically-minded and may be regarded as typical products of the West Aryan civilisation. But neverthelesss Mysticism survived for many centuries in Alexandria and at the beginning of the Christian era formed an alliance with scholarly Christianity the product of which was the Gnosis. Gnosticism was revived by German scholars during the last century and the result of their labours will be found set forth in Harnack's *History of Dogma*, Vol. I, and Mead's *Fragments of a Faith Forgotten*. Plotinus and Apollonius of Tyana carried on the Pythagorean teaching during the post-apostolic age, but found no successors. A great revival of Eastern mysticism took place in Europe during the Middle Ages, to which Christian Rosenkreutz and the Alchemists made considerable contributions. The mystical philosopher, Jacob Boehme, who has many followers and interpreters even at the present day, adopted the symbolism of alchemy in most of his mystical writings. But the revival of Eastern mysticism from which Modern Theosophy emerged was accomplished by Madame Blavatsky, a Russian lady who, towards the end of the last century, visited India and unearthed from the monasteries the archaic "Stanzas of Dzyan," upon which she wrote an elaborate commentary called *The Secret Doctrine*, which was followed by *The Voice of the Silence*. She had previously produced a commentary on the Egyptian Mysteries, called *Isis Unveiled*. There remains, however, a vast deal of mystical knowledge in India and Tibet which no Westerner has been permitted to tap as yet. The fundamental principles of Eastern Mysticism can be classified with fair success by *The Philosophy of Analogy and Symbolism*.

(2) LOGICAL

Aristotle is universally recognised as the founder of the science and art of Logic. The principles of Logic which he enunciated received little notice, however, until over a thousand years had passed, when they were studied at the educational institutions founded by Charlemagne. Here they were made the foundation of Dialectics, the study of which was regarded as calling for a high order of intellectuality. It formed part of the Quadrivium of the time, according to Dean Milman, and speedily became the handmaid of controversial theology. It then gave rise to a wordy warfare which persisted until the Renaissance, in which desire to exhibit intellectual adroitness far exceeded that to investigate and propound truth. It throve on argument and might well have died out but for the disputatious temper of its exponents. War broke out when the Nominalist Roscelin denied the real existence of universals and was quickly adjudged to be a dangerous heretic, the champion of orthodox Realism being Anselm, Archbishop of Canterbury. The system culminated in the five great schoolmen, Albertus Magnus, Thomas Aquinas, Bonaventura, Duns Scotus, and William of Ockham, who began to arise towards the middle of the thirteenth century. Vast tomes of scholastic divinity were written in which some profess to discern Arabic learning, but it is generally agreed that none repay the labour of perusal, being in the main mere labyrinthine curiosities. The conflict between Anselm and Roscelin was revived by the followers of Scotus and Aquinas under different names and waged with dialectical fury. Aquinas, the Angelic Doctor, was certainly no heretic, though his Conceptualism perpetuated certain features of Nominalism.

The logic of the Schoolmen, as subsequently developed by post-Renaissance dialecticians, was summed up by Emmanuel Kant in his logical judgments, principles of the pure understanding, and categories, which, however, remain till to-day as dialectical curios having never been applied to solve problems of psycho-philosophy either by the Master himself or his legions of admirers. They can be classified and analysed in accordance with the principles of *The Philosophy of Analogy* and bear some fruit if treated thus. Within the last thirty years or so the study of logic has been revived at Cambridge and some useful advances have been registered. The science of Dialectics may, however, be regarded as a characteristic product of the Latin mentality of Southern Europe in view of its intimate association with Roman theology.

(3) Psycho-philosophy or Aletheianism

The Twelve Fundamental Processes of Thought were enunciated and elaborately analysed by the late Dr. (Col.) Sir Arthur Lynch, who embodied his results in a monumental work called *The Principles of Psychology*, which unfortunately has not yet received the intensive study which it merits, in view of the fact that it summarises and makes a tincture of the collective teachings of the psycho-philosophers of the nineteenth century, the majority of whom belong to Germany. Dr. Lynch proves that all his processes of thought are inevitably employed in reasoning and shows by elaborate explanations the precise part played by each. The general analytical treatment is in harmony with the mentality of the Anglo-Saxons rather than with that of Germans or Latins and it may well become the foundation of the Psycho-Philosophy of the West.

(4) The Philosophy of Grammar

The philosophy of Grammar has hardly been developed at all. It belongs to the Science of Linguistics, which itself rests upon the foundation of Philology laid by the great German exponents of that science during the nineteenth century, of whom Müller was by far the most notable. Skeat, in England, has also written important works on the subject. The science of Philology involves intensive study of the various leading languages of the nations of the earth, such as Hebrew, Arabic, and the Indo-Germanic family of tongues, which leads inevitably to the comparative study of their grammar and syntax. But if logic reveals the structure of the mind, as logicians claim that it does, the grammatical parts of speech do so no less clearly from another angle, and to do this is the appointed task of the Philosophy of Grammar, which yet remains to be developed. The German mentality is best adapted to perform this task, which justifies us in connecting the science in question with the North. Speech is the most objectively materialistic element of the Four Categories and is part and parcel of both Grammar and Philology. The precise method by which intelligible sounds are produced by the speech organs can be minutely studied and described but no one has yet been able to observe the brain producing concepts.

The utilisation of the Four Categories as components of the mechanism of thought enables the toughest problems connected with the classification of the arts and sciences to be resolved. The understanding of the mode in which the brain is organised and equipped to conduct analyses and syntheses is of far more importance than knowing its structure as a registry of facts or what people suppose to be facts. A brain should be able to use its faculties as powerful reagents analogous to those to be found in every well-appointed laboratory, by which a skilful chemist is able to make the most refractory substances reveal their true nature and composition.

The Four Categories will be analysed in the following order: (*a*) Psycho-philosophical (Fundamental Processes), (*b*) Logical, (*c*) Grammatical, (*d*) Analogical and Mystical.

THE TWELVE FUNDAMENTAL PROCESSES OF THE MIND

In 1923 Colonel Sir Arthur (otherwise Dr. Arthur) Lynch published the compendious work already mentioned called *The Principles of Psychology* in which he claimed that all possible modes of of thought and reasoning could be defined by combinations of twelve fundamental processes of the mind which he analysed and set forth in considerable detail. The subject was one which had interested Dr. Lynch from his early youth and to which in later life he devoted fifteen years of intensive study. The following article in no way claims to be a précis of this work, but rather an application and expansion of the fundamental processes dealt with subject to certain modifications which the present writer regards as called for. The Processes in question, set forth in the order in which they will be expounded, are: (1) Generalisation. (2) Association. (3) Sense of Effort. (4) Memory. (5) Conception of Time. (6) Conception of Space. (7) Agreement. (8) Hedonism.

(9) Impulse. (10) Unit Concept. (11) Immediate Presentation. (12) Negation. They will be dealt with under somewhat more cumbrous titles in order to clarify their essential nature, namely (1) Equilibrative Association. (2) Directional Association. (3) Constructive Association. (4) Conception of State. (5) Conception of Time. (6) Conception of Space. (7) Constructive Individualism. (8) Constructive Hedonism. (9) Constructive Impulsiveness. (10) Unit Concept. (11) Immediate Presentation (of sense data). (12) Realism. The second scheme differs from the first in that it assumes association in the sense of centripetal attraction as being inherent in all the Processes, its negative being centrifugal dispersion. This in turn necessitates Negation being treated as inherent in all the Processes and therefore Realism which is the negation of Idealism is placed in (12), although Dr. Lynch did not treat it as a fundamental process, but included it under Immediate Presentation (11).

When seeking to condense a complex subject into a limited space it is desirable to utilise, if possible, an appropriate system of imagery, for this, if handled with discretion, will enable comments and explanations to be reduced to a minimum compatible with lucid exposition. A system of this kind lies ready to hand in the prismatic spectrum of colours which corresponds with the conscious mind or personality. In the same connection we may take the ultra-violet rays as corresponding with the super-conscious mind and the infra-red with the sub-conscious mind. The Fundamental Processes are capable of being ranged in four groups of three which find their counterpart in the blue, green, yellow, and red rays. Although we cannot permit ourselves to stray far into the subject of colour symbolism in an article of limited dimensions it may be said that blue suggests rational rule and volition, green the subjective mind, yellow the objective mind, and red rational materialism in human beings and instinct in animals. In diagrammatic form these may be numbered tiers IV, V., VI, and VII, with the First Process starting in (10). Below the last named we have brown corresponding with selfishness and grey with fearfulness, both self-preservative instincts common to human beings and animals. It is, of course, recognised that infra-red rays do not appear to our eyes as grey, brown or black, but then we have no areas of the retina capable of interpreting them as colours at all. Above tier IV we have the purple of idealism, which in the prismatic spectrum is divisible into indigo (9), purple (8), and violet (7). The peoples of ancient times who studied the symbolism of colours, such as the Babylonians and Egyptians, recognised five, amber or pure invisible yellow, purple-blue, green, orange or visible yellow, and red, and the former coloured their five-tier pyramids accordingly, a tier being reckoned as a number of courses of the same colour. Archæologists have been puzzled as to why yellow should have been placed at the top while the remaining colours followed the order of the spectrum, and here we have the explanation. In harmony with the scheme as developed so far we have the amber tier numbered II and above that we may place an electrum numbered I. For practical purposes, however, we must concern ourselves almost entirely with the blue, green, yellow, and red tiers, IV to VII, in this article. The way is now clear for the fundamental processes to be considered seriatim in such detail as space permits.

(10) EQUILIBRATIVE ASSOCIATION

Dr. Lynch in dealing with Generalisation associates it with Symbolisation and Classification. To gain a complete picture, however, of these operations performed by the brain we must provide subject matter upon which they may be made to work. This subject matter is under ordinary conditions a Master-concept divided into subordinate concepts. To bring the question down from the region of ideas to that of facts let us take any government project which a department or office is called upon to put into effect. The first step to be taken is to organise a registry in which the subordinate concepts appear under the familar name of headings of subjects. The naming of these subjects starts the process of Symbolisation which is elaborated by the use of letters and numbers to identify files. The latter, all of which must have headings of some kind, are then organised by the processes of Generalisation and Classification. If we represent the first of these by horizontal lines and the second by vertical lines then we obtain a framework of pigeon-holes which give us a picture of the conscious memory as well as of the wooden framework usually constructed to accommodate files. To illustrate the distinction between Generalisation and Classification let us suppose the Master-concept is the organisation of an army. Then generalisation concerns the organisation of personnel into (a) General and Staff Officers, (b) Regimental Officers, and (c) N.C.O.s and men (other ranks), while classification concerns the organisation of personnel into, say, Artillery, Cavalry, Engineers, and Infantry. On a larger scale it is seen in Army, Air Force, Naval, and Supply organisations. Schemes created by the brain of man inevitably shape themselves on the line of the thinking machine which elaborates them and afford us an enlightening imagery of its constitution. If psychologists would but refrain from multiplying technical terms which have no existence but in the region of abstract ideas and descend to the use of familiar illustrations drawn from everyday life they would certainly clarify the subject for students and possibly even for themselves. The reason for calling the first process by the name of Equilibrative Construction will now be clear since the four sub-processes of concept-generation, symbolisation, generalisation, and classification, automatically bring all the concepts, great and small, into equilibrium, and it is the operational methods by which the human brain enables this to be done which places it far above the animal brain. Concept-generation finds its simplest expression in the generation of all numbers from unity by a process of addition, while generalisation and classification find their counterparts in multiplication or heaping up and in division or dividing up heaps of the aggregates so obtained in accordance with the analytical requirements of symbolisation. Naming is rendered necessary by progressive diversification which is akin to subtraction, for just as multiplication is integrated addition so division is integrated subtraction. The brain is in truth a calculating machine which unconsciously works by the rules of simple arithmetic. The four sub-processes of Equilibrative Association have a special value in that the last three throw considerable light upon Processes (11), (12), and (13). In fact, Classification, which completes the pigeon-holes of Memory, links up with Conception of State so intimately that Dr. Lynch is certainly justified in regarding memory as a fundamental process, for it is unquestionably associated with Conception of State.

The foregoing enumeration and arrangement of brain functions are, needless to say, inadequate from the point of view of the particular type of brain specialist known as the logician, but this is due to the fact that only the organisation of the central registry of a government department has been selected for purposes of illustration, whereas the logician is interested in the working of the department and the practical use made of the registry by government officials in transacting business, which entails correspondence, conferences, and the issue of rulings and regulations. For the logician every concept centre or departmental head is one who performs the mental operations of induction, the adoption of working hypotheses, and the testing of them by deduction in order that beliefs of varying degrees of comprehensiveness and reliability may be constructed. The sub-process of generalisation as already referred to is equivalent to the explanatory generalisation of logicians which aims at discovering laws capable of being incorporated into beliefs, which may be graded as certainly, possibly, or probably true. Classification corresponds to the logician's empirical generalisation, the purpose of which is descriptive though it paves the way for explanation. Logic is a highly developed science, which is full of complications, as may be realised by the fact that Professor J. M. Keynes has written a treatise on Probability alone. Logicians have not much to say about Symbolisation, but it comes into operation during the process of language enrichment requisite for the formulation of beliefs which are of the nature of abstractions.

(11) DIRECTIVE ASSOCIATION

Directive Association derives its importance from the fact that it is by far the most powerful of centripetal forces in uniting human beings who have otherwise nothing whatever in common. We may seek for its philosophic basis in radiation, say, of heat-rays from a fire or stove, which continuously subtract heat energy from the source and exhausts it altogether in course of time if no fresh fuel is added. But radiation is nothing if not directional, for if we do not place ourselves in the directions of the waves we do not feel them at all. Light rays are even more directive, as illustrated in the use of an electric torch at night. One of the best examples that can be cited of directive association is provided by crowds which stream in from all directions to a popular race meeting and whose only bond of unity is interest in horse-racing, for they disperse in all directions after the races are over. Such crowds are from their very nature extremely diversified. Rising up to the institutional sphere we have examples of directive associations in joint-stock companies and banks in which the natural desires of shareholders and depositors to make and conserve money are afforded outlets. When some enterprise such as the South Sea Bubble is boomed those who risk their savings are drawn from every rank and class of society, from every conceivable form of occupation, religious belief, educational and cultural level, in fact from almost every variety of grouping known to a civilised community. In the metaphysical region the philosopher is above all others subject to the urge of directive association, for whatever be the reasons which he gives or the facts which he collects to support his theories all alike are directed to prove a few specific theses. The mind of the philosopher radiates outwards as it were into space where it is liable to lose its impetus if not halted within reasonable limits. As regards the association of symbolism with directive association and still more with dispersion, the greater the variety of elements in a particular group the more important it is that each should receive a recognisable label or means of identification. One of the first acts of Adam after his creation, so we are told in the second chapter of *Genesis*, was to give names to the great variety of animals with which he found himself surrounded. The Greeks, who were the greatest philosophers among the ancients if not of all time, evolved a language from which we draw freely in order to coin names, that is, symbols, for the elements of innumerable sciences. The Greek mind was intensely speculative, and there are few problems of philosophy with which it did not concern itself at one time or another. It was never necessary to ask a Greek *Quo vadis?* for moving forth intellectually into the unexplored regions of the mind was the essence of life to him, except in so far as he selected the alternative attraction of politics or art. Where will-power is usually characteristic of the man of equilibrative association imagination is the badge of the man of directive association. A special kind of effort is needed to initiate Directive Association which is easily confused with the Effort dealt with under (12), but whereas the former has for its physical counterpart the effort needed to overcome inertia and set bodies in motion, the latter has for its counterpart the effort needed to lift weights against gravity and overcome frictional resistance. Once inertia has been overcome it then becomes one's ally and helps to maintain the directional mobility of the mind so that it may have to be restrained to avoid mental exhaustion. Nervous people are traditionally slow to make up their minds to act and are noted for the difficulty with which their purpose is diverted or held up by others once they have got fairly under way.

(12) CONSTRUCTIVE ASSOCIATION

It is abundantly evident that much greater physical efforts are needed to construct a substantial edifice than, say, to go to race-meetings, or to create a large commercial organisation involving transportation over long distances, financial trusts, combines, banks, or limited liability companies. The test of the amount of effort used up in the creation of any system or institution is its endurance, and so we find that the Romans who were the most energetic if not the most artistic architects and engineers of the ancient world have bequeathed to civilisation their monumental body of law, not to mention other institutions such as the Holy Roman Empire, which had its roots in Imperial Rome and only expired officially about a century and a half ago. The amount of physical energy which human beings are able to expend in raising heavy weights against gravity for architectural purposes is made evident by a study of the cities which the Peruvians under the Incas constructed on the summits of Andean mountains and of the great road which traversed the empire from north to south and which was constructed at a considerable elevation in spite of the prodigious amount of excavation and bridge building which this involved. In the mental sphere a vast amount of effort has been expended in the construction of religious beliefs, and it should not be forgotten that the Romans and Latinised peoples were mainly responsible for the development of the chief elements in the ecclesiastical organisation, law, and dogmatic theology of the Christian religion and that the Roman Catholic Church is still numerically the most powerful of all the Christian communions. By putting forth efforts to raise weights against gravity a reserve store of potential energy is created which under suitable conditions can be recovered as in the case of a pile-driver or water-tower. Similarly the energy stored up in metaphysical creations of the brain, mind, spirit, or soul is always available to do mental work if needed. The association of Generalisation with Constructive Effort is plain enough, for all generalisations in the region of ideas, laws, creeds, and systematised philosophies require a considerable output of mental energy to establish just as if they had to be raised against some metaphysical downward pull of gravity, and it is for this reason that people of primitive minds such as one finds among savages have so few names to denote classes or species of plants and animals as well as objects such as mountains, valleys, or rivers, whereas they are able to particularise with almost bewildering facility and give names to nearly every physical object of note in their vicinity. Hegel was the great authority on generalisations among the Germans of the nineteenth century and insisted that most apparent contradictions could be resolved or explained by the free use of common denominators. There are definite sense organs terminating in the tendons which inform the brain as to the amount of energy expended in the contraction of muscles, just as most animals, especially migratory birds, have a remarkably acute sense of direction, while man himself has a highly acute sense of balance located in the semi-circular canals of the middle ear without which he would find it difficult if not impossible to maintain an erect position, much less walk and run.

(13) CONCEPTION OF STATE

Few, if any, philosophers show any appreciation of the fact that state makes a triad with time and space, yet so far from the metaphysical conception of state being difficult it enters so much into our ordinary conversation that even children soon learn to use the word freely. The ideas suggested by state are those of continuity and resistance to change, as the adjective static proves. To the Greeks the most deadly disease which could infect a state was stasis, that is incapacity to progress or adapt itself to changing conditions of environment. Static people are conservative and live in the past, finding solace in plumbing the depths of long and accurate memories. Stasis usually sets in through an autocratic clique of elderly men clinging to power as long as possible and bequeathing it at their death to those who are likeminded. The type of mind involved is that which psycho-analysts call introversial because it looks inwards and feeds upon its own innate ideas oblivious of what the minds of others are thinking. If we set ourselves to describe the state of a country at any particular epoch, provided we do not dive too deep into the past, we find ourselves embarrassed by the amount of material available and could easily fill a volume with our conclusions. When a general inspects a battalion he is handed a document called a state which shows the number of officers, N.C.O.s, and men serving on the strength and this might be called an arithmetical state. But before he can report on the state of the battalion, that is, upon its state of efficiency, he will have to submit to a few appropriate tests. Now efficiency is only acquired by training in the past which has been carried out continuously and this connects up with what we have seen to be the essentials of state. A state may be inherited from a condition in which potential has been created by constructive effort, but if this be drawn upon till exhausted a state of deterioration will set in rapidly and become permanent. Of the three kinds of motion, rotary, vibrational, and linear, state is related to the first provided the axis of rotation is fixed as in a flywheel or is vertical as in a gyroscope. No linear motion can be set up in this latter case except one which is vertically upwards as in a helicopter. But gyrostatic movement affords an excellent example of the manner in which the static or introversial mind works because its ideas always revolve in a circle. Considerable stability is obtained by vertical rotary motion but at the expense of all possibilty of progress. The condition of the East Roman Empire and even more so of the Byzantine Empire into which it developed, provides a striking example of an introversial political organisation which remained vigorous for a time under the inherited potential of Imperial Rome, but then disintegrated because it failed to renew the original source of energy. The negative of consolidation by centripetal forces is disintegration by centrifugal forces and this is precisely what happened to the Western half of the Empire. A good illustration from physics is afforded by a seemingly permanent colloidal sol which can be made to precipitate or flocculate almost instantaneously by a current of electricity. Another example is supplied by a millstone or grindstone which breaks up if rotated too rapidly for its modulus of cohesion to hold it together.

(14) CONCEPTION OF TIME

We are not concerned here with giving laborious abstract definitions of the philosophy of time-conception but rather with tracing out the characteristics of those people whose conception of time is markedly stronger than their conceptions of state or space. We say that time flies and most people in whom time-conception is active seek to fly with it and sometimes try to be ahead of it. They are haters of stagnation and pay small regard to traditions which stand in the way of their own progress. They are active, optimistic, fond of planning and intensely vital. Life is not measured by state or space, but by time. The characteristic mode of motion is vibratory, which in the case of a metronome or pendulum clock is the prime cause of ticking out time. Breathing itself is of the nature of slow vibration. Space people are phlegmatic and sometimes lethargic, whereas time people are tense and excitable, vibrating with energy, so to speak. From their ranks come the Liberals and Radicals of politics who hope that given time they may be able to plan a new earth if not a new heaven. Such people show love of changes, of scenery, environment, occupations, ideas, and even beliefs. A war correspondent or newspaper reporter is a typical time-subject. If we hark back to past historical ages we have excellent examples of time-subjects in the highly mobile barbarian tribes of Slavonic and Teutonic origin which overran the Western Roman Empire and even large tracts of the Eastern Empire. The barbarian tribes gloried in their freedom and ability to move where and when they liked, and settling in whatever country took their fancy. State is liable to be earthy in character, but time is airy, it flies like the wind, which supplies the breath of life to the lungs. The life of a time-subject consists of ups and downs like a temperature chart, of crises which resemble the crests and troughs of waves. He would sooner face the risk of calamity than endure monotony and servitude to fossilised authorities.

(15) CONCEPTION OF SPACE

The man who has an active conception of space is primarily concerned with equilibrating with his environment, being what psycho-analysts call an extravert. He also equilibrates the conceptions of state and time and seeks a *via media* between the extremes to which those who hold the latter conceptions tenaciously are liable to go. No man can get in touch with his spatial environment and all that it connotes as being the ground-basis of the social sphere, without spending a certain amount of time in one locality and sensing the state of those who inhabit it, but he cannot afford to become rooted to one spot without his mentality becoming unduly static. Linear motion is appropriate to space and a country cannot be understood and appreciated merely by reading guide-books, it must be traversed by rail, car, or airplane. The space-man, if he makes a hobby of equilibrating with his environment, is liable to become all things to all men even at the sacrifice of principle and to be perpetually wondering if he is making a good impression. He seeks for a variety of sense-stimuli and in most cases is a lover of nature and art. But above all he seeks to preserve his mental equilibrium and to avoid unwholesome excitement and anxiety. Just as the ear is the sense organ which appreciates time-rhythms so the eye is the organ of space-perspectives and for that reason a blind man finds it hard to make contact with novel surroundings, having only hearing and touch to guide him. Of course, time enters into all appreciations of space since motion in space must be carried out at some velocity, however small, and velocity is space divided by time, provided we take it as a measure of slowness and not quickness. To pass to historical illustrations, when the barbarian tribes settled down into the various countries of Europe the officers became feudal magnates and the freemen townsfolk or serfs. Both set themselves forthwith to equilibrate with their environment and thus there grew up in the Middle Ages a picturesque form of feudalism in which chivalry, heraldry, pageantry, and prestige played important parts. The political and ecclesiastical spheres were dominated by emperors and popes respectively, both essential heads of the system of the Holy Roman Empire whose form was derived from Christian Rome as the name implies, but whose spirit came from the dynamic Barbarians. The contemplation of the majesty of the Empire with its two great lights, the planets of which were the kings and princes of most of the countries of Western and Central Europe, made a powerful and vivid appeal to mental spaciousness, as may be seen from Dante's *De Monarchia*, in which he extolled the theory of the Empire as representing the high water-mark of human wisdom. Had the sun of the Empire and the moon of the Papacy been content to live in equilibrium and harmony Dante's extravagant laudations might have been justified, but as things turned out both parties became equally discredited by their virulent animosities.

(16) INDIVIDUALISTIC CONSTRUCTION

The three forms of constructiveness characteristic of the objective mind may be regarded as being derived from Constructive Association (12) brought down to a lower region of consciousness. Here we are concerned with Dr. Lynch's process of Agreement and Disagreement, taking the positive and negative together. Now Agreement is mainly a matter of intellectual harmonisation but it often happens that the more intelligent a number of men are the more acutely they disagree among themselves, partly because of the personal equation of each and partly because of the complexities of the problems with which those who seek to regulate human affairs have to deal. It was to counteract the anarchy liable to be caused by individual men of forceful character being able to have their own way in everything that Law was adopted by the peoples of the earth, both civilised and barbarian, and this applies specially to constitutional law. It is generally agreed that the spirit of the Renaissance centred upon the assertion of the rights of the individual, and the virtual dissolution of the Empire as an effective system of government in international affairs caused the individualism of the various nations to awaken into unprecedented activity, with the result that national bodies and codes of law were perfected and the principles of constitutional law and organisation were hammered out in each country, not without considerable bloodshed, especially in the early stages when the issues were clouded by acrimonious religious discord. If the political individualist is a problem to his fellows the religious individualist is twice as difficult to deal with. The Reformation was to religion what the Renaissance was to culture and in both cases men were compelled to hasten with constructive work designed to regulate and control the eccentricities of individualism, because for a time the lid was taken off the bottomless pit of human lawlessness and the alternatives presented were "Organise and obey the laws or perish." It was primarily because the Poles refused to face this situation that their country was partitioned between their three unscrupulous neighbours while small individualistic nations like the Dutch and the Danes throve apace.

Individualism lies at the head of the objective mental activity and manifests itself above all in Opportunism, which involves seeking opportunities and not waiting for them to turn up. Partly on this account, partly from curiosity, and partly because of uncongenial happenings at home, multitudes of the inhabitants of Europe set forth during the next three centuries to explore the far regions of the earth and to settle in those in which the climate was suitable for the upbringing of children. Constructive Individualism then appeared in the building up of communities abroad which became first colonies, and then dominions, while in the case of the United States an independent state or rather federation of states emerged.

(17) Hedonistic Construction

Hedonistic constructiveness is the mighty urge which impels those who have formed the political constitutions of new states to clothe them as it were with the things that make life worth living not only from a materialistic, but from an æsthetic and ethical point of view. If Law dominates Individualistic Construction, Administrative Method on equitable lines dominates Hedonistic Construction, and it is this latter fundamental process which lies at the root of the civilisation of the present day. Autocracy has given way to bureaucracy, but whether this means that we have exchanged king log for king stork remains to be seen. The real and pressing danger, however, which the hedonistic urge is liable to bring in its train is to afford opportunity to the selfish to accumulate wealth and revel in the so-called good things of life while the masses are deprived not merely of the amenities of civilisation but even of much of its necessities. Such is the situation in which we find ourselves now and for which capitalism is blamed rather than the inherent self-seeking which would make any financial system subserve its own ends. Hedonistic Constructiveness reached its apex early in the twentieth century, but since then two devastating wars and a major revolution in Russia have introduced an era of destructiveness the outcome of which may be complete disaster. The aim of the hedonistic urge is to bring the greatest happiness to the greatest number according to the philosophers who have expounded it to us, and if this be the case it has failed lamentably to justify itself in the age in which we live. The sense associated with hedonism is taste.

(18) Impulsive Construction

We may take it as generally true that while political organisation is a test of individuality and the nature of civilisation is a test of character, impulsive organisation is a test of personality, since, as a rule, the maintenance of order and the subjugation of social unruliness bring to the top persons who command general approbation on account of their capacity to enforce obedience upon those whom arguments cannot convince nor threats intimidate. Impulsiveness is fiery in character and if not restrained within bounds may cause irreparable havoc. It feeds on grievances as a fire feeds on fuel and revels in the delusion that change for the sake of change will improve the general lot of mankind. The urge of impulse exceeds both that of individual opinion and that of cultural progress in its power for moving men to violent action and though it has to be restrained by a police organisation forcible repression is liable to leave fires smouldering which burst once more into flame as soon as the heavy hand has been lifted. A good example of the operation of Impulse is afforded by Trotskyite Bolshevism which only recently threatened to reduce Greece to chaos. Fenianism and allied Irish disorders of recent date had or have their root in unregulated impulse. In its essence Impulse is intensified wilfulness if permitted to run riot, but energetic drive if directed on right lines. At all times it is liable to be "agin the government," but usually respects the police. Bergson has dealt with its philosophic implications under the name of "élan vital." Just as individualism works off surplus energy by expansion in space and distributing mankind throughout the habitable places of the globe, and just as hedonism aims at producing a healthy state of civilisation, so impulse is allied in nature to Conception of Time (14) and manifests the same tendency to produce irrational optimism and an even greater liability to exaggerate and to be deceived by mirages. Time-conception, as a reaction against state-conception, invariably gives rise to love of change and reform, but is liable to carry them to a point at which chaos supplants order through the jettisoning of the wisdom gained in past times by hard experience. Its emotional content renders it at times impervious to reason, though it can always be set in motion by tub-thumping and mob oratory.

The sense corresponding with Impulse is an intensified kind of taste which has something of tactile sensitiveness in its composition, causing palatable food to be greedily swallowed or unpalatable food to be violently ejected. Those who have the related psychic sense are characterised by strong likes and dislikes.

(19) Unit Concept

We shall find that all the processes are reproduced in a similar form in the fourth tier both upwards and downwards, and in this case we have what we might call the unit of Equilibrative Association, that is the sub-concept analysed with special reference to the associated presentations or sense data which impinge on the consciousness from the external environment, that is the percepts which, when they reach the brain, becoming organised or manifolded as concepts. The brain in forming the Unit Concept organises percepts by symbolisation, generalisation, and classification, and when this is done they are packed into the sub-conscious memory if suitable for storage there, or else pushed up into the higher strata of consciousness plus the intensification of feeling supplied by Impulse and the refinement of feeling supplied by Hedonism. The man in whom the process of unit conception is active places great reliance upon his own judgment which is, as a rule, sound in purely material things because he seeks to make use of all sense data that have a bearing upon any particular concept and incorporate them all as elements in his final decision or plan of campaign. Stalin affords a striking example of a man in whom this process is highly developed.

(20) IMMEDIATE PRESENTATION

The associated sense data or external presentations of (20) are the sensory counterparts of the motor impulses which radiate outwards in the compartment of Directional Association (11). They are from their very nature highly diversified and need, therefore, to be subjected to association before being sent up to the brain, which would otherwise become bewildered and overloaded. The type of person in whom the process of Immediate Presentation is active hardly calls for much imagination to describe, for he must first and foremost have keen perceptions combined with a capacity for recognising, identifying, and describing whatever stimuli impinge upon his perceptive consciousness from without. He is active and alert, but sceptical of everything that he cannot sense directly and explain, as well as measure in terms of some standard unit.

(21) REALISM

Realism, the lower harmonic of Constructive Association, seeks to examine the foundations of all things rather than to raise edifices. It expresses itself in particularisation which it carries to extremes, often keeping its eyes so glued to the ground that it loses all capacity to take wide views. It is a truism to say that the process of Realism assures us of the objective existence of the material world in which we live. It discourages us from paying heed to the erudite philosophers who would have us believe that the only world that exists for us is what is pictured in our own inner consciousness. Realistic people play an important part in the economy of this world because they have an active appreciation of its material needs and as often as not labour assiduously in one way or another to supply them. They are frankly utilitarian in their outlook, but when, as in the case of the Swedes, they combine utilitarianism with hedonism they raise the general level of civilisation and set their face against all devices for money-making which result in creating glaring inequalities between rich and poor. But their keen discrimination in material things renders them liable to become over-critical and fault-finding so that their merits are as often as not belittled if not ignored. The senses associated with Processes (19), (20), and (21) are three forms of Touch which may be described as Sensitiveness, Perceptiveness, and Pressure.

A brief consideration of the associated colours will serve to bring into further relief the essential nature of the Fundamental Processes.

Tier VIII

The Brown tier VIII is the lower harmonic of the Green tier V and includes the three subconscious forms of Conception of State (Memory) (22), Conception of Time (23), and Conception of Space (24). It is the seat of the vice of selfishness which mars so much of the constructive activities of tier V. These are altruistic in their nature and become ruined out of recognition if exercised in a spirit of self-seeking and self-glorification.

Tier IX

The Grey tier IX is the lower harmonic of the Yellow tier VI and is the seat of the vices of fearfulness, over-anxiety, and self-distrust which exercise a paralysing effect upon the constructive activities of Individuality, Hedonism, and Impulsiveness producing a condition of mental indecision which results in the frittering away of energy.

Tier III

The Purple tier III is the upper harmonic of the Yellow tier VI and is the seat of the idealisation of the Constructive Processes (16), (17) and (18). The idealisation of Law leads to high conceptions of just and fair dealing as between man and man in the competition which is inevitable under present conditions, thus reducing litigation to a minimum. The idealisation of administrative method in the region of hedonism by which alone civilisation can advance appears in the formulæ of ethical and humanitarian philosophies, of which that of Confucius affords an example. The idealisation of orderliness in the relationship of men to each other, considered as beings in whom impulses and desires make imperative demands on self control, results in the acceptance and development of religions by which alone men can be united in the bonds of brotherhood (cf., religio-binding).

Tier II

The Amber tier II is the upper harmonic of the Green tier V and is the region of intellectual purity of a kind that leads to the powers of the mind being employed altruistically in the ecclesiastical, educational and social spheres.

Tiers I and X

Tier I is concerned with pure and selfless motivation which inspires rulers to govern solely in the interests of the ruled. Its colour is electrum and its lowest harmonic is black, from which emanate cruelty, tyranny, and treachery, and in fact most of the vices which have rendered Nazism odious in the sight of all mankind.

CHAPTER IV

THE FUNDAMENTAL PROCESSES AND THE ANALYSIS OF LOGIC

See TABLES B and C.

LOGIC is a word which is used in two senses, either as the art or science of reasoning as exercised by the mind as a whole or in a narrower sense as the art or science of argument. It is in the former sense that it will be dealt with here. Firstly we may recognise four major elements in logic, Proposition, Belief, Explanatory Generalisation and Empirical Generalisation. The Proposition in Logic has much the same signification as the Concept in Psychology, that is to say both are self-contained and are sources of operative power. Belief implies the existence of believers in a proposition and its acceptance by them as true, whether capable of proof or not. The Explanatory Generalisation, as the name implies, aims at explaining facts and understanding the laws governing them. It involves the exercise of the understanding. The Empirical Generalisation is closely connected with Classification and is exercised upon observed facts so that it involves discovery and description. In constructing a Key Table one may either take the four leading elements and see if there are eight others of approximately equal importance which may be placed with them in 12 compartments, or if we find the latter do not exist, as in the present case, then we may write down the leading elements in four tiers and divide them up among the 3 compartments composing each tier. Applying the latter to Logic we obtain 12 Principles of Logic the first 6 of which equate more or less with the first 6 Processes of Psychology and are as follows:—Proposition (10), Deduction (11), Induction (12), Certainty of Belief (13), Possibility of Belief (14), Probability of Belief (15). There are three kinds of Explanatory Generalisations excluding those which are necessary, certain, and axiomatic and which may be placed in tier VI, viz. those which affect the Laws of the Natural Sciences (16), those which affect the membership of objects in particular classes or positions in symmetrical schemes of arrangement (17), and those dealing with explanations of biological facts as consequences which operate in time and are known as Teleological (18). (16) may be described briefly as Regulative or Ordinant and (17) as Classificatory. Empirical Generalisations are divisible into three kinds, two qualitative and one quantitative, and the two qualitative may be divided into Sequential and Simultaneous, (19) and (20), the last being defined as Statistical

(21). There is also another logical principle, the Subconscious Belief or as it is usually called Superstition, which has much in common with the Certain Belief of (13) but has no evidential basis of the kind usually recognised as such by scientists and logicians. The seven modes of generalisation from (16) to (22) inclusive may be classed together as evidential because they furnish the necessary data for inferences to be drawn from facts, either directly or indirectly. The principles connected with the 13 compartments, otherwise "the contents" of the same will now be considered seriatim, beginning with the lowest, in order to preserve the inductive sequence which works from the factual to the metaphysical.

(22) SUBCONSCIOUS BELIEFS

The Subconscious beliefs, which are held by crowds rather than individuals, or at least preserved and transmitted by them as part of their ancestral heritage, might be classified under (22), (23) and (24) according as they are Certain, Possible, or Probable in regard to their truth, but for present purposes all three may be included under (22). The same compartment will serve for the subconscious memory of events in the past lives of individuals, since these with subconscious beliefs furnish the pabulum upon which Psycho-analysts rely to prove their theses. The latter certainly come under the headings of generalisations performed by mass-reasoning while the former usually appear as generalisations of a series of events or as the abstraction of the psychological quantum of some event of special importance. This whole subject, however, belongs to psychology rather than to logic.

(21) QUANTITATIVE EMPIRICAL GENERALISATIONS

The object of the empirical generalisation is not to ascertain the laws governing the facts so generalised but rather to marshal them in groups to provide evidential data for explanatory generalisations, so that once they have been described the object for which they have been made may be regarded as having been achieved. Quantitative generalisations are well represented by statistics, which while they may suggest the operation of laws to experts, do not of themselves prove them. Most commissions appointed by governments to consider complex social problems make free use of statistics to guide them in their findings. Now statistics are notoriously dry and uninviting to the average man, but they have the advantage of compelling him to face facts, especially disagreeable ones. Human beings are all prone to form opinions which have a hedonistic appeal and cling to them tenaciously for that very reason as if part of themselves. One often hears people say that they like to think this or that, quite unconcerned as to whether their opinions are probably true or valid. Whenever they can be induced to consider statistics which bear upon the particular subjects on which they hold opinions, they are liable to be brought down to earth with an uncomfortable jolt. All the hedonism which inflates their convictions oozes out and perhaps for the first time in their lives they are compelled to face grim realities. Thus we see the almost exact correspondence between the 12th principle of Logic and the 12th Fundamental Process of Realism, by which, as the name denotes, facts are realised and recognised, instead of being set aside with ostrich-like disdain. We must also take into account the individual who is determined to make statistics support his opinions and who shamelessly fakes them until they furnish the particular kind of evidence which he desires. Honest statistics cannot lie, provided they cover the facts involved, but most people at one time or another find themselves floundering in quicksands of faked statistics.

(20) QUALITATIVE EMPIRICAL GENERALISATIONS
    SIMULTANEOUS

A great deal of empirical generalisation of the qualitative kind is performed unconsciously and instinctively by the organs of physical perception, particularly those of special sensation such as the eye, the ear, and the nostril, as part of their allotted functions of keeping the individual fully informed as to the conditions of his environment. The qualitative character of visual impressions, sounds, and scents is obvious enough, and furthermore these are usually interpreted as agreeable or the reverse. Even the various impressions grouped as tactile may render us comfortable or otherwise. Furthermore a large number of sense impressions of inconceivable variety are received simultaneously every second by individuals in the waking state and pursuing their customary avocations. If they themselves move or observe external objects in motion then clearly the question of succession comes into the picture but not in such a manner as to eliminate that of simultaneity. Part of the sense data which impinge upon the perceptive organs are manifolded by the brain into concepts but the remainder are conserved as percepts of varying degrees of integration, and as such become available for service in the making of Explanatory Generalisations of the Classificatory group (17), in which objects are arranged and graded in accordance with the kind of stimuli which they impart to our sense organs.

What is known to psychologists as the behaviour of animals, especially that which is revealed in the co-operative activities of insects such as bees or ants, is determined, apart from hereditary predispositions, by the nature of the empirical generalisations of a simultaneous qualitative origin which they make. The science of Behaviourism involves the study of nervous structures and functions with special reference to the activities of the reflex centres. One school, the Gestalt, regards behaviour as resulting from tensional systems with laws of characteristic patterns (gestalten). Another school postulates as the explanation of specific behaviour a faculty of extra-sensory perception.

(19) QUIDDITIVE EMPIRICAL GENERALISATIONS
    SEQUENTIAL

The second class of Qualitative Generalisations would be more accurately described as Quidditive because they are formed by abstracting the essences of sense-impressions for the purpose of manifolding as concepts, and in the course of this process the hedonistic elements become eliminated to some extent. Now concepts cannot be entertained by the brain simultaneously when first formed. They must of necessity rise up into consciousness in succession but once they have risen they can be integrated. This is what happens in a very primitive manner in counting, for this operation consists essentially in the addition sum of $1 + 1 + 1 + 1 = 4$, to take a specific example. All generalisations of events or of appearances of moving objects made sequentially, that is in time, come under the heading of (19), and these being dynamic in origin provide data which are appropriate to the formation of Regulative Generalisations in which the explanation of law is the object of search. If we leave out of account Quantitative Statistics and Qualitative generalisations of Sense Data then all that remain of Empirical Generalisation belong to the Sequential kind.

Sequential generalisations made by the brain which provide an inner urge for purposive action may be correlated with the Propensity school of psychologists, which includes all the psycho-analytical schools. This school is concerned with Dispositions whereas that of the Behaviourists is concerned with Reactions.

(18) Explanatory Generalisations
    Teleological

The connection of the 9th Principle of Logic with the fundamental process of Impulse is clear enough, for the latter furnishes the motive power for all generation, which is the primary means utilised by the forces of biology to perpetuate mankind and the existing species of animals and plants. The teleological implications of generation are well exemplified in the promise made to Abraham by the Almighty that in his seed all the nations of the earth should be blessed. Here we have teleology made to coincide with the utmost limits of prophetic forecasting. As already pointed out, sequential orderliness distinguishes the operations of all biological processes but there are sharp conflicts of opinion as to whether the biological forces now in operation were at any time competent to produce new species from old, and thus biological generalisations by no means lead inevitably to the formulation of laws upon which all scientists are agreed. True that the majority believe in some sort of evolution but the most responsible ones admit freely that they are no nearer understanding the mechanism of evolution than they ever were since the days of Darwin and that for the time being therefore Evolution must be treated as an unproved hypothesis. Comparatively few of the lesser lights, on the other hand, have accepted this cautious advice.

(17) Explanatory Generalisations
    Classificatory

We cannot do better than take the science of Chemistry as an example of the operation of the principle of Classificatory Generalisations. Biological generation is under the Control of electro-magnetic laws to a greater extent than is even realised by advanced authorities on the subject for the fertilised sex cell has not only polarity but is a miniature battery. And in addition animal magnetism lies at the root of all sex-attraction. Chemical laws are, it is true, profoundly affected by those of Electro-magnetism on the one hand and by those of Solution and Diffusion on the other, but when we eliminate these we have still the powerful structure-building forces of chemical affinity to give rise to the complex forms of the organic and inorganic kingdoms. To begin with, all the known chemical elements have been classified according to the Periodic Law which within certain limits tabulates if it does not wholly explain the properties of the various elements. But when we come to the inorganic and organic substances formed by the combinations of the elements according to the laws of chemical attraction their number defies computation, though the exact nature of most can be defined by formulæ. The majority assume crystalline forms, wholly or partly, and all possible crystal forms have been described and classified by the pioneers of the science of Crystallography. Protoplasm, the substance from which all living forms have been created, belongs to the category of organic chemical compounds, and even minerals assume many forms resembling plants, of which the most familiar is the crystallisation of fern patterns on window-panes in frosty weather. These are however evanescent, whereas the forms assumed by many minerals are characteristic and permanent. Many of the material symbols which we employ to describe human and animal psychological characteristics are drawn from the chemical world, for the illustrative art is sculpture and character comes from the Greek charassein, to engrave. Large numbers of mineral forms look as if they had been either moulded or sculptured and the living bodies of human beings, whose chemical constituents are accurately known, have been from the earliest times utilised as models by artists of the hammer and chisel fraternity. It may be objected that classification is static whereas laws are dynamic and the latter alone can explain sequences of cause and effect but on the other hand when some new element is found it fits readily into a vacant space reserved for one of the same atomic weight and after that a whole series of properties can be predicated about it with a high degree of probable correctness. The relationship between Hedonism and æsthetic form calls for no demonstration, for it is self-evident and the two entities are almost interchangeable.

(16) Explanatory Generalisations Regulative or Ordinant

It is difficult to find a suitable title for the Explanatory Generalisations which deal with natural laws, for words legal and juristic obviously have no bearing on the case. Ordinant is an adjective formed from ordinance and Nature's laws might fairly be called her ordinances. Regulative might be adopted as alternative title. The Regulative is the highest of the Evidential Generalisations, inclusive of the three distinguished as explanatory, because they define the conditions that fix the nature of the elements of empirical generalisations, and also because they do

THE FUNDAMENTAL PROCESSES AND THE ANALYSIS OF LOGIC

in fact explain what the latter cannot do. Explanation of a kind that can be appreciated by the understanding of the ordinary man is the avowed object of educational science. In the absence of such explanation phenomena appear to follow their own sweet will and do what is right in their own eyes, but lawlessness of this kind in natural events and processes is from its very nature revolting to the judgment of every thinking man. Particular irregularities and eccentricities are however to be expected in the behaviour of objects in the natural world as of living things. Theoretical knowledge is expected to demonstrate how the problem to be solved is associated with other problems that are more easily and perfectly apprehended. It may be noticed incidentally how instinctively we apply the metaphor of solution, which is a physical process, to an analogous mental process. Some problems like certain intractable substances cannot be dissolved except by specially powerful reagents. Few explanations can be regarded as completely satisfactory in that even when one has discovered a law, verified it, and defined it with mathematical symbols, the question still presents itself as to why that particular law should operate at all and not one which we might consider more practical. Problems of regulative generalisation have usually to be solved piecemeal, here a little and there a little, partial generalisations of a similar character being established seriatim. In fact it is often essential to divide up major problems into subsidiary ones before any headway can be made at all, oblivious of the urgings of impatient people who seek to make grandiose regulative syntheses which would soon disintegrate under the scrutiny of analytical minds.

(15) PROBABILITIES OF BELIEFS
   EVIDENCE AND INFERENCE

The Social Sphere is the region of beliefs which are probably true. This will become clear if we commence with the Religious Sphere (13) which until recently used to be hardly separable from the Home Sphere, and regard it as the region of settled beliefs which were always taught as certainly true, and then pass on to the Educational Sphere (14) in which beliefs are usually classified as possible or impossible. In the Home Sphere parents used to bring up their children in their own faith and teach them the tenets of the same as doctrines to be received and believed without argument. By this means, for better or for worse according to the creed inculcated, the child was enabled to form a metaphysical core or armature which served to give it stability of outlook for the rest of its life, especially if its mentality were introversial. In the school or university, on the other hand, young people are being taught increasingly to think for themselves and not to receive as final what they are taught without acquainting themselves with the arguments which support the teaching given to them. But as the life of the schoolboy or the university student is relatively uncomplicated because he has no occasion to face up to the real problems of life, so his mental outlook becomes academic and he views the world with intellectual detachment. Under these conditions he comes to regard everything that cannot be justified by logical argument as impossible and to adopt a cocksure attitude on the matter, just as the child who has been rigorously instructed in some particular creed is dogmatic in its outlook, because it cannot conceive that its parents or religious instructors should have been mistaken. But as soon as boys and girls pass from the educational atmosphere to the social atmosphere they find out very quickly that their views are far too naïve to be of practical use to them and proceed to absorb the social beliefs of their set without inquiring too closely into the evidence on which such beliefs are based. They are frankly uninterested as to whether social beliefs have evidential support or not because they intend to adopt such beliefs in any case on the ground that acceptance of them makes the wheels of life go round smoothly. They want to be in the fashion and to be thought good company. They soon learn that dogmatism and cocksureness get them nowhere and are considered bad form. Social beliefs are accepted by them because they are probably true and afford a reasonably safe guide by which to direct their activities and ambitions. The boy soon moves on to the business sphere where he encounters innumerable laws that have to be obeyed but even then he spends the recreational part of his life in the social sphere. Girls, until recently, lived almost entirely in the social sphere. In both adaptability is a *sine qua non* for success, but life is far more leisurely and free from tensions and problems in the former than in the latter. The Social Sphere is the region where young people learn the practical knowledge of the kind that is the metaphysical counterpart of sight, for in it they see life as it is. When they begin to understand its principles they say, "I see what you mean," to their monitors whereas at school and college they were told to give ear to the precepts of masters and professors. Inner sight or intuition under the new conditions is of far more value to them than inner hearing and they are satisfied with seeing propositions and beliefs as probabilities spread out before their eyes in panoramic fashion. This mental attitude is unsatisfactory to the logician but it is that of the average person, who says he knows this and that without having the slightest notion as to what evidence he can adduce to justify his views and opinions. His usual attitude towards beliefs is to inquire whether they are likely to smooth the path of life before him and then if challenged to cast about for any evidence which on the face of it supports them and to imagine that he has thereby rendered them critic-proof. A few young people however to whom a rational attitude towards life is attractive set themselves to infer beliefs from the evidence furnished by the seven kinds of generalisation. It is not to be supposed from the foregoing that social beliefs of a traditional character are unsupported by evidence of any kind. On the contrary when they first acquired ascendancy the supporting evidence was doubtless paraded and publicised in an adequate manner. But as time passes on interest in the rational basis of beliefs of probability fades away and only the beliefs themselves persist. Many people leave it to neighbours whom they consider to be wiser than themselves to do their thinking for them and accept the conclusions of their guides without undue scepticism.

Comparatively few people have the leisure, much less the inclination, to probe into the foundations of the prodigious quantities of popular beliefs with which they come in contact. If however they do set themselves to infer their beliefs from the ample supply of evidential generalisations at their disposal, they have first of all to satisfy themselves that the propositions which they accept are true and secondly that the inferences which they make from the same are logically valid. If reassured on both points they can then claim with justification that the sum-total of their beliefs constitutes real knowledge even though held as probably and not certainly true. As it has been stated succinctly, "Probability is the rule of life," which is in effect the pith and marrow of the philosophy expounded by the eminent philosopher, John Locke. There can be no question that there are endless degrees of probability ranging from the improbable though possible to the certain and reliable. But since there exists no means whereby degrees of probability can be measured the average man must rest satisfied if he succeeds in acquiring insight into the relative values of the numerous beliefs which in the aggregate pass for knowledge of the world and its ways. The classification of beliefs does not appear to be dealt with on sufficiently comprehensive lines by most authorities on logic and the following remarks on the subject must not therefore be regarded as reflecting the official view. Firstly as regards the classification of beliefs into certain or uncertain (13), possible or impossible (14) and probable or improbable (15), in this work certain or uncertain is taken as including moral truths and untruths. Now moral truths cannot be proved to be certainly true by any process of logic except in so far as it is possible to prove from history that moral virtues pay and immoral vices do not. The difference between what is moral on the one hand and what is immoral or at least unmoral on the other is a matter to be determined by ethical instinct and the traditional views and actions of the best of mankind. The question of religious belief is closely connected with moral and ethical beliefs, but the history of Christianity, to take only one religion, is a record of the continuous raging of bitter controversies over what was to be regarded as true or false, the penalty of falling into error being too often insisted upon as eternal condemnation. For psychological purposes one must accept the belief of an individual or a religious community as a fact whether one regards it as true or untrue, and moreover one must expect every sincere man to be certain about his belief, and if he is not certain to abstain from trying to propagate it. It is however in the region of the intellect, that is the philosophic and educational sphere, that we find the distinction between the possible and impossible most sharply defined, for the very word impossible has an absolute meaning, there can be no degrees in it. What is impossible cannot be done and if any man claims that he has achieved the impossible he proves, provided his success is admitted, to have achieved what is possible though perhaps difficult. There are three main kinds of intellectual belief, namely the axioms and postulates of mathematics, logic, and geometry. What they assert to be untrue is impossible. If we confine ourselves to elementary mathematics we know that if the rules for adding, subtracting, multiplying, dividing, and extracting roots are followed the results obtained are infallibly correct. The laws of logic, of which there are four basic ones, are so self-evident that no-one who was not mentally unbalanced could question their validity. Lastly the axioms and postulates of Euclid are incontrovertibly true for tri-dimensional uncurved space, and it has yet to be proved that any other kind of space exists. By a process of elimination we arrive at a group of somewhat ill-defined beliefs which may be classed as social, artistic, or salutary, the third indicating what is good for health or otherwise. The most important of the social beliefs is that of the divine right of kings which has been held as true and incontrovertible with but few dissentient voices in both East and West for thousands of years. The first time that it was challenged in the East was in the Chinese Revolution which was staged early in the present century. If we except the Greeks and Romans of republican times before the Christian Era and some of the barbarian Celtic and Slavonic tribes we may say the Divine right of kings was acknowledged as a truth until challenged by the French Encyclopædists of the eighteenth century, making due allowance for the brief period during which monarchy in England was in abeyance during Cromwell's régime. It should be borne in mind that the doctrine in question teaches that monarchy as an institution is Divinely ordained and not that every king who occupies a throne should be permitted to exercise authority whatever his vices or eccentricities. Next we come to the canons of art which have remained virtually unchallenged since the Age of Pericles in Greece to the beginning of the present century. They have been universally accepted as probably true and valid by all artists, taking the word in its widest application. For instance it was held that if a painter set out to draw the human body or a sculptor to model it, he should select physically perfect types to copy unless of course he was commissioned to paint a portrait or make a statue of some particular celebrity. But only a generation which held traditional artistic canons in profound contempt could find anything to admire in much that passes for poetry, music, painting, or sculpture at the present day. Salutary or healthsome beliefs are not so much the edicts of medical science as the rules of health universally recognised as sound from ancient times, such as the need for a certain amount of fresh air, relaxation and recreation to preserve health and youthfulness. There is a high degree of probability that these are medically true, as most doctors readily admit.

(14) POSSIBILITIES OF BELIEFS
    ARGUMENT AND THE LAWS OF LOGIC

Compartment (14) might be called the natural home of logicians owing to its connection with intellectuality, universities, professors, and everything associated with the dissemination of pure knowledge. The Scholastic Philosophy which prevailed in the educational institutions of Europe from the ninth to the fourteenth centuries was mainly concerned with formal logic in its relation to religious philosophy. During the latter part of the thirteenth century the wrangles between the Scotists and Thomists, the advocates of Realism and Conceptualism respectively, were carried on with such vigour, both claiming the science of logic as supporting their respective teachings, that Europe became sickened of the whole subject and the opinion prevailed that logical argumentation was necessarily as arid as the sands of the desert. Every argument is made up of propositions of which one constitutes the conclusion while the others are treated as evidence. The latter are called premises and may be either positive or negative, while propositions may be general or particular. Arguments are classified into four main groups according as their conclusions belong to one or other of four types. The principles of deductive reasoning are derived from a fundamental axiom and three laws of thought, those of Identity, Non-contradiction, and the Excluded Middle. The whole subject is however intricate and technical and no analysis of it can be attempted here. The axiom and the laws of formal logic are so self-evident that they appear as mere truisms, but when applied with precision they suffice to detect flaws in arguments which render the conclusions invalid, or in other words impossible. Axiomatic truth cannot be violated by any contradiction which can even claim to be possibly true.

There are, it is true, some mystical philosophers, such as Ouspensky, who say that the laws of logic are not valid in the psychic state of consciousness and that an idea or thing called A can be different from an idea or thing called B and yet identical with it. But anyone who asserts this can be challenged to prove that the idea or thing which he calls A is not in fact Ax and that which he calls B is not in fact Bx and that the nexus of identity which he perceives is not in fact x, which A and B qualify in different ways. Any assertions that the absolute laws of logic, mathematics, and geometry are only valid in this world are emphatically propositions which must be proved and not assumed.

(13) CERTAINTIES OF BELIEFS
BELIEFS AND FACTS

If we distribute the triad of Evidences, Arguments and Beliefs into compartments (15), (14), and (13) we observe to begin with that evidences may be regarded as so far spatial in that they partake of simultaneity and nearly all are derived from observations of environmental conditions in the first instance. Logical argument, on the other hand, is referable to time, nor merely because argument takes up time and frequently a good deal of it but because the science or art of logic has a long history behind it, dating from Aristotle who lived in the fourth century B.C. Lastly, believing is generally admitted to imply a state of mind in which one or more beliefs are firmly rooted, at any rate when they are religious, moral, or in any degree traditional. We naturally think of beliefs as fixed because experience teaches us that they are adhered to with tenacity by those who entertain them, as if they were interwoven in the substance of the soul. A belief in order to be worthy of the name must have some fact or occurrence, perhaps belonging to the distant past, to support it, and the more of these which can be adduced as evidence the better for the belief. A belief necessitates the existence either in the past or present of one or more believers who held or hold it. Again an inquirer into the tenets of a creed which is new to him passes through several states of mind wherein he investigates the evidence for it, judges its merits, compares it with other beliefs, studies the arguments for and against it, during which he may be doubtful, hopeful, pessimistic, or enthusiastic in turn until finally he grasps its inner significance and becomes a convinced convert. These states of mind are subjective and the belief remains objective until such a time as its truth is recognised and it becomes absorbed into the religious fabric of the convert. The connection between beliefs and facts is illustrated diagrammatically by the process of expanding the contents of compartment (13) into those of tier VII which relate to the empirical generalisation of facts.

(12) INDUCTIVE PROCEDURE

The purpose of Inductive Procedure is to discover and tabulate the underlying conditions which give rise to objects and their distinguishing characteristics. In the language of the builder it quarries stones and excavates foundations in order to be able to erect structures, for the explanatory generalisations of tier VI, the expansion of compartment (12) may be compared both with architectural edifices and with the geological strata which the earth has formed for itself during millions of years by earthquakes and inundations. In order however to effect an inductive generalisation use has to be made of two higher principles. A start having been made with an empirical generalisation of facts which entails observation of resemblances and differences, a Hypothetical Proposition (10) is then formulated to account provisionally for the existence of the empirical generalisation, taken in conjunction with the knowledge which has already been obtained bearing upon the aforesaid facts. The next step is for the investigating scientist to trace out deductively the consequences which follow inevitably from the hypothetical proposition, assuming it to be dynamically active. Deduction inevitably suggests to the mind a chain of reasoning which descends from above, as rain does from the clouds, or which radiates from the proposition as emanations do from the sun, and for this reason it is the logical counterpart of the process of Directive Association (11) which is analytical in its mode of operation. Deduction is clearly distinguishable from the laws by which the validity of deduction is tested, and those who deduce consequences from causes are of a philosophic bent of mind, whereas the mentality of the logician is scholastic and academic. The deductive process must be regarded as being effected in a direction which brings it back to the starting point, somewhat after the manner of a water-cycle in which water is evaporated from a lake, condensed into a cloud, and then precipitated in the form of rain upon the surface of the same identical lake. The end-products of the deductive chain are then tested out against the original facts to ascertain whether they agree or disagree with them. If the former happens then the hypothesis becomes a reliable proposition worthy of belief and if the latter its utility is finished and it is discarded. Strange to say Newton stated that he never had anything to do with hypotheses, but he could not have been a logician otherwise he would have realised that he could have made no discoveries without them. Certainly the laws of gravitation and motion were entertained by him as hypotheses before they were announced to the world as in accordance with known facts. When a hypothesis has been confirmed by tests with known facts it can then by a process of trial and error be formulated in such a manner as to render it unchallengeable. Induction of the higher order of (12) summarises explanatory generalisations as these in turn summarise empirical generalisations, and is the means whereby new theories are formed. A theory is however something more than a super-generalisation, for it must be capable of deduction from one or more propositions, in fact it could not be formed without the operation of deduction. The logical justification of theories comes within the province of the philosopher who is the recognised expert on deductive reasoning. The procedure here described is by no means inevitably fruitful of results because of psychological twists which urge us subconsciously to select facts as evidence which support whatever theory we are testing out, especially if already held tenaciously as a private and personal belief. As Jevons put it, "it is difficult to find persons who can with perfect fairness register facts for and against their own peculiar views." There has been some controversy among logicians as to whether inductive reasoning provides rules which enable discoveries to be made but the majority undoubtedly hold that the primary function of induction, working in conjunction with the proposition and the deductive method, is to prove the reliability or otherwise of discoveries suggested by empirical generalisations. There is a danger, in earmarking compartments (10), (11), and (12) for Proposition, Deduction, and Induction respectively, of suggesting to the reader who is versed in logic that their activity is restricted to tier IV. But like the corresponding fundamental processes of thought they are free to range as may be required over the remaining compartments, for no explanatory generalisation can be utilised to prove the soundness of a belief without them, as no belief which rests upon inductive proof can be utilised to prove a theory without them.

(11) DEDUCTION
  THEORY

As already pointed out logic can prove whether deductive reasoning conforms to its laws, but it cannot act as a substitute for it, and the philosopher, who from the nature of his outlook relies primarily upon deduction to describe and justify his theories, seldom troubles to test out his reasoning by their conformity or otherwise to the canons of logic, though on the other hand he usually refrains instinctively from violating them. But if, by any chance, he makes use of analogy to furnish collateral proof, he then uses a method of reasoning about which logicians have little to say, except of a disparaging nature. Yet in occult and mystical reasoning proof by analogy is accepted by general consent as indicating probable truth on the ground that it conforms to the axiomatic dictum, "as above, so below," which may be expressed as, "the microcosm is organised so as to be the image in miniature of the macrocosm."

(10) PROPOSITION
LOGICAL GENERATION

The proposition is to Logic what the Master concept is to Psychology in the sense that both exercise generative as well as operative powers, just as does the process of Addition in arithmetic, which creates numbers by addition from unity and then operates upon the numbers so formed in conjunction with its derivative operations of Subtraction (which is addition in reverse), Multiplication, and Division, to which we may add Extraction of Roots. In all our reasonings propositions abound in such quantities that it is difficult to see the wood for the trees and to perform the integrations necessary to enable complex problems to be effectively handled. Handling by the brain, incidentally, is no mixed metaphor, since we can grasp by the brain. In all the tiers the Proposition is king, whether of Theories in IV, Beliefs in V, Explanatory Generalisations in VI, and Empirical Generalisations in VII.

THE FUNDAMENTAL PROCESSES AND THE PARTS OF SPEECH

(10) PRONOUNS

JUST as the metaphysics of the Fundamental Processes deals with the operations of the Mind in the widest sense, so Grammar deals with the operations of Speech as the external revealer of the mind. In this paper we will confine ourselves to analysing the parts of speech which constitute the foundational elements of Grammar, using the human skeleton and its component parts for purposes of illustration, since grammatical speech may be regarded as the skeletal framework of thought. In this connection it should be remembered that the skeleton combines rigidity with flexibility to a remarkable degree, this being especially true of that of the monkey, and it is universally recognised that one of the chief desiderata for language is flexibility, otherwise speech and writing are bound to appear stilted and tend to cramp thought rather than reveal it. It is evident that we must seek to extract the pith and marrow of the fundamental processes to obtain the necessary linkages with the parts of speech, since the latter must needs express simple and rudimentary conceptions, if for no other reason that it must serve to clothe the thoughts of the uneducated as well as the educated. The first part of speech is the pronoun, which enshrines the conception of Intelligent Agency because no animal can use the first person singular I. The adoption of the word pronoun does not exhibit much inventiveness on the part of the grammarian who first brought it into use, for to call such an important part of speech as "I" or "You" a mere substitute for a noun conveys a very inadequate idea of what it really is, and that is in most cases the designation of a self-conscious individual capable of initiating chains of causation by design. Pronouns are more universal in their significance than nouns and may be used to denote a greater variety of objects without specifying in what respects they vary. For instance "it" is a more universal conception than mammal or bird and may include both. Religion deals with the government of conscious agents on earth by Conscious Agents in Heaven, a Trinity of Persons Who make use of the pronouns I, Thou, and He in speaking of Each Other. One of the most imposing titles of God is "I AM that I AM."

As the pronoun is the most universal part of speech so the verb is the most diversified with the sole exception of the noun. If we compare the pronoun with the brain whence decisions emanate from the ego, we may compare the verb with the peripheral motor nerves which actuate the muscles, governing them as transitive verbs do nouns. It is by the brain that we manage or handle our affairs but fingering objects denotes something very different and is equivalent to investigating them. Whereas the first fundamental process is the performance of operations on concepts, the second is concerned with symbolisation and movement in a determined direction both of which, as we shall see, are connected with the functions of verbs and enable their inner nature to be investigated. The main divisions of pronouns are those which are used only as nouns, those used as adjectives also, and those used solely as adjectives. The two latter classes will be dealt with together with the Demonstrative Adjectives, *the* and *a*, under that heading. The distinction between pronouns and nouns has been defined briefly as follows:—Pronouns indicate, nouns identify, which means that nouns are more precise in their functions than pronouns.

(11) VERBS

The Fundamental Process of (11) is related to the radiation of energy from a central source and the basic idea behind radiation is direction as well as transfer of energy from the parent body to the confines of space. Direction in the full sense is hardly separable from motion though a static object such as a signpost can be used for directive purposes. Now a verb is a part of speech with which we are able to make assertions about things, that is predications, and what we may predicate is either action or state, the former being associable with motion which is dynamic and the latter condition which is static. Furthermore, if action is not directed intelligently it cannot achieve the purpose with which it was initiated. Since most verbs predicate action of one kind or another we must clearly place them in a dynamic column, and space (11) appears suited in every way to accommodate them. A transitive verb indicates an action towards some object and intransitive verb indicates an action not directed towards some object or a state. Certain prepositions prefixed to intransitive verbs makes them transitive. Verbs are also inflected to denote distinctions of Voice, Mood, Tense, Number, and Person. Voice is active or passive according as the subject of the sentence stands for the doer or for the object of the action expressed by the verb. (11) is the lower harmonic of (2) as (10) is of (1) and consequently we may expect to find duality brought out in the classification of verbs. It is however true that in Greek we find a mean between the two called the Middle Voice. Moods are changes of form assumed by a verb to indicate different ways in which action can be conceived as stating facts, asking questions, expressing suppositions, giving commands, suggesting contingencies and denoting actions. Tense indicates the time at which action is described as taking place and also shows whether the action was completed or not at the time. The Verb is thus pre-eminently a philosophic part of speech which makes refinement and copiousness of ideas expressible with ease and precision. In order to bring out this characteristic more clearly let us consider the answers expected to the queries who? why? what? and how? In the first we seek for the identity of an agent or cause of action as when we ask, "who did it?" In the second we seek for information regarding causation and expect an answer which begins with "because," which means "by cause of." To state the cause of a phenomenon is to some extent to give the reason for it and a reasonable man is one who takes into account the fact that all effects are the results of antecedent causes and who regulates his acts and speech accordingly. In the third we seek as a rule to ascertain the identity of some object, that is of a noun, though we may, it is true, expect an answer by a verb, as when we ask, "What did he do?" and get the answer, "He ran away," but even then an action of running is described, which is a noun. In the fourth, "how" is often answered satisfactorily by the use of an adverb, though if information is required about a complex process then a description of method or procedure becomes necessary. Verbs are the most flexible of all the parts of speech, for this is what inflection denotes. In this respect they resemble the fingers which are the most flexible organs of the body. Furthermore they can "touch the spot," with unique precision, being able to be inflected in such a way as to express the most minute shades of meaning.

Theosophists teach that the three aspects of the Supreme Being are Power, Wisdom, and Activity. Power renders Agency (10) effective. Wisdom directs and controls Activity as transitive verbs do nouns for without rational direction designed to achieve some specified object activity becomes purposeless and results in waste of energy. Verbs are far more susceptible to symbolisation than nouns, though of course both are in themselves symbols, verbs being names of modes of action and nouns names of objects. But the whole utility of gesticulation resides in the fact that it can be used as an adjunct to the expression of ideas denoting action. On the other hand it is difficult to describe a noun, especially a concrete one, by gesture. Animals are usually represented by the sounds which they make and noise-making is a form of activity. Verbs rather than nouns lie at the basis of dramatisation and histrionics. The inflexion of verbs is effected in English by a large number of auxiliary verbs which greatly reduce the number of terminal modifications of the principal verbs.

(12) Nouns

A noun is the name of a thing, that is of any object of thought, which may be real or imaginary, live or dead, material or immaterial. Every sentence is composed of at least one noun and one verb, either stated or implied. A noun used as the subject of a sentence verges towards Agency (10) in its essential meaning, whence we may infer that Objectivity (12) is the true mark of a noun. The chief point to note about nouns is that they are capable of being generalised and particularised to an extent and with a degree of accuracy impossible in the case of any other part of speech. A common noun is a name which can be given to an indefinite number of things in the same sense and thus exhibits generalisation at its maximum. A singular noun is one which cannot be applied to more than one thing in the same sense and exhibits differentiation at its maximum. A proper noun is a name assigned to an individual person or object or to a group of the same having a basis of affinity as a distinguishing mark or means of identification and thus approaches the principle of Symbolisation (11). Animals and plants can be classified or rather stratified in seven degrees of descending generalisations, Kingdom, Sub-kingdom, Class, Order, Family, Genus, and Species, to which we may add an eighth, Variety, after which we come to an individual animal or plant. Domesticated animals are usually given human names for purposes of singular identification. We may thus picture to ourselves both the Animal and Plant Kingdoms as pyramids of seven or eight tiers or courses each and this emphasises the general static character of nouns. Concrete nouns are characteristic of (12) and abstract nouns verge towards (11). Verbs in the infinitive mood, gerunds, and verbal nouns are all abstract nouns. Abstract nouns may also be formed from verbs by the addition -ion, e.g. attraction. Others are formed by adding the terminals hood, age, dom, ship, etc, to other nouns, or ness, th, ity, ce, etc, to adjectives. Adjectives may be used as abstract nouns, e.g. the beautiful, the wonderful, and so on. In general we conceive of abstract nouns by the exercise of imagination which belongs to (11), rational common-sense which prefers the concrete and objective being usually exercised in dealing with concrete nouns. The very word concrete as applied to a solid substance used in architecture and engineering gives us a good mental picture of what a concrete noun is in relation to an abstract one. Nouns can be inflected like verbs but on different principles, three being the maximum, Gender, Case, and Number. Gender in the Noun is the equivalent of Person in the Verb, for agents can be male, female, or neuter. Case in a Noun is the equivalent of Voice in a Verb, for "govern or be governed" is the counterpart of being active or passive. The hall-mark of case is however relationship to other words in a sentence. All cases can be analysed in accordance with the Fundamental Principles, the nominative as indicating the subject agreeing with (10), the vocative as indicating the opposite number with whom one is in communication agreeing with (11) and the objective or accusative indicating relative passivity with (12), which is a static number. The corresponding limbs of the skeleton, the arms, are very flexible but cannot be used for fine work or manipulation. So the inflection of nouns is not capable of being carried to the same degree of refinement as that of verbs. Nouns on account of their prodigious number and case modifications may fairly be described as "all embracing." A nominative pronoun, a verb agreeing with it, and a noun which is the object governed by a verb provide us with a graphical picture of the joint operation of brain, nerves, and muscles, especially if the noun in question is concrete. The verb enables the sentence to be dynamically or statically balanced according to the selection made by the pronominal agent. All architectural or engineering works, as well as upright trees and plants, are of necessity statically balanced.

Adverbs

An adverb is a word which modifies the meaning of a verb, adjective, or other adverb. In order to work adverbs into the Table it will be necessary to classify them first into nine main kinds and then generalise so as to accommodate them in three spaces, which is the most that they can be allowed in order to maintain their proportionate value relative to other parts of speech. The scheme of division is as follows:—Adverb of Affirmation. Yes. (10). Adverb of Negation. No. (11). Adverbs of Certainty (12), of Manner (13), of Time (14), of Place (15), of Consequence (16), of Quality (17) and of Quantity (18). (10) and (11), as equivalent to (1) and (2) set forth the primary positive and negative uses of adverbs. We say that no is an answer in the negative and it would be equally logical to say that yes is an answer in the positive. Next to these we must obviously place Adverbs of Certainty such as certainly, not, perhaps, possibly, positively, surely, mayhap, etc. We habitually join the latter with yes or no to reinforce them and give them balance and weight, as in yes certainly and surely no. (12) is a number connected with force and massiveness. Adverbs of Manner (13) describe how actions are performed and qualify states of being; examples being well, properly, accurately, ill, badly. As already mentioned (13) is concerned with answers to "how?" Adverbs of Time (14) are answers to the questions when? how long? and how often? such as now, then, soon, always, rarely. Adverbs of Space (15) are answers to the questions where?, whence?, whither?, and in what order? such as here, hence, hither, and lastly. Adverbs of Consequence (16) are used in reasoning and logic, such as therefore, thus, so, consequently, hence. They introduce answers to puzzles and problems, and clinch arguments. Adverbs of Quality (17) are sometimes classed with those of Manner but they approach more closely to the qualitative character of adjectives from which they are all formed by the addition of the terminal -ly, which is an abbreviation of -like. But on the other hand it does not follow that all adverbs so formed are those of quality. Adverbs of Quantity (18) are sometimes called those of Degree, examples being scarcely, quite, exactly, and are the counterparts adverbially of the indefinite Adjectives of Quantity. We now proceed to generalise these nine kinds of adverbs in groups of three, Adverbs of Fixation, Condition, and Adaptation.

(13) Adverbs of Fixation

Life would be impossible in a world in which beliefs, institutions and customs were in a perpetual state of uncertainty and flux and a man who is without convictions makes no headway in life. Fixation is one of the chief characteristics of the abstract condition called state, which is from its very nature static, if nothing else. State is allied with memory and unless we have a reliable memory we perpetually find ourselves uncertain about facts and past actions about which it is imperative that we should be well informed and often lie about them without any intention of being untruthful.

(14) Adverbs of Condition

Modality, time, and space are conditions which limit our freewill in a number of ways but without them the possibilities of choice would be infinite and we should be unable to make any plans for the future. The laws of Modality, that is of the methods which must be employed under existing circumstance, of the time these methods take to put into operation and bring to condition, and of the space and other factors in our environment which must be taken into consideration, introduce limitations which are often irksome, but which enable us to distinguish between the possible and the impossible.

(15) Adverbs of Adaptation

In our daily lives we have to take into account the elements of fixation which derive from the past, including our own habits and beliefs as well as the laws and customs of our country, and the elements of conditioning which we must take into account in planning for the future. Then with these governing factors in mind we have to equate ourselves to our environment and act in such a manner as our reason tells us will enable us to do what we want, subject to the laws of probability which operate in the present. If we scrutinise environment we see that it consists mainly of objects which are described by adjectives of quality and quantity and equally so living and acting in this environment is describable by adverbs of the same kind.

As regards the associated parts of the skeleton, the backbone is freely used as an emblem of fixation and erectness, and we call a man of backbone one who knows his own mind and is not easily swayed by the wishes of others. But the ribs, as the symbols of the breath of life, the laws of life, and the expectations of life, have never appealed to the imagination of language-builders. Neither do we speak of the breastbone or breast of the earth and the sea but we do speak of the bosom of both and our environment is the bosom of the former if landsmen and of the latter if seafarers.

(16) Pronominal Adjectives

The Pronominal Adjectives of (16) are pronouns which are used as adjectives and are classified as possessive, definite, indefinite, distributive, demonstrative, relative, and interrogative. Taken as a whole their functions are primarily demonstrative and distributive. They either enable persons and things to be identified or make it clear that precise identification is impossible though their existence is not questioned. Their analytical value surpasses that of all other forms or parts of speech, and their pronominal affinities bring them within the sphere of agency and origination. Take for instance the forcefulness of such a phrase as "Each man for himself" which denotes the maximum of individualistic action. Here again the corresponding parts of the skeleton are not specially informative, for they are the spines of the pelvis which, though they do not meet in front, are completed to constitute the pelvic girdle by strong muscles. The thoracic girdle is formed by the shoulder blades and the collar-bone. Girdles are symbols of the strength conferred by respect for law and order, law in front and order behind, the law of the judge backed up by the order enforced by the police. Law arises, as already pointed out, from the paramount necessity of curbing excessive individualism in which each one does what is right in his own eyes. Taken as a whole, Pronominal Adjectives assist us in forming a vivid and instructive picture of the struggle for existence between all sorts and conditions of men and animals for the means of surviving which constitute life on this planet.

(17) Qualitative Adjectives

The true Adjectives are divided into qualitative and quantitative. The pronominal adjective already dealt with is a close relation of the Demonstrative Adjective and the two may be classed together under (16) together with the Ordinal Numerals, first, tenth, etc. An Adjective is defined as a word which is associated with a noun to limit its application and elucidate its nature. The Qualitative Adjective alone possesses the attributive character which constitutes its primary value as a part of speech owing to its capacity for lucid descriptiveness, as the French understand better than any other people, but it is too often put to the baser use of exaggeration and inflation, to which it lends itself by reason of its three degrees of comparison. The adjective should assist us to assign proportionate value to all nouns which it qualifies. It gives potential to speech, for potentials can be graded from zero to the highest point attainable by the use of the degrees of comparison. Adjectives have the same discriminative value as adverbs and enable the classification of nouns to be carried to any degree of differentiation desired. Adjectives and adverbs together form the backbone of speech, the former having the massiveness of the lumbar vertebræ and the latter the flexibility of the dorsal vertebræ. Most qualifying adverbs are formed from adjectives by the terminal "ly," meaning like. In the analysis of the speech organs they correspond to the base and the tip of the tongue, the second of which is prolonged in some animals to form a lash.

(18) Quantitative Adjectives

Whereas Qualitative Adjectives answer the question what sort? Quantitative Adjectives answer the definite question how many? in which a precise answer is expected and the indefinite question how many? or how much? in which an answer in exact figures is not expected. Answers to the definite question are given in cardinal numerals or in the adjectives no, none, or both, while those to the indefinite question are given in such words as many, any, some, few, most, or several. The conception of number is inherent in (18). It belongs to the harmonic series (0), (9), (27) and the ancients always regarded zero, not one, as the source of all numbers. The corresponding process of the mind is Impulse and of all impulses the generative is the most insistent and powerful in order that the human race may be propagated indefinitely in time. The associated part of the skeleton—the pelvis or loins—is frequently used in Scripture to indicate the source of generative power, not only in the female but the male, for the Israelites are spoken of as having come forth from the loins of Abraham. In mathematics intensification of quantity to obtain numbers like the stars of heaven or the sand of the sea is secured by the use of powers. The generation of numbers by addition belongs to (19).

(19) Conjunctions

A Conjunction is a word which is used to join words and sentences. Certain relative pronouns and conjunctive adverbs can be used for the same purpose. Conjunctions are divisible into co-ordinating, correlative, and subordinating. The first is characteristic of (19) and the second and third have affinities with (20) and (21). Conjunctions might be called the locomotive organs of speech without which it would be jerky and discontinuous, consisting of terse clauses or sentences lacking any links to indicate their relationships or mutual dependence. The co-ordinating conjunctions join co-ordinate or independent clauses on an equal footing just like the feet of poetical lines, common examples being "and" and "but." They are clearly additive in nature for we can say either one plus one plus one make three, or one and one and one make three. This reminds one of the operations performed by the brain upon unit concepts which arise into consciousness successively and are then summed up. Admittedly the brain reduces them to a condition in which some concepts have greater importance than others, but as concepts they enjoy substantial equality, unlike percepts. These conjunctions usually join sentences even when they only appear to join words, and thus bridge the gulf between etymology and syntax. Subordinate conjunctions join a dependent clause to a principal clause, examples being "if," "though," "because," "till," and "after." Good literature depends mainly upon the skilful use of subordinating conjunctions, though sentences become involved if they are used too much and in such cases it is as well to introduce co-ordinating conjunctions to restore simplicity or else start new sentences. The subordinating conjunction introduces on a restricted scale the principle of stratification in rising layers which in the classification of nouns is illustrated by the general, the particular and the singular, for it is manifest that the last two are dependent on the first or if preferred support it. Finally Correlative Conjunctions can only be used in pairs, common examples being "whether" . . . "or," "either" . . . "or," "neither" . . . "nor," "so" . . . "as," "so" . . . "that," "as" . . . "so." Their scope of activity is wider than that of the simple co-ordinating conjunction and in this respect they bestow greater mobility upon speech and language. But all conjunctions play a part in conferring fluidity on speech just as interjections impose discontinuity. They furthermore give a broad basis to speech and language and greatly enhance their capacity for expressing thoughts in appropriate clauses and sentences. There is also a forcefulness in the double conjunctions which is lacking in the single.

(20) INTERJECTIONS

An Interjection is a word or maybe a sound without any definite meaning which expresses an emotion but does not enter into the construction of the sentence. It is thus the opposite of the Conjunction, which unites and adds, for it divides and subtracts. In the general symbolism of numbers we may take (19) as a dynamic human number, (20) as a dynamic animal number, and (21) as a static plant number. Now if most animal cries are analysed it will be found that they express emotions which they share with human beings, in fact interjections might be said to constitute the sum-total of the language of animals. They occupy the lower harmonic of the Verb space (11) and most call-cries of animals might be translated into, "Come here" or "Take care." Imperatives such as, "Go" or "Stay" are of the nature of interjections and are often spoken with emotional force. Some interjections of an observational kind are merely expressive of conventional politeness and are devoid of emotional content. The true interjection, as the word denotes, is thrown in between two sentences or clauses and momentarily interrupts the natural sequence of thought or grammatical expression in order to emphasise a point or rivet attention. It is a part of speech which is freely used by orators and actors and makes a strong appeal to massed audiences. Apart from the "inter," "jection" comes from the Latin, *jacere* to throw, and abusive interjections are thrown about or projected like missiles in verbal conflicts in which adjectives and nouns of an uncomplimentary character are conjoined and used interjectively. But, unlike brickbats and cobble-stones, hard words break no bones. The interjection "oh" was included in the vocative case by the Latins in the conjugation of nouns. Many interjections which are now classed as profane had a religious origin and were cries to the Persons of the Godhead for help in danger or distress. Others classed as oaths are used to emphasise meaning and these are peculiarly representative of the mental process of Impulse which always tends to intensify speech and the feelings which speech seeks to interpret. Some swear-words are however simply used to express irrational anger or annoyance such as animals express by growls and snarls. But the greater number of interjections are uttered as the outcome of encountering the unexpected in one's environment. However alert and keenly observant one may be and whatever precautions one may take against being surprised, there are many times when the unexpected is encountered with suddenness and, if unpleasant, may give rise to interjections of pain, annoyance, or consternation. Since human beings and mammals habitually walk and since the toes are in the front of the foot, they, like the nose, are the first parts of the body to encounter unexpected obstacles, especially in the dark. And if one drops a heavy object the chances are greatly in favour of its falling upon one's toes. The simple process of stubbing the toe has probably given rise to more imprecatory interjections than any other form of impinging upon unexpected obstacles.

(21) Prepositions

A preposition is a word which is used with a noun or pronoun to show its relation to some other word in the sentence. To a certain extent the cases of inflected nouns, the parts of speech belonging to the upper harmonic compartment (12), supply the place of prepositions. Adverbs are easily confused with prepositions but these never govern nouns or pronouns. A preposition (21) and a noun (12) may together form a phrase which is equivalent to either an adjective (17) or an adverb (13), all four parts of speech belonging to the central static column. Thus a man of power is a powerful man and entering by force is the same as entering forcibly. Even languages which inflect their nouns most freely are compelled to include many prepositions to define the relationships of nouns or pronouns to other words. They are classifiable on the same principles as adverbs. They are the most realistic of all parts of speech, especially those which relate to position in space, which animals are able to appreciate almost as accurately as human beings even though they have no words for above or below, in front or behind. Prepositions correspond with the legs because of their implications of structural support in the phrases and sentences into which they enter, and we naturally say that they illustrate the relationship in which objects stand with regard to each other. Legs can move as well as support when they form limbs of live creatures, but their use in language to describe supports forming parts of inanimate objects is widespread as in tables and chairs. The very word preposition meaning something placed before something else is static in its implications. Prepositions are so numerous that they enable the relationship of objects in state, time, and space to be defined with detailed accuracy and moreover the commoner prepositions bear several meanings according to context in which they are used. The case prepositions can be classified with some degree of certainty but the remainder present difficulties in this respect. In the declensions of nouns we have Nominative or Subjective (10), Vocative (11), Accusative or Objective (12). Ablatives By (13), From (14), and With (15). Datives To (16), For (18). Possessive Of (17). As regards others we have At (19),

Up Above (20), In and Out (21), and Down Below (22). It is difficult to generalise the meaning of most of the case prepositions but "By" denotes certainty, proximity, "From" denotes origin, "With" denotes companionship and agreement, "To" denotes progressiveness, "Of" denotes ownership, connexion, and quality, and "For" denotes desire, quest, and exchange.

In conclusion we have one good means of checking up on the correctness of the general scheme of classification set forth in the preceding pages and that is its conformity with the law that the 2nd tier expands the meaning of the 2nd space or compartment, the 3rd tier does the same thing for the 3rd space, and the 4th tier for the 4th space. Thus we have the Adverbs in tier V expanding the meaning of the Verbs in space (11), the Adjectives in tier VI expanding the meaning of the Nouns in space (12), and the Conjunctions and Prepositions of tier VII being in many cases words which can also be used as Adverbs. Adverbial clauses are introduced into sentences by means of subordinating conjunctions. Prepositions are much easier to distinguish from Adverbs than are Conjunctions. "Yes" and "No," classed as Adverbs, are often used as Interjections.

FOREWORD TO CHAPTERS V, VI, X

THE System of Mysticism which is the basis of the above-mentioned chapters is founded upon the teachings of the following schools, all of which have a claim to be considered in dealing with this vast and complex subject. They are as follows:—

(a) Blavatsky Theosophy which is a Western exposition of the theosophy of the Hindu Scriptures. These are usually regarded as having been composed between 1500 B.C. and 500 B.C., and in turn are founded upon the Stanzas of Dzyan or at any rate are regarded as expositions of them. The Gnostic *Book of the Saviour* contains a passage to the effect that Christ communicated Two Books of Jeou (Dzyu?) to Enoch and if these are to be identified with the Two Books of Dzyan, then they may be dated about 3000 B.C.

(b) The Rosicrucian School of whose teaching Max Heindel is the leading exponent, his most important work being *The Rosicrucian Cosmo-conception*.

(c) The Rosicrucian School of whose teaching Richard Ingalese is the leading exponent, his most important work being *The Greater Mysteries*.

(d) Hebrew Mysticism or Kabbalism as set forth in the Book of the Zohar and various apocalyptic works of which the three Books of Enoch and the Third Book of Baruch are the most important.

(e) Egyptian Theosophy of which Pythagoras gave a Western exposition, the details of which have been for the most part lost. The subject has been dealt with by many Egyptologists.
(f) Alexandrine Gnosticism of which a fairly exhaustive account will be found in *Fragments of a Faith Forgotten*, by G. R. S. Mead.
(g) The Behmenist School of Christian Mystics of the seventeenth century A.D., of which Jacob Boehme was the founder and John Pordage and Jane Lead the leading exponents.

All these schools view Mysticism from different aspects and though it may be conceded that Blavatsky Theosophy is the most important in view of the number of able writers who have published books upon it, yet the other schools have undoubtedly a right to be heard. As a result of a close study of the teachings of these seven schools I have come to the definite conclusion that the region below the Great Boundary, generally known as the World Egg or Ovoid, is divisible into either eight worlds or twelve spheres, every alternate world consisting of two spheres.[1] This mode of classification is not accepted as here defined by Blavatsky Theosophists but I do not regard it as inconsistent with their teachings. It should be perfectly obvious that a system of Mysticism which claims to be a synthesis of the teachings of seven schools which have arisen independently at intervals during the past 4,000 years or so and which view their subject from widely different angles and expound it in different idioms, cannot be in complete agreement with all of them or any one of them. There must be give and take in any effort to seek a *via media* between schools of thought, which, though not opposed to each other in the essentials of philosophy and psychology and, what might be termed, "celestial geography," appear nevertheless to differ in many important respects.

CHAPTER V

THE TWELVE FUNDAMENTAL PRINCIPLES OF MYSTICISM

See TABLE D.

THE Twelve Fundamental Principles of Mysticism, Theosophy, or Occult Philosophy are (10) Repetition. (11) Involution. (12) Evolution. (13) Karma. (14) Time Organisation. (15) Space Organisation. (16) Incarnation. (17) Incorporation. (18) Generation. (19) Government. (20) Conduct. (21) Environment. No claim is made here that the foregoing titles are fully descriptive of the principles; their main purpose is to serve as convenient identification labels. The full signification of the 12 Principles is too recondite to make it possible to find verbal headings which adequately summarise their characteristics.

[1] *See* Table F.

(10) Repetition

Repetition is the name given by theosophists to the primary principle that all things generated and created by the Supreme Being are organised on one plan which confers unification upon them all. Hence the symbolic number of Repetition is (1) or (10). *The Philosophy of Analogy and Symbolism* is the exposition of the key to Recapitulation in so far as it reveals the constitution of Western sciences and philosophies, though it is impossible to make use of this key without frequent reference to Eastern philosophies, especially in their relation to the organisation of worlds and spheres and the constituent parts of human personality. One of the basic elements of Repetition is the doctrine that Man, the Microcosm, is the measure of the Cosmos or Macrocosm, known to mystics as the Grand Man of the Universe. For that reason the correct organisation of the principles of Human Physiology is of great importance, especially in view of the admitted fact that physiology is a far more exact science than psychology, mainly because its elements are more susceptible of demonstration by inductive proofs. The following definition of the Law of Repetition by a theosophist of wide experience who has a special gift for condensing information in tabloid form is worth recording. "It asserts that the same system of form, time, and motion runs through the whole universe so that if we properly study an atom or cell we will obtain the key to the workings of a man, a planet, or a constellation. . . . This great Law of Repetition declares that there is an ordered arrangement within the universe, with certain periods of time and patterns of form repeated up the scale and governing the tiniest to the greatest. It asserts that the little things are a mirror of the larger ones, and everything is not only a replica of, but is intimately concerned with, everything else. For instance, if you want to study a solar system you can study an atom. And, if you want to study animal, plant, mineral, or even solar life you will find it all represented in the body of man himself. 'Man, Know Thyself,' was the ancient command written above the temple door. If we persevere with this fascinating study we will find that in the form of every human being the universe is presented to us; we can inspect the solar system of his atoms, the mineral world in its most active and creative form in his interior laboratory, and the physical development of animal life from its lowest to its highest form in his embryo. In his nature we will find a mixture of the passions and peculiarities of all living creatures. We can also trace an intimate relationship with all the planets through the interplay going on in his body with the cosmic and planetary rays, and a connection with the world of magnetism and electricity as well. And finally we will discover that man has in his puny frame the capacity to connect his mind with the highest unseen cosmic intelligence—the mind of 'Nature.' "[1] We may reflect at this point that since man's greatest gift from God is that of his separate individuality and self-consciousness it is hardly rational or logical to deny these attributes to the Giver. All phenomena coming under the heading of Repetition fall within the sphere of operation of

The Finding of the Third Eye, Vera Stanley Alder, 1937, pp. 47, 48.

the First Logos, the Father of Christian Theology. It should, however, be recognised that Repetition is a method which is energised by Epigenesis, a force which Rosicrucians rightly place first in a triad of which Involution and Evolution form the other two members. Epigenesis means generation by the union of the masculine and feminine principles.

(11) INVOLUTION

Involution is the mode whereby spirit descends into matter and purifies it, its ultimate purpose being to initiate and complete Evolution. Matter is not inherently evil though from its very nature it affords a lurking ground where evil can hide undetected. Spirit is the expression of the masculine principle of the Godhead symbolised by the sun, and matter is the expression of the feminine principle of the Godhead symbolised by the moon. The former is the Great Father and the latter the Son-Daughter of indeterminate sex. Thus involution and evolution working in conjunction afford an example of Marriage working in its cosmic form, the masculine descending from above to meet and intermingle with the feminine rising up from below. There is however a feminine element in both, since spirit cannot operate except as bisexual because it makes its first contact with the feminine matter-principle or "Great Waters of the Mother" through the feminine element in itself. The work of Involution is carried out by the Second Logos, the Son-Daughter, Who, though masculine in some respects, is feminine in other respects in relation to the First Logos. The characteristics of Christ are recognised to be feminine not only by those who believe that He incarnated as Jesus of Nazareth but by those who recognise a Christ-influence as operating in the Cosmos. Vishnu, the Preserver, is more feminine than Brahma or Shiva. Christians appreciate the involutionary nature of the ministry of Christ more than people of other religions because Christ, the Scond Logos, according to their belief, incarnated as a Man, that is to say He took manhood into permanent union with Himself. The whole Christian Church is involutionary in its attitude because of the example set by its Founder, Who, though He was God, divested Himself of the prerogatives of the God and took upon Him the form of a Servant. The Church has always looked askance at Eastern faiths and at theosophy because of their evolutionary character, holding that the very depths of humanity must be purged and purified before it can go forward upon its evolutionary course with confidence. Therefore the Christian Church has on the whole been that of the masses and has recognised no untouchables. It started as a Church of the lower orders and was established by Twelve Apostles who were nearly all drawn from the ranks of the Galilaean peasantry. It was as a peasant carpenter that the Christ elected to move amongst the Jews of Palestine, for such was his trade even though He may have worked very little at it. The Church realises that its ministry must reach down to the masses throughout the world before the consummation of its hope can be accomplished. "Hath not God chosen the poor of this world, rich in faith, and heirs of the kingdom which He hath promised to them that love Him," wrote James, the Apostle of the underdog. Paul is even more explicit in his description of the involutionary character of the Church's mission. "God hath chosen the foolish things of the world to confound the wise, and God hath chosen the weak things of the world to confound the things which are mighty, and base things of the world and things which are despised hath God chosen, yea and things which are not to bring to nought things which are, that no flesh should glory in His presence." (I Cor. i, 27-29). Glorying in the flesh must be confined to those who have endowments of wealth, talent, beauty, or some other asset that the world considers desirable.

(12) EVOLUTION

The work of the Great Logoi in creating and administering the Cosmos is cumulative, that is to say, as already indicated, the Second Logos works in close collaboration with the First and carries out His general instructions. The Son does the will of the Father in all things and leaves the initiation of all plans to Him, and the Third Logos works under the direction of the Other Two. The Bible is the Book of the first Two Logoi, the Old Testament being the Book of the Father and the New Testament the Book of the Son. Similarly the First Book of Dzyan is the Bible of the Third Logos and deals with the Divine Dragon of Wisdom, the Seven Fighters or Builders Who are His Seven Breaths, and their Mother. The Third Logos, also called Oeaohoo the Younger to distinguish Him from the First Logos, Oeaohoo the Elder, represents the Father in carrying out the work of evolution. The Seven Spirits represent the Third Logos in carrying out the same work. And finally the Mother of the Seven must also be regarded as exhibiting the fundamental qualities of the Third Logos. The Gnostics recognised the same triad of Powers, the Great Light of Lights, the Seven Spirits of Whom Jeou and Melchizedek are the chief, and the Virgin of Light, Who was worshipped in a pagan form as Diana of the Ephesians, the Many-breasted One. The Christian Church has had very little revelation concerning the Mother, except in Prov. viii and ix, and parts of the Wisdom of Solomon. The greetings sent to the Church through John in Rev. i, 4, 5 are from the Father, the Son, and the Seven Spirits, the last being worshipped collectively by the Church as the Holy Ghost. One of the chief points of controversy between the religions of the West and those of the East is that the Christian peoples of the former worship the Third Logos as a Masculine Holy Ghost and the non-Christian peoples of the latter worship the Third Logos as a Feminine Holy Ghost. The teaching of the Gnostics which reconciled the two was rejected by the Episcopacy when the Creeds were drawn up, but most Christian mystics, especially Jacob Boehme, John Pordage, and Jane Lead, have distinguished between the Spirit and the Mother. Jane Lead calls the latter, "The Spirit of the Spirit of God." It will be seen that in proportion as we descend in the scale of the Logoi they become increasingly feminine. The Law of Evolution is expounded in more than one passage in the First Book of Dzyan but deals with it solely as it affects the Sun-gods or Progeny of the Fourth Logos whose inmost Divine principles are called Sparks. "The Spark hangs from the Flame (its particular one of the Seven Spirits) by the finest thread of Fohat (Fourth Logos). It journeys through the Seven Worlds of Maya. It stops in the First and is a Metal and a Stone; it passes into the Second and behold a Plant; the Plant whirls through seven changes and becomes a Sacred Animal. From the combined attributes of these Manu, the Thinker, is formed." (*Stanze*, VII, 5). The First World is really a sphere, the Upper Plutonic. The second is the Subphysical World. The next seven are the Lower and Upper Physical, the Astral, the Lower and Upper Mental, the Buddhic, and the Atmic or Lower Nirvanic. The last-named is the Fifth Heaven of Rev. iv and v, the sphere of the Four Living Creatures or Sacred Animals. From thence the Spark passes to the Sixth Heaven, the sphere of the Manus or Thinkers, the Upper Nirvanic or World of Virgin Spirits, ruled over by the Fourth Logos. The Law of Evolution is defined by Vera Stanley Alder as follows:—"Everything in life is evolving upwards and onwards to a higher and more perfect state, having had its beginning in an uncreative, unconscious, and elementary form, and growing and progressing through striving, sacrifice, and struggle to a condition of creative self-conscious potent strength." (Ibid, p. 49). Minerals furnish the food of plants and plants furnish the food of animals, who could not absorb minerals directly, except perhaps in small quantities, and in the form of water, which must be classed a mineral, together with air. The various evolutionary grades are admirably illustrated in the phyla of plants and even more so of animals which ascend from single-celled Protozoa to the kingdom of the Mammals.[1] Man in turn absorbs the flesh of animals into his system though he is able to feed directly upon plants as they are. Animals such as apes, cats, dogs, and horses can be trained by association with man to become highly intelligent, and totem aborigines such as the Australians keep in very close touch with the animal creation. In human affairs the process of Evolution is patent, though much of it is illusory because the involutionary work needed to give it a stable foundation has not been completed. Consequently when we begin to flatter ourselves that man is evolving his civilisation to higher levels we find ourselves rudely disillusioned by the outbreak of devastating wars which set back our progress by centuries. Unseen beings such as sun-angels of the Sixth Heaven (the Host of Heaven worshipped by the Sabaeans) and Race and Group Spirits of the Second Heaven are largely engaged upon assisting mankind to evolve upwards spiritually, mentally, and æsthetically, but find their efforts wasted time after time by the fact that the involutionary work of spiritualising the lower strata of human consciousness has been far from completed. Man has made a god of evolution because it promises to him a multitude of benefits which he urgently desires but he almost ignores involution

---

[1] Evolution of plan is referred to here, not that by successive physical changes, the mechanism of which is still unknown in the West.

because it calls him to self-discipline, self-examination, and self-sacrifice, and discourages groundless optimism and swelled-headedness. The involutionist is dubbed a pessimist because he refuses to be led astray by the roseate dreams of the evolutionist, who seeks to fly before he can walk, and is in danger, like Icarus, of losing his wings and breaking his neck, if he has not already done so.

(13) STABILISATION—KARMA

The essence of the 4th Principle is stabilisation but it is revealed in what is known as Karma in Eastern phraseology. Its custodian is the Fourth Logos Who is seldom distinguished from the Third, though in the First Book of Dzyan a great deal of information is given us about Him under the name of Fohat. The Fourth Logos is fourfold in constitution and embraces and brings into manifestation the powers and prerogatives of the First Three Logoi. Here we come to a somewhat controversial question which has not been so far satisfactorily explained, namely the correct mode of setting forth diagrammatically the Four Persons of the Divine Family, as recognised by most mystics. The correct correspondence appears to be Father, Daughter, Son, Mother with Lion, Eagle, Man, and Ox. The question is complicated through each Person being bisexual, that is to say there are feminine elements in the Father and the Son and masculine elements in the Daughter and the Mother. The most accurate way of representing the situation is to say that the principles of Repetition and Epigenesis belong to the Father, that of Involution belongs to the Daughter, that of Evolution belongs to the Son, and that of Stabilisation or Karma to the Mother. It is true that the Fourth Logos as corresponding with Fohat of the 1st Book of Dzyan, Ptah of the Egyptians, and El Elyon, the Most High God of the Hebrews is masculine, but He has a feminine consort called the Great Virginal Spirit, and together they stand for the Mother Principle which is frequently symbolised by the Cow.

The Great Four are also symbolised by the Sun, the Moon, the Surface of the Earth, and the Interior of the Earth and this correspondence further illustrates their bisexuality for some nations regard the Sun as feminine and the Moon as masculine while the earth is associated with both gods and goddesses. The net result of the operation of the powers of the Four Logoi is stabilisation without impairment of progress, but the Fourth acting by Himself maintains the *status quo* and does not readily sanction changes. He is the Lord of Individualisation under Whose rule the Virgin Spirits of mankind are placed when they are given the endowment of self-consciousness in its first aspect of the Ahamkara of continuity. The substance of the Sixth Heaven is the Akasha, the sensitive medium which preserves a photographic record of all the words and works of the beings of the Cosmos below the Great Boundary. The Keepers of the Records, the Book of Life and the Book of Works, are called the Lipika or Scribes in the First Book of Dzyan. Thus we see how the Fourth Logos comes to be associated with the Law of Karma of which Vera Stanley Alder says rightly, "This word has not even an equivalent in the English language. Its meaning is 'cause and effect' or 'action and reaction'." She continues, "We are told that all life is built upon the law of opposites, as in the negative and positive poles of electricity, day and night, heat and cold, summer and winter, good and evil. The constant friction between these opposites causes development, change, adjustment—in other words originality, or the free will which functions throughout all creation, and through which creation itself learns eventually to become creative." (Ibid., p. 51). Strictly speaking the great Karmic forces are fourfold and are symbolised by the Four Great World Rulers who are subordinate to the Fourth Logos, the Mahadevas of the Cardinal Points. The operation of these Four is revealed in most of the well-known groups of four in nature, morning, afternoon, evening, and night; spring, summer, autumn, and winter; east, south, west, and north, right, left, front, and back, and so on. The term Karma appears, however, to be often used to define if not describe the state of a man's inmost spirit at any given time or as expressed in Scriptural language, his precise condition as assessed by a balance sheet struck in the Book of Works. Most men have in them both good and evil Karma, for nothing that a man does is inoperative. What he sows that he also reaps. A man has in his heart both good and evil treasure which he has laid up for himself in the course of innumerable lives on earth and until he learns to discriminate between the two he can never be fit for the Kingdom of God. At the same time it should be clearly understood, what theosophists as a class often studiously ignore, that the Law of Karma is the law of the Fourth Logos and the Sixth Heaven, and is capable of being considerably modified by the Laws of the first Three Logoi. The special witness of the Christian Church is to the possibility of the Law of Karma being substantially modified by the Forgiveness of Sins, which is designated in the *Pistis Sophia* as the First Mystery. The Gnostics believed in Reincarnation but taught that the process of purifying mankind by the Law of Karma was so slow that Christ incarnated to hasten the process by the introduction of speedier methods, which to a large extent are effected by the Christian sacraments and Mysteries, though these may be and are greatly misused by those who seek salvation without sacrifice and genuine repentance.

(14) LAWS OF TIME CYCLES

The Gnostics recognised other Logoi besides the first Three or Four, and just as we may regard the Fourth as assisting the Third so we may regard the Fifth as assisting the First and the Sixth as assisting the Second. The First Logos is the God of Time-cycles but not as measurable by the time divisions known to man. He is El Olam, the Everlasting God, He which is and was and is to come. The work of the Fifth Logos is to order all the events in the Cosmos beneath the Boundary according to definite programmes of time cycles, the units of which are supplied by the motions of the sun, moon, and stars which were created for that purpose as well as to give light upon the earth. Students of prophecy are familiar with recurrent cycles of 1,260 years, 1,335 years, 2,300 years, and 2,520 years, to mention only a few. Then there is Drayson's processional cycle of 31, 752 years. Hindu chronology takes account of vast time cycles running into hundreds and even thousands of millions of years. Reasons have been given in chapter X for allotting 180 millions of years to the Creation evening-morning and 4,320 million years to the Cosmic evening-morning. The conception of motion lies at the root of time cycles, not only because they are defined by movements of celestial bodies but because time itself is conceived of as moving backwards from future to past or because we think of ourselves as moving forwards through time. (5) contains the mystery of predestined dispensations or elections and of plans and purposes of the Deity as progressively manifesting themselves under conditions of time and space. When a Virgin Spirit moves down from the Nirvanic to the Atmic Sphere it becomes endowed with a reformative Ahamkara in addition to the conservative Ahamkara conferred upon it in the Sixth Heaven and this gives it power to view its states and Karmic aggregations with a critical eye in order to ascertain how far they may be improved by intelligent planning and forecasting. All processes require time to enable them to develop and produce results under conditions of space and matter, and frequently these cannot be accelerated from their inherent nature no matter how much space and material are available. If the rates of maturing of such processes are not correctly estimated they are almost certain to result in chaos.

(15) Laws of Space

The Laws of Space are in their lowest form those of Euclidean geometry, leaving out of account speculations as to the possible curvature of space. In their highest form they relate to the conformation and disposition of the heavens and spheres below the Boundary, but not to their grades of density which appear to be regulated by the Third and Fourth Logoi. There are Eight Worlds and Twelve Spheres below the Boundary exclusive of regions called the Outer Darkness and the Hells. These are usually conceived of as being in motion. Motion itself can only be measured by space and time units used in conjunctions and the worlds and spheres could not be created until not merely material had been provided and time-schedules drawn up but space or "elbow-room" made available and geometrical boundaries fixed. The organisation of the subspheres of the Sixth Heaven is given in the First Book of Dzyan and these are spoken of as seven wheels disposed in the six directions of space with one in the centre, evidently to form a model of the disposition of the worlds and spheres below on a much larger scale with the Seventh Heaven at the zenith, the Sixth Heaven at the centre, the Second Heaven at the nadir, and the Fifth, Fourth, Third, and First Heavens in the four directions of horizontal space. This geometrical disposition is doubtless symbolical but it is symbolical of something which is governed in principle by the higher Laws of Space. Some occultists insist that the worlds beyond this have more than the three co-ordinates of space with which we are familiar but the ordinary man can form no conception whatever of even a four-dimensional space, let alone a five- or six-dimensional.

(16) INCARNATION AND REINCARNATION

The Laws of Incarnation and Reincarnation are those of birth, life, and death in so far as these relate to the entry into and departure from the Physical World, though something resembling birth and death may take place when the Ego descends into or ascends from the Mental, Astral, and Subphysical Worlds. All religions take cognisance of Incarnation but all Eastern religions, except the Hebrew Faith, recognise Reincarnation. The Christian Gnostics believed and taught it, and it is remarkable that since then all branches of the Church should have rejected it, in view of the immense importance attached to the life a man lives on earth. But at the same time the Christian Church is justified in teaching that those who make right and proper use of the means of grace which she dispenses will not be compelled to reincarnate again. The Gnostics were very insistent upon this truth. Yet on the other hand it must be recognised that a large percentage of human beings die before they have had a chance of choosing between good and evil or have reached years of discretion. Similarly the majority of human beings pass seemingly uneventful lives as members of uncivilised and even savage tribes, or as proletarian workers in civilised countries. What adequate chance have any of these categories in creating a Karma representative of their real tendencies under such conditions? It is by their Karma as assessed by the Book of Works that they will be judged and allotted positions of trust or of service in the regions of the Blest or condemned to punishment outside the confines of the New Jerusalem. Their condition will not be eternal in a mathematical sense but will continue unchanged for a large number of years. The most elementary requirements of justice seem to demand that men shall be given several opportunities of proving what they can make of life on earth under varying conditions. Moreover if each soul born into the world is a visitor to its surface for the first and last time and we take into consideration that such visitors have arrived for millions of years, the total number of souls must reach figures which stagger the imagination. The association of reincarnation with Karma is so close and intimate that most theosophists treat them as coming under one Law, yet they manifestly embody different principles. As Vera Stanley Alder writes, "The Laws of Rebirth and Karma work hand in glove, so to speak. We are told that mankind came into being because Spirit, or the life-force behind everything, wished to develop more creative power. This development could only be accomplished by Spirit being so imprisoned and confined in matter (flesh) that It forgets Its oneness with Wisdom, and has to find everything out afresh through fighting and experience. So we are told that the Virgin Spirit divided itself up into fractions and by ensouling the egos of men and all other forms of life, sank itself into the heavy imprisoning matter of this world, and is slowly and patiently fighting its way back to Truth, Light, and Power. The human egos evolve steadily, each undergoing constant rebirth, until it gradually attains to a knowledge of the universe through Karma—or the effect of its own acts and thoughts, achieving power and strength through the mastery of one law after another until at last it reaches omnipotence both physical and spiritual." (Ibid., pp. 51, 52).

(17) INCORPORATION

The principle of Incorporation is seen in the formation of groups of every description. These are much more than mere aggregates of units for they are composed of units which specialise in a diversity of functional activities so that each makes some special contribution of the life of the group-form which no other could make. The materials from which human groups are formed are the jivas of human monads which incarnate by taking to themselves substance of the Upper Mental Plane and then all pass downwards to the Lower Mental where they come under the organising control of vast numbers of group-forming Beings belonging to the hierarchies of the Second Heaven, who are ruled by an inferior Logos called the Aethereal Jesus by the Gnostics and Metatron by the Kabbalists. These beings are often called Angels but they represent a class which lies mid-way between the Sun-angels of the Sixth Heaven and the Nature-spirits of the Subphysical world. The Gnostics describe them under various official titles and they may be regarded as a formative administrative angelic bureaucracy. They include Race-spirits which form and administer human groups of every sort and kind, together with Animal, Plant, and Mineral Group-spirits. Human groups are formed by a number of agencies as an examination of any catalogue of human institutions speedily reveals, and these will be further considered under Principles (9) to (12). Here we are primarily concerned with groups whose nexus is provided by common mental conceptions, laws, doctrines, and modes of reasoning. Let no one underrate the power of the mind as a group-forming agency, for history is crowded with examples of men who will cheerfully sacrifice all, even life itself, for ideas. It is now being realised that conflicting ideologies, such as Fascism, Democracy, and Bolshevism may cause more devastating convulsions in human civilisations than any other motive-spring of action. In addition to organising and controlling groups of living beings the hierarchies of the Lower Mental World provide designs for the Elemental Kings and Nature-spirits of the Subphysical World to copy faithfully in the formation of the geographical features of the earth's surface, which have such a powerful influence in moulding the activities of groups of living creatures. A consideration of these belongs to the 12th and last principle. All groups as here marshalled are regarded primarily as coming under the centralised state-forming force which was examined in connection with Karma. State and the maintenance of the *status quo ante* are bound up with historic continuity and become greatly consolidated under the march of time. Human mental groups, once formed, manifest an extraordinary persistence in conserving their functional characteristics, and when they come into conflict the struggles which ensue are correspondingly ferocious, the wars of 1914-18 and 1939-45 affording perhaps the most striking examples that the history of mankind has hitherto recorded. In dealing with groups we feel that we have to do with something objective and tangible even though they have their vital springs in the region of mind. Industrial projects as a rule remain projects and no more until companies have been incorporated to materialise and operate them. The Christian Church, the greatest of all groups hitherto formed on earth, has enabled the teachings of Jesus Christ to be propagated and carried out in greater or lesser measure throughout the world, and but for the Church His doctrines would at the most have been preserved in libraries mainly for the information of those engaged in the study of comparative religions. The Gnostics died out and their doctrines almost perished because they were constitutionally incapable of forming stable groups. The 8th (or 17th) Principle enables us to visualise in our minds the conception of mental form as opposed to physical form, and these mental forms may be moulded, cast, sculptured, or hammered out in the same manner as material shapes. If cast they are brittle and if sculptured there is much wastage of material. Groups which are hammered out suffer considerably in the process. Civilisation makes the easiest and pleasantest progress when subjected to moulding forces.

(18) GENERATION

The 9th Principle is concerned with generation as a means of propagating, enlarging, and conferring longevity in groups as well as a means of effecting incarnation and reincarnation. The 8th Principle looks back upon the past with pride and boasts of the stability which it produces by historic continuity but the 9th Principle looks forward to the future and visualises with enthusiasm a situation being produced in which its ideas and aims are universally accepted and followed. The Gnostics recognised 12 Depths of the Godhead, the 8th and 9th being Forefatherhood and Fatherhood. In its simplest form Forefatherhood finds expression in the ancestor worship of the Chinese and Japanese but it is a term which may be extended to cover pride in all institutions which are able to trace back their origin to the remote past. It is emphatically a principle of static implications. Fatherhood on the other hand is dynamic and comes into the Time Column under the Time-cycle Principle (5). It is seen in the patriarchal ambition so common among the ancient Hebrews and focused in Abraham, to be the father of a great nation whose descendants should be as the stars of heaven and the sand of the sea for multitude, and for the even greater ambition that all the nations of the world should be blessed in consequence of the spiritual seed which should be sown among them. Principle (9) is that of the Container and in its mechanical aspect is seen in the hammering out of a rod into a plate and bending it over to form a hollow cylinder. Biologically it is seen in the folding of a group of flattened cells to form a gut cavity, a process known as gastrulation which produces the cœlenterates. Taking the analogy supplied by the skeleton we see the operation of the principle in the outgrowth of ribs from a chain of vertebræ to form the bony framework of a creature such as a snake. Shoulder and hip bones, and even the bones of the skull, may be regarded in the light of specialised ribs which have become adapted to enclose cavities and afford protection to soft and delicate tissues. The first stage in the generation of the race of Adam, according to the account given in Genesis, was the formation of the woman from the body of the man by taking one of his ribs as the basis of her framework. The Hebrew word for rib in this connection has the fundamental meaning of side. Man was not adapted to become a container of offspring before birth, but the pelvis of woman was so formed that she is enabled to carry offspring in her womb for nine months from conception until the time for parturition arrives. All generative groups may be regarded in the light of containers or wombs from which new adherents may be generated, and the entire process by which religious groups spread their doctrines and make converts is frequently spoken of under the imagery of generation. The Church is, for instance, often mentioned as bearing offspring for Christ. The generative process is very much under the control of Principle (5), that of time cycles, and physical generation cannot be expedited by any means known to man without producing abortions. The very word generation has by now acquired a time-signification and is usually regarded as equivalent to about 30 years. Just as the whole mechanism of group-formation is operated from the Lower Mental World, so that of generation is operated from the Astral World, one of the first steps in conception being the effecting of a union between the astral vehicles of the parents to provide an astral vehicle for the child, without which it would be impossible for the fœtus to grow in the womb. The generative instinct in man which leads him to seek to impregnate the woman and the corresponding instinct in woman which responds to his advances is electro-magnetic in character and finds expression in the creation of a strong difference of potential in animal electro-magnetism which can only be equalised by coition. Human beings, animals, and to some degree perhaps even plants, become restless, excitable, and even ill when supercharged with animal electro-magnetism. There is no respect in which the Fall of man has produced more lamentable consequences as in the corrupting of the natural and lawful instinct of procreation. In the Biblical story of the Fall, one of the first consequences of the eating by Adam and Eve of the forbidden fruit was the realisation that they were naked, which prompted them to make aprons of leaves to conceal their organs of generation.

(19) GOVERNMENT

The symbolism associated with the actual birth into this world of children is that of the number (10) in the science of numerology, though, as we have already seen, it is brought out to some extent in (1), (4), and (7), all numbers of the same series. Children (1), Parents (2), Marriage (3), and more Children (4) constitute a recurring series throughout the whole gamut of numbers. All ancient cosmogonies, especially the Egyptian, employ the imagery of parturition to explain the generation of the Manifested Godhead from the Unmanifested, one of the favourite instances utilised being that of a hatching of a chick from an egg. (0), the upper harmonic of (9), is the symbol of an egg or container, while (1) and (10) are symbols of the Living Contents after they have been extruded. Again we can predicate next to nothing about the Unmanifested Godhead but we think primarily of the Manifested Godhead as the ruler and governor of the Cosmos. So it comes to pass that in Scripture the birth of the Manchild is usually correlated with the exercise of the functions of government. "Unto us a Child is born, unto us a Son is given, and the government shall be upon His shoulder. . . . Of the increase of His government and peace there shall be no end, upon the throne of David, and upon His Kingdom, to order it, and to establish it with judgment and justice, from henceforth and for ever." (Is. ix, 6, 7.) "And the Woman brought forth a Man-child who was to rule all nations with a rod of iron." (Rev. xii, 5.) In all monarchical countries the birth of an heir to the throne is an event which is celebrated with national rejoicings and many desolating civil wars have been caused by the lack of a direct heir to the throne whose right to reign was beyond the power of any faction to dispute. The type of government resulting from the patriarchal instinct of (9) is patriarchal and history has abundantly proved that such a mode of rule is incapable of keeping under control the unruly wills of mankind. But often the transition from (9) to (10) has been from the frying-pan into the fire when the king has proved a selfish and cruel tyrant, obsessed with the notion that he has been given a Divine right to rule or misrule as it pleases him. The Romans always looked back with longing to the age of Saturn (whose number is (10) or (19)) when a series of Etruscan monarchs governed justly and firmly during what came to be known as the Golden Age. Similarly all creation looks forward consciously or subconsciously when the whole race of mankind shall be perfectly governed,[1] this earnest longing being at the basis of the abortive efforts made during the last few years to establish a League of Nations to secure that end and of the attempts now being made to create a United Nations Organisation to replace the League and deal with international problems on new lines. The fact that (10) is the lower harmonic of (1) denotes that Man, the Microcosm, seeks to acquire the art of perfect government in imitation of God, the Macrocosm, Who governs perfectly except in so far as He is hindered by the beings upon whom He has conferred the sovereign gift of free will. But man knows little or nothing of the Law of Repetition, and the record of his civic history shows that he cannot visualise the supreme importance of giving each class an adequate voice in government. In countries such as Sweden where this principle is recognised and applied there is more peace and contentment than anywhere else in the world. The history of mankind pivots upon the exercise of rule by one class or another in

[1] Romans viii, 22, 23.

an irresponsible or arbitrary manner until the remaining classes become so exasperated that they combine to overthrow it, and then before long one of the allies will establish predominance over the others and exploit it without shame. Political involution is well portrayed by the Great Image of Daniel in which rule begins in the kingly head of gold, passes on to the aristocratic breast of silver, then devolves upon the brazen thighs of the middle classes, and finally ends up in the iron legs and feet of the proletariate, which being mixed with clay have no stability or permanence. The ideal set before us in the Millennial Reign of Christ is the establishment of a form of government which shall not merely be a wise and benevolent autocracy, but one which shall enable every subject to develop his will-power and capacity for rule in accordance with his station and class, whether on a large scale or a small, so that if he cannot exercise high authority he can at any rate familiarise himself with right principles of government and be ready at any moment to assume authority over ten cities because he has shown that he has been able to administer one justly and efficiently.

(20) Conduct

The 11th Principle comes directly under the 7th and like it is individualistic. (20) is the symbolic number of the physical world in which we live and of the senses by which we take cognisance of our environment. All studies in mass-psychology must at one stage or another take account of the behaviour of the individual, the units from which masses are formed. All institutions depend in the long run upon the temper of the men who work them. Switzerland thrives under a democratic régime, Portugal under a dictatorship, because the peoples of these countries are desirous that these forms of government should be worked. Sweden, Norway, Denmark and Holland are content to preserve monarchical constitutions for the same reason. Men conduct themselves as they should when they subordinate the animal nature in them to the human, and the animal nature belongs to principle (20) because animals are the natural preordained inhabitants of the physical world. Many, though not by any means all, of the evils which afflict mankind arise from the readiness with which men become animals and bite and devour each other. (20) is also a lower harmonic of the principle of Involution (2) and represents its end-product. If the involution of spirit into matter fails to spiritualise the animal nature then there is little more that it can do. Reference has already been made to the Christian teaching that man's future destiny is determined by the manner in which he behaves on earth under the same physical conditions as animals, and it is under the symbols of sheep and goats that Christ spoke of the ultimate characteristics of two great divisions of mankind, usually designated "the saved" and "the lost," sheep representing those who suffered the animal nature in them to be spiritualised and goats those who resisted the process. The acid test to which they were subjected to prove to which category they belonged was not whether or not they loved God with all their heart but whether they loved their neighbours as themselves. Animals do not love their neighbours, nor, with rare exceptions, their own kind when they become old and feeble, suffer from some physical infirmity, are maimed by an accident, or are tamed by mankind. In the animal world it is each one for himself except in so far as the herd instinct dictates a contrary course or mother-love intervenes. Theosophical creeds do not prescribe belief in a day of settlement of accounts such as the Judgment Day, but they do make provision for the judgment of those who persist in subjection to the animal nature. All the fundamental principles so far considered have their Christian equivalents: (7) in the Incarnation of Jesus Christ, (8) in the formation of the body of Christ, (9) in the taking of the Bride of Christ from the body that She may be the Bridegroom's helpmeet, (10) in the Millennial Reign of Christ, and finally (11) or (20) in the Judgment Day.[1] The Book of Works keeps indelible records of the deeds done in the body of flesh and by those same records it will be decided whether the sons of men have free access to the New Jerusalem or have their portion with the evil beings who are without the City, dogs, sorcerers, whoremongers, murderers, idolaters, and liars.

(21) ENVIRONMENT

(21) is the number of the material environment of mankind, and especially of the Plant Kingdom. Both in Scripture and mystic literature one is continually coming across symbolic Twelve Trees, and these appear in the New Paradise, as, according to Gnostic teaching, they did in the old. The future environment of the saved is determined by the City of Gold with its twelve foundations, its twelve gates and its walls twelve times twelve cubits high. Man is tested and trained in a double environment in this life, symbolised by the earth and the sea, the former representing stable and organised conditions of society, whether civic or ecclesiastical, and the latter unstable and chaotic conditions. The emblems of these in ancient times were Ceres and Neptune in the Latin pantheon and Demeter and Poseidon in the Greek. Both provided food for mankind, Ceres being the goddess of the earth harvests and Neptune the god of the sea-harvest. But in the New Earth no sea was seen by John because all conditions will be stabilised and made permanent for the nations of the saved after the Old Earth has passed away. The sea, if it remains at all, will be a fit emblem of the six kinds of sinners who are barred from access to the New Jerusalem. One might almost discern in the anti-symbols of the earth and the sea the kinds of environment in which the sheep and the goats found satisfaction, the latter being the type of men who fish in troubled waters. It is significant that the sign of Capricorn is a Goat with a fishlike tail and contains the decanate of the Dolphin, whereas the Ram is always depicted as a perfect animal. The sheep is peaceable but the goat is contentious. The actions of sheep are usually foreseeable but not those of the goat

[1] *cp* the 20th Tarot Card—*The Judgment.*

who loves to spring surprises on others. No man can ever feel secure under goatlike conditions in which great military powers like Germany can reduce civilisation to chaos by suddenly launching attacks upon their neighbours when the latter desire above all things to work out their national destinies in peace. In the 7th chapter of Daniel a picture is given us of four wild beasts which arise from the sea—caricatures of the cherubim—who spread devastation and destruction. In the 8th a picture is given us of a Goat attacking and destroying a Ram. In the 13th chapter of Revelation a Beast is seen arising from the sea who claims worship as a god and throws the civilised world into the melting pot, a counterpart of the Leviathan who makes the deep to seethe like a cauldron (Job, xli, 31). It is true that another Beast follows him from the earth, but it is rooted in an historical past and its acts can to some extent be foreseen and its machinations countered in advance, but no one can predict what the First Beast will do next.

It has already been stated that the physical environment of man, otherwise the geography of the earth's surface and the plant world which can only flourish in solid earth or at least fresh water, are designed and regulated by Group-spirits in the Lower Mental World. Geography makes contact with geology, meteorology, astronomy (in so far as the movements of the earth relative to the sun and moon are concerned) and finally with botany. By the interaction of these four the physical environment of man is determined and the character of the groups which he forms is profoundly affected. Therefore it is evident that the Controllers of Human Groups must be given a predominant voice in the designing and regulation of all that constitutes their physical environment. Of recent years geography, which used to be mainly descriptive, has given rise to sciences such as political geography, economic geography, ethnographic geography, and botanical geography (or if preferred, geographical botany). The entire distribution of men, animals, and plants over the face of the globe has been determined by climatic conditions, mountain ranges, forests, rivers, prairies, deserts, islands, and oceans. But as often as not man's environmental conditions are made inimical to existence in peace, comfort, and security, for the cataclysms of nature afford a valuable means of disciplining him and destroying peoples who have become incurably corrupt. Therefore just as man longs for a Millennium of perfect government, for a world in which wars are impossible and animals from the highest to the lowest are friendly to him, so he earnestly desires a physical environment which can be counted on to preserve life and not destroy it. (12) is the lower harmonic of (3), the number of Evolution, and the perfect evolution of physical conditions can only provide an environment for him which will assure him of food, warmth, and seasonable weather conditions generally. Those who picture the New Earth as representing a state in which none of these things will matter are imagining a vain thing. Finally, if we desire to proceed to the limit, we can postulate a principle (22), a lower harmonic of (4) in which these conditions will be rendered stable and permanent for æons of time.

CHAPTER VI

MYSTICAL PHILOSOPHY. PRINCIPLES, HEAVENS, AND CREATIVE HIERARCHIES

See TABLES E., F., G., H., I.

THE archetypal principles of Mystical Philosophy present the constitution of the Cosmos from an angle which is different in many ways from that already used as a point of observation, though the two groups of twelve must of necessity be closely affiliated. The members of the second group are (10) Fiat, (11) Symbol, (12) Configuration, (13) Number, (14) Tone (Sound), (15) Colour (Light), (16) Letters, (17), Geometry, (18) Speech Sounds, (19) Mantras, (20) Acts, (21) Sacraments, Charms.

(10) FIAT

The Fiat stands for the output of Energy under the direction of the Word by which the mighty act of Cosmogenesis was performed at the opening of the present Cosmic Day and of those Days which preceded it. The Cosmos in the full sense denotes far more than the sum total of the Nebulæ of Stars, it is the manifested Heavens from the 9th downwards to the 1st, the Physical Creation, and the regions of the Underworld and the Outer Darkness. But the Cosmos includes even more than this and far more, for it covers the inhabitants of the Heavens from the Powers of the Father-Mother in the 9th Heaven to the elementals of the Underworld. Our word Universe combines the ideas of one and turning which as applied to the earth denotes one planetary body turning on its axis and so producing alternations of night and day in relation to the sun. Similarly in the Spiritual Cosmos there are alternations of Nights and Days, the duration of each of which, according to tradition, is 4,320 millions of years.[1] The Law by which the Fiat works is Repetition, and its power is continuously in action, even though not put forth creatively, for the administration of the Super-cosmos and its myriads of Inhabitants calls for unceasing Divine supervision. The First Book of Dzyan, which with the second and a number of unpublished stanzas constitute the oldest documents in the world's history, gives a full account of various stages in which Cosmogenesis and the generation of the Sparks or inmost life-principles of angels and men was carried out.

Theosophists and Mystics describe the involution of the mighty process in various symbols, including that of colour, but in regard to the latter their schemes vary in many respects so it will be as well to give the correct one as indicated by the Philosophy of Analogy. Invisible

[1] This figure is not accepted however for reasons to be given later.

white and invisible yellow or amber set forth the positive power of the Father which corresponds with the light of the Sun. Purple and blue, appearing as amethyst when combined, set forth the power of the Daughter which corresponds with the light of the Moon. Green and visible yellow set forth the powers of the Son and the Seven Spirits respectively, corresponding with the earth's surface, which is partly cultivated as represented by green vegetation and partly desert as represented by yellow sand. Red, brown, and grey set forth the powers of the Mother, the Creator of the Eight Worlds and Twelve Planes of the Cosmos below the Great Boundary which divides the 7th Heaven from the 6th. Jacob Boehme calls them collectively by the name of the Universe (or Ovoid) of Eternal Nature. The highest world consists of two planes and the next of one plane and so on alternatively. In the above analogy the domain of the Mother corresponds with the interior of the earth, but if we regard the latter as being expanded to the dimensions of the World-Egg, then we view the limiting boundary or shell of the Egg from the inside, as if it were a planetarium with a star-spangled roof. Red, grey, brown, and black afford a good symbol, if not description, of the soils and rocks of the earth's crust and interior. The 6th Heaven is the special abode of Fohat, from which He rules the World-Egg. Fohat is "the Son left out," that is outside or below the Great Boundary, above which are the Seven Fighters or Planetary Logoi.[1] A volume might easily be written about the mode of operation of the Fiat which consolidated the Cosmos by the Divine Pronouncement—"Let there be" uttered by the Voice of the Word. The first two hours of the twelve of the Cosmic Day were preparatory in character for the six days of creative work which were to follow, and they were preceded by the process of Cosmogenesis as described in the *First Book of Dzyan*. Stanzas I to III inclusive of the Second Book describe the events leading to the bringing forth of an abortive creation by inferior powers, which had to be totally destroyed before the real creative work could start at 8 a.m. The operations of Cosmogenesis and Destruction are described in Gen. i, 1, 2 as "In the beginning (of the Cosmic Day) God created the heaven and the earth, and "And the earth became without form (defined surface) and void (of inhabitants)." A more detailed description of the havoc resulting from the abortive creation is given in Jer. iv, 23-27. Then from 8 a.m. to 2 p.m. the Six Days work of Creation as described in Gen. i, 3-31 and ii, 1). We are now in the early part of the 7th Day which is the 9th hour of the Cosmic Day.

(11) SYMBOLISM

The vastness of the space covered by symbolism is best appreciated by realising that it is difficult if not impossible to cite the name of any act or thing which has not a symbolic value. Furthermore we must think of symbols as forming chains, for each symbol, starting from below and working upwards, has a corresponding anti-symbol and this in turn

[1] *First Book of Dzyan.* Stanza IV, 5.

is a symbol whose anti-symbol is one link higher up. But we are not compelled to work upwards in thinking of symbols, in fact it is more profitable to reverse the process and think of the mysteries of God as being revealed downwards from anti-symbol to symbol. This is the highest signification of Aquarius, God the Revealer of Mysteries by metaphorical raindrops which come down from heaven. The region of the personality given to man to unlock the mysteries of symbols and anti-symbols, types and anti-types, the literal and the metaphorical, the physical and the metaphysical, is the imagination, the reflecting boundary surface of the mind whose planetary symbol is the moon and whose metallic symbol is mercury. The Egyptian Thoth, the equivalent of the Roman Mercury, was originally a moon-god and also a money-god, and it is from Mercury and merx that we get our word merchant. The upward and downward chains of symbols have their physiological equivalents in the sensory and motor peripheral nerves and also in the perception of mysteries and the revelation of mysteries, the afferent and efferent aspects of dealing with mystical truths. Mercury or quicksilver is the symbol of nerve-energy, which makes man behave as a human barometer in crises, especially of the financial kind which threaten his means of livelihood or life's savings.

The necessity of names, symbols, marks, brands, tokens, entitlements, seals, and impressions arises from the paramount importance of identifying large numbers of highly differentiated acts, states, and objects. An army consisting of a rabble of men, without anything whatever to distinguish one from another or the whole crowd from a hostile army, would be worse than useless and the initial steps which would be needed to convert it into a fighting force would be to give each man a uniform, badge, identifying number, personal name, rank, regimental or corps designation, etc., which would make it possible to put him in his right place along with others who bore similar marks of identification. In Rev. xiv we read of a body of people who are numbered and sealed, and on that account occupy a special position of honour and privilege. A symbol is like a globule of quicksilver which catches the light and reflects it back by means of an identification mark. Thoughts emanate from the brain like radiations and would be lost in space but for the imagination which arrests their outward course and reflects them back. This is the function of the Divine Daughter in the economy of the Godhead, symbolised by the eagle, the bird of mystery, which is able to mount up to great elevations by means of its powerful wings. Both the Syrians and the Copts assigned five rational processes to the Persons of the Godhead, or maybe Aspects of the Same, which they called Limbs of the Ineffable. They were Thought, Mind, Reflection, Thinking, and Reasoning and are exemplified in the rational faculties of the Mental, Astral, and Physical vehicles of man. Thought is the power of the Higher Mind which generates ideas and fixes them in the Lower Mind so that they form groups, complexes, and patterns in the Web which traverses this vehicle. Reflection is the mode of reasoning characteristic of the Astral Mind as seen in initiates, recluses, and students who meditate, reflect, and perceive truths by the agency of the imagination. Thinking is rational planning and reasoning is rational philosophising. The Gnostics, and especially the Sethians, taught that "All genera and species and individuals, nay, the heaven and earth itself, are images of "seals"; they are produced according to certain pre-existing types. It was from the first concourse of the three original principles or powers that first great form was produced, the impression of the great seal, namely heaven and earth."[1] In this case the Fiat stands for the signet or impressing seal. The Ancient Mysteries were celebrated and the Initiations accomplished amid a profusion of seals and symbols of every kind, every act having a symbolic value as being the outward expression of an inward and spiritual process. Many were dramatic representations of events in the lives of gods and heroes. The Docetæ taught that the souls of men were impressions, types, or seals of the Third Logos. Seals were acts which bound the recipient to God as His servant and so Paul exhorts his converts not to grieve the Spirit of God whereby they were sealed to the day of redemption, that is through the laying on of hands administered by the Apostle. So also the powers of evil were regarded as affixing their seals to the souls of men which had to be broken before they could ascend to higher realms. The Gnostics speak much of the seal on the forehead of Jeou, Lord of the Seven Planetary Logoi, the Image of the True God. The 8th Heaven is the Region of Mysteries and the Dramatic Mysteries of the Ancients were designed to give spiritual access to it. The 9th, 8th, and 7th Heavens are the domains of the Three Logoi whose primary attributes are Power, Wisdom, and Activity respectively. The Hebrews alone of the nations before the Christian Era obtained access to the spiritual atmosphere of the 9th Heaven because they have always set a high value on Power, Law, and Organisation, and still do so, all the more so because for 1900 years they have had no country of their own to rule. The Babylonians, Syrians, Phœnicians, Egyptians, Persians, and Greeks for the most part sought spiritual advancement through the various mystery cults which they originated. Christians have long recognised the extent to which the Egyptian Mysteries of Osiris prepared the way for the advent of Jesus Christ. It is to be regretted that when the Mysteries first emerged into history they had reached a state of deterioration and in some cases of degradation, as in the Dionysian orgiastic festivals, but those who seek information about the mysteries and rites of initiation in their purest state cannot do better than read *The Great Initiates* (Sketch of the Secret History of Religions, 2 Vols.) by Edouard Schuré.[2] The spiritual beings who inhabit the 8th Heaven are the Elohim, a title which is sometimes erroneously applied to the Seven Spirits of the 7th Heaven. The hierarchies of all three of the highest heavens were known to the Hebrews as the Angels of the Presence. The speciality of the Elohim and Their Angels is teaching men the esoteric Wisdom of the Mysteries, which they did in times past by instructing them in the significance of

[1] *Fragments of a Faith Forgotten*, C. R. S. Mead, 1906, p. 214.
[2] Rider and Company, 1912.

dramatic representations. In the language of the Grammarians the three Heavens above the Great Boundary illustrate the significance of the Pronoun, the Verb, and the Noun respectively.

(12) CONFIGURATION

The principle of Configuration dominates the 7th Heaven, the Anupadaka of Theosophists. It is associated with the conceptions of Skeletal Frameworks, Diagrams of Static Organisation, and Architecture. It we assign the Old Testament to the 9th Heaven with its volitional ordinances and the New Testament to the 8th Heaven with its mysteries (*cf.* "Unto you it is given to know the mysteries of the Kingdom of God," Luke viii, 10), then assuredly the *First Book of Dzyan* is the Bible of the 7th Heaven. Dzyan comes from a root meaning to shine (*cp.* Greek *zeein*) and in the *First Book of Dzyan* we find the Seven Spirits called the Seven Shining Ones (stanza III, 7) and their Lord, the Living God (El Chai) called the Radiant Child of the Father-Mother, the Unparalleled Refulgent Glory, Bright Space, and the Blazing Divine Dragon of Wisdom. He may be identified with the True God of the Alexandrine Gnosis, the Great Light of Lights. The Seven Spirits are also called the Seven Fighters (stanza IV, 5) which agrees with the meaning assigned to Zain, the 7th letter of the Hebrew Alphabet, viz. a sword or weapon with a cutting edge. Finally they are also called the Seven Builders, though somewhat obscurely, in stanza IV, 3 for the Flames, the Elements, the Builders, and the Numbers, are the hierarchies of the four highest of the Manifested Heavens, the Essences being the hierarchy of the Unmanifested 10th. In Physiology Configuration is illustrated by the Skeleton, which is the framework of the human body. It is allied in significance with the Grand Man of the Universe who furnishes the heavenly pattern of the entire Cosmos, both above and below the Great Boundary. Modern constructional work in steel concrete finds its counterpart in the framework of bones and ligaments which supports the body, and the muscles which for the most part cover them and which constitute the edible flesh of animals. For this reason all the architectural symbolism of Masonry throws considerable light upon the essential principles of the 7th Heaven, which are all related to Creative Wisdom (Dzyu) in one or other of its aspects. Whereas some of the books which expound the theory of Freemasonry are hostile to orthodox Christianity, this is not the case with those of Manly Hall, the most valuable of which is *The Lost Keys of Masonry*. In it he says, "True Masonry is esoteric. It is not a thing of this world. It has nothing to do with the things of form, save that it realises that form is moulded by, and manifests, the life it contains, and the student is seeking to mould his life, that the form will glorify God, within whose temple he is living." The names of some of the Seven Spirits have come down to us from the Gnostics, Jeou, Tsabaoth, Zarazar, and Melchizedek. The last-named should not be confused with the Melchizedek of Gen. xiv who was one of the Elohim of the 8th Heaven, though both may have been concerned in the founding of the Order of Melchizedek to which all circles of Christian Mystics are affiliated. Much space is given in the Book of the Great Logos, one of the chief Gnostic books, to the description of diagrams or configurations showing various aspects of the organisation of the 7th Heaven or Treasury of Light, otherwise the Middle Light World, the 8th being the Higher Light World. These are very complicated and include diagrams of no less than 28 Jeous. The Gnostic Books confine themselves almost entirely to the hierarchies and organisations of the three highest of the Manifested Heavens which are known collectively as the Pleroma or Fullness of the Godhead.

The Esoteric Buddhists of India and Tibet resemble the Alexandrine Gnostics in being far more interested in the cultivation of Creative Wisdom than in the celebration and perpetuation of dramatised mysteries, and regard the Stanzas of Dzyan as containing all the Wisdom that is worth knowing, but they appear to have lost the meaning of most of the stanzas of the First Book, judging from the commentaries made upon them by Mme. Blavatsky, though the contents of the Second Book of Anthropogenesis are well understood. One must be well grounded in the doctrines of the Alexandrine Gnosis to grasp the meaning of the First Book.

(13) NUMBERS

Numbers may be generated by any one of the four processes of Arithmetic, Addition, Subtraction, Multiplication, or Division, but in so far as those of the 6th Heaven are concerned only the last operation comes into the picture. The inmost spiritual principles of angels and men are called Sparks, which are united in the cosmic consciousness of the 7th Heaven to form Flames, and are differentiated in the 6th Heaven in order that they may acquire the highest form of Ahamkara or Individualised Consciousness. This is the first step which they take in their downward descent into the material world. The Sparks are divided into three classes of which the first has the same name, the second is called that of the Sacred Animals, and the third is called that of the Messengers of the Sacred Fathers, that is of the Seven Spirits. The Hebrew mystics called them the Angels of the Sanctuary, the Angels of Wind and Fire (Ps. civ., 4), and the Angels of Heat and Cold.[1] All incarnate in due course in the Adamic Race, the first two constituting the upper and lower divisions of the 7th subrace of the 5th Root Race and the third the 6th subrace. The corresponding religious organisations are the Order of Melchizedek, the Order of the White Knights, and the Christian Church. These with the Hierarchy of the 7th Heaven are symbolised by the Four Rivers of Eden, Pison, Gihon, Hiddekel, and Euphrates. The natural homes of the three last hierarchies are the 6th, the 5th, and the 4th Heavens respectively, otherwise the Spheres of Numbers, Tones, and Colours. According to occult teaching the Sparks proper, also known as Sun-gods, inhabit the stars of the cosmos of universities as their bodies, and

[1] The two latter are identical with the Spiritual and Celestial Angels respectively of Swedenborg.

their number is incalculable. Below the Boundary they are ruled by the Holy Four, known to the Hindus as the Mahadevas of the Four Cardinal Points. When the promise was made to Abraham that he should be the ancestor of innumerable descendants he was invited by God to number the stars if he sought to estimate the number of his descendants. As the power of telescopes increases so large numbers of nebulæ are seen to consist of countless multitudes of stars, and the expression "astronomical" figures has now come into common use, not only to express distances but numbers. The 6th Heaven is the Upper Nirvana of Theosophists, the World of Virgin Spirits of the Rosicrucians, the Still Eternity of the Christian Mystics,[1] and the Spiritual Temple of the Book of Revelation (ch. i). The 5th Heaven is the Lower Nirvana or Atma of Theosophists, the World of Divine Spirit of the Rosicrucians, and the Heaven of Rev. iv, v. The 4th Heaven is the Buddhi of the Theosophists, the World of Life Spirit of the Rosicrucians, and the New Jerusalem of the Christian Mystics. The ideas of the 7th Heaven, Anupadaka, are clothed and expressed in six veils or classes of symbols, viz. numbers, tones, colours, letters and written words, geometrical forms, and spoken speech sounds and words. The symbolism of numbers is the ground basis of this book. In addition all the classes of symbols are related to each other and in particular a vast science called the Gematria has been built up in which numbers have been assigned to all the Hebrew letters, written and spoken, so that every word has a corresponding symbolic number. One of the Gnostic books was called, *The Number-Symbolism of Marcus*, and according to Irenæus opened with these words, "Now the utterance of the Great Name was on this wise, The Father spake the Word; the first note of His Name was a sound of four elements; the third of ten; and the fourth of twelve. Thus the utterance of the whole Name was of thirty elements and four sounds or groupings." Numbers may be regarded as including all units of measurement and capacity and the activities of the 6th Heaven are concerned with the careful and meticulous ordering of details under the supervision of the Holy Four. The lowest hierarchy of sun-gods, the Asuras, is partly evil and is called the Satanic Hierarchy by Theosophists.

Numbers represent the principle of differentiation in state and are connected with methodical examination and detailed procedure. One department of numbers, and an important one, relates to money values and thus makes contact with accountancy. A balance sheet when accurately drawn up gives an exact indication of the "state" of a firm's business and the principle can be extended to throw light on the nature of Karma. Next we have numbers in their relationship to population and voting. Governments are always particularly interested in the taxpayer, and in the Roman Republic taxation came under the purview of the Censor. Nations are vitally interested in statistics which show whether their population is increasing or decreasing. But the utility of these examples in the present case depends upon the light which they

---

[1] *A Manifestation concerning the Eight Worlds or Regions.* Jane Lead, 1695.

throw upon the essential nature of numbers, about which Mme. Blavatsky wrote with truth, "Every cosmogony, from the earliest to the latest, is based upon and interlinked with and most closely related to numerals and geometrical figures." And again, "Numbers and figures are used as an expression and a record of thought in every archaic symbolical scripture."[1] Pythagoras used to tell his disciples, "If the world is built upon the power of numbers, then numbers must be the key to the understanding of the universe." And Skinner writes in this connection, "The power of expression of the law (creative law or design) exactly by numbers clearly defining a system, was not the accident of language, but was its very essence and of its primary organic construction."[2] Not the least part of the value of numbers consists in the fact that mathematical laws are absolutely true and accurate, beyond possibility of doubt and denial. In the dimension of time the part played by numbers in measuring time-cycles and fixing dates is of incalculable importance and but for their intervention no science of history would be possible. The mystery of the Number of the Beast has always intrigued students of prophecy. It is 666 which by reduction becomes 9, pointing to the Beast himself and his 8 heads.

(14) SOUNDS

A perusal of Rev. iv. and v shows that the 5th Heaven is above all others consecrated to music, and the songs and ascriptions of praise which proceed from it contrast strongly with the silence of the Still Eternity. The 24 Elders are seen with harps and vials full of odours which represent articulate liturgical worship. Seven groups of Beings are depicted as singing praises or worshipping the Lamb, Elders, Living Creatures, Angels, and all the Inhabitants of heaven, the earth, and the underworld. The Sacred Animals include six orders of Angels, Ministers or Elders, Living Creatures, Seraphim, Cherubim or Ophannim, Thrones, and Dominions. They are the Agnishvatta Pitris of the Hindus. The Music of the Spheres is no pictureque metaphor, according to many mystics, but is composed of harmonies which may be heard with the inner ear. Pythagoras claimed to be able to do so. Job wrote that when the work of Creation was completed the Morning Stars sang together and all the Sons of God shouted for joy, referring perhaps to the twice-six orders of Angels. We may discern five primary elements in music, tone or timbre, pitch, harmony, tempo and rhythm, and loudness or softness. There are 5 staves to the bar. In modern orchestras we find wood-wind instruments, brass and silver instruments, stringed instruments, pianos, and organs or harmoniums, five kinds in all. The xylophone comes under the same category as the piano. Music belongs to the 2 series which is seen in the major and minor keys, while 8 is seen in the octave. The sphere of Music has seven spheres below it

---

[1] *Secret Doctrine.* Vol. III, p. 69. Vol. I, p. 341.
[2] *The Source of Measures*, p. 204.

before we reach the 12th, the lower octave. Shakespeare wrote of the music of the spheres:—

> There's not the smallest orb which thou beholdest,
> But in his motion like an angel sings
> Still choiring, to the young-eyed cherubim;
> Such harmony is in immortal souls.

Towards the end of the last century Sedley Taylor invented an instrument called a Phoneidoscope which reproduced sound in colour and projected the latter upon a screen. Clairvoyants claim to be able to see beautiful forms and colours arising from orchestras and choirs which give performances of musical masterpieces. Handel's *Messiah* is said to fill a hall with waves of pure tints of orange, pink, purple, and blue.

Music appropriate to certain states of mind has undoubtedly a great therapeutic value, though not so pronounced as that of colour. While no music is able to convey precise ideas on any subject from mind to mind yet it is able to work people up into exalted emotional and even passional conditions of soul. The subject will be further dealt with under the arts.

The Greek word for letter, *gramma*, meant also a musical note. This is the true gramma in time as the letter or character is in space. The revealing powers of sound and music are symbolised by the lungs by which the breath of heaven is inhaled. Exhaling should not be a convulsive output of breath such as "the blast of the nostrils" but the quiet and easy expulsion of air working in rhythmic agreement with inhalation. The Gnostics taught that at the opening stage of Creation the Great Voice uttered the seven notes of the scale in conjunction with the seven vowels of the Greek alphabet, and that these vocal sounds penetrated through the heavens below the Pleroma and multiplied themselves. The gramma may also bear another signification, namely the cry of the creature which expresses its needs, sufferings, hopes, and aspirations. Music itself thought inarticulate has much the same emotional content as the spontaneous cry, as may be seen in the joyous singing of birds.

(15) COLOURS

The 4th Heaven is called the New Jerusalem by Jane Lead and the New Paradise appears to be part of it. In the vision of the New Jerusalem in Rev. xx the description is concerned entirely with colours, appearance, and dimension in space. We are told of 12 foundation stones of all the colours of the rainbow, of light of the appearance of crystal, of walls like jasper, of gates of pearl, and of streets of gold. We read that it had no need of sun or moon because the glory of the Lord lightened it. Nothing is said about sound, all is light and colour. Paradise is lit by the same agency, the glory of God, and trees, leaves, flowers, and fruits are of various colours. Colours have outlines, sometimes clear and sometimes ill-defined, but in the former case their limitations can be depicted by form-lines. Both forms and colours can be applied to plane surfaces by brush, pencil, crayon, or pen. The representation of form bridges the gulf between Painting and Letters. The most important mystical aspect of colour relates to the Rays which emanate from the Seven Spirits of the Seventh Heaven (Anupadaka) and which set up currents in the Fourth Heaven. These are controlled by the Planetary Logoi and constitute its blood-stream, which circulate in the inferior worlds and planes down to the Chaotic World. The colours are white (invisible), electrum (invisible), amber (invisible), purple, blue, green, orange, red, brown, and grey and they circulate chiefly in the inferior worlds as follows:—Upper Mental—Electrum. Lower Mental—Amber. Astral —Purple. Upper Physical—Blue. Lower Physical—Green. Subphysical —Orange. Upper Plutonic—Red. Lower Plutonic—Brown. Chaotic— Grey. Every star and planet as well as every element has its characteristic spectrum by which it can be identified, provided the emanated rays can be collected in sufficient quantity and intensity. Elaborate systems of colour therapeutics have been devised by various medical men and healers, beginning with that of Babbitt, some of which have proved remarkably successful, especially in dealing with neurotic subjects.

Every colour has a numerical value, just as every tone has, which is bound up with its rate of vibration. Every substance in nature has a colour of some kind, if we include neutral tints, and of course white and black. The characteristic colours of substances extend beyond the visible spectrum which clairvoyants and occultists are able to see if not describe. The silvery violet rays of a high-frequency electrical machine which merge into pure luminescence give us some idea of the nature of invisible colours as do also certain metallic sheens. Occultists have from time immemorial correlated vowel sounds and colours. Every planet is believed to have its characteristic colour though unfortunately authorities are by no means agreed as to what they are. Similarly the signs of the Zodiac have all been allotted symbolic colours.

The New Jerusalem, Jerusalem the Golden, is the permanent spiritual home of the Solar Logos, the Planetary Logoi or Genii, and the spirits who have incarnated in Vulcan, Mercury, and Venus, who are more advanced than those of the Adamic Race on this planet but certain pioneers of the 6th and 7th Races, advance contingents who are Fifth Race men by nature but whose evolution is proceeding rapidly, have made their home in the New Jerusalem with the higher planetary spirits. Reverting to the Archetypal Man we have up to the present referred to three of his physiological organs and systems as affecting the Heavens of the Pleroma, namely the central nervous system of the brain, the cerebro-spinal system, and the muscular-osseous system. The systems corresponding to the 6th, and 5th, and 4th Heavens are the Thyroidal-mammary, the Respiratory-urinary, and the Cardiac-Thymic or Circulatory. The functions of the thyroid are numerous and varied and include control of growth and size, preservation of the elasticity of the tissues, regulation of the generative functions, and maintenance of the acuteness of perception of the senses. Mentally it gives an active memory and the capacity to form fixed habits. The Respiratory system by which we breathe is associated symbolically with Mercury and the air, which is the medium by which sounds travel and are distributed as already mentioned. But the important point to be borne in mind by the members of the Churches is that their calling is to be the Heart and Arterio-venous system of the Archetypal Man. It is doubtless for this reason that the spirits of the Fourth Heaven, the true Sixth Creative Hierarchy of the Cosmos, were known as the Angels of Heat and Cold. For we speak instinctively of a person as having a warm heart and being hot-blooded or having a cold heart and being cold-blooded. The circulation of the blood serves among other things to keep the temperature-balance of the body. Light rays and heat rays are branches of a common group of thermo-luminous radiations though they are not convertible terms. Beauty of complexion and colouring is largely produced and maintained by the blood and here we have one of the distinguishing Venusian characteristics, for the traditional goddess was above all a being who rejoiced in life, light, and colour, all emanations from the World of Life-spirit. As Venus-Urania the goddess was the embodiment of the most exalted forms of human affections. It is hardly necessary to comment upon the vast influence of sex-relationships in the world day, apart from all procreative functions of the sexes, and it is, or should be, to the Christian Churches to which the world should look for enlightenment as to how co-operation between the sexes can be furthered to the glory of God and the benefit of humanity.

(16) LETTERS

The whole subject of the formation of letters and scripts is so far-reaching and complex that one hardly knows where to begin in attempting to cope with it. From letters are formed words, from words sentences, and from sentences in accordance with the rules of syntax, are formed languages. Up till the invention of wireless transmission, and to a lesser degree of telephony and telegraphy, no method of communication between man and man, business and business, could compare with script, and its modern substitutes and aids of printing and typewriting. (16) is the number of Gemini whose house, the 3rd, is said to be associated with all forms of writing and communications other than vocal. Letters may be defined as arbitrary diagrams or glyphs which represent affiliated ideas and sounds. It is probable that originally all letters, excluding some hieroglyphs and cuneiforms, were rationally diagrammatic but in nearly every case the primary designs have become so much simplified or altered in the process of time that the original reason of their adoption cannot be traced. The mystical meaning of letters is a science in itself of which Hebrew furnishes the securest basis. Consonants are far more important than vowels in the Hebrew alphabet, which as we have it now consists almost entirely of consonantal sounds, vowels being represented by pointing. The most ancient Hebrew manuscripts contain no vowel pointings at all. The invention of the alphabet, if indeed we should not rather say the revelation of the alphabetical principle, marked a notable advance in the resources of civilisation, for it enabled words to be permanently recorded on parchment, clay tablets, or stone. Without writing or inscribing the only means until recently of perpetuating ideas was committing words, sentences, and stories to memory and transmitting them orally from generation to generation as the Maoris and many African tribes have done with astounding accuracy and fidelity. The letters of the demotic script of Egypt were based on the pictorial representation of objects, most of which are recognisable to-day. A considerable number of American Indian tribes use picture-writing to convey ideas and instructions, thus providing a firm linkage between the arts of writing and drawing. Chinese characters are pictorial representations of ideas rather than of letters, which eliminates spelling. Association glyphs are used with numbers in the science of mathematics which have virtually the force of words. Religious records and revelations have been extensively perpetuated by oral traditions but business contracts and bargains have always had urgent need of being recorded in some permanent form so as to be available for later reference independently of the testimony of witnesses. Written records are not infrequently a source of embarrassment to priesthoods, when, as often happens, their doctrines and practices degenerate with the lapse of time and some reformer gains access to the original records and uses them to test the reliability of the teaching given to the people in his own day.

The race belonging to (16) is the upper half of the 5th Root Race, called Aryan by some theosophists, though the Aryans we know most of are descendants of Japhet. There seems to be no doubt that many civilisations which were fairly advanced in many ways were in existence before the Adamic Race appeared nearly 6,000 years ago, in China, India, Babylon, Egypt, and perhaps Mexico and Peru. At any rate we have no ground for asserting that communication by script was unknown to them. There can be little doubt that large numbers of individuals of the 5th subrace of the 5th Root Race survive at the present day though inextricably mixed up with the descendants of Adam. The region from which most of these incarnating egos came was the 3rd Heaven, the Upper Mental World of Theosophy and the Region of Abstract Thought of the Rosicrucians. No name has been given to it by Christian mystics but it might be called Mount Moriah since the Region of Concrete Thought is identical with the Mount Zion of Jane Lead and Rev. xiv, 1. The natural inhabitants of the 3rd Heaven are the six inferior orders of Angels, Mights, Powers, Principalities, Archangels, Angels, and Decans. The heads of those members of the orders which remain faithful to God are apparently the six men with slaughter weapons of Ezek. ix, 2 who were used for punishing the guilty city of Jerusalem. The activities of the six orders are punitive and bellicose since they belong to the Martial Sphere (16). The chief of the six is called the Scribe or Man with the Writer's Inkhorn, in other words a Man of Letters. St. Paul had no high opinion of the Angels of the 3rd Heaven, to which he was caught up at one time. He told his converts of his wrestlings with Principalities and Powers, of World-rulers of Darkness (Mights) and of Wicked Spirits in high places (Archangels) (Eph. vi, 12). It was from the last-named, also known as Watchers or Sons of God, that the angels came who cohabited with Sethite women before the Deluge and who produced a race of giants and war-lords who filled the earth with violence, so that God repented that He had made man (Gen. vi). Swedenborg called all the inferior six orders Angels of Power and the superior ones Angels of Love. The inferior orders are the Makara or Crocodile Spirits of Theosophy, the administrative angels of the 2nd Heaven being the Barhishad or Lunar Pitris and the Astral Angels of the 1st Heaven being the Solar Pitris. The evil Makara Pitris made common cause with the turbulent and bellicose Asuras on many occasions in times past. Mrs. Besant calls the Makara spirits the 5th Hierarchy, placing them above the Agnishwatta Pitris, but they constitute the 7th.[1] It seems probable that the Egyptian Crocodile-god Sebek, the symbol of the Pharaohs, was the chief of them. Yet the Egyptians also depicted ordinary human spirits by crocodiles and one picture has been found which shows the goddess Neith as suckling seven young crocodiles. The Hebrew prophets, Enoch and Baruch, had no high opinion of the 3rd Heaven as the result of their visits to this place. In the Book of the Great Logos and other Gnostic works we read of a Ruler called Adamas Sabaoth who led astray the apostate members of the six inferior orders. He is said to have been a Tyrant, that is one of the Thrones, and was punished by being confined with his dupes in the Astral World. In general the apostate angels of the 3rd Heaven manifest all the qualities arising from perverted wills, wrathfulness, arrogance, violence, self-sufficiency, and love of despotism. Adamas Sabaoth is said to have ruled over 365 aeons, the same number as that of the days in the year. It is worthy of note that the Hebrews called the Angels of the 3rd Heaven by the name of the Angels of the Four Seasons, which together make up the year and consist of about 91 days each. The symbolism of the year has many implications but it represents a cycle of birth, life, and death, of change and renovation, and of capacity to adapt oneself to extremes of climatic changes. Now Gemini people are the most physically adaptable of all types and seem to be able to thrive in parts of the earth which are unhealthy for most people. For that reason they make excellent explorers and prospectors.

(17) FORMS

There seems to be general agreement among Theosophists that the Lower Mental World of Concrete Thought is *par excellence* the region of geometrical forms, patterns, and designs. It is here that all the schemes for making changes in the earth's crust and forming mountain ranges, continents, islands, and seas are modelled, so to speak, before they are put into effect. This is the sphere where, according to E. L. Gardner, the learned author of *The Web of the Universe*, the three-dimensional lattice-work is seen in its clearest form and with innumerable geometrical

[1] *The Pedigree of Man.* 1904.

figures interwoven with or embroidered on its strands. These figures convey very precise information to those who are able to interpret them and even on earth diagrams play an important part in many abstruse sciences, mathematics above all, in illustrating and explaining the nature and operation of principles which would otherwise be obscure. The geometry of the generation of plane and solid forms, and of the innumerable surfaces obtained by taking sections of them, is a science in itself as is also that of the classification of crystals by means of space-lattices. The Formative Hierarchy of the 2nd Heaven is that of Race and Group Spirits of Animals and Plants and of the spirits, who, as already mentioned, control the form of all continents and seas. They have various names indicating their administrative functions, including the titles of archangels and angels which renders them liable to be confused with the preceding hierarchy. The Hebrew mystics called them angels of clouds, rain, hail, snow, mist, frost and ice, not because they controlled terrestrial weather, which is the task of elemental kings, but because they disposed of forces of which the physical phenomena just mentioned are types. Cold for instance is a crystalliser as seen in its effects in producing frost patterns and snow crystals. The chief administrator, as already mentioned, is the Aethereal Jesus or Jessu, sometimes confused with Jesus Christ. Hebrew mystics sensed him as a White Swan and also as a Cloud which prevented the heat, that is the despotism, of the Crocodile Spirits from interfering with the work of form-building. In the 2nd Book of Dzyan, stanza VI, he is called, "The White Swan from the Starry Vault." The Gnostics preserved much lore concerning the Aethereal Jesus, who was also known as the High Priest, and is perhaps to be identified with the Child or Lad of the Hebrew mystics and the Gnostics, so-called because of his eternal youthfulness. The 8th Hierarchy incarnated freely in the first four subraces of the 5th Root Race.

The associated Physiological systems are the Lymphatics, Hepatic, and Alimentary in the case of principles (16), (17), and (18), the leading characteristics of which are Adaptability and Distributiveness, Regulation of Growth and Metabolism, and Absorption and Excretion respectively, but the correspondences cannot be dealt with here.

(18) SPEECH-SOUNDS

We take the utterance of words as a matter of course without pausing to think how mysterious they are. We have become accustomed to think of them as little more than compounds of elementary sounds represented by letters of the alphabet. But just as a building is something more than the aggregate of the stones of which it is constituted, because they are arranged after a specified design to form a noble structure, so words are something much more than a synthesis of the elementary sounds of which they are composed. All occultists insist on the coercive power of words when uttered by those who understand the operation of the finer forces of nature. Much more is this true of the Voice of the Word. "By the Word of the Lord were the heavens made and all the host of them by the Breath of His Mouth. . . . For He spake and it was done, He commanded and it stood fast."

In considering the use of words in conversation and speech-making it is important to bear in mind that this form of communication is an important equaliser of potential. There are three kinds of conversationalists, the positive who desire to impart information, the negative who seek to acquire it, and the neutral who like to exchange ideas. We all know what it is to meet people who are bursting with information like overcharged thunder-clouds. They literally cannot keep silent and prefer to talk to those who take no interest in what they have to say or even ridicule them, rather than keep silent. Such people may be heard orating in the parks every Sunday. One of their less obvious but equally exasperating relatives is the club bore. The craving to acquire information may be a virtue or a vice according to the kind of information sought. The avid inquirer in important matters is usually kindly treated and helped by those who are in a position to tell him what he wants to know, whereas the curious busybody who seeks to probe into the private affairs of his friends and neighbours is a public pest. The man who has learnt the true art of conversation, which is a giving and receiving of information in approximately equal quantities, can always count on making many friends and keeping their friendship.

The development and regulation of speech sounds and the pronunciation of languages falls within the province of the Astral Angels, the leaders of which are the gods and goddesses who were assigned various names in the ancient pantheons of the West. In the Gnostic *Book of the Saviour*, Zeus or Jupiter is represented as a real being who rules the Fate-Sphere, a name given to the Astral Plane because the stars to some extent rule the fate of men and nations by the emanations, now called cosmic rays, which they send forth. Four other deities are mentioned as ruling under him, Hermes, Aphrodite, Ares, and Kronos. Many long speeches by the gods of Greece are reported by the poets and dramatists of that country, and they are always represented as conversing freely with each other. Both they and the Romans, who worshipped the same beings under other names, rated the art of Eloquence very highly, the Romans in particular encouraging forensic eloquence. The Hebrews called these beings, the 9th Hierarchy, by the names of Angels of Thunder and Lightning, terms which are commonly used as descriptive of impassioned oratory. When mighty Jove assembled the massed artillery of heaven for action it was regarded as a sign that his anger had been aroused by some evil deeds of mankind. In general the inhabitants of Olympus, and still more those who, like Poseidon, sought to be admitted to that hallowed spot but who were prevented from doing so, behaved very much like human beings in their loves and hates, or in other words were dominated by the astral forces of emotion, desire, and passion. According to the Phœnician historian Sanchoniathon they all incarnated in or near Phœnicia after the Deluge, apparently in the descendants of Cain, and added much legendary lore to that which was already set forth concerning them in the signs and decanates of the Zodiac. All astrology is astral in origin and character. It is remarkable that the Hindus have so little to say about the 9th Hierarchy, which they classify as Solar Pitris.

(19) MANTRAS

With mantras, magical acts, and sacraments we come to a series of processes or occult practices of which free use is made either for good or evil according as to whether the exercise of white or black magic is meditated. The essence of mantras and all similar invocations is that they should be presented in rhythmic form, which was as essential to the invocation as the words employed, perhaps more so, because there is a cumulative power in rhythmic words or acts repeated continuously over a period of time. There can be little doubt that peasants in Roman Catholic countries often repeat their Paternosters and Aves as if they were mantras though not uttered in rhythmic form. The use of mantras, a term also applied to Vedic hymns, might be called a kind of mechanised intercession. No Christian doubts the power exercised by intercessory prayer even though the requests preferred cannot always be granted, but in this case the power comes from a concentration of spiritual desires directed upwards to heaven. It is needless to enlarge upon the diabolical uses to which incantations are put by black magicians, whose power is proportionate to the ignorance and timidity of those who approach them or become subject to their influence. The utterance of incantations can and does set evil forces in motion which may do incalculable harm before their potency becomes exhausted. Even as the Great Fiat in the upper harmonic compartment was the source of all creative power in the beginning of the Cosmic Day, so the incantation is the source of all destructive power on earth other than that which is exercised by physical force.

The lowest of the seven forms of Yoga is known as the Mantra and includes rhythmic dancing, marching, military ceremonial, group-singing and certain kinds of religious ceremonial. Even music is reckoned to come under the heading Mantra Yoga, with colours and perfumes. It acts by setting up rhythmic currents in the Etheric Vehicle.

(20) MAGICAL ACTS

The power put forth by magic acts is clearly dramatic rather than poetic in its nature but is furthermore to be distinguished from that resident in mantras by the fact it calls for a certain amount of knowledge of mysteries to be exercised effectively. The agent used in the performance of miracles was nearly always a rod, a copy of the Caduceus of Mercury, a divining rod, a magic wand, or even a pointed finger. It must not however be supposed that any rod could ever be used effectively by untrained persons to counteract the normal forces of nature or supersede them by forces operating under different laws. Those who sought to make use of the powers of white magic to work wonders had to undergo a gruelling training and master the intricacies of many laws, natural and supernatural. The black magician likewise could not control the powers of evil without knowing a good deal about the laws governing their mode of operation, even though he may have made free use of elementals, either natural or of his own creation. Inexperienced magicians who sought to make elementals do their bidding were liable to be attacked themselves by the entities which they had sent forth to destroy or injure others. But there is one series of events recorded in Sacred History in which a rod of power, Aaron's, was used to transmit power provided by Jehovah Himself to inflict the Ten Plagues on Egypt. Moses and Aaron were learned in the wisdom of the Egyptians, which in matters of science was the only one to which they had access, but it does not appear that anything which they may have learnt concerning magic was of value to them during the infliction of the Plagues. The magicians of Egypt used enchantments to imitate some of their miracles, though presumably on a restricted scale, but were completely baffled by the later ones. The rod of magic always served to point out the direction in which the power was required to flow in order to produce a maximum effect, unlike the mantra. The wielding of a magical rod was in itself a dramatic act but the manipulation of the forces of black and white was effected by the agency of other acts too numerous to mention. Divination may be regarded as the negative of miracle-working, for its purpose is sensory, that is to obtain information, not motor to produce positive results. The divining rod was however somewhat of an adjunct to divination which could be practised by interpreting omens, observing the flight of birds, investigating the appearance and arrangement of entrails, and by countless other methods. Divination by crystal bowls, cards, tea-leaves, sand, or even by holding an object belonging to a person about whom one seeks information, is commonly practised to-day. A great deal of legitimate and non-miraculous diagnosis may be performed telepathically by observing the movements of a rod used for water-divining or a specially constructed pendulum, as is done by those who are developing the new therapeutic science of Radiæsthesia, which may well revolutionise in process of time the medical art as practised to-day.

(21) SACRAMENTS—CHARMS

Under the general heading of Sacraments we may include all substances and objects which are believed to be the seat of spiritual or supernatural powers of one kind or another, transferable without any mantras or divinatory measures being employed in the process. Apart from such substances as have been used sacramentally for many ages, bread, wine, fire, water, oil, incense, and salt, we have relics of saints preserved for centuries in order that the powers inherent in them can be called forth from time to time by acts of faith. Then we have charms and mascots which even in this sceptical and science-worshipping age are being increasingly used by all those engaged on dangerous work or locomotion, especially by airmen.

So far no reference has been made to the last three hierarchies, if indeed such an exalted title can be applied to them. The Hindus refer to them vaguely as classes of pitris in the case of spirits which we should classify as solar or lunar, but there seems to be a general agreement as to the nature of the 12th hierarchy, which is composed of Elemental Kings of four classes, spirits of fire, air, water, and earth. The country folk of every country in the world have their own special names for the Little Folk, some of which however are the size of human beings while others are mere midgets. These should not be confused with the geometrical elementals which are said to reside in trees and inorganic substances.

The Astral Angels probably incarnated largely in the Atlantean or 4th Root Race and perhaps sun-spirits in the second half of the Lemurian or 3rd Root Race. The Rulers of the last three orders of beings belong to a far higher order than the so-called hierarchies, for they appear to be the Regent of the Sun,[1] the Regent of the Moon, and the King of the World or East, concerning whose recent activities Dr. Curtiss had much to say in a book which he published called, *Coming World Changes*.

Position of Adamic Humanity

It is a remarkable fact that the true position of the spirits of the Adamic Race should not have been accorded them by theosophists. Rosicrucians call them Virgin Spirits and place them in the 12th and lowest Creative Hierarchy. The English Behmenist, John Pordage, in the description which he gives of the Virgin Spirits of the Still Eternity (6th Heaven) in his booklet, *Mystica Teutonica*, calls them Sparks and says that they are spirits destined to incarnate in human bodies. The Sparks of the 1st Book of Dzyan, as we have seen, include three Hierarchies, the 4th, 5th, 6th, that is Sun-gods, Sacred Animals, and Messengers of the Fathers (Adamic spirits). The breath of life which God breathed into the nostrils of Adam to make him a living soul was the immortal spirit-soul which had passed down into the 5th Heaven. The immortal souls of the Adamites are the gods of Plotinus and the Augoeides of the Neo-Platonists. When we read in *Porphyry* that Plotinus was united six times with his god we are to understand that he made conscious contact with his own immortal spirit-soul on six occasions. Theosophists have much to say on the subject of the immortal spirit-soul, Atma-Buddhi, but fail to recognise it as the unit of the 6th Hierarchy. Its highest faculty is Intuition, of which Mrs. Besant writes, "Intuition, as we see by its derivation, is simply insight—a process as direct and swift as bodily vision. It is the exercise of the eyes of the intelligence, the unerring recognition of a truth presented on the mental plane (Buddhic plane?). It sees with certainty, its vision is unclouded, its report unfaltering. No proof can be had to the certitude of its recognition, for it is above and beyond the reason.' "[2] The most serious of the consequences of the Fall of Adamic Man was his inevitable separation from his immortal soul which was as completely driven forth from the

---

[1] This Being should not be confused with the Solar Logos or Lord of the 4th Heaven, the Abraxas of the Gnostics.

[2] *The Seven Principles of Man*, p. 54.

MYSTICAL PHILOSOPHY

garden of his astral body as he was driven from Paradise. As long as his immortal soul was in the garden of his astral soul it was impossible for him to die. The complete salvation of man will be accomplished when he has regained the close companionship of his immortal soul and not till then.

The 4th, 5th, and 6th Creative Hierarchies, the chiefs of the Adityas, Rudras, and Vasus, are known to Theosophists as the Manasuputras of Sons of Mind and are called the Lords of the Dark Wisdom or Asuras, the Lords of the Flame or Agnishvatta Pitris, and the Lords of Venus or Dragons of Wisdom. The difference between good and evil Asuras is very pronounced, there being no doubt whatever which are Angels and which are Devils. They are either Lords of the Dazzling Face or Lords of the Dark Face. Both are extraordinarily knowledgeable and subtle. The Agnishvatta Pitris are sometimes called the Pentagon which agrees with their symbolic number and sometimes the Lords of Yoga. They are the Lungs or Breath of the Body of the Grand Man and not the Heart as Mrs. Besant says. They are Kumaras who are too spiritual to create bodies of flesh. The Lords of Venus are the Planetary Spirits of the Second Order, the Lords of Wisdom, and should not be confused with the Seven Great Planetary Logoi of (12). They include orders named after the sun, moon, and planets, which means that there are lesser Lords of Venus included in the main order. Whereas the 4th Hierarchy is symbolised by Mammals and the 5th by Birds, the 6th is symbolised by Dragons. (Table Q). The 6th Hierarchy is that of the Six-fold Dhyanis though this name seems to be applied also to the three inferior orders of ths six which constitute the Agnishvatta Pitris. These orders of Cherubim, Thrones, and Dominions mostly work in the 4th Heaven with the Dragons of Wisdom. Mme. Blavatsky describes the Lords of Venus as, "towering giants of godly strength and beauty."[1] Taking the sub-orders in detail the Lords of Mars are said to have been active during the first three Rounds in preventing the human spirit from becoming too closely identified with the body until the 5th Root Race appeared. The human spirit acts on the body through the lymph and the Lords of Mars kept its heating powers latent, probably by reducing its copper content. It is lymph corpuscles and not red corpuscles which are the causes of fevers arising through fighting hostile microbes. The Lords of Mercury have now taken charge of the 2nd half of the 5th Basic Race and are striving to teach its members the art and virtue of self-mastery and to prevent them from falling into the snare of regarding their physical bodies as prison-houses.

The Supreme Lord of the Messengers of the Gods is the Angel of the Sun. He is probably the Being mentioned in Rev. xix, 17 who calls upon the fowls of the air to come and feast upon the flesh of those who are slain at Armageddon. To the Gnostics he was the Immortal Adam, the spiritual prototype of the historical Adam. He is probably the Aryaman of the Iranians, and is also the Word of the Lord mentioned in Ps. xxxvi, 6 who was used by the Elohim to give artistic form to the

[1] *Secret Doctrine*, II, 181.

Universe. Kon-fu-tyu says of him, "The Dragon feeds in the pure water of Wisdom and sports in the clear waters of Life." He is closely associated with the mysterious Narada, also called Pesh-hun the Messenger whom Mme. Blavatsky says is the executor of the decrees of Karma and Adi-Budh (the Ruler of the 5th Heaven). He is instructed by Brahma to make all men believe in Vasu-Deva, the Liberator, that is the Christ. He is said to have inspired all the greatest heroes of the present Cosmic Day and to have calculated all cosmic cycles to come and to have set them down in a book called the *Mirror of Futurity*. Many thousands of stanzas have been written to record his activities.

The Hierarchies of the 5th and 3rd Heavens

It is important to distinguish between the 12 Creative and Formative Hierarchies which span the Cosmos from the 9th Heaven to the earth and two bands of six hierarchies each which have their seats in the 5th and 3rd Heavens and whose lower orders reside in the 4th and 2nd Heavens respectively. The Chief sub-order of the first six is that of the Flames, Ministers, Elders, or Thrones. These Higher Thrones are frequently confused with the 5th sub-order of the Lower Thrones, the Dignities or Light-Beings of Jude, 8, who often act as the chief of a group of 8 sub-orders composed of Lesser Thrones, Dominions, and the 6 sub-orders of the 3rd Heaven. The Living Creatures are distinct from the Cherubim, and the Ophannim are a branch of the Cherubim. The Cherubim are sometimes called Lords of Form, which causes them to be confused with the Powers. Rosicrucians call the Thrones, Dominions, Mights, Powers, and Principalities by the titles —Lords of Flame, Wisdom, Individuality, Form, and Mind.

Mystical Experiences

Many records have come down to us of mystical experiences undergone by seers and initiates but the region to which they penetrated in spirit is seldom if ever defined. All mystics seek to drink of the waters of the Rivers of Eden, Pison, Gihon, Hiddekel, and Euphrates, which flow through the 7th, 6th, 5th, and 4th Heavens respectively. Jacob Boehme penetrated to all four as his books show, and in an early vision he was shown the mysteries of the 3rd Heaven when he perceived the essences, uses, and properties of plants as illustrated by their figures and signatures (*cf.* mystery of letters) as the result of which he wrote, *De Signature Rerum*. He spoke of the 4th Heaven as the Heart of God where the love of the Bride and Bridegroom was manifested. The 5th Heaven was to him the region of the sharpness of eternal liberty and was filled with music and praise. The sixth Heaven was the house of the six inferior forms where desire was fixed and the Eye of God searched out the limits of the globe of Eternal Nature, the first and highest of the Eight Worlds. He speaks of the 7th Heaven as, "the Royal Palace of the Holy Ghost." Dr. John Pordage, the English Behmenist, called the 4th, 5th, and 6th

MYSTICAL PHILOSOPHY

Heavens, the Heart, the Breath, and the Eye (Pineal Eye) of God and spoke of the 7th as the region of the Seven Spirits. The treatise of Plotinus on *Intelligible Beauty* is concerned with the 4th Heaven where, "the gods are venerable and beautiful and their beauty is immense." The gods are the 6th Creative Hierarchy and the spirits of just men made perfect. In the 4th Heaven light meets light everywhere and the splendour is infinite. The Christian sings of it as "Jerusalem the Golden, with milk and honey blest." This is likewise the heaven of the Sufis, the essence of which, according to Max Müller, is "a loving union of the soul with God." Its poetry is that of the Song of Solomon in which what the world calls sensuous imagery is used to reveal the most sacred relationships between God and humanity. It is the Golden Flower Heaven of Lao Tse which leads to Tao, the 6th Heaven. The Heaven of the Vedanta is the 6th and the Middle Light World of the Gnostics is the 7th. It is from the latter that the inequalities generated by the laws of Karma from the 6th are rectified by "the Gods of Compensation."

The Iranian Heaven with which the mysticism of Zarathustra is concerned is the 5th, the New Zion of Rev. iv and v. The Seven Amesha Spentas are not the Seven Supreme Logoi, who are far more powerful beings, but the Seven Spirits of Rev. iv, 5, the Eyes of the Lord which run to and fro through the whole earth. (Zech. iv, 10). Fechner has expounded fully the mysticism of Iran in his book, *Zarathustra*. The theology of the Zoroastrians places the total irreconcilability of good and evil in the forefront of its tenets. Such is the holiness of God that He can consent to no sort of compromise with evil. War to the knife must be waged by Him against the Powers of Evil. It was the holiness of God which impressed Isaiah when he was privileged to hear the Trisagion of the Seraphim (Is. vi), and John heard the same hymn sung by the Four Living Creatures when he was taken in spirit to the 5th Heaven. The Iranian saw in stories of the conflicts of the elements and the flash of the lightning, Athar, the fire from heaven, appropriate emblems of the conflicts of "the Spirits of Fire and Wind" waged against the legions of Angra Mainyu. The Hindu god Rudra, whose voice roars like the tempest, the Lord of the Maruts, resembles Ormazd of the Iranians in many ways, but the Hindu is far more anxious for the silence and peace of the 6th Heaven of Nirvana than for the sound and ceaseless activity of the 5th, and for him the Divine Breath is of value chiefly because, by following the disciplinary precepts of Yoga, he can prepare himself for admission to a region where he can meditate upon and contemplate the power of God as revealed in and through Krishna or as manifested direct to him. Max Müller in his book on the Theosophy of the Hindus says, "That which we can study nowhere but in India is the all-absorbing influence which religion and philosophy may exercise on the human mind." He sums up the essence of the Hindu religion in the words, "Thy soul is the Brahman." There exists a remarkable religious system of Christian Theosophy, which is concerned almost entirely with the 6th Heaven, known as the Doctrine of the Order of

Melchizedek. It has been fully expounded by Dr. W. G. Hooper, Ph.D., of recent years in a series of remarkable booklets called collectively, *Secrets of the Universe.*[1]

The Yoga of India has no counterpart among Western Nations. It may be described as an elaborate educational system for developing the vehicles of man other than the physical, i.e. the etheric, the astral, the mental, and buddhic, the atmic, and the nirvanic. The ultimate aim of Yoga is to attain to spiritual perfection and in some it may aspire even beyond the nirvanic state to the monadic. There are seven forms of Eastern Yoga which may be regarded as synthesised in the Monadic World. These will be considered working upwards from the etheric, but first a brief reference may be made to the nearest approach to Yoga that exists in the West, Bodily Culture and Mental Culture.

(21) Bodily Culture

Bodily culture includes the performance of physical and gymnastic exercises, scientific dieting, and in some cases irradiation, either by sun-bathing or artificial rays. In the East it would be regarded as coming under Hatha Yoga, but the general purpose of all the forms of Yoga is to divert attention from the physical vehicle of man rather than to concentrate upon its development.

(20) Mental Culture

By mental culture is meant the development of mental power by exercises of the Pelman type and also by increasing the awareness in relation to the physical environment by the cultivation of observation and concentration of attention upon specific objects. Mental culture should sharpen the acuteness of all the senses and develop the capacity of discrimination to a maximum. Hindus would classify it as a form of Hatha Yoga with some elements of Mantra Yoga.

(19) Mantra Yoga

The following descriptions of the Hindu Yogas are taken from Furze Morrish's comprehensive work, *Outline of Metaphysics*, pp. 171, 176. Mantra Yoga causes the will to function by creating and destroying forms of power and makes abundant use of nature rhythms to regularise the personality. Repetition-rituals are known to have a powerful influence upon the finer ethers of the physical vehicle. Rhythmic dancing, marching, group-singing, and religious and military ceremonial. The Nazis made considerable use of certain forms of Mantra Yoga in their training of the Hitler Youths. Incense affects not only the etheric vehicle but also the astral and mental by sympathetic vibrations.

(18) Bhakti Yoga

Bhakti Yoga is concerned with the purification of the higher astral centres. It eliminates the intolerant fanaticism and aggressive argumentativeness of primitive astral personalities and sublimates their ideals,

[1] Publications obtainable from the Author, address, Wheaton Lodge, Bournemouth.

often by encouraging them to admire and imitate some great master or teacher. It tends to accentuate the sky-blue tints of the aura and produce self-sacrificing devotionalism.

(17) Hatha Yoga

Hatha Yoga works by means of the lower or concrete mind and seeks to sensitise the consciousness by sympathetic vibrations. The exercises should, however, be prescribed and supervised by experts, for they may have dangerous results if performed by novices and even produce insanity and other mental disturbances which affect the lower manas, such as undue exaltation, irrational anxiety, and so forth. Order should reign in the lower manas and it should serve as a mirror to reflect a perfect image of the true self and to quiet astral emotionalism.

(16) Laya Yoga

Laya Yoga is called the Yoga of Fire and to utilise it rashly is literally to play with fire. It works through the causal body which rules the inferior vehicles by the counterpart of fiery heat. If practised by ignorant novices it may wreck the moral nature which is above all subject to law. When rightly used it sublimates the kundalini or serpent fire and teaches the pupil to restrain all attempts to gain worldly success at the expense of others by questionable means. It thrives on a rigorous sense of justice and respect for the liberties of mankind. It is said to be bound up with the essential significance of Leo, the sign of rule by love.

(15) Gnana Yoga

The purpose of Gnana Yoga is to bring the powers of the universal mind, Mahat, to bear upon the buddhic vehicle. Its effect is to sharpen the intuition and spiritual vision of that important part of the human incarnating ego. Buddhi is the seat of the spiritual understanding, and when we desire to indicate that we understand someone who speaks to us we say, "I see what you mean." The Hebrews regarded the heart as the seat of the understanding and the buddhic vehicle is closely linked with the heart chakram. Gnana Yoga promotes the recognition of the single Truth which underlies everything and gives power to recognise the unique fragments of truth in all beliefs, however incompatible they may appear. It elevates the pupil to an eminence from which, as from Pisgah, he may view the Land of Promise. It confers the priceless gift of panoramic vision, by which alone the basic realities of life can be appreciated. It bestows the Libran gift of sympathetic adaptability, the readiness to be all things to all men, provided no sacrifice of principle is entailed.

(14) Raja Yoga

Raja Yoga is the most important of all the branches. It acts positively in both the initiation and inhibition of thought, feeling, and action. It develops the spiritual will and makes the atma-buddhi-manas its obedient instrument. It cannot operate apart from high moral development and when its authority had been established it confers immunity from the tyranny of fixed beliefs and opinions and assists Bhakti Yoga in sublimating the feelings. It enables Hatha Yoga to achieve complete tranquillity of mind. Its associated colour is the pure yellow of perfected intellectuality. It is under the rule of the First Logos as Gnana Yoga is under that of the Second and Karma Yoga is under that of the Third.

(13) KARMA YOGA

Karma Yoga is the agent for developing the Nirvanic vehicle. It procures the intensification and sublimation of the love-nature into complete universality and impersonal union with every form of life. Krishna says concerning it, "Such earthly duty free from desire and thou shalt well perform thy heavenly purpose." Its watchword is service. Nirvana is the region where the records of Karma are preserved by the Lipika and where the karmic balance is periodically struck.

CHAPTER VII

THE FUNDAMENTAL PROCESSES AS ILLUSTRATED BY THE GRAECO-LATIN GODS AND THE SOLAR SYSTEM

See TABLE J.

THE thesis to be established in the following pages is that the functions and characteristics of the chief gods of the Graeco-Roman Pantheon, arranged in the order of their identification with the sun, moon, and planets, accord with the fundamental processes of the mind, item for item, if taken in the theoretically correct order. No theosophist would be surprised that this is the case, for a fundamental point of his teaching is that man is a microcosmic replica of a macrocosmic universe. We know too little about the constitution of the Cosmos of Universes to prove this theory on the largest scale but we do enough about that of the solar system to make a good case for the theory on a more restricted scale. The solar system must be viewed from a geocentric standpoint with sun, moon, and earth taking the lead. Then follow 12 Planets, Vulcan, Mercury, Venus, Mars, Minerva, Jupiter, Saturn, Uranus, Neptune-Ceres, Pluto, Adonis, and Proserpina. Minerva is the name given provisionally to the planet which æons ago became disrupted to form the minor planets. Ceres[1] is a companion planet of Neptune and has been erroneously called Pluto by astronomers. It probably formed a single planet with Neptune when first condensed, but afterwards it

[1] The names of Minerva and Ceres have unfortunately been given to two minor planets.

would seem that the solid nucleus broke through the outer crust and so two planets were formed. Prof. Pickering has proved the existence of two planets beyond Neptune and has calculated their distance from the sun approximately and Prof. Forbes has calculated approximately the distance from the sun of a third planet even more remote, which may well be the outermost member of the sun's family. It seems evident from Joseph's dream as recorded in Gen. xxxvii, 9 that the Hebrews believed in the existence of 12 planets, mistranslated stars in the Authorised Version. Joseph was represented by Venus, for he was the eldest son of the beautiful Rachel and had a comely appearance according to tradition.

The gods of all the national or racial pantheons of ancient times had much in common with each other, though in the case of complex pantheons like those of the Hindus and Egyptians we find many of the gods associated with one or more companions who illustrate phases or aspects of their own characters, e.g. Horus and Anubis. The second leading triad of the Babylonians consisted of Anu, a sky-god, Ea, a water-god, and Bel, a storm-god. The Egyptians visualised these as An or On (Helios), Aton, and Amen. Eros was said to have been the first god born from Chaos and was originally a deity who hallowed friendships between man and man as well as love between the opposite sexes. Hesiod speaks of him as one who forms worlds by the inner union of separated elements. As such he may have been conceived of as a generator of the sun and planets and also as one who keeps them united in one system. But in course of time Eros degenerated into a mere masculine counterpart of Aphrodite (Venus). In Homer Zeus (Jupiter) took his place as the Father of the Gods and was identified with Amen by the Egyptians, who erected a temple dedicated to Jupiter Ammon in an oasis in the Libyan Desert. There is no doubt, however, that Phœbus-Apollo was the sun-god of the Greeks and Romans and as such the equivalent of the Babylonian Shamash and the Egyptian Ra.

(10) APOLLO

The basic significance of Apollo as a god of imperial and domestic politics has been somewhat obscured by the emphasis laid upon other qualities of his which depict him as a sort of masculine Venus. The Delphic Apollo, whose temple and oracle at Delos were the most hallowed spots in Greece, was a veritable Mecca for those who sought for supernatural counsel through the Pythoness, and these included not only Greek politicians but Asiatic monarchs such as the kings of Lydia. Delos was the chief seat of the Inter-Hellenic Amphictyonic Council and was for many centuries the central point of a theoretically united body of City-states. The Scythians, who were Cymri, had a sun-god of similar qualities but of unknown name, and sent annual offerings of amber, "the tears of Apollo," to the Delphic shrine. It would seem that the Scandinavians at one time venerated a similar god, later overshadowed by Odin, for Rendel Harris has traced him to Abalus, on the coast of Frisia, from which the apple was named, so that we find Apollo called Aploun in Thessaly and Maleates (He-of-the-Apple) in Athens. His name Hyperboreios is alone a witness to his northern affinities. His names of Phœbus and Lycius mark him out as a god of sunlight and so of the illuminating and fructifying power of the solar orb. His title of Far-darter evidently came from the shafts of light emitted by the sun which we call sunbeams. His festivals were all in the spring or summer, and he was venerated as a sort of celestial farmer and cattle-breeder. Armed with his silver bow he stood forth as a warrior-god in times of crisis and his name was invoked at weddings because of his generative powers. The single peony, which may be golden as well as crimson, was dedicated to him, hence his name Pæonian Apollo. His association with Delphinus, the Dolphin, made him the patron of navigable seas and he was also a guardian of streets and highways. His reputation as a healer, especially through the mistletoe, was unchallenged, but above all he was a god of truth and high morality, especially in the estimation of the Dorians. Homer represents him as a master of poetry, dancing, music, and song. His name of Pythian testified to his oracular powers. Enough has been said to prove the astounding variety and comprehensiveness of the attributes of Apollo, who was a synthesis of the remaining gods in the same manner as the sun may be regarded as the synthesis of the collective planets, all of which owe their origin to it. His chief affinity was with the sunny goddess Venus-Aphrodite, for they had a great love of the fine arts in common and both were avowed pleasure-seekers. Astrologers connect the 5th House of Leo, the Sun-sign, with pleasure, society, love-affairs, and children, which also come under the domain of Venus, and connect the heart with both. There can be no question that the sun bears the same relationship to the earth and the rest of the planets that the head does to the body or the brain to the remaining physiological organs, and that the latter, as the organ of thought, takes cognisance of everything that affects both head and body. So also in a metaphysical sense the brain is associated above all with the first fundamental process whose function it is to organise all the concepts generated in the brain.

(11) DIANA

Diana, like her brother Apollo, was armed with a bow, and under the name of Artemis was said to have often associated herself with him in slaying monsters and giants. If we compare the processes of Concept-formation and Direction with the sun and its beams the analogy is obvious and in dealing with the senses it was shown that dynamic equilibration was inseparable from a sense of direction affecting short distances. Now the sun and its rays may be compared with a bow and arrow and we often speak of the sun shooting forth its beams, consequently the favourite weapons of Apollo and Diana afford important clues to the principles underlying the conception of their functions, both physical and metaphysical. The Moon, the orb of Diana, is also an emanator of rays, though they are not self-originated but reflected. But the fact that Diana was a noted huntress connects her with long-distance direction, for a hunter to be successful must be prepared to go far afield in search of game and to ascertain the direction in which his quarry is moving as soon as he locates it. He may use dogs to follow up the scent of game in order to direct his path aright. Whether he uses bow and arrows, slings stones, or fires a sporting gun, his aim must be sure as regards direction to within a high degree of accuracy. Direction need not of necessity follow a straight line and the moon herself follows a somewhat eccentric course in revolving round a body which itself revolves round the sun. In some pantheons the moon-god was masculine. The Syro-Phœnician Mene and the Egyptian Min afford examples, as well as Month from whom we derive our word denoting the period of revolution of the moon. All these and many cognate words are said to be derived from an Idg root Ma meaning measure, the moon being the measurer of time. Clearly the principle of measurement appears in aiming for the angles made by the missile or projector with the horizontal and fore-and-aft vertical planes have to be judged to a nicety to get good results. Diana was also the patroness of all wild animals, especially the bear and the hind. The former animal is a confirmed nomad and is endowed with an excellent sense of locality which is bound up with that of direction. But indeed all animals have a far more acute sense of direction than have human beings. The name of Artemis was frequently given in Asia Minor to Mother-goddesses or Earth-goddesses who were entirely distinct from the chaste, swift, and elegant Moon-goddess and some of these so far from being fond of animals ordained wholesale sacrifices of the same in their honour. The zodiacal sign affiliated with Diana is Aquarius.

(12) THE EARTH-MOTHER

The Greeks and Latins did not pay homage to the Earth Mother unless we connect her with Ge or Gaia, the consort of Uranus and Saturn. But the Earth Mothers of the Near East do not appear to have been burdened with husbands and showed no disposition to have their liberty of action restricted by male gods. The earth itself together with its geological strata affords the best testimony to the material aspect of Effort, for the law of gravity renders it inevitable that any architectural or engineering structures raised on its surface should call for sustained efforts to erect and man himself cannot move on its surface, other than down-hill, except by muscular exertion. The successive layers of aqueous rocks required the unleashing of gigantic forces, chiefly generated in the earth's interior, to deposit, fold, crack, and fault, as the outcome of which mountain chains were thrown up and ocean basins were formed, the geographical configuration changing perceptibly every few million years. The Earth Mothers of various peoples seem to have partaken of the earth's forcefulness for, as already mentioned, the sacrifice of animals and even human beings was demanded by them, a notable example being furnished by Artemis of the Tauri of whom Euripides said, "Herself doth drink the blood of slaughtered men." The only zodiacal sign appropriate to the Earth Mothers is the sinister and revengeful Scorpio, though it may be said in its favour that it includes the decanate of Ophiucus, the Healer. But the decanate of the Serpent reminds us of the belief common among so many ancient peoples that the earth itself was encircled by a gigantic snake. A gem found at Knossos shows the Great Mother of the Cretans standing majestically on a high mountain with Mycenæan columns behind her. Paul nearly paid with his life for his courage in preaching doctrines which deprived Diana of the Ephesians of all importance and threatened to reduce the rich priests and attendants of her celebrated temple to penury. The building itself was a masterpiece of the architectural art and took many years to complete because of its swampy foundations. Ephesus was at that time the most important commercial centre and port in Asia Minor and we can hardly doubt that Diana, the Many-breasted, was not only an emblem of the fruitfulness of the soil but also a patroness of trade and commerce. The Great Mother's name figured in the Delphic Liturgies although she was never admitted to Olympus, as in the passage "First in my prayer before all other gods, I call on Earth, primæval prophetess." Homer records a hymn in her praise in which she is adored as the Being who nourishes all things on the land, makes the man whom she honours the possessor of fertile fields, gives him fine cattle, and fills his house with good things. But the average man, in spite of the good intents of the Earth-Mother, has still to eat bread by the sweat of his brow. Rhea, the daughter of Uranus and Gaia, became a Great Mother in due course and was worshipped as such all over Asia Minor and a temple was erected in her honour on the Palatine Hill in Rome. She is often mentioned as Rhea-Cybele and those who sought admission to her rites had to be purified by baptism in blood-baths of bulls and rams. Her attendant priests were known in Asia Minor as Corybantes and indulged in the wildest orgies, even wounding each other or mutilating themselves. They were cordially detested in Greece because of their persistent mendicancy.

(13) Vulcan

Vulcan, the Latin equivalent of the Greek Hephæstus, was honoured as a fire-god and smith, though in earlier times he was credited with having produced exquisite works of art in gold and silver. Hephæstus or Hypsistus was connected with El Elyon, the Most High God of the Hebrews and Ptah, the Creator-god of the Egyptians, one of the most powerful of all their gods, as well as the most ancient. His chief shrine was at Memphis, where the bull Apis in which he was believed to incarnate in later times was kept. The priesthood of Memphis was always an institution to be reckoned with in the internal politics of Egypt and during the later dynasties exercised important administrative functions, ultimately taking charge of the government of the country, securely entrenched in fortified temple enclosures. To the Egyptians, Ptah was the embodiment of their earliest form of religion and was the symbol of the historic continuity of the country and its rich store of archaic mystical traditions. Even the Ptolemies saw the wisdom of abstaining from interference in the legal and religious institutions of the Land of the Pharaohs. But for all intents and purposes the cult of the World-Creator vanished after the Roman conquest, which indeed may be regarded as an exemplification of the fall of Hephæstus before the conquering armies of Zeus-Jupiter. Thereafter the Temple of Jupiter-Ammon at Thebes was rated as of higher rank than that of Memphis. Thebes or "Populous No" had from time immemorial been the headquarters of On or Helios, in conjunction with Heliopolis. But the cult of Ptah had always been the backbone of the Egyptian religion and was aptly symbolised by Apis and the sign of Taurus, for the bull has the most massive backbone of the Ruminants, in fact of all mammals except the great pachyderms. There should now be little difficulty in appreciating the connection of the cult of Ptah with the fourth process of the mind which is concerned with memory and historic continuity and which in a degenerate form manifests itself in mummification and functional atrophy. According to Greek legend the fall of Hephæstus was brought about by presumption in that he endeavoured to patch up the quarrels between Zeus and Hera on one particular occasion, but no such story would have found credence in Egypt at any time. The priesthood of Egypt was celebrated throughout the civilised world for its esoteric wisdom and many of the Greeks, including Orpheus and Pythagoras, became initiates of the Mysteries. But once the fossilisation of a religion sets in there appears to be no means of arresting the process. The priests of Memphis inherited and perpetuated a spiritual technique which utterly failed to keep pace with the expanding intellect of the centuries immediately before the Christian era and in the face of such obstinate conservatism its ultimate downfall was a foregone conclusion.

(14) MERCURY

Mercury and his counterparts in the other Pantheons fall into two classes, a fiery type which is volitional and somewhat bellicose and an airy type which is intellectual and pacific. Among the former we have the Babylonian Nebo (*cf.* Samgar-nebo, Sword of Nebo, Jer. xxxix, 3) whose name means "Interpreter of the gods," the Assyrian Asshur (in whose honour the celebrated library of Nineveh was established), the Canaanite Chemosh (meaning Conqueror), the Hindu "Roaring Rudra" (a strict disciplinarian of stormy temperament), and lastly the Scandinavian Odin, lately renovated as the Nazi god. Among the latter we have the Egyptian Tahuti or Thoth, the Phœnician and Greek Hermes, and the Roman Mercury. The Iranian Mithras had affinities with both types, and as the Bull-killer he was the sworn foe of intractable ecclesiasticism. Thoth-Hermes also was hostile to the secretiveness of the Memphite priesthood and is said to have written many philosophical and scientific books to improve the educational standard of the Egyptians who were fast becoming priestridden. Both Thoth and Hermes were the accredited mouthpieces and messengers of their respective sun-gods, Ra and Apollo, but the latter also took orders from Zeus. Hermes was noted for his swiftness in the Homeric Epics, "Straightway Hermes bound beneath his feet his lovely golden sandals, that wax not old, that bare him alike over the watery ocean and the boundless land, swift as the breath of the wind." Rudra also rode upon the wings of the wind, the steeds of the Maruts. Under the symbol of a simple stone or Herm, the Greek god guarded the sanctity of boundaries. Here, however, something must be said about the associated zodiacal sign of Aries which differs from that assigned to him by astrologers, Gemini. The traditional correspondences between planets and signs only take into account the sun, the moon, and five planets, and being obviously incomplete may well be erroneous in some respects. There is no doubt that the moon is the negative aspect of the sun and therefore its affiliated sign should be Aquarius, the polar opposite of Leo. Scorpio, which stands for the earth's surface, is the polar opposite of Taurus, which together with Vulcan may be taken as symbolising the earth's interior. Now we come to Mercury and Venus whose zodiacal signs are the polar opposites Aries and Libra. Hermes was a shepherd god and wore a shepherd's cap. He was "the Lord of Wide Pastures" and one of his names was Criophorus, the Ram-bearer. Perseus, one of the decanates of Aries, has much in common with Hermes as being the Messenger of Athene. Finally Hermes was a musician, for he invented the chelys, an instrument resembling a lute whose sounding-board was a tortoise-shell. When shown the instrument Zeus said of the tortoise, "Living thou shalt be a spell against all witchery, and dead, then a right sweet music-maker." If we consider all the gods of the Mercury class together we see the extent to which they conform to the conditions of time and the ideas linked with it, wings, wind, swift motion, a quick ear to receive commands, writers of history and makers of history. Reflect how the whole history of Germany is bound up with the Teutonic gods, Odin and Thor, and how the long-foretold twilight set in a short time ago. But who could have foretold that the worship of Odin and Thor, fired by the wild tempestuous music of Wagner, should have inspired a power-drunk maniac to aim at the domination of the world? Nearly 3,000 years ago the Assyrians, intoxicated with the bellicose cult of Asshur, sought to create a similar world-despotism, and in 625 B.C. perished in the destruction of Nineveh. Mithras, the idol of the Roman soldiery, exercised no small influence in shaping the military history of Imperial Rome. Thoth, Hermes, and Mercury were pacifists in comparison, but as educationalists we must credit them with an interest in history and doubtless the Hermetic literature included works on the religious and intellectual development of Egyptian culture. The sign of Aries marks the beginning of an annual time-cycle beginning on 21st March. Aries was the sign of Rama, one of the great makers of history in ancient times who led his followers from the forests of Lithuania to found empires in Persia and India. Astrologers credit Arietians as being planners who look far ahead in time in order to realise grandiose schemes. The type is common in Bavaria whence Nazi-ism took its origin and it is significant that the Nazis rewrote most of their history books in order to educate the German youth in the principles of their debased ideology and promised them as a reward for obedience an empire which should last 1,000 years. It is difficult to understand how any people should make a god of good character the patron of thieves, but if Mercury approved of plunder his heart would surely have been rejoiced by the spectacle of the armies of Hitler looting nearly all the countries of Europe. For 12 years the Nazis were the Rams of Germany whom the masses followed to utter destruction with sheep-like docility. Finally we may notice how shepherds are dominated by seasons and time schedules by the very nature of their calling, often travelling long distances annually to find suitable pasturage for their flocks. This is one of the features of Spanish rural life.

(15) VENUS

The character of Venus is as simple as that of Mercury is complex, though one must discriminate between the chaste Uranian Aphrodite and the sensuous Cythereian, with a few intermediate types. Venusian people hate complications, disagreeables, and ideologies which are calculated to cause bad feeling. They are ready to be all things to all men and all women for the sake of peacefulness and popularity. There is no Mercurial intensity about them and they are perfectly happy resting in the sunshine and enjoying the beauties of nature, gazing with mingled amusement and wonder at those of their fellows who feel that they must be up and doing something or degenerate into loafers. In philosophical language their consciousness is focused on space and conditions of environment to which they seek to equate themselves in accordance with the significance of their sign of Libra. Space means for them the created world, replete with natural objects of art, rich in colour-schemes and harmonies of all kinds. With Stevenson they say, "The world is so full of a number of things we think we should all be as happy as kings." Venus is the patroness of the social sphere as Mercury is of the intellectual, and is therefore associable with royal and aristocratic classes who lead society and lay down the laws of etiquette and ceremonial, for all devotees of Venus love pageantry and display and venerate prestige, as the devotees of Mercury do knightly courage and venturesomeness.

(16) MARS

Ares, the Greek war-god, was a professional shedder of blood and nothing else, for which reason he was not held in high esteem. It appears that riots, plagues, and disasters of all kinds were attributed to him. The Thracians, however, exalted him almost to the level of Dionysus and Helios or On, seeking to bring out the respect for law which is one of the chief virtues of upright Martians. The Hindu equivalent was Indra, who was a warrior sun-god and a mighty slayer of dragons and serpents but who absorbed many gallons of soma to sustain his efforts. The Egyptian equivalent was the Elder or Hawk-headed

Horus, a god who had a high reputation for justice and integrity. The Latin Mars and his Sabine alter-ego Quirinus were originally nature-gods who protected fields and herds, warding off pests, storms, droughts, and bad weather generally. As a war-god Mars was known as Gradivus, the Rapid Strider. The first thing to note about a Martian is that he can only spend certain periods of his life fighting and during the rest of it he must earn his living. The early business of the Latins was farming, with little trading or what we call business these days. But if we were to create a modern Mars we should have to make him a patron of all kinds of business and lawful occasions upon which man expends energy in times of peace. The soldier with a little business experience and the business man with some military experience both make good in civil life as a rule because their success under both conditions calls for opportunism, powers of observation, endurance, quick decision, and respect for orders issued by superiors. Nowadays the importance of developing a sense of individuality in every soldier however humble his rank is fully realised and governs the whole character of his training. Though taught to obey instantly the orders given to him by a superior he is held responsible for interpreting them intelligently and if faced with an emergency must be ready to act on his own responsibility as he believes his superior would act if on the spot. In short, he must develop the mental process of constructive individualism to the full, that is individuality as controlled by law, which in an advanced state becomes the perfect law of liberty.

The burning torch was one of the symbols of Mars, suggesting a love of incendiarism. The associated sign is that of the Twins, Gemini, which contains the mighty sun Sirius, after whom Helios, the sun-god of Egypt was named, Ra being the sun of our own system. The Romans regarded the Twins as representing Apollo and Hercules and the Greeks called them Castor and Pollux, both able naval and military commanders. Gemini includes the decanates of the Greater and Lesser Dogs, Sirius being in the former. It was regarded as the cause of the Dog-days in summer. Homer spoke of it as a star "Whose burning breath taints the red air with fevers, plagues, and death," and Virgil said that, "with pestilential heat it infects the sky." Precisely the same disasters were placed to the credit or discredit of Mars. We habitually speak of an outbreak of hostilities as "loosing the dogs of war" and trained dogs now play important parts in military operations. To go to the dogs, however, means to waste one's life and miss one's opportunities. At Sparta dogs were sacrificed to Ares under the title of Theritas. The Martial Romans believed that their ancestors Romulus and Remus, the Twins of their day, were suckled by a she-wolf and adopted this animal as a symbol of the Republic. Astrologers are agreed in regarding Geminians as smart and versatile, quick-fingered and sometimes light-fingered, fond of correspondence and careful about business files, good mixers, usually free with their money which they make to spend, great travellers, and fond of solving problems of all kinds. Indecision is their worst fault from a business point of view but on the whole they are quick to scent good business propositions. All of them have marked individualities in which they differ from Arietians which contain a goodly proportion of sheep.

(17) MINERVA

There is no planet Minerva, but according to Bode's Law there is room for one between Mars and Jupiter. Her sign is the Fishes, and the various groups of asteroids strongly remind one of shoals of silvery fish when they become luminous or shoot. The Minervan goddesses were important in most of the Pantheons. The Tyrians had three, Pallas, Athene, and Britannia. Pallas and Athene were united and became the guardian and protectress of Athens, and the Phœnicians introduced Britannia to England. The Egyptian Neith was venerated as the guardian of the ancient civilisation of Egypt in the days when the Atlanteans who worshipped Poseidon threatened to overrun Europe and the Near East. The ancient name of Athene was Tritogeneia, "born of Triton, the roaring flood," and thus like Neith she was also a water-goddess. The sign of Pisces is water. In due course a belief arose that there might be Tritons living with Poseidon and Amphitrite in the ocean. Some had the body of a horse and were called Centaurotritons, obviously copied from sea-horses. The Minervan goddesses were, however, more concerned with streams and rivers of fresh water than with the sea. Athene-Minerva was the goddess of civilisation but also a warrior-goddess who taught men to protect their possessions against unscrupulous robbers. She befriended many doughty champions, Perseus, Bellerophon, Jason, Heracles, Diomedes, and Odysseus. She dispensed the blessings of nature, the olive being her especial symbol among the trees. She was clever, witty, clear-headed, and discreet, and many discoveries were credited to her ingenuity. In fact she was regarded as the source of expertness in every art and science. Shipbuilding and horse-taming also came within her sphere. Every form of art was encouraged by her, especially sculpture, and numerous statues were erected to her, the chief of which was Athene Parthenos, wrought in ivory and gold and 30 feet in height with its pedestal. It stood in the Parthenon. Even more gigantic was the bronze image of Athene Promachos which stood near the sea at the Piræus. The forms of all the statues of Athene were as much masculine as feminine and she was always shown with a military helmet. There is hardly need to adduce fresh evidence to prove the connection of the process of hedonistic constructiveness, the driving force of civilisation, with Minerva. Typical civilisations of the kind are those of France and China, yet the explosive elements in them accumulated to an extent which brought about the revolutions of 1793 and 1906 respectively. Another illustration of the same condition of affairs is provided by a boiler unprovided with a safety valve in which steam pressure is raised to a point at which an explosion becomes inevitable. As already made clear, if the operations of hedonistic constructiveness are performed in such a manner that a great chasm is created between the upper and cultured classes and the masses, so that the former despise and oppress the latter and the latter hate and envy the former, the outbreak of a major revolution is merely a question of time.

(18) JUPITER

The sign of Jupiter, Sagittarius, is the polar opposite of Gemini, the sign of Mars, and there are many resemblances between the two gods of these names. Both disposed of a considerable amount of energy which found vent in their individuality and personality respectively, the psychological basis of the latter being animal electro-magnetism, which is much the same as the astral force of theosophists. Jupiter and Juno, otherwise Zeus and Hera, were a married couple with strong personalities which were perpetually clashing. According to Homer Zeus had little self-control and his wrath was aroused by the smallest semblance of opposition. Yet in process of time he appears to have improved out of all recognition, for Dio Chrysostom wrote of him, "Our Zeus is peaceful and altogether mild, as the guardian of Hellas when she is of one mind and not distraught with faction, an image gentle and august in perfect form, the common father and saviour and guardian of mankind." Here we have a more exalted phenomenon than the control of personalities by police methods, namely the control of them by an appeal to religion, which is the spiritual power maintaining order in heavenly places. Every schoolboy knows that Jupiter is the god of thunder and lightning, and the Scandinavian equivalent Thor, who was much more powerful than the war-god Tiu or Tyr, illustrated to perfection this aspect of the functions of Zeus, as did the Slavonic thunder-god Perun. The name Zeus, which is cognate with the Sanskrit Dyaus, means sky-god, and so we find the Greeks attributing to his moods all changes in the weather, including the sending of gentle fertilising rain. His oracle at Dodona was greatly venerated and frequently consulted. The remarkable sublimation of Zeus may be illustrated diagrammatically by elevating him from space (18) to space (9), that of the Egyptian Amen and also of the Babylonian Marduk in his later and higher character when he became merged with Bel as Bel-Marduk. The sublimated Zeus gods, with whom we may include the Hindu Brihaspati, specialised in ceremonial, self-purgation, and self-sacrifice, as symbolised by the decanate of the Burning Altar in Sagittarius, and abundant praise and worship was accorded to them as symbolised by the decanate of Lyra. But in his terrestrial capacity Zeus was attended by Victory, Force, Might, and Strife, all fiery powers. As a generator of many gods and goddesses he was the protector of the home and family and defender of the hearth (Ara). He was the sealer of covenants and the avenger of perjury and the guarantor of personal and national freedom. All these functions and attributes illustrate the fundamental process of Constructive Personality. The Italian Jupiter is hardly distinguishable from Zeus as regards personality and the same applies to Juno and Hera. In some places Jupiter was worshipped as a sun-god and Juno as a moon-goddess.

(19) SATURN

Saturn, the god of the æther of space, introduces us to the deities of the physical elements, Uranus of the air, Neptune of the sea, and Ceres of the earth, and their psychological counterparts are those functions of the brain which are exercised in forming concepts of the sense data of the physical world supplied by the end-organs of special and general sensation. The Greek Kronos first emerges into mythology as a harvest god Kronion, but later on became identified with Kronos, the god of time and mundane time-cycles and rhythms. The Roman Saturn was worshipped as a god of Etruscan affinities who, at a remote time in the past, had introduced a golden age into Italy, ruling the country with strict justice and impartiality. During the Saturnalia, a feast celebrated annually in his honour, temporary freedom was given to slaves, and they were entertained and waited on by their masters as a reminder that under the rule of Saturn all men had been treated as equals in the eyes of the law. The Egyptian counterpart, Seb or Geb, was highly honoured and by some sublimated to a sun-god almost equal to Ra. In Syria and Canaan similar deities were worshipped under the names of Moloch, Chiun, and Remphan. Moloch was undoubtedly a physical sun-god whose symbol was a fiery furnace into which children were cast. The Babylonian Ninib was a martial deity. To the astrologer Saturn is the symbol of binding, restricting, and disciplining. He stands for strict justice without the mercifulness of Jupiter. "He binds in fetters and limits all things," exercising a power symbolised by gravitation in the solar system and gravity on earth. The symbolism of Cancer, the Crab, agrees generally with that of Saturn. The Arabic name is Al Sartan meaning the Binder. It is cognate with the Hebrew satar which means to cover, hide, and keep secret, as in Dan. ii, 22. The Greek name is Karkinos, meaning encircling. The claws of the Crab are a symbol of great tenacity. The general symbolism agrees with that of Moloch, the sun, as holding all the planets of his system in a firm grasp. The original meaning of the Great and Little Bears was that of Folds or enclosures erected to prevent domestic animals from straying. The Hebrew Dhover means a Fold and Dhov means a bear. In short, Saturn stands for agricultural and Cancer for pastoral activities. It is not, however, denied that Cancer has lunar affinities since it represents the headship of the negative or material part of human personality where, Leo and the Sun represent the positive or spiritual centre of the same. In other words, the physical sun bears the same relationship to the spiritual sun as the moon does to the sun. The bear was sacred to Artemis, the moon-goddess.

(20) URANUS

Uranus under the name of Varuna was accorded great veneration by the ancient Iranians as the god of the night-sky, with the star-spangled robe, and with the moon as his eye. In view of his relationship to Mithras we must think of him not only as a moon-god but also as a negative aspect of the sign of Aries, Mithras being the positive. The associated sign of Uranus in (20) is Capricorn, and the Goat as an animal has much in common with the Ram. Just as restraint is the conception underlying Saturn and Cancer so liberty is that underlying Uranus and Capricorn, the polar sign of Cancer. The mountain goat is as freedom-loving and agile as the mountain sheep, and the Eagle and the Dolphin which constitute two of the decanates of Capricorn are free to range where they will through air and sea respectively. Capricorn is the sign of wild animals who follow their sweet wills as Cancer is of domestic animals which are either penned in or watched by cowherds and shepherds who prevent them from straying too far. The third decanate of Capricorn, the Arrow, also suggests freedom of a kind such as an inanimate object might possess and in any case it indicates the swiftness of movement which mountain goats, eagles, and dolphins exhibit. Capricorn is peculiarly the sign of animals and of uncivilised man in which the traits of animals are more prominent than in civilised man. Now animals have keener perceptions than men and in many cases have to act upon the sense data presented to them in a reflex manner without deliberate thought in order to catch the prey necessary for their sustenance or to escape capture by stronger and fleeter animals. Life is full of surprises for weaker animals and their young are carefully trained from the beginning in the precautions that they have to observe to prolong their lives. This is specially true of the Rodents. The Greeks and Latins paid scant attention to Uranus and have told us nothing about his character but astrologers call the planet of that name "the planet of surprises and sudden events." The goat is noted among zoologists for the quickness of its perceptions and those who resemble this animal have external minds and often sensual natures. Even the domestic goat is fond of springing surprises upon man and butting him from the rear when he least expects to be attacked.

(21) NEPTUNE

Neptune has a companion planet, the true Ceres, wrongly called Pluto, and the two may have formed one originally, as mentioned previously. The extreme denseness of Ceres indicates that it formed the core of the original planet and burst through the envelope which then condensed into Neptune. The god of that name was no denizen of Olympus but was probably an Atlantean importation. Under the name of Poseidon he was worshipped or rather propitiated by the Cretans, for they feared him rather than loved him. He was originally a fisherman's god and his trident was a fishing implement. He was perpetually at war with Zeus, a conflict which was reflected in the hostility with which the Cretans and their kinsmen the Mycenæans treated the Hellenic invaders from the north. Poseidon was known as the Earth-shaker but probably without reference to any volcanic activities. He was the embodiment of the furious dashing of stormy seas against the coastline. Homer addresses him as a dark-haired god who was an appointed Tamer of Horses and Saviour of Ships. Foam-capped waves have often been likened to white horses, like clouds. Ultimately the Greeks became reconciled to Poseidon and treated him with respect if not with affection. To the Cretans he was a bull-god and they held bullfights in his honour as the Spaniards do to-day for their entertainment. Both the Illyrians and the Argives sacrificed horses to Poseidon. The Bull on which Poseidon is sometimes shown as seated may be a symbol of the Underworld beneath the ocean bed. Herodotus tells us that the Libyans, who were great horse-breeders, were the original worshippers of Poseidon in so far as the Mediterranean peoples were concerned. The marine subjects of Poseidon were depicted as centaurs with dolphins' tails. The Centaur is one of the decanates of Virgo.

(21) CERES

Ceres, the Latin counterpart of the Greek Demeter, was a Grain-goddess and was on this account associated with Virgo, the sign of the Virgin who carries ears of corn in her hand as a symbol of her functions. Just as the earth always suggested feminine functions to primitive man so also its produce was supposed to come under the domain of woman rather than man and for that reason many African tribes leave agricultural work to women lest the profane masculine touch should interfere with the growth of grain or other plants. Demeter was also regarded as the guardian of earth-bound spirits who for some reason or other were prevented from passing down to the depths of Tartarus, the domain of Pluto.

The salient characteristics of the domains of both Neptune and Ceres are flatness, for corn grows at its best on plains, and the delta of Egypt, which is only a trifle above sea-level, was once known as the granary of the Roman Empire. Now flatness in this case is connected with the principle of the datum level, which for purposes of survey and contouring we take as mean sea level. This varies within very narrow limits in the Mediterranean. Psychologically the datum level represents the sense of ultimate reality. Virgo is the polar sign, of Pisces as Taurus is of Scorpio and in the case of both pairs there is a permanent fall of potential. The principle of hedonistic constructiveness may be compared to a high-pressure steam boiler because it is liable to inflate the mind, but the principle of realism, which brings one down to earth, may be compared to a condenser. The amount of work obtainable from a steam boiler depends on the lowness of the temperature of the condenser and so the actual permanent value of a civilisation depends upon the realities upon which it is founded. This fact is what renders Swedish civilisation so stable, for the cultural level does not vary within wide limits among the classes and the upper have never sought to oppress the lower to the same extent as in France and elsewhere. Sense data approximate to the real because they are derived from material objects of one's environment but they are liable to be deceived and wrongly integrated. There can however be no deception as regards the reality of the existence of land and water, which are tangible though we can feel air when in motion.

(22) Pluto

The boundary between the domains of Neptune and Ceres and that of Pluto clearly represents the threshold of the subconscious, or more accurately the preconscious state, and the latter can be classified on the same principle as the upper harmonic tier in which we have Consciousness of State, Time, and Space. According to theology those who are in a state of condemnation (which need not be permanent) pass down into the Underworld, which is often spoken of as a state rather than a place though it may well be both, a place suited to a certain state. But for psychological purposes the planet Pluto simply represents the preconscious memory which is an index to the preconscious state. It is this state, with all its complications and intricacies, that the psychoanalyst or psychiatrist seeks to unveil by hypnosis when he desires to resolve subliminal complexes. All three spaces of the preconscious, (22) in elderly people and (23) and (24) in young people, may harbour most undesirable predilections and urges, which periodically force their way upwards past space (21) to space (20) where they are dramatised as dreams at night. For this reason psychiatrists consider dreams as affording valuable means of diagnosing nervous complaints and their causes. Sometimes the sufferer resorts to drugs which have a strong effect upon the process of state (21) and prevent the complexes generated in the preconscious self from extending their influence to space (20).

(23) Adonis
(24) Proserpina

Adonis, the Thammuz of the Syro-Phœnicians and the Attis of Asia Minor, together with Proserpina, the Persephone of the Greeks, were the subjects of Mysteries which were designed to awaken young people to the folly of becoming wholly immersed in frivolities and pleasure-seeking, on the ground that if they refused to ascend upwards morally and spiritually they were certain to sink to the regions where evil was generated. It is true we have to infer this in the case of Adonis but the details of the Eleusinian Mysteries prove the thesis to the hilt. The fall of Proserpina into the clutches of the preconscious region (24), which is the source of all Venusian evils, was symbolised by her capture by Pluto, after having been tempted by Eros. Adonis appears to have entered the regions of the Netherworld by an untimely death, which was symbolised ritually by the setting sun and also by the burning up of spring vegetation by the fierce rays of the summer sun. The evils of the Adonis space (23) are those to which degenerate Mercurians are subject, which the Nazi worshippers of Odin have manifested in a manner that the world is unlikely to forget for many a long day. One of the features of their training was gymnastics to improve their physique and appearance.

THE OUTER PLANETS. THEIR DISTANCES AND NOMENCLATURE

By the term "Outer Planets" is meant a group of four planets beyond Neptune, the first of which is the recently discovered Trans-Neptune, to which the name Pluto has been given. Since there are good reasons for questioning the appropriateness of this name the four planets will be called A, B, C, and D for the purpose of discussing their distances from the sun and their orbits. A, though beyond Neptune, is its companion planet, their respective average distances from the sun being 2,793 and 3,665, taking the unit as 1,000,000 miles. If we treat them as a self-contained system whose respective masses are as 22 to 1 then their common centre of gravity is 38 beyond Neptune and 2,831 from the sun. If we take the average distance of the system from the sun the figure is 3,229. The mean of these two figures is 3,030. Planet B is Pickering's Planet S, whose average distance from the sun he gave as 4,450. He based his calculations upon the effects produced by it in two perturbations of Uranus and the aphelia (furthest distances from the sun) of a group of visible comets associated with it. Lowell and Gaillot working independently upon perturbations of Uranus fixed the distance of the same planet from the sun as 4,480. Since the corresponding periods of revolution round the sun were given as 333 years and 335 years respectively we may regard the position of the planet as fairly accurately fixed. Planet C is Pickering's Planet P, which he calculated to be 6,290 from the sun, judged by perturbations produced upon Uranus, and 7,410, judged from the position of a group of associated comets. The mean of these two values is 6,850. The corresponding orbital periods were given by him as 557 and 656 respectively, the mean being 606 years. Assuming that we are concerned here with one planet and not two the results are seen to give nothing like the accuracy secured in the case of Planet B. Finally we have the outermost Planet D, which was studied by Prof. George Forbes, of whose existence he had no doubts. He gave the mean distance from the sun as 9,755 and the orbital period as 1,100 years. Let us now consider Bode's Law of Planetary Distances from the sun and the modification needed to make it applicable to the Outer Planets. Bode's Law, as it stands, gives us a simple formula for determining the approximate distances of the planets from the sun, from Mercury to Uranus inclusive. 9 millions of miles is taken as the unit for calculation, that is one fourth of the mean distance of Mercury from the sun, which is 36 millions of miles. The distances of the remaining planets are then found to be approximately 4 + 3 units, 4 + 6 units, and so on, doubling the second term each time. In this reckoning the planet whose rupture many æons ago resulted in the formation of the asteroids is taken into account. The formulæ works out fairly well for Uranus, the distance according to Bode's Law being 1,764 as against a measured distance of 1,783, the discrepancy being about 1 per cent. But beyond that the Law as it stands fails to give results. Let us however take Uranus as the basis of reckoning instead of Mercury and utilise a new unit of one fourth of its distance from the sun (Bode's figure), that is 441. We then proceed as before, taking Neptune's distance as 4 + 3 units, Planet B's as 4 + 6 units and so on. Bode's figure for Neptune—Planet A is 3,087 as against a mean figure of 3,030 already obtained. It must be admitted however that not much can be proved from this comparison, but when we come to Planet B the agreement is striking, for Bode's figure is 4,410 as compared with a calculated 4,450 according to Pickering and 4,480 according to Lowell and Gaillot, the mean being 4,465 and the discrepancy about 1 per cent. In the case of Planet C Bode's figure is 7,056 and Pickering's figure (mean of two calculations) is 6,850, the discrepancy being about 3 per cent which is about equal to the discrepancy of Jupiter and half the discrepancy of Venus. Bode's figure for Planet D is 12,348 as against Forbes's figure of 9,755 but Prof. Crommelin stated in a letter to the writer that he considered Forbes's results of doubtful value. Prof. Pickering, in one of his contributions to *Popular Astronomy*,[1] calls attention to the fact that the orbits of the planets from Uranus outward double the values of their periodicities, taking the figure for Uranus as 84 years. According to this the figure for Neptune should be 168, that for Planet B 336, that for C 672 and that for D 1,344. Planet A with a periodicity of 247 lies half way between Neptune and B, the mean of whose periodicities is 252. The agreement with the figure for Planet B, 334, is striking as in the case of the figure for the distance from the sun in comparison with the Bode's Law figure. The theoretical periodicity for C is somewhat higher than the larger figure given by Pickering, 656. The theoretical figure for D 1,344, is much higher than Forbes's figure of 1,100, but if we increase his figure of 9,755 in the proportion of 1,344 to 1,100 we get a distance from the sun of 11,919 which approaches much closer to the Bode's formula distance of 12,348, the discrepancy being only 3½ per cent.

The identification of the Planet A (Pickering's Planet O) with Pluto, the god of Hades, because a little girl thought it a good idea, was a calamity. Prof. Pickering protested as soon as he heard of the proposal, but could only suggest the name of Neptune's wife, Salacia, as an alternative, which naturally proved unacceptable, as few people had ever heard of the lady. The true companion of Neptune, the Fisherman god, was Ceres, the Corn-goddess who presided over the kindly fruits of the earth. The Greeks knew her by the name of Demeter, meaning grain-mother. Pandora had affinities with her and so had the Mountain-Mother of the Cretans, Diana of the Ephesians, Cybele, and Semele. In Crete Neptune (Poseidon) and the Mother reigned supreme, their only rival being Jupiter. Clearly the deities of the sea-harvests and the earth-harvests were closely akin. Unfortunately Ceres had been already given as a name to an insignificant minor planet but this could have been adjusted. Uranus and Neptune were named correctly with uncanny intuition but the naming of Neptune's companion was a blunder of the first magnitude.

[1] *The Three Outer Planets Beyond Neptune.* Vol., xxxvi, 7. Aug.-Sept. 1928, p. 423.

The total number of original planets of our system was probably twelve, excluding the earth which, from a geocentric point of view, forms a triad with the sun and the moon.[1] The first is Vulcan in whose existence the sages of the East have always professed a firm belief. The inductive evidence for believing in the existence of this small planet between the sun and Mercury is as follows:—on 26th March, 1859, Lescarbault claimed to have seen a planet close to the sun and correctly named it Vulcan. Watson made a similar claim on 29th July, 1878, during the solar eclipse which occurred on that date. Trouvalot saw a red planet near the sun during the eclipse of 6th May, 1883, which he took to be Vulcan. These are three items of positive evidence which are worth more than the negative evidence of any number of astronomers who have failed to see a small planet near the sun, which from its situation and orbit is necessarily difficult to detect. The distance of Vulcan from the sun according to the principle of Bode's Law should be to that of Mercury what the distance of Saturn is to that of Uranus (900 to 1,764), which gives a figure of about $18\frac{1}{4}$ millions of miles. The next planet, or rather ex-planet, that calls for comment is Minerva, the parent of the minor planets, the orbits of which lie between those of Mars and Jupiter. The cataclysm occurred many æons ago and the probable cause was either the sudden generation of vast quantities of volcanic gases in the interior or the speed of rotation overcoming the cohesion of the crust. As regards the erroneous naming of Neptune's companion planet, one is reminded of a story told about Abraham Lincoln in which he propounded the following conundrum to one of his secretaries. "How many legs has a cow?" "Four," came the reply. "And supposing you call a cow's tail a leg how many legs would it have?" "Five," replied the unwary secretary. "Wrong," said Lincoln, "the cow would still have four legs, for calling its tail a leg would not make it a leg." Similarly calling the real Ceres Pluto will not make it Pluto.

CHAPTER VIII

THE PSYCHOLOGY OF MATHEMATICS

See TABLE K.

THE late Dr. Arthur Lynch frequently stressed the truth that mathematics was the basis of psychology on the ground that the process of reasoning on material things was fundamentally the same as that employed in counting and in performing simple arithmetical operations, and that algebra was in its essence a complex branch of arithmetic in which the methods of calculation were simplified by the use of letters to symbolise numbers. In a similar manner the metaphysical conceptions of language are developed from words which describe simple objects, acts, and relation-

[1] This was apparently the ancient Hebrew belief judging by Joseph's dream, Genesis xxxvii, 9.

ships in everyday life and which become adapted by convention to describe analogous elements in the operations of the mind and the emotions. While the origins of words belonging to the world of outward sense are often difficult to trace, those belonging to the regions of the objective and subjective minds can nearly always be made to yield the secrets of their ancestry by intelligent examination. In investigating the relationships between the chief branches of mathematics and the corresponding psychological processes the same system will be followed as that employed in the analysis of the Fundamental Processes.

(19) ARITHMETIC—UNIT CONCEPT

The psychological counterpart of the arithmetical calculator is the man to whom we apply the adjective calculating, in the sense that he takes no chances, but carefully considers all factors bearing upon a project or situation before he commits himself to any definite line of action. In arithmetic four operations can be performed upon numbers, addition, subtraction, multiplication, and division, the first and fourth of which can be used to generate all numbers from unity. Similarly in psychological calculation four operations can be performed upon concepts, generation from a master concept, symbolisation, generalisation, and classification. Particularisation is a step from generalisation to classification, and memory is the end product of the second. Symbolisation is used to identify subsidiary projects which are related to subtraction in that their generation subtracts energy from that which is available to operate the master-concept, just as radiation of heat waves from a hot body necessarily reduces its store of heat energy. All generation involves subtraction of energy from the parent. Furthermore symbolisation is often of a philosophic kind which abstracts qualities from concepts to provide suitable names for them, for unless a symbol is a mere letter, number, or sign it gains in value by describing something about the concept which it identifies. Generalisation, which involves a species of mental heaping up, is equivalent to multiplication, though the concepts of which the heap is formed must be multiplied before they can be aggregated. We may collect numbers of objects of different kinds to form a heap, in which case this very word constitutes a generalisation regarding them, for each is part of a heap. Similarly division is equivalent to particularisation and to a specifice kind of it calling for more discrimination, that is classification. In short the mind in order to think at all must do so arithmetically. We think of a calculating man as a human machine which moves as regularly as clockwork and which inevitably gives correct results, subject to possible mental flaws in the agent's mind. The calculating man backs his own judgment against anybody else's and is often inclined to be censorious, stern, autocratic, and a lover of discipline.

(20) THEORY OF NUMBERS—IMMEDIATE PRESENTATION

The identification of external stimuli is bound up with measurement and this in turn is inseparable from numbers. These stimuli or sense data reach our consciousness for the most part through our five primary senses and we are able to identify different sound and light waves by their frequencies of vibration. We have good reason for anticipating that as scientific knowledge progresses other stimuli such as scents will become susceptible to measurement. In mathematics and especially in arithmetic, numbers take the place of sense data as may be seen in the simple case of a schoolboy who is given two numbers to multiply together. The numbers come to him from without and he is then called upon to perform an easy operation upon them. We expect our senses to inform us with reasonable accuracy what is the nature of the stimuli which impinge upon them and the answers which we get from them would for the most part prove to be very complex if we could unravel them and subject them to measurement. In the same way the arithmetician who desires to explore his subject must endeavour to obtain answers to the question, "What are numbers in themselves, what is their essential nature?" and must master the branch of mathematics known as "The Theory of Numbers." Numbers have characteristic modes of activity and we often find these discussed in popular articles with examples given which anyone can understand. But the pure theory deals with the properties and behaviour of numbers, both prime and composite, and bristles with technical headings such as totients, residues, congruencies, ideals, class numbers, etc. The basis of the theory is the division of all numbers into elements and aggregates. Then we have what might be called the mystical properties of numbers with which the philosophy of Pythagoras concerned itself and which must be taken into account in framing key-tables of classifications of phenomena, unless the employment of numbers is to be merely arbitrary. Ordinal and cardinal numbers which are used haphazardly merely as convenient symbols to identify individuals or groups, naturally have no mystical meaning, though on the other hand we find people frequently giving remarkable examples of the part certain specific numbers have played in their lives, and numerologists identify all human beings by characteristic numbers based on calculating the dates of their birth. People in whom the corresponding mental process is strong take naturally to divination in one form or another, if of a mystical temperament, but if they are practical and materialistic they compare phenomena with each other and with accepted standards of measuring and weighing, and consider no external stimulus as properly defined except in standardised units. They are precise, exacting, and sceptical, and are found in considerable numbers in Prussia and North Germany.

(21) Partition of Numbers—Realism

When one proceeds from endeavouring to find answers to the question "why are phenomena?" to find answers as to "what are phenomena?" one must generalise and particularise with special reference to essential qualities. This calls for close analysis and discrimination. The mathematician Euler developed the branch of mathematics known as "the

Partition of Numbers" in order to try and explain the inner nature of numbers and subjected them to a process of internal analysis accordingly. The type of mind adapted to pursue such investigations is one which loves detail and minute inspection, especially with the object of increasing the sense of the reality of matter. Philosophers who concentrate upon immediate presentations are liable to become bemused by the complications with which they find themselves faced and to propound theories which bear little relationship to the objective reality of matter, so that those who start with the conviction that matter exists and that it is our business to find out why it behaves as it does perform useful services to science and humanity, although they are usually lacking in breadth of vision.

(22) Combinatorial Analysis—Subconscious Memory

The branches of mathematics numbered (22), (23), and (24) find their psychological counterparts in the preconscious stratum of personality, sometimes called the subconscious, though the true subconscious is lower down. This stratum is divisible into preconscious apprehension of State or Memory, of Time, and of Space; also of Past, Future, and Present. The principles involved are certainty, possibility, and probability, and their negatives uncertainty, impossibility, and improbability. Nicholson defines the Combinatorial Analysis as "a branch of mathematics which teaches us to ascertain and exhibit all the possible ways in which a given number of things may be associated and mixed together so that we may be certain that we have not missed any collection or arrangement of these things that has not been enumerated." This subject is taught in schools under the more familiar title of Permutations and Combinations. If a collection of objects are all of a similar nature they are said to be unipartite and if divisible into two or more classes they are said to be multipartite. It should be observed that here we have a branch of mathematics which takes account of the existence of different objects and of their classification, thus making contact with Memory, which is the end product of Particularisation and Classification. Furthermore, the main thing that we require of memory is that it should be accurate and should preserve all the facts which are deliberately consigned to its keeping. In many ways the preconscious (subconscious) memory fulfils these requirements more efficiently than the conscious memory, hence the extent to which psychiatrists seek to dive into its recesses in connection with their diagnoses of nervous diseases. The more exhaustive the memory is the more useful it is to its possessor, whether it be conscious or preconscious, and many instances have been recorded of individuals having committed the whole of the Scriptures or all the plays of Shakespeare to memory. On the other hand, nothing is more of a handicap to a man than an uncertain memory, not so much the kind that forgets, but the kind that thinks it remembers correctly and fails to do so. Little practical use is made of permutations and combinations except by bell-ringers in bell-pealing competitions. Of course words are combinations and permutations of letters but from the point of view of the mathematician they are haphazard and do not lend themselves to treatment by his instrument.

(23) Progressions—Preconsciousness in Time

It is evident that irrational numbers such as π, $\sqrt{2}$, recurring decimals, and the three progressions, arithmetical, geometrical, and harmonic, all bring before us a procession of figures which are lost in the dim future, in fact the very word progression is allied in meaning to procession and both are concerned with the march of time. If we know the law governing a progression we can predict the value of a term any distance in time ahead. The notion of the possible with its negation the impossible comes into the picture when it concerns the summation of the terms of a progression to infinity, for this is impossible if the terms increase in value. It is also impossible to express any irrational number accurately in figures, hence its name. Progressions have in them the essence of vitality, in fact of endless life, especially when their terms increase in value and so become incapable of summation except within arbitrary limits fixed by the calculator.

(24) Probabilities—Preconsciousness in Space

The theory of Probabilities is put to a number of practical uses. Laplace defined it thus:—"The probability of an event is the ratio of the number of cases which favour it to the number of all the possible cases when nothing leads us to believe that one of these events ought to occur rather than the others, which renders them for us equally possible." This theory, in view of its value in calculating out mundane matters, is associated with space, environment, and the present to a peculiar degree of it is a science of events. It combines law with chance, the law of the past with the chance of the future and equilibrates between the two just as the present fixes the boundary between past and future. The laws of averages and errors are dependent on similar considerations and the whole subject has been extended into many branches of physics, especially those which deal with the structure of the atom and the behaviour of electrons. In business the laws of Probabilities are used in actuarial calculations of risks and their costs, if they produce accidents, in relation to the total of the premiums paid by insured persons. Gamblers make use of the same laws in framing the systems which sooner or later prove their undoing. There seems to be something in the nature of free will in the behaviour of electrons regarded as individuals and yet collectively they are amenable to law. The science is also known as one which relates to determinacy and opens up a strange vista in all that concerns the behaviour of small particles.

The branches of mathematics numbered from (21) to (24) form a small inter-related group which dovetail into each other in innumerable ways though they make contact also with pure algebra at certain points.

(18) Logarithms—Powers—Impulses—Passion

Logarithms were discovered by Napier in 1614. If a, x, and m are any three quantities which satisfy the equation $\frac{x}{a} = m$, then a is called the base, and x is the logarithm of m to the base a. The science of logarithms was a development of the arithmetical process of powers by which numbers could be multiplied by themselves any amount of times, and thus large quantities could be obtained with rapidity. Roots may be regarded as the negative aspects of powers. The philosopher Fechner sought to measure passion quantitively with indifferent success but the principle on which he worked was justifiable. Multiplication by powers finds its physical counter-part in explosions in which large volumes of gas are suddenly generated and these in turn provide images of conflagrations of passion and rage. Passion need not, however, be selfish, for we can have passionate resentment against injustice and passionate love of country. The magazine of forces from which passion takes its rise is virtually the same as the Impulse of psychologists, which is often regarded as the driving power inciting men to purposiveness and the formation of concepts (19), but on the other hand as often as not the latter furnish the fuel on which the fires of passion feed, enabling it to become a ruthless agent of destructiveness. Passion belongs to the astral world of theosophists who connect it with star emanations or as we should term them to-day cosmic rays. Passions of refined kinds acting in conjunction with the thinking brain give rise to the formulation of idealistic plans in which irrational exaggeration becomes prominent, of the kind that induced the three sons of Noah to say "Let us build a tower which shall reach to heaven." People of this type are often fascinated by the marvels of astronomy and find a ready means of calculating star positions in the logarithmic tables used to solve spherical triangles. We sometimes speak of large mathematical quantities such as those which define stellar distances as astronomical figures. Passion includes crude desires and emotions, but refined desire may be identified with hedonism and refined emotion often appears in love of competition, emulation, and interest in the solution of puzzles and problems.

Passion belongs to the Time-column I rather than the Space-column II or the State-column III because it is the driving force of physical generation by which human beings and animals propagate their species and thus enable their stock to endure from one age to another. We often think of time as flowing like a river and passion as rushing along like a mountain torrent. The heavenly bodies, especially the sun and the moon, are time-measurers and were set in their places to measure seasons and years. Astronomers measure time with extreme accuracy and become perturbed if they are a second out of their reckoning in sidereal time over a period of a few years.

(14) Expanding Algebraic Functions—Series and Sequences—
    Conscious Conception of Time

Expanding Algebraic Functions are clearly the algebraic equivalent of Arithmetical, Geometrical, and Harmonic Progressions and as such belong to (14), the upper harmonic of (23) in the time-column. If we take Arithmetic as the mathematical basis of the mental processes which are concerned with material things as well as of the instincts and preconscious mechanisms, then Algebra stands for those far more complex processes of the higher parts of personality in which the will, the mind, and the emotional nature are concerned. Preconsciousness in time, like other preconscious and subconscious processes which operate in the lower parts of the personality and also in groups and masses, are usually simple enough to define in words once they can be unearthed, and mainly centre on some primitive urge such as fear, lawlessness, selfishness, or sexuality. Consciousness in time, on the other hand, leads to intellectual planning for the future, taking time by the forelock, and sometimes, in the case of unpractical people, in building castles in Spain. It leads also to methodical reasoning in which certain premises are made, a series of logical steps taken, and then a definite conclusion reached, all of which take time. The successive steps may be taken as analogous with the terms of an expanding algebraic series and the ultimate conclusion with the summation of the terms.

Expanding functions which reach out into the future have a suggestion of vitality in themselves, for life is measured in terms of time, not state or place, and alternate expansions and contractions bring before one the acts of respiration by which life is maintained and prolonged. A man is usually far more concerned with how long he is likely to live, which is beyond his control, than with where he lives, which he can usually decide for himself. The very word function is suggestive of life and we recognise death as the cessation of all the bodily functions. Logarithmic series make contact with Logarithms in the space below (18) and so we find that vital consciousness in time plus impulsive passion constitute the two main ingredients in what Henri Bergson calls, "the élan vital."

(10) THEORY OF GROUPS—ORGANISATION OF UNIT CONCEPTS

The Theory of Groups is the algebraic equivalent of simple arithmetic and occupies the upper harmonic space (10). Arithmetic is the theory of the performance of operations on numbers and the Theory of Groups is that of the performance of operations on algebraic expressions. Naturally it is an abstract and complex branch of mathematics which comparatively few mathematicians explore thoroughly. Sophus Lie, the Norwegian, laid the foundation of the science in his Theory of Continuous Groups and Galois in his Theory of Discontinuous Groups. Both operations and groups are classified and the latter are divided into subgroups called conjugate, isomorphous, etc. Here we have the mathematical ground-basis of the highest kinds of mental operations of which man is capable, involving the creation and working of complex organisations of human groups whose characteristics may be regarded as suggested if not definable by algebraic expressions and equations. Mankind seems to be testing its brain upon a sequence of related groups, royal, aristocratic, plutocratic, and democratic, and rejecting them in turn. Ochlocracy or mob rule is the only form that all are agreed upon in rejecting. Cerebration, no matter how abstract and philosophic may be the raw material on which it works, inevitably follows the procedure of generating minor concepts from major concepts, symbolising them, generalising them, particularising them, classifying them, and memorising them. Plans and projects are then given paper form in files with headings and subheadings which are treated in a similar manner in offices and registries, after which they are given objective existence in organisations which are cast on the same lines as the files and which are themselves also the product of brain-pictures. The combination of the Theory of Groups with that of Expanding Functions sets forth that of Institutions with Historical Development.

(17) Theory of Forms—Civilisation

The branches of the Theory of Forms dealt with under (17) concerns form as visualised by the builder, the sculptor, and the moulder rather than the draughtsman and painter, unless the latter be designers of buildings and statues. We commence with linear, plane, and solid figures, examples of the latter being spheres, cylinders, cones, and the polyhedrons. Since none of these is more than three-dimensional they provide points of contact between the algebraic equations which represent them and the science of the geometrician. Gauss developed a co-ordinate system for measuring curved surfaces which compounded features of spherical trigonometry with those of cartesian and polar co-ordinates, (18) and (13). Then Riemann, Petersen, and Clebsch began to investigate forms of more than three dimensions, combining them with various kinds of curved surfaces. Minkowski and Einstein followed on with theories which asserted that it was possible for one or more of these forms to have objective existence whence the Relativists derived their notions of four-dimensional curved space. To correlate geometrical forms with civilisation and the constructive hedonism which is at the back of it we may consider the former in so far as they are illustrated in the contoured surface of the earth, which has become moulded and sculptured in the course of millions of years into watersheds and basins, hills and valleys, mountains and plains. These furnish striking pictures of the development of civilisations, difference of class being represented by difference of elevation. Class may be defined by birth, wealth, or culture, but whatever be its origin it is distinguishable from the masses which are the counterparts of low-lying plains. It is generally agreed that civilisations can only be created by classes who have sufficient personal wealth to exempt them from the need of toiling for their daily bread and to enable them to devote sufficient leisure to respond to the hedonistic urge in humanity. Civilisation may express itself in idealised ethical philosophies or in the multiplication of material luxuries and physical comforts, as well as in systems of administration which insist on a measure of justice and fair treatment being meted out to all classes. If the upper classes in a civilisation become powerful enough to corrupt justice then its doom is sealed though its dissolution may take time. Crystalline forms provide good types of civilisers since the latter usually have clear-cut minds and express themselves lucidly.

(13) CO-ORDINATE FRAMEWORKS—CONCEPTION OF STATE—MEMORY

Co-ordinate frameworks, whether of the visible geometrical kind or the invisible mathematical kind, agree in being the central stabilising factors in the allied sciences. They are of two main kinds, Cartesian and Polar, though there are one or two other varieties. They are also known as frames of reference and are of great value in theoretical discussions in providing something that the imagination can catch hold of. Their metaphysical and psychological equivalents are the organised memories which are the prime agents in producing permanent states. They furnish the central armatures without which metaphysical conceptions become either flabby or hopelessly fluidic. If we consider the lines defined by the intersections of Cartesian planar co-ordinates, then the vertical line conveys the notion of perpendicularity which is inherent in that of stability and which is a distinguishing feature in the skeletal structure of nearly all trees and most shrubs and plants. Cartesian co-ordinates provide such an obvious and convenient method of measuring the positions and directions of motion of points in space that one is surprised that they were not thought of long before the eighteenth century. The general significance of principle (13) in whatever branch of knowledge it appears centres on the point of origin of all systems of co-ordinates, without which the mind wanders in vain for a pivot or centre of fixation. Psychologically a well-organised and retentive conscious memory resembles an upright framework of girders such as builders of steel-concrete structures make use of, and because it is rooted in the past ministers to the consciousness of continuity which lies at the root of individualised being. Every new experience is automatically tested against the consciousness of continuity to ascertain if it harmonises with it or opposes it, and when this consciousness becomes fossilised, as often happens, then a condition of obstinate and irrational conservatism supervenes which the Greeks called stasis and regarded as the most dangerous disease which could afflict a civilised state.

(12) INFINITESIMAL CALCULUS—GENERALISATION AND PARTICULARISATION

The mathematical process of the Infinitesimal Calculus is divisible into two stages, the first that of differentiating which is analytical and the second that of integrating which is synthetic. If we seek to follow the pathway of a moving point as defined by the terms fx, f_1y, and f_2z where f, f_1 and f_2 are functions of the co-ordinates x, y, and z by which the law of the point's motion is regulated, then we commence by regarding the linear co-ordinates of the starting point as increasing by small increments called differentials. At any stage we select we can ascertain the position of the point by integrating, that is summing the increments, and this summation is equivalent to the generalisation of particulars in reasoning. Analysis is sometimes regarded as involving at least the three elements, the general, the particular, and the singular, and in this case the increment corresponds to the singular with the particular omitted. The geometrical uses of the calculus are innumerable, not the least of which is that by which volumes and increases of volumes can be measured within any limits desired. One of the most ambitious generalisations ever made by any scientist was that of Natural Selection as enunciated by Charles Darwin in which he sought to account for primitive species developing into higher and more complex forms by innumerable incremental changes. When a new and stable species was ultimately produced by this process then an integration or summation of the increments was deemed to have been effected. Owing to the fact, however, that fossils obstinately refuse to provide evidence of any successions of minute changes, the latter are now regarded by some evolutionists as potential increments which do not materialise until a new species emerges into the light through integration. We may also correlate the calculus with such operations as making a heap of myriads of grains of sand, or building a gigantic pyramid with small stones such as are used as aggregate for concrete. Actually we need to visualise in the second case the preliminary task of separating the pebbles from matrices of clay in which other pebbles of an unsuitable kind are embedded. Thus Darwin in propounding his theory of the origin of species carefully selected from his store of observed facts those which seemed to support his theory and discarded those which did not, a not uncommon practice among scientists and philosophers. Generalisation involves a special mental effort as if one were lifting weights against a metaphysical pull of gravity, and this Effort is recognised by most psychologists as a fundamental process of the mind. The Calculus is the last of three mathematical processes of the central column III whose characteristic is their intimate relationship with Geometry.

(16) ALGEBRAIC EQUATIONS—INDIVIDUAL DISCRIMINATION

It is to be regretted that the term, "personal equation" should have been coined to mean "aberration from strict accuracy, or personal error" since its simple and straightforward interpretation is distinctive individuality, with special reference to competence to perform a task. If a man who is not strong is given arduous work we instinctively seek to know if he is equal to it. That is the test of his personal equation in that particular case, for individuality is not something that appears on the surface but rather the root essence of a combination of qualities the nature of which is revealed in reaction to emergencies. The proverb *Quot homines tot sententiae*, means that individual opinions or equations are more likely to differ than agree and the fundamental process of the mind involved when two men propose to unite in a common cause is that of agreement or disagreement. If a number of men of differing personal equations agree to adopt a common formula we say that they have found a solution and that is precisely what we set out to do in connection with mathematical equations, namely to solve them. People who enjoy solving puzzles and problems often find pleasurable relaxation in solving arithmetical puzzles, which usually yield to the appropriate algebraic equation. Thus we find a refined kind of emotionalism of a hedonistic kind appearing in mental activities which are usually regarded as purely intellectual. The personal equations of competitors for a well-paid post are what the prospective employer wants to know and what he takes the needful steps to find out. The kind of man who succeeds in practical everyday affairs is one who lives in the present, keeps his perceptions alert, and seizes favourable opportunities before they pass him by. This is virtually equating himself to his professional or business environment. A man who finds that he fails to achieve this turns the searchlight of analysis on to his own individuality to ascertain if possible by close examination what term, sign, variable, or coefficient in his personal equation is at fault and needs to be eliminated. The equation is itself the essence of Algebra and defines its inner nature. Solving an equation involves asserting equality between two classes of quantities known and unknown and defining the unknowns separately in terms of the knowns. But this is equally true of the process by which all language itself is developed, for we use words of known meaning to define analogous ideas which for all practical purposes remain unknown to the average man until they have been clothed, as it were, in appropriate words. Life itself in this world presents to us a continuous series of problems which call for solution and is on that account generally regarded as the greatest of all problems, in fact as being the *fons et origo* of all other problems.

Individualism in the sense of capacity to seize opportunities and solve the problems of life belongs to the space column because it enables one to equate oneself with one's environment. Those who live in little worlds of their own or shun their fellows, preferring as it were a stable state to changing surroundings, greatly reduce the number of problems which they are compelled to solve.

(15) THEORY OF FORMS—TRANSFORMATIONS, ETC.—CONCEPTION OF SPACE

In the space above (16) we have (15) the number of Conception of Space. The principle of equating with one's environment still predominates but without any complications resulting upon active competition, for the notion of relaxation and restfulness is prominent in this case. The individual in whom the mental process of conception of space is strong combines appreciation of form (13) with that of life (14) and seeks to keep his body in health by conforming to the natural laws of his environment. Walking, running, swimming, motoring, and flying all give him sensations of pleasure. The algebraical counterpart is found in those branches of the Theory of Forms which are concerned with draughtsmanship rather than the plastic arts. One of the chief of these branches is that which deals with the effects upon equations of transferring them from one set of co-ordinates to another, for some change their forms while others remain invariant or are classifiable as covariant or contravariant. Another branch, that of Projections, invades the domain of optics since the shape of all objects which we see are projected on the retina of the eye. What we call transformations in nature are best illustrated by the protean metamorphoses which are commonest in the insect world though not unknown in the amphibian, e.g. the change of a tadpole into a frog. The most artistic of insect metamorphoses are those in which caterpillars become butterflies and larvæ dragon-flies after passing through a chrysalis stage. If we regard water, earth, and air as being of the nature of co-ordinate frameworks in a somewhat metaphysical sense then we find animal equations undergoing such astonishing changes of form that no one but a zoologist is able to know from what grub or larva the end-product or imago emanates. These are, however, extreme cases and it will serve our purpose better to call attention to the countless cases in which the higher animals, even man himself, undergo marked anatomical changes when transferred permanently from one environment to another, even though both be terrestrial. Some races, however, preserve invariance of form much better than others and resist absorption by the inhabitants of the countries to which they migrate. Admittedly it is not always easy to distinguish between visual form and sculptural form and it is equally difficult at times to know whether to place certain branches of theory of forms under the heading of (15) or (17). Changes of complexion and colouration obviously come under (15) but most branches of the Theory are capable of geometrical affiliations. In the analysis of environment (15) relates to climate and temperature and (17) to mountains, valleys, and plains. In optics sculptural forms all appear on a series of flat planes at receding distances and only training in perspective vision enables us to know that they too are not flat. The eye is without doubt the king of the sense organs in all that relates to spatial environment.

(11) Theory of Forms—Determinants, etc.—Directional Symbolisation

The most abstruse branches of the Theory of Algebraic Forms are those known as Determinants, Symmetrical Functions, Enumerating Generating Functions, and Binary Forms. We shall confine ourselves to the first as being the least complex. The basic principle of (11) is that of Diversity, as that of (10) is Unity, and that of (12) is Totality. As in the case of the Immediate Presentations of the lower harmonic (20) we may picture diversity as revealed in radiations coming from a luminous or hot body, in which case the idea of Direction is as important as that of Diversity. But the complications introduced by diversification are so serious that to be able to handle them we must associate them in groups or bundles and give them identifying symbols, names, or labels. The individual "ray" corresponds in most respects with the individual equation and also with the individual man if we take institutions into account. Thus we may expect to find a branch of mathematics which deals with the grouping of equations and such exists in the Theory of Determinants. A determinant is a function which appears or results from the joint solutions of a group of equations, and which consists of a number of coefficients, algebraically related, which can be arranged graphically in what is called a matrix and is symbolised by Delta. Jacobi linked them up with the Calculus and Cayley with linear transformations. Determinants are applied largely to the solution of semi-geometrical problems resulting from the intersection of three planes, the relationship of lines to planes, in fact to almost all the problems connected with co-ordinate geometry. The corresponding psychological process is that made use of by philosophers and speculative thinkers who radiate their concepts into space and then arrest or terminate them on the screen of the imagination, which reflects them back duly grouped and tabulated so that they can be examined at leisure and utilised to create philosophical systems and throw light on the hidden questions to which the ordinary man craves for answers and, it must be regretfully admitted, seldom receives.

This concludes a brief survey of the principal branches of mathematics and geometry and of the mode in which they throw light on the fundamental processes of the mind, taking the last-named to include all conative, intellectual, practical, and instinctive functional activities, whether exercised in the conscious or subconscious regions of individuals and groups. It is obvious that only the barest sketch of this new science can be given within the limits of a single chapter and that its treatment could be expanded much further.

CHAPTER IX

THE ARTS AND THE FUNDAMENTAL PROCESSES OF THE MIND

See TABLES L AND M.

THE classification of the arts has often been attempted in the past but with little or no success. The reason is clear, psychology was antecedent to art and made art possible, from which it follows that the correct classification of the processes of the mind must be made the ground-basis of that of the arts. Furthermore since the aesthetic satisfaction which we obtain from contact with the arts is sensory, we must seek for their psychological correlatives in the sensory rather than the motor elements in the processes of the mind. In the case of two at least of the arts, music and painting, this presents no difficulty at all since the former without possibility of contradiction appeals to the ear and the latter to the eye. The minute anatomy of both these sense organs reveals the reason for the extraordinary accuracy with which they have been rendered capable of receiving the vibrating waves of sound and light respectively and discriminating between their frequencies and even overtones. In these cases, although there are æsthetic conditions of a very definite kind which are induced by music and painting, we can proceed straight from the associated sense organs to the corresponding mental processes of consciousness in time and space, for music, except as regards chords, involves the production of sounds in succession, whereas painting presents its subjects in simultaneity for all practical purposes, though admittedly the eye has to travel over the canvas to some degree, especially if a spacious one. In the matter of discrimination of vibrations and rhythms in time, the ear's capacity is far in advance of the eye's, whereas the opposite is the case when it is a question of estimating distances, directions, and localities in space. In the case of two more senses, namely smell and taste, the arts to which they give rise, perfumery and gastronomics, can certainly not be placed on a level with any of the major arts which we are considering here, and consequently we must in these cases seek for a metaphysical bridge which will carry us from the literalism of smell and taste to the recondite conceptions which link our minds with the arts symbolised by smell and taste, to wit, literature and sculpture, which are of the highest rank.

(10) POETRY

The aforesaid metaphysical bridge comes at once into prominence when we proceed to trace the affiliations of poetry with the sense of balance whose organs are the semicircular canals of the ear. These organs are not merely designed to enable man to maintain static balance in state but to achieve the far more difficult object of enabling him to maintain dynamic balance in time. In plainer English they do not merely enable him to stand but to run, skate, jump, ski, and perform gymnastic and acrobatic feats, which may be divided into movements on solid ground or ice depending on the use of the feet and legs and movements in the air depending upon use of the hands and arms. Doubtless the canals are also of use in swimming in which both arms and legs are used. The art associated with movements with the feet on a solid surface is obviously dancing but this is connected in turn with another sense, æsthetic contact, which, except in ballet and tap dancing, enhances considerably the enjoyment of the art, because ball-room dancing involves joint movement by people of opposite sex. We may, however, use dancing as a bridge to carry us to the upper harmonic art of poetry, which in view of its mental and metaphysical associations is represented better by the feats of acrobats performing on the flying trapeze or of the agile ape-monkey, the gibbon, even than by the evolutions of expert skaters. The unit of poetic measurement is, however, called a foot, which indicates a natural linking in the mind of walking or running with poetry, the former suggesting the religious ode and the latter the lyric. But against this we have the syllable into which the foot is divided, which means to grasp with the hand (Gk. *sullambanein*) and one of the best-known feet of Graeco-Latin poetry is the dactyl, which means finger. If there is one feature above another which distinguishes the great poets, especially the epic, it is the grasp they have of stupendous subjects which transcend the capacity of the ordinary mind to handle. This is no mixed metaphor for we handle concepts with the brain just as we do objects with the hand, and although the many may understand sublime poetry only the few grasp its full significance. It should be noted furthermore that gymnasts and acrobats do not normally progress forward but revolve in circles, though the monkey on the other hand covers considerable distances by swinging from tree to tree. So also a good deal of poetry impresses one as circulating round a fixed theme, though this is obviously not true of dramatic poetry or its near relative the epic. As a rule the individual is free to perform agreeable movements and avoid disagreeable ones, though tastes vary in this matter since some enjoy fun-fair rides which cause others giddiness and apprehension. Most people find rolling and pitching at sea intolerable, for the canals dislike these motions and give instructions to the vagus nerve to upset the stomach and to warn its possessor to give as wide a berth to sea-voyages as possible, thus imposing a most unreasonable restriction on freedom of travelling by sea, not to mention air. Even train-sickness is a common complaint. One must remember in investigating the problems of æsthetics that of recent years most of the canons of this science have been and are now being openly defied for the first time in the history of the world, so that bastard offsprings of poetry and prose which are completely devoid of artistic merit are being forced upon the public, which is gullible enough to accept them as shining examples of progressiveness in the divine art. Much the same is true of all the other arts and never within the memory of man has the Temple of the Muses been subjected to such unscrupulous desecration as at present or more grotesque caricatures palmed off upon the public as inspired creations.

If we were to make a composite picture or photograph of the world's great poets we should obtain the likeness of a man whose ambition is to originate world-movements in which he himself is the central disturbing force. He visualises his influence as flowing outwards in concentric waves until all peoples, nations, and tongues guide themselves in accordance with his ideals. His motive is unconnected with exhibitionism and its fuel is the urge to attack stagnation wherever it threatens to establish itself, and disperse it before it has time to become entrenched. If the poet's sympathies are rooted in the past he marshals his events so as to manifest the undercurrents which have determined the cyclic evolution of history, he dwells upon the deeds of great men who have given the destinies of nations new orientations. Or he may create imagined characters who may be taken as standard representatives of their age but who yet stand head and shoulders above their fellows, and celebrate their successes. Poetry is rightly regarded as the racial art of the Anglo-Saxons, that is of a people which has organised itself into a world-wide system of free commonwealths which, with the exception of the United States, look in every case to the British Crown as the symbol of its unity of purpose and of high endeavour. Poetry in its earliest stages was the means by which the official records of nations and peoples were preserved and handed down to posterity, especially such as reflected credit on kings and national heroes. Dramatic poetry served a somewhat similar purpose except that incidents of special significance were detached from the general record and grouped so as to produce consecutive dramatic stories. The spirit of poetry is incarnated in the British Race to an exceptional degree. While the Greeks delineated powerful characters in their dramatic literature they always regarded Fate as dwarfing the individual to insignificance. The British, on the other hand, regard the individual as captain of his fate, provided he chooses to put forth his inherent capacities and makes the most of his endowments. Their national heroes are men who seek to bend Fate to their will and never submit to be carried along by it as corks in a mill-race.

(11) Drama

The Dramatic Art, restricting the term to written plays or dramatic poetry, involves the pleasurable exercise of the sense of direction which is that given to man and beast for the exploration of space, subject to the restrictive limitations of gravity and the earth's surface. Undoubtedly the sense of direction affects to some degree the organs of balance, for changes of direction producing corresponding changes of inertia would certainly be registered by the canal in the forward vertical plane. But the directional sense here contemplated is that which enables migrating birds to return to their exact starting point and migrating fishes, such as salmon and eels, to perform similar feats. The sense organ involved may possibly be the archepallium in the forepart of the brain, which is well developed in relation to the cerebral hemispheres in the lower animals. Certainly sight would not be sufficient, for birds fly to their objective over trackless oceans at night and fish swimming at sea have even less to guide them. Man however possesses the directional sense to some degree, for some individuals, especially explorers or roamers over wide open spaces, are able to find their way, even without the aid of the stars, with uncanny precision. Animals, which most certainly cannot guide themselves by the stars at night, exhibit remarkable capacity for keeping track of their location even in the dark. But granted that the archepallium is the sense organ involved the mechanism of directional pathfinding remains obscure. Some call the sense magnetic and if the recent alleged discovery, suggesting that magnetic currents may flow along the magnetic meridians, proves to be true this may be the explanation or part of it. In dealing with the mental processes it was shown that the second was directional in character and corresponded with radiations emanating from a source of radiant energy, but nevertheless subjected to grouping in bundles. If we think of poetry as represented by the grasping hand, drama is equally well represented by the extended fingers, especially the index finger, which is so frequently used to point the way. For drama is nothing if it be not the unfolding of a plot which develops in a fixed direction, even though minor deviations may be permissible. This is especially true of the Greek tragic drama which visualised the affairs of mankind as governed by an inexorable fate moving relentlessly along a prescribed path towards an inevitable goal. The word direct may mean to advise or it may mean to govern, just as the directors of a financial concern direct its policy and order their activities accordingly. Tragedy means goat-song and was doubtless so called because the goat loves to climb persistently and laboriously to lofty eminences whence it is able to command a wide view of the surrounding country. Historical drama, which is a record of fact, though it may be presented in orthodox dramatic form, should not be confused with fictional drama which proceeds from the imagination. The effective settings for historical dramas are unlimited areas of country and ocean routes which afford unstinted scope for the directional movement of groups of adventurers or colonists. Nothing produced by the imagination has ever approached the conquest of Mexico and Peru by the Spaniards, the foundation of British Colonies by Merchant Adventurers such as the Hudson Bay Company, the conquest of Siberia by the Cossacks, and the vast trek westwards towards the Pacific by American pioneers which began about the middle of the nineteenth century, many phases of which have been presented to us in films of outstanding merit. There is no doubt that full historical dramatic effect calls for numbers of people as well as unlimited space but there must also be persons of conspicuous ability as leaders to explore the full grandeur of the situations. The Drama is as much an art of space as Poetry is one of time, as is seen by the fact that dramas are divided into acts and scenes. Drama must, of course, progress in time but its rate of advance is more leisurely than that of poetry and reminds one of a river which takes its origin from a high mountain range and suddenly reaches a plain in its course which it overspreads in many channels so as to form a delta or even a lake.

(12) ARCHITECTURE

Architecture is a natural development of the pleasurable exercise of the sense of effort which seems inseparable from a psychological sense of achievement. The poet and the dramatist can never be certain that their work will endure for ages but the architect who builds solidly has no doubts on that score and as he sees his labour crystallising into a mighty pyramid or temple or defying gravity, as it would seem, in the roofing and spanning of a lofty Gothic cathedral, he has the immense satisfaction of knowing that not an ounce of his efforts has been wasted. As the Hebrews produced the master-poets of the ancient world and the Greeks the master-dramatists, so the Romans created vast megalithic structures, aqueducts, viaducts, amphitheatres, and public buildings which, if not exhibiting such delicate artistic sensibility of design as the Greek architectural monuments, far outdistanced them in public utility and outranged them in number. But of all the architects who excite our admiration and deserve our gratitude, the travelling masons of the Middle Ages who raised up Gothic cathedrals to the glory of God in most of the countries of Western Europe, notably in Spain and France, lead the way, for their wages were scanty but the efforts which they put forth were energised by zeal for God and an intense urge to create buildings in which the worship of His Name should be conducted with befitting majesty of liturgy and ceremonial.

The contemplation of massiveness in static space, that is state, has always fascinated the human mind. Our admiration is excited by cyclopean buildings and megalithic terraces and pyramids, not merely because vast numbers of men had to be collected to erect them, nor even because of the engineering skill displayed in the transportation and elevation of ponderous stones, but because massiveness when contemplated from a reasonable distance gives us an inward sense of security and stability. We experience a similar kind of satisfaction when we gaze upon Nature's architectural masterpieces, mountain ranges, towering peaks, sheer precipices, and gloomy chasms. Immensity and immobility belong to the very essence of architecture in its most grandiose natural examples. Martin Hume, the eminent authority on Spain, acclaims the Spaniards as the greatest of the European architects. "Clearer than in their literature," he writes, "more distinctly even than in their institutions, the special characteristics of the Spanish people are set forth in imperishable stone in the great architectural monuments produced in the early stage of their evolution as a nation. Profound veneration allied to exaggerated self-respect, proud reticence easily aroused to florid vociferation, vivid imagination overleaping material limitations, these and much more may be seen in the severe spaces and massive walls, pierced by doorways and windows overloaded with ornament; in buildings whose vast breadth of span are still the wonder and despair of all architects, and whose bold arches springing from magnificent clustered columns are surrounded on all sides by an ornamentation so luxuriant, so varied, so overflowing with detail as to seem the work of fairies rather than men; in cloisters whose staid and stern background is veiled by beautiful lacework of stone, the exquisite tracery of which, growing ever more florid, conceals its own massive strength."[1] It is small wonder that the handful of Spaniards under Pizarro should have been amazed and fascinated by the mighty road which traversed Peru from north to south winding its way at a high altitude along the mountains of the Andes and by the cities and terraces which were built on the very summits of peaks which were sufficiently truncated to provide level sites.

(13) MOSAIC

It is less easy to find the art associable with the atrophied pineal sense because no one is quite certain what it was but it probably served partly as a means of internal diagnosis for ascertaining if the body-machinery was working properly and may have been a synthesis of the senses below it with vision predominating. It is also said that the external pineal eye, of which we have the rudimentary remains preserved in the tuatera lizard as a true organ vision, was able to react to luminous rays beyond the present limits of the visible spectrum. The pineal gland is an appendage of the thalamus, which is almost a closed chamber in the brain. The primary interest of the affiliated art may therefore be anticipated to be internal, which suggests that it may be mosaic. The corresponding mental process, which concerns memory and the preservation of the continuity of state and produces ultra-conservatism, was characteristic of Byzantine civilisation which was also conspicuous

[1] *The Spanish People*, 1901, pp. 228, 229.

for the extent to which it developed the mosaic art in the interior decoration of its buildings. We may possibly be justified in including all forms of internal decoration in the artistic equivalent of pineal sight. The idea of fragmentation is also inherent in mosaic and this is seen in the associated science of colloidality, for colloidal solutions are essentially suspensions of minute particles of solid matter. Fragments of stone, glass, pottery, etc., which would be unsuitable for the external ornamentation of buildings as being inconsistent with their massiveness, except in the case of windows, can be readily adapted to mosaic work of a highly ornamental character. Thus the pictorial character of the pineal art is preserved and the predominance of vision in the synthesised sense is justified. At any rate there can be no question that mosaic is far more nearly allied to painting than it is to music, the arts of the external eye and ear respectively. Mosaic is derived from the same word as Music, that is Muse, and there are even points of resemblance between Mosaic and Music, since both harmonies and noises are mosaics of sounds, the former arranged either in symmetrical or at least recognisable patterns and the latter mingled together without any design. Mosaic must be provided with plane surfaces, flat or curved, on which to rest or be made to adhere by cement and from an architectural point of view it is somewhat of a parasitic art.

(14) Music

The scientific basis of music, that is organised vibration, is as simple in principle as the proportionment of form on which statuary is based, yet it explores the mysteries of time just as the statue does those of mass-form. Time, as we have seen, is not so much a metaphysical clock as a measure of the development of successive states, with peaks and troughs of tensional activities resembling a temperature chart. That which is inherent in state must have time to express itself fully, its historical cycles must be permitted to unfold themselves without check, revealing the potentialities of the initial state in innumerable aspects. The initial state of a musical composition is the theme, and all but the very simplest compositions are mainly concerned with thematic development. Once this has been successfully accomplished the third stage of recapitulation or restatement is comparatively easy to traverse. Music explores and exploits the time factor in thematic treatment, and its power of portraying the spirit of a cycle or epoch is altogether unique. No other art can approach it in this respect. One reason of this is the extent to which music entrenches itself in the memory, and dwells in the subterranean chambers which store the archives of historical fact. So that when the chords of memory are plucked, airs and melodies come tumbling forth mingled with mental images of scenes, crises, entertainments, romances, so that they can hardly be distinguished apart. The joys and sorrows of life express themselves through the medium of music with a vividness and intensity which only those whose souls are saturated with the art can understand.

(15) Drawing and Painting

Drawing and painting are closely allied, but whereas when we speak of drawing a house everyone understands that we mean drawing a picture of one, when we speak of painting a house we might either mean drawing a picture of one or covering the walls with paint. Drawing is the foundation of script without which the production of literature would have been impossible until the invention of printing. Colour exhibits more continuity than sound, as tints and hues blend into each other by nature; and since sight conveys impressions of simultaneity to the brain, painting partakes more of continuity than melodic music. Certain kinds of orchestrated music are called colourful, especially those of the later Romantic school, and coloratura in music denotes the art of embellishing melody with variations, trills, and similar ornaments. The joys of sight and of painting are near of kin but the former is bound to predominate in intensity by reason of the fact that Nature's colour schemes are more gorgeous, arresting, and kaleidoscopic than paintings or films in technicolour can possibly be.

(16) Literature

The metaphorical implications of scent are so numerous and varied that the difficulty is rather to exclude what does not concern it than to catalogue what is related to it. The corresponding mental process of constructive individualism predominates in the regulation of what we call active life, in which all sorts and conditions of men mingle together indiscriminately and strive to earn a living under the competitive stimulus, being sometimes driven by urges which pay scant heed to the canons of ethics. Scent plays a much more important part in the animal world than in the human, where its value is utilitarian rather than æsthetic. Dogs, which of all four-footed animals have the keenest sense of smell, do not appear to enjoy what we call perfumes but on the contrary find satisfaction in the unsavoury odours of decaying carcases of a kind that make human beings retch. To a large number of animals the scent of the genus man, *homo sapiens*, conjures up the picture of a ruthless killer, to whatever race he may belong. Dogs, on the other hand, distinguish between the body-odours of individuals and probably interpret them as denoting either friendliness or hostility. The extent to which bloodhounds are able to recognise, identify, and follow up the scent left on the ground by individuals is nothing short of phenomenal. A dog would probably say, "I do not like you, Dr. Fell, the reason why I cannot tell, but this I know and know full well, I simply cannot stand your smell." If a human being of observant habits were to become a dog for no more than an hour he would probably find that his sense of smell opened up a new world to him and invested every new object with intriguing attributes. One has only to see how an active dog, such as a fox-terrier, behaves himself when given the run of a field, to appreciate the utilitarian value of smell to him, though we have no means of knowing its æsthetic value. There is, however, a strong satisfaction which is derived from the mere use of a sense quite apart from the

THE ARTS AND THE FUNDAMENTAL PROCESSES OF THE MIND 167

agreeableness or otherwise of the objects which furnish it with sense data or afford it exercise.

To the human being the metaphorical sense of smell denotes a capacity to sum up quickly his fellow's individual characteristics in so far as they affect the ordinary issues of competitive life. The business man is seldom interested in the politics or religious views of his competitors, and is concerned with their ethical views only in so far as the latter are put into practice. It is said of many business men that they are able to smell a new proposition from the point of view as to whether it is sound and money-making or not. Similarly many professional men and trading firms hunt up clients by a process which suggests to us a dog following up a hot scent. Whenever we judge an individual, no matter if only for a moment, we sniff him in a metaphorical sense. Thus the human counterpart of smell provides its possessor with a series of novel experiences even in the dullest of days. Dogs are notorious for their love of novelties in their surroundings and the owners of many barking dogs make themselves a nuisance to their neighbours simply because they will not accord freedom to their pets to investigate the countless objects of interest which the outside world provides for their entertainment. Thus we arrive, by a somewhat circuitous route, at the art which corresponds with scent and smell, namely literature, with special reference to the novel, which is more interesting to the average man and woman than all other kinds of literature put together. The very word novel suggests something new and the comparatively recent popularity of the novel arises from the fact that life is yearly becoming more complex and charged with new possibilities and fresh situations. The novel, as an environmental art, is more nearly allied to drama than to any other, its chapters being acts and scenes under other names. But unless the novel deals with the life of an explorer or traveller, it does not demand spaciousness for self-expression nor does it concern itself except incidentally with the fortunes of associations or groupings of men. What we demand of all novels is consistency in the individualisms and qualities of their principle characters, and when this is done we use a metaphor from the draughtsman's art and say that the novelist's characters are well drawn. If they are devoid of appeal we say that they are colourless, or we may take a metaphor from the culinary art and speak of them as insipid. Just as the exercise of constructive individualism involves a maximum of discrimination, keen observation, and analysis, so also does the novel which depicts situations arising from the free mingling of human beings in countless spheres of activity, the outcome of which may be either constructive or destructive, according as to whether the laws of the land are good and enforced by the infliction of punishment for infringing them. Dogs are law-abiding in their relationship to man but shameless law-breakers in their relationships with each other, starting ferocious dog-fights upon the least provocation, or what we might perhaps regard as a considerable provocation if a dog, the emission of an objectional body odour. If a dog does not like a canine Dr. Fell he seldom troubles to conceal his aversion, and as likely as not is soon vigorously supported by associates who share his animosity. It is a regrettable fact that what seem unreasonable dislikes manifested at sight are part and parcel of life in the world as it is to-day. Literature, as an art, must have freedom of expression and be untrammelled by the limitations and conventions to which drama, its near relation, is subjected. It binds the whole world together as no other art can possibly do. Most writers on the ways and habits of peoples of foreign countries make a point of visiting the said countries, and if possible acquainting themselves on the spot with their languages, literatures, and traditions. Literature was not the cause of man being fruitful and multiplying and replenishing the earth but it has provided priceless records of the manner in which he has carried out the Divine command. Literature must be placed in a compartment in diagrammatic contact with that of drawing and painting, not only because script is a form of drawing, but because the novelist is the preordained depictor and describer of human environment, natural, geographical, scenic, social, and communal. He must be more than a word-painter, he must be an illuminator, a colour-specialist in the fine shades of the meanings of words. Writers must be prepared to forge ahead of contemporary thought and visualise the potentialities of new states into which society is evolving, seeking to discern through the mistiness of the future the shape of things to come.

(17) Taste—Relish

The affiliation of the sense of taste with the fundamental process of hedonism is easy to see. A child is soon taught to understand the distinction between what is tasty and what is tasteful but nevertheless to connect the two qualities in its mind as having something in common. Some people write of civilisation as if, from its material side, it consisted mainly in the enjoyment of luxuries, but unless these are in good taste the hedonistic urge which produces such a civilisation is not of an exalted kind. A dictionary definition of the higher taste is "the mental faculty or power of apprehending and enjoying the beautiful and the sublime in nature and art, or of appreciating or discerning degrees of artistic excellence; also manner, style, or execution as directed or controlled by this faculty." Taste is essentially the kind of discrimination which ranges objects of art, luxury, or comfort in various degrees, being what one might call adjectival in this respect. China, which claims to be the oldest civilisation in the world, is celebrated for the tastefulness of all its artistic products as also for their refined quality. The associated art is sculpture but we need not restrict this to statuary, which in China is confined to the images of corpulent Buddhas, but may legitimately extend it to cover the exquisite and intricate ivory carvings produced by its artists, not to mention carvings in wood and jade. True hedonists have also a keen appreciation of form both in a literal and a metaphorical sense, for the terms "good form" and "good taste" are both recognised attributes of good breeding. The leisured, wealthy, and aristocratic classes lead the way in the demand for and enjoyment of luxuries, and the latter through centuries of interbreeding produce finer and more delicate bodily forms than the masses. These are truisms which approach the banal but they must be set down to clinch the argument. Hedonism makes a strong appeal to the desires but does not arouse passions unless upper strata of society are gradually formed whose acquisitiveness leads them to reduce the lower strata to poverty of a kind which denies them not merely the comforts but the necessities of life. Then the lower classes start to envy the upper and the stage begins to be set for revolutionary activity. The ideal of all sculptors who follow Greek models is to obtain perfection of form conjoined with reposefulness, without which statuesque effect is impaired. In like manner a civilisation in order to survive must possess certain elements of reposefulness to counteract the strenuousness of life as illustrated by the metaphysical sense of smell. Reposefulness is the leading characteristic of the Eastern Buddhas and also of religious statuary in the West. Needless to say, there are times when the sculptor seeks to exercise his art to depict action, in which case the representation of energy is incompatible with that of peacefulness and beneficence. Just as taste comes into the foreground when the contours of the human body have to be carved or modelled in stone or plaster, so also it reigns supreme in the sphere of the clothing of the body, especially when the feminine sex is affected.

(18) INTENSIFIED TASTE—NAUSEA

In order to connect the next art of eloquence with the unnamed form of taste which appears equally in greed and nausea it will be necessary to carry out some more metaphysical bridge-building. There are two kinds of taste buds in the mouth, one of which tends to crowd towards the back of the tongue and the throat and produce what might be called intensified taste. When we stimulate the first kind we speak of liking or disliking food, whereas in the second case we speak of loving it or hating it, and the same distinction may be seen in our attitude towards persons who may or may not be to our taste. The anterior buds encourage us to eat and drink daintily whereas the posterior cause us to gorge and swill with small regard for refinement of manners. It we do not like a certain kind of food we swallow it under protest and avoid it for the future, or at the worst voluntarily spit it out. But when the posterior buds are offended, which usually happens when food is nauseous or decomposing, they may set up violent reflex actions such as choking and forcibly ejecting the contents of the throat. Intensified taste approaches more closely to the tactile sense than ordinary taste, for part of the enjoyment of swilling consists in the flowing of liquid down the gullet and the contact of a small foreign body such as a fish-bone may produce choking. The stomach if not violently fond of some kinds of food is violently antipathetic to others and may cause vomiting of an unpleasant and painful severity. We may classify the arts of columns I, II, and III as passional, emotional, or desiderative, and so in the first case we may have passionate poetry, passionate music such as Wagner's, passionate oratory of either a patriotic or tub-thumping kind, and passionate dancing of either an erotic or war-mongering variety such as savages indulge in. Acting is primarily concerned with emotional people, for however passionate may be a lover whom an actor impersonates we are conscious all the time that his passion is simulated. Similarly erotic literature which reaches us *via* the eyes may make a strong emotional appeal, whereas erotic oratory which reaches us *via* the ear makes a passionate appeal. When we describe individualistic activities we instinctively adopt physical metaphors such as diffusion, solution, and precipitation and when we deal with the association of people of marked characters we often find chemical metaphors of use such as arise from the affinity of certain elements for each other and in extreme cases of the explosive violence of certain chemicals which furnish us with revolutionary similes. But in the case of the strong affections and antipathies which correspond with intensified taste we find electro-magnetic phenomena of great descriptive value and call to mind thunderous oratory followed by thunderous applause or lightning thrusts aimed by the speaker at the weak points in the opponent's armour. In the sphere of eloquence personality is far more effective than either individuality or character and a man of magnetic personality carries all before him, often when his oratory is illiterate and illogical. Animal magnetism which plays a predominant rôle in courting and amatory advances has so much in common with physical magnetism that it is often hard to distinguish between the two. The clashing of personalities which are antipathetic produces much stronger antagonisms and dislikes than the clashing of individualities, in fact veritable thunderstorms are not uncommonly the outcome. Homicidal crimes arising solely from sex-jealousies are common. Passionate eloquence of the Cyrano de Bergerac type goes far with women, especially if of Latin affinities. Rhythm and vibration are characteristic of the Arts of Col. I, the former predominating in poetry and dancing and the latter in oratory (*cf.* a voice vibrant with passion) while music occupies a position midway.

(19) DANCING

With the arts of Dancing, Acting, and Moulding (Ceramics) we come to the regions of the instincts which we share with the animals, who dance, impersonate, and construct like mankind and in some cases, such as nest-building by birds, achieve more than man could do with all his resources. Not many animals are architects in the strict sense of the term, though the huts made by beavers and the mounds made by termites show great constructional ability. On the other hand, they mould and weave with consummate skill and the honeycomb made by the bee is a geometrical wonder. Dancing occupies the lower harmonic space of poetry, and, as mentioned, ball-dancing is alone symmetrically rhythmic for ballet-dancing is partly dramatic in form. But besides the sense of balance that of æsthetic contact based on sex-attraction must be given due weight. Both sex-dances and war-dances are performed by savages but among civilised nations the latter finds no place.

Practically all enjoyable ball-dancing bears, however, a sex aspect of a perfectly respectable and legitimate kind as a rule, based on the simple satisfaction experienced in the conjunction of the polar opposites, positive and negative magnetism. This satisfaction is enhanced by actual contact between partners which can hardly be avoided even in the most formal and ceremonious of ball-dances. There are four kinds of tactile senses, first that which is associated with pleasure or pain, from which we derive the adjective touching, meaning affecting the sympathetic emotions; second, that which is discriminative but unemotional, which seeks to measure and identify tactile data; third, that of light pressure which is used mainly to assure oneself of the reality of the material world; and fourth, that of heavy pressure which comes into play when muscular power is exerted. Sensations of irritation and tickling belong to the first kind, for if accentuated they can become as unendurable as severe pain. Mere sense data are in themselves neutral in regard to the feelings but when they reach the thalamus they are then interpreted as pleasurable or painful quite apart from the information they convey, so that, strictly speaking, the unit concept is not a purely intellectual manifolding of percepts but can be pleasurable or painful in a crudely hedonistic sense. The concept, as already pointed out, is associated with the brain in the same manner that the percept is with the sensory peripheral nervous system and the organs of sensation. It has been known for some time that the brain was the centre for rhythmic pulsation but comparatively recently Dr. Golla of the Burden Neurological Institute near Bristol has discovered three kinds of rhythms of different tempos by means of an instrument called the encephalograph. These are normal in a healthy person but he has also found a fourth which is pathological. Furthermore, as pointed out in analysing the nature of poetry, the movements of dancing are made possible by the unique structure of the semi-circular canals of the inner ear. Whether the brain actually thinks rhythmically remains to be proved. The association of the passions with dancing is seen in characteristic form in the war-dances and erotic dances of savages, the latter being often needful to enable the race to reproduce itself. As regards the sense of contact of the first kind, namely that which is associated with pleasurable feelings, it is hardly needful to dilate on the part this plays in the mechanism of generation but it also enters largely into the enjoyment of dancing in an innocent and legitimate manner. When we make use of this sense metaphorically we speak of an episode as being touching if it makes a strong appeal to our sympathies or affections. It may well be that attractions and repulsions in love and friendship are partly determined by the synchronisation or otherwise of psychical rhythms.

(20) ACTING

The art of acting or impersonation involves the exercise of the second tactile sense and its associated psychological equivalents, all of which are sensitised by awareness and minute discrimination. A successful impersonator, besides natural aptitude, must have the capacity for minutely observing every trick and trait of gesture, expression, voice, intonation, and accent, not to mention eccentricities of habits, dress, and deportment of his subject or model. Acting is in fact the expression of the dramatic by mimicry and in a primitive form is known as miming. While rhythmic movements of arms and legs are the essentials of dancing, non-rhythmic movements of the same with a view to interpreting emotions by gesture lie at the root of acting. Interpretive or ballet-dancing bridges the gulf between the two. Furthermore, facial gestures are part and parcel of acting but find no place in ballroom dancing and very little in interpretive dancing, except among savages. The ground basis of true pantomime is the fact that practically every gesture expresses a meaning of its own and on that account it should not be treated as merely amplifying the meaning of speech. This is a point upon which Charlie Chaplin always laid great insistence and for that reason adhered to the silent film long after it had been abandoned by the film industry as a whole. If the meaning of gesture be standardised and conventionalised then gesture itself affords a valuable means of communicating over distances at which speech or even shouting is inaudible. As children grow up they accumulate a large stock of instinctive gestures which express their individuality with precision and are readily understood by those who have cultivated the art of gesture-interpretation. The mobile gesture, as opposed to the mere static gesture associated with expression of face and posing, is unrivalled as a means for expressing the emotions. Speech itself is produced by tongue gestures which, as Sir Richard Paget has demonstrated, are symbolic of the acts they describe. Pantomime, which occupies the lower harmonic of Drama, is the obvious and natural means whereby Drama is brought down from the region of the universal to that of the particular. Originally the two arts were one and the actor composed his drama and acted it himself.

(21) Pottery—Ceramics

Pottery is the only true plastic art. Architecture is plastic in so far as plastic materials are used in buildings, such as mortar, cement, concrete or moulded bricks but very little art is needed to manipulate these, however expert the craftsmanship. The true art of architecture lies more in design than in execution, and ornamentation is primarily sculptural. Sculpture is plastic only in so far as plaster models of the subjects are made first. The art of the potter calls for the skilful use of the palms of the hands in conjunction with the potter's wheel, a mode of making earthenware vessels which even modern science cannot improve upon. It is probably the most ancient of all the arts. The sense organs which are actuated in the art are those of light contact as applied by the palms, for the fingers are seldom used separately. Glass-blowing is a specialised branch of ceramics in which air pressure takes the place of hand pressure. Ceramics occupies a humble place among the arts, for more than all the others it is the servant of mankind, and the most beautiful examples of pottery are those in which the painter, drawer, or colour specialist has exercised his art upon the finished articles. Nevertheless there are no more delicate and beautiful *objets d'art* in the world than the finest Chinese porcelain jars or vases judged by their form alone. Pottery faces up to the reality of human life more than any other art, for man must eat to live and needs vessels in which to cook and store his food. Nature supplies caves for shelter but not pots and pans. There is a 13th art, the lower harmonic of Mosaic, which is developed from that of the smith, namely the artistic working of metals, of which the finest examples are, as might be expected, executed in silver and gold. Here we admittedly begin to encroach upon the preserves of the manufacturer as we do in the case of the arts lower down, gramophone manufacture, the photographic art, cinematography, weaving, and radio-transmission. The smith works more by the sense of heavy pressure than that of light pressure, whatever metal he uses, and the ancients emphasised this in another way by locating Vulcan's workshop in the depths of a volcano where the pressure of the atmosphere would be greater than at the earth's surface, so that a general air of stuffiness and compression would inevitably predominate.

CHAPTER X

GEOLOGY AND THE GENESIS STORY OF CREATION

See TABLES N, O, P, Q, R.

THE Science of Geology lends itself readily to analysis on the general principles of the Philosophy of Analogy and Symbolism provided one is content to take a very broad view of the subject. The diagrammatic result is shown on Table N from which it will be seen that the Six Creative Days are shown as coincident with Tiers X to V. It is quite evident that we must adopt an evolutionary mode of classification and work upwards to ensure a correct picture of the situation. The time-period of each complete Night-Day is taken as 180 million years. Since each of these periods is one hour of a Cosmic Night-Day of 24 hours the total duration of the latter is 4,320 m.y. The German astronomer Mädler is said to have calculated that the sun takes 180 m.y. to make a complete circuit round Alcyone in the Pleiades but details of his calculations are not available. The fact is however worth mentioning. The figure of 180 m.y. is convenient because the hours expended on creative activity at its maximum may be estimated roughly as eight, which is one-third of a Night-Day or Evening-Morning of 24 hours and 180 m.y. is readily divisible into 3 periods of 60 m.y. each. The question then presents itself as to how far this time-scale fits in with that of the recognised geological epochs. The various estimates made of the age of the earth do not help us unless by that term is meant the age of the aqueous strata, for by no possible means could we make the vaguest estimate of the age of the igneous strata. Reference should be made at this juncture, if possible, to a most instructive booklet called *The Age of the Earth*, by Prof. Arthur Holmes, of Edinburgh University,[1] who gives figures for the time taken to deposit the primary strata based on observations of the radio-activity of certain rocks. Full details of these will be found on p. 178 of Prof. Holmes's book. The calculation of the age of any particular stratum is effected by taking a representative sample of it and ascertaining both the percentage of uranium in it (if present at all) and that of the uranium-lead which is formed as an end-product of its period of radio-activity. Then the proportion of lead to uranium multiplied by 7,400 m.y. gives an approximate figure for the age of the sample. Thorium may also be taken into account when present as a check on the figures obtained with lead. It is true that some geologists do not attach much importance to the time-periods obtained by this method of calculation but they have no other means of estimating the ages of individual strata with anything approaching the same degree of accuracy and their objections can all be satisfactorily met. In order to construct a table we commence by placing the Tertiary strata in compartment (13), for this is the pivotal compartment of the Table and the Tertiary Age coincides roughly with the last third of the 6th Day's work when mammals were produced and man made his appearance. If we now write down the remaining strata in the accepted order of their deposition we have Cretaceous (14), Jurassic and Triassic (15), Permian (16), Carboniferous (17), Devonian and Silurian (18), Ordovician (19), Upper Cambrian (20) and Lower Cambrian (21). We must allot 60 m.y. to each as a very approximate allowance, based on the subdivision of 180 m.y. into 3.

The details of dates of samples of various strata as obtained by tests of the same by the Helium and Lead Methods (*Age of the Earth*, p. 178) fit in remarkably well with the dates of the limits of strata as shown in Table N. The system adopted here of allowing 60 m.y. per stratum (or pair of strata in some cases) makes the datum date for the Lower Cambrian 540 m.y. before the Quaternary. The most recent date for samples from the Upper Pre-Cambrian (22) is 530 m.y. B.Q. with a possible error of 15 m.y. either way. The basic date of the Upper Pre-Cambrian is about 900 m.y. B.Q. as fixed approximately by the Bröggerites of Norway. The limits of the Middle Pre-Cambrian are from 900 m.y. to 1,260 m.y. B.Q. and the basic date of the Lower Pre-Cambrian may be taken as 1800 m.y. B.Q. On p. 78 of *The Age of the Earth*[2] Prof. Holmes gives a list of revolutions or geological cycles marked by upheavals involving changes of the earth's surface. He calculates that there were 20 of these and that the average interval between each pair was 30 m.y. making a total of 600 m.y. to the beginning of the Pre-Cambrian. The figure shown on Table N for the same stage is 540 m.y. The difference

[1] *Nelson's Classics*, 1937.
[2] *Benn's Library*, No. 102, 1927.

is due to three revolutions of 90 m.y. being allotted by him to the Carboniferous and Devonian periods instead of 60 m.y. each. The Silurian is given 30 m.y. and the Ordovician 90 m.y., which adds another 30 m.y.[1] It is of great importance to appreciate the significance of the major revolutions shown on p. 49 which belong to the pivotal compartments (13), (16), (19), and (22). In Europe they were the Alpine, the Hercynian, the Caledonian, and the Charnian, the counterparts in America of the first two and the last being the Cascadian-Laramide, the Appalachian-Ouachita, and the Killarnean. Now in these compartments we have the operative thirds of the 6th, 5th, 4th, and 3rd Creation Days when the maximum amount of creative energy was put forth in the form of evolutionary activity. Evolution as used here is confined in meaning to evolution of plan about which there is no conflict of opinion. In view of the fact that the leading evolutionists admit frankly that no mechanism of evolution has yet been regarded as satisfactorily proved, no process of gradual changes from one species to a higher can be assumed as having taken place, apart from the argument that such an idea is negatived by the fact that all fossils consist of perfect specimens of their own species and no transitional or transformative types have ever been found. Favourable reception was given to a theory propounded by Prof. Joly to account for the regular periodicity of the revolutions. He assumed with good reason that the continents are irregular slabs of granitic rocks embedded in a deep substratum of plastic basaltic rock. "The source of the earth's short-period pulsations lies in the alternate accumulation and dissipation of the latent heat of fusion of basaltic material, fusion and expansion being followed in every cycle by consolidation and contraction. As fusion becomes general, the crust as a whole is heaved slowly outwards; but the continents sink a little in the substratum, and their lower levels thus come to be invaded by the transgressional seas. As consolidation supervenes, the outer crust has to settle down on the contracting interior, and the weaker rocks are folded and otherwise deformed like the skin of a withering apple. At longer intervals, involving perhaps six or seven of the basaltic cycles, the still deeper layers of the earth become fused and set up a similar process, though on a more extensive scale. To this the author refers the greater revolutions of earth history, marked by the crumpling, overthrusting, and uprising of great mountain ranges and accompanied by igneous activity on an exceptional scale." (Ibid., p. 50.)

CREATIVE EVOLUTION OF ANIMALS

Table P is taken in anticipation from the Major Work to illustrate the relationship of the various orders and species of animals to the geological periods during which they either originated or became especially prolific. The Algonkian strata of the Upper Pre-Cambrian, deposited during the 3rd Creation Day, are definitely fossiliferous and traces of worms, brachiopods, and trilobites (primitive crustaceans)

[1] Prof. Holmes reduces the figure of 600 m.y. to 500 m.y. in his book of 1937.

have been found in the Grand Cañon and New Brunswick strata, while the existence of graphite proves that plant life must have appeared by then. The Upper and Middle Pre-Cambrian strata are called Proterozoic in America and the Lower Pre-Cambrian are called Archæan or Archæozoic, though no convincing evidence has been adduced that the beginnings of life are to be reckoned prior to the Middle Pre-Cambrian.

Trilobites flourished and multiplied to a prodigious extent in the Cambrian period. Other animal fossils include radiolaria (protozoa), sponges, graptolites (hydrozoa) corals, annelids, brachiopods, starfish, snails, and cephalopods. The fauna of the Cambrian, Ordovician, and Silurian periods manifest a marked family resemblance. They differed largely from modern fauna in general and were highly diversified. The strata were deposited in shallow water, thanks to the uplifting of ocean beds effected by the Charnian and Killarnean revolutions. Even cracks made by the heat of the sun and pitted marks made by hail have been preserved. It is quite conceivable that the sun radiated heat long before it radiated light, for it did not become luminous until the Ordovician period, according to the Theory of Creation here advanced. It is true that our sun belongs to the category of the red dwarf stars which are in process of cooling down over periods of many millions of years but this does not preclude the possibility of intermittent bursts of activity during which the process might be reversed. The Cambrian strata in British Columbia are about 40,000 feet thick. The Ordovician and Silurian periods were originally included under one heading but were later separated in spite of Geikie's objections. It is a matter of choice whether we speak of the Upper Ordovician or Lower Silurian so close is their resemblance. The creatures which appeared in the Cambrian period are all present but elaborated and diversified. In addition we find insects in the strata of Sweden and Colorado and scorpions elsewhere. A revolution which might almost rank as a major one occurred in America between the Ordovician and Silurian periods. It is known as the Tacomic. During the Silurian period we still find corals, echinoderms, and brachiopods in abundance but polyzoa are less conspicuous than before.

In the Devonian period the formation of the Old Red Sandstone in Europe preserved for us a more complete record of flora and fauna than any deposit which preceded it. The most striking development in the animal kingdom was the great increase in the ganoid fishes, "the knights in shining armour." For this reason the Devonian period is called by common consent, "the Age of Fishes." Corals continue prolific, crinoids and echinodermata multiply but trilobites decrease in number though the mighty eurypterid is common and attains a length of 6 feet. The Devonian period marks the peak of brachiopodal activity but a gradual extinction of Silurian fauna is observable. Even the corals of the Devonian period differ from those of the Silurian. Myriapods, which are crustaceans together with orthopterous (such as locusts) and neuropterous insects are common in the Old Red Sandstone. The Carboniferous period, as the name implies, witnessed the creation of the bulk of the world's supplies of fuel, both solid and liquid, by the action of the sun's rays on decaying vegetation. It is usually taken as closing the Palæozoic Era with the Permian period acting as a bridge to the Mesozoic. It is true that the carboniferous strata contain only 2 per cent of coal but even this amount required vast quantities of vegetable matter to produce. It is hardly too much to say that the progress of civilisation has been largely dependent on the amount of fuel available for the inhabitants of cold and temperate climates, not only for domestic comfort but for industrial development. The climate was uniform in character, warm, and very moist. The highest type of life reached was amphibian, as illustrated by the extinct order of the Stegocephalia, salamander-like creatures reaching 8 feet in length. Corals and crinoids multiply and cover large areas of the ocean bed. Spiders make their first appearance and scorpions flourish in large numbers. There was a marked increase in size of many creatures, huge insects coming on the scenes with three pairs of wings and a 30 inch wing-span. A large brachiopod, *productus giganteus*, also belongs to this time. Molluscs too become much bigger and armoured sharks predominate among the fishes. The conditions were generally favourable for the preservation of fossils. The introduction of the Permian period was effected by mighty revolutions in the Old and New Worlds which brought about a titanic redistribution of continents and oceans. Two great land masses emerged as the result, which were divided by a continuous sea linking the Atlantic with the Pacific by way of the Mediterranean. The northern mass comprised North America, Northern Asia, and Europe, and the southern South America, India, Australia, and most of Africa. Geologists are of opinion that these cataclysmic changes were carried out on a universal scale within a comparatively brief space of time. The salient feature in the animal world was the appearance of reptiles in large numbers and many varieties but not of great size. New arachnids, crustaceans, and insects are found but corals remain of the Palæozoic type. We witness the advent of new dipnoi among fishes and larger amphibia such as *eryops megacephalus*. The atmosphere was evidently much drier in the Permian period than in the preceding one.

With the Triassic period we find ourselves fully launched into the life of the Mesozoic Era. The intercontinental sea known as Thetys still covers large tracts of Southern Asia and deposits oceanic Trias there. Reptile life registers a striking development in every respect. Ichthyosaurs, plesiosaurs, and giant land saurians such as the dinosaur appear for the first time, to be followed by the pterosaurs or winged-reptiles. Amphibians reached the peak of their development in the labyrinthodont. Turtles are found in two varieties but no snakes or lizards. The Jurassic rocks are in high favour with geologists because of their fossiliferous character and over 30 subdivisions have been made of them. During the early part of the Jurassic period one of the most formidable of the marine transgressions occurred, submerging large tracts of Europe and Southern Asia. A notable feature of the times was the commencement of the formation of climatic zones. Small and primitive mammals came into evidence during the Triassic period but made little progress in the

Jurassic. Articulata such as echinoderms become definitely Mesozoic and molluscs are found taking up whole strata. Modern types of sharks and rays appear though the ganoids still lead the way among the teleostome fishes. Many geologists regard the Jurassic period as marking the culminating point of reptilian development. Crocodiles, ichthyosaurs, and plesiosaurs abound together with huge pilosaurs, rendering the existence of fishes precarious in the extreme. The giant land-saurians were, however, mostly herbivorous and would have paid little attention to other animals. The hideous pterosaurs became if anything more numerous and revolting, and one mesozoic bird, the archæopteryx, entered into the picture. Cretaceous formations are remarkably well-developed in America, reaching a thickness of 46,000 feet in the West. The sea made further incursions during the Lower Cretaceous period, after which a general uprising of land surfaces occurred. All types of animal life increased in size and variety, with the exception of the mammalian. Molluscs, insects, fishes, and birds advanced apace and many bony fishes of a modern kind emerge on to the scene. A powerful carnivorous fish, the saurodont, is characteristic of the period and has fortunately not survived to modern times. Cephalopods, ichthyosaurs, and plesiosaurs attained to gigantic dimensions, some of the last named reaching a length of 50 feet. Carnivorous marine lizards made the lives of fishes more than hazardous and the pterosaurs developed a wing-span of as much as 20 feet. Birds with toothed beaks became common and the largest, *hesperornis*, was 6 feet in height.

With the Eocene subperiod of the Tertiary Period we enter the Cainozoic or "Modern Life" Era. Volcanic activity became far more pronounced than in any previous epoch and the architecture of the earth's crust as we know it now, with its great mountain ranges, was developed apace under the stress of the titanic forces unleashed by the Cascadian-Laramide and Alpine Revolutions. The climate of the world became much colder, so much so that the mesozoic monsters began to die out with rapidity. Marine, winged, and terrestrial they all vanished, leaving few fossil remains as mementoes of their unlovely presence on this planet. There is no need to enter into the varieties of animal forms which began to appear as the influences of the Tertiary period gained impetus. We are familiar with most of them to-day though some, such as the mammoth, the woolly rhinoceros, and the cave-tiger, have vanished.

If we now compare the Geological Table N with the Zoological Table Q, we observe striking correspondences from (18) to (13) inclusive. Below that one of the chief points to note is that Protozoa fall into compartment (25) which is that of the operative third of the 2nd Creation Day, between 780 and 720 m.y.s ago, and this is well within the Algonkian limits of fossiliferous strata. We cannot however deduce from the comparison of the two tables that the phyla from Anthozoa to Crustaceans made their appearance as indicated at first sight by the coincidences of compartments of the same number, for we find crustaceans in the form of trilobites in the upper Pre-Cambrian strata while they appear as thoroughly acclimatised and multiplying themselves apace in the Cambrian period (21). In short, the lowest members of the highest phyla below the fishes make their début very early in the history of organic life. When we reach the Fishes of the Devonian period we come within the orbit of the Fundamental Processes, for these creatures exhibit the characteristic features of Impulse as it appears in animals in a striking manner. Fishes are dominated by the sense of Intensive Taste in its positive aspect for there is not much that nauseates them. They mostly seem to be the victims of chronic hunger or it may be that they make a cult of voracity. It is said that the shark is never satisfied. Impulse leads inevitably to Contest and the fish is in such a hurry to swallow a dainty morsel before any other fish can get it that it can hardly enjoy its food much. Its appetite is rapacious and as soon as it has swallowed one morsel it looks out for another. One has only to realise how completely different is the mental attitude of the Reptiles towards food to appreciate the degree to which the Fishes are slaves to their appetites. In the matter of reproductiveness which is effected by the sexual appetite the fish leads the way. When Jacob blessed Ephraim and Manasseh he expressed the desire that their descendants should multiply like fishes in the midst of the earth. Frogs and Toads manifest the particular aspect of Hedonism (17) that appears as self-inflation, which in the world of thought and aspiration translates itself into impracticable idealism. The frog combines something of the lethargy of the reptile with the impulsiveness of the fish for it enjoys taking prodigious leaps after resting without having the remotest idea where it is going to land. Again the progress of civilisation is bound up with the attachment of great importance to clothes, especially by women, and fashions usually revolve round batrachian puffings and inflations of one kind or another. Even men are not above going in for padding to improve their figures. It was doubtless partly the historic fondness of the French for inflated garments which led the English to compare them to frogs. Serpents and crocodiles, on the other hand, are canny, calculating creatures, who, however lethargic they may appear, have usually an eye to the main chance. They are individualists by nature however much they may herd together under the compulsion of natural surroundings, as in the case of crocodiles. The deliberation of the tortoise is proverbial. The wisdom of the serpent, which has been a byword in the East for thousands of years, largely consists in its capacity for exercising rigid self-restraint until the moment has come for it to strike effectively. With the Dragons of (15) we come to an order of creatures unrecognised by zoologists, although evolutionists are never tired of asserting that birds ascended from reptiles by the process of generation. In that case one would expect to find multitudes of missing links whereas, beyond revealing the presence on earth of pterosaurs for 50 million years or so, fossils furnish no examples of intermediate types. We may however class as dragons the countless sea-serpents of whose existence since the earliest of times we have abundant evidence. There are insistent traditions in India of the existence in that country of gigantic snakes which caught elephants and sucked their blood, indicating that they were warm-blooded. The Chinese Wingless Dragon is a heraldic representation of an animal which the people of China say was once fairly common in their country. Of all mythical monsters the fiery flying serpent has the biggest weight of testimony to prove its one-time existence. Josephus says that the deserts between Egypt and Ethiopia in the days of Moses could not be traversed because of the number of "saraphs" which inhabited them. Large parts of Arabia had to be vacated by human beings for the same reasons. If the saraphs which attacked the Israelites in the Wilderness had been wingless they would easily have been disposed of with sticks. Pliny visited Arabia to investigate the stories which he had heard concerning the deadly nature of saraphs but as they had been largely exterminated all he saw were their bones. So-called mythical animals such as basilisks, wyverns, cockatrices, and hippogriffs may have some foundation in fact though invested with an element of the marvellous by popular tradition.[1] Experienced native hunters in Central Africa state positively that a snake exists there which crows like a cock. Then there is the gigantic cattle-thieving swamp-boa of the Great Lakes called the lukwata by native hunters whose booming cry has been heard by many responsible Europeans. But though we have no materials for assessing the psychology of dragons there is no difficulty in estimating their effect on the psychology of the people of the Middle Ages. The dragon with two wings and four legs is of course a zoological anachronism but leaving that out of account there was a glamour about it which made it a figure of public interest. There is no doubt that it had an eye for beauty and gave full-time employment to gallant knights who preferred to win their brides at the point of the lance to adopting more prosaic methods. We have all the familiar Venusian atmosphere surrounding the dragon and romance was the loser by his extinction. The symbolism of birds is bound up with principle (14) which is associable with the ideas of the wind, flight, swift movement, vitality conjoined with those of ephemeral lightness and absence of permanent solidity. Finally we reach the mammals of (13) which with the exception of the sea-mammals have mostly four legs which enable them to stand firmly and move about without undue risk of falling over. They convey to us precisely those conceptions of fixation and perpetual contact with solid earth which is lacking in birds.

CREATIVE EVOLUTION OF PLANTS

The most striking feature about the evolution of Plants (Table R) is the extent to which it lagged behind that of animals, which is easily accounted for by the theory that the sun did not become an active source of light until the working part of the 4th Day which coincides with the Ordovician period. Up to that time plants would have been entirely dependent upon the solar luminosity light which was created on the 1st Day. Very few fossils of plants belong to the Cambrian period and

[1] A marine creature answering to the Egyptian conception of the hippogriff was seen and described by independent observers at Weymouth and Portsmouth during 1945-46.

not many more to the Ordovician but ferns are definitely identifiable in the Silurian, while gigantic seaweeds are known to have grown on the ocean beds in that period. The whole scene changes, however, when we come to the Devonian period by which time the sun would have been able to get into its stride, so to speak. Vegetation is now found to be luxuriant as if the plants had been touched by a magic wand. Ferns, calamites, mosses and horsetails abound and even a few gymnosperms can be found among them. In the Carboniferous period these are supplemented by cycads and coniferæ in abundance, the resinous pines being especially valuable for conversion into coal measures. One thing is quite certain, namely that the sun must have become a source of intense heat and light before coal could have been produced and deposited. The moist damp climate of the Palæozoic Era would have been eminently favourable to the development of the chemical fermentation necessary to convert vegetable matter into coal and oil. In the Permian period the cordaiteæ and lycopods which swarmed in the Carboniferous period are unrepresented, but tree-ferns, cycads, and conifers increase and multiply. Conditions remain much the same in the plant-world during the Triassic and the Jurassic periods. Primitive Angiosperms appear in the early Cretaceous period but later on palm trees and forest trees are found in abundance and the flora generally asume a modern character. With the advent of the Ternary period mesozoic flora vanished like mesozoic fauna.

Creative Evolution of Man

No human remains have been of earlier date than the Pliocene subperiod and if we seek for any further information about the origin of man we must turn to the 2nd Book of Dzyan which deals with Anthropogenesis and the advent of a succession of Basic Races up to five. A Shadow or Pattern Race appears to have been formed on the 1st Day during the working third of it, which was followed by the 1st or Polarian Basic Race on the 2nd Day (Upper Pre-Cambrian), the 2nd or Hyperborean Basic Race on the 3rd Day (Upper Pre-Cambrian), the 3rd or Lemurian Basic Race on the 4th Day (Ordovician), the 4th or Atlantean Basic Race on the 5th Day (Permian) and the 5th or Himalayan Basic Race on the 6th Day (Tertiary). The Book of Dzyan only refers to these races by the ordinal numbers and gives them no names. Since only 4 of the 7 Branch Races of the 5th Basic Race appeared during the Tertiary period and the remainder belong to the Quaternary, we must apply the same principle to the preceding Basic Races, which means that the 2nd half of the Lemurian Basic Race belongs to the Silurian and Devonian periods, in which reproduction by two sexes as it functions at present commenced both among human beings and animals, the symbolic number of which is (18), *vide* Table H. The Book of Dzyan is explicit about the fact that man had not developed to a point at which he was able to reproduce his kind sexually until the 2nd half of the Lemurian race, and it was not until then that the incarnating egos from above were willing to take up their abode in the bodies of humanity. Following the same lines the 2nd half of the Atlantean Basic Race must be associated with the Triassic and Jurassic periods. The Atlanteans were the first to be given a fully organised animal soul. After that the 1st half of the 5th Basic Race were given a fully-organised mind or mental soul (concrete mind) early in the Tertiary period and the 2nd half were given a fully-organised spirit (abstract mind) in the Quaternary period. Apes and monkeys originated from degenerate Lemurians of the 1st half of the race. Perfect man in the physical sense did not appear until the 6th Day when the 1st half of the Himalayan Basic Race were formed. The Atlanteans were the first to acquire speech. (Stanza ix, 4). The 1st or Polarian Basic Race is said to have been extoplasmic while the 2nd or Hyperborean Race was made of solid matter, as we know it, but spongy. The 3rd or Lemurian Race was the first to be provided with hardened bones. Stanza VIII, 2, reads, "Animals with bones, dragons of the deep, and flying sarpas (reptiles) were added to the creeping things. They that creep on the ground got wings. They of the long necks in the water (sea-serpents) became the progenitors of the fowls of the air." And VIII, 3, "During the Third (Race) the boneless animals grew and changed, they became animal with bones, their chhayas (ectoplasmic or spongy bodies) became solid." This reads as if the Reptiles were contemporaneous with the 3rd or Lemurian Race but according to the geological record they did not appear until the Permian period,[1] which agrees with the account of Genesis placing the creation of the monsters of the deep on the 5th Day. The general character of the Atlanteans of the Left was reptilian and draconian, judging by tradition, for they were bellicose, domineering, inflated with pride, and addicted to the worst forms of black magic. They were the prototypes of the Titans of Greek legend. The whole subject of the Races is however complicated by the fact that it is often impossible to know whether Theosophists or Rosicrucians who discuss them are referring to the Basic Races or to Branches of the 5th Basic Race. Since the latter recapitulate the former they have been given the same names, so that we have a Polarian Race which appeared on the 2nd Day in the Middle Pre-Cambrian period confused with a Polarian Race which appeared on the 6th Day during the Eocene subperiod. It is highly unlikely that the latter was made of ectoplasm and looked like a bag as the former did. The term Root Race is often used and on the whole it is best to apply this term to the Branches of the 5th Himalayan Race. For practical purposes we may say that the 1st Root Race appeared early in the Eocene subperiod, the 2nd in the Oligocene subperiod, the 3rd in the Miocene, the 4th in the Pliocene, and the 5th early in the Quaternary period in the Pleistocene subperiod. Each of these Root Races was divided into 7 Subraces but in the case of the 5th or Aryan Root Race only 5 subraces have been fully manifested so far, though the Adamic is the forerunner of the 6th and many 7th subrace types are on earth at the present time, especially in California.

---

[1] Occultists maintain that reptiles appeared in the Devonian period but they were probably pioneer types.

Another question on which orthodox theosophical teaching appears unsatisfactory relates to the periods of time assigned to the Rounds, that is the Seven Revolutions of the Life Wave round the Seven Globes. The whole subject bristles with difficulties and pitfalls and gives more headaches to students of Theosophy than any other branch of the science. We are, however, here concerned solely with the question of time-periods and not with the precise nature and purpose of the revolutions. First of all it should be made clear that there is an interval of rest between rounds and it is by no means certain as to how long this interval is calculated as lasting, but since a complete Chain Period coincides with a Cosmic Day of 12 hours we should expect a Round or Revolution to coincide with a Cosmic half-hour, that is with a Creation Day of 12 hours. Now it is highly probable that the active period of the 4th Round began on the 6th Day when the 5th Basic Race appeared and the passage of the Life Wave through the Seven Globes is reflected in the appearance of the Seven successive Root Races. Reasoning backwards it would seem certain that the active period of the 1st Round began during the last third of the 3rd Day when the 2nd Basic Race made its appearance. Yet many competent theosophists start the 2nd Round during the 2nd Preparatory Day, thus rendering all coincidence with the history both of the Basic Races and the Root Races impossible. A convenient rule of thumb is 1st Round—2nd Race—3rd Day, all three of which in the Involutionary Scheme of the Key Table are located in compartment (14). Now the 1st Round is the equivalent in a cosmic hour to the 1st Chain Period in a Cosmic Day and it is agreed that during the latter the Sense of Hearing was developed in its essential nature, from which it appears probable that the literal sense organ of the ear was developed archetypally during the 3rd Day in the 2nd Basic Race, and this belongs to (14) *vide* Table M. Similarly the eyes were developed archetypally in the 3rd Basic Race during the 4th Day when the sun and moon, the two Eyes of the Sky, were illuminated with the result that their light would tend to stimulate the spots on the skin most sensitive to light. Following the same line of thought the sense of smell, which is keen in Reptiles, was developed archetypally in the 4th or Atlantean Basic Race and the sense of taste is now being perfected in the 5th or Himalayan Basic Race. It is eminently fitting that the Life Wave should first have been openly manifested towards the close of the 3rd Creation Day and at the end of the Proterozoic Era when we have proof positive of the appearance of animal and plant life on this planet. (5) and (14) are essential Life numbers whereas (4) and (13) relate rather to form.

ANALYSIS OF THE COSMIC DAY

An analysis of the Cosmic Day on an Involutionary basis is shown on Table P. The primary division of the 24 hours of the Night-Day will naturally be into a Night and a Day of 12 hours each but the division into 3 groups of 8 hours should not be overlooked since at 10 a.m. the Seven Revolutions of the Life Stream round the Seven Globes of our Earth System began, of which the outcome was the appearance of the

Basic Races in which incarnations began. According to the 1st Book of Dzyan the Deity slumbered during the Cosmic Night for 7 Eternities. Since the Cosmic night consists of 8 Eternities of 270 m.y. each and it is probable that the 8th Eternity should be placed after the hour of awakening we may take it that the Deity became active about 4.30 a.m. of the Cosmic Day. The theory that our earth was in any sense created in the early hours of the present Cosmic Day or that it was cast off from a molten sun to cool down at say 4.30 a.m. is rejected because for one thing it is contradicted by the evidence of the radio-active rocks which give dates far older than the B.Q. 1,710 m.y. which corresponds with 4.30 a.m. The planets including our earth were probably brought into being on the Fourth Cosmic Creative Day when the stars became luminous, which is about 10,000 m.y. ago, so that we need not trouble ourselves about problems connected with cooling down from a molten state. For present purposes we may assume, in the absence of evidence to the contrary, that the 1st Preparatory Stage starting from 6 a.m. of the Cosmic Day may be taken as marking the opening events of the 2nd Book of Dzyan. These were initiated by the Earth Spirit asking the Solar Logos or possibly the Solar Regent for inhabitants and receiving the reply that she must first get rid of three useless strata, presumably igneous, and create seven new ones. Judging from Stanza II, 1 these operations took 300 m.y. (30 crores) to complete, that is from B.Q. 1,440 m.y. (6 a.m.) to B.Q. 1,140 (7.40), so that the strata in existence were all Lower and Middle Pre-Cambrian. Then about 7.40 a.m. the Earth Spirit produced a brood of horrible monstrosities which were destroyed before 8 a.m. after having been in existence say 50 m.y. 8 a.m. corresponds with B.Q. 1,080. The allocation of the 7 Days of Genesis to compartments (12) to (18) is in accordance with the symbolism of numbers as applicable to the character of the work performed on the 6 days. There is nothing whatever in the foregoing scheme which conflicts with the evidence supplied by the radio-activity of rocks although these give dates of origin as far back as 2,000 m.y. ago while Prof. Paneth of Durham University has assigned an age of 7,000 m.y. to some meteorites. It is possible that the whole process of radio-activity remains in abeyance during a Cosmic Night, so that the total age of a meteorite might be 7,000 m.y. plus 2 Cosmic Nights, that is over 11,300 years.

Objections to Duration of Rounds Considered

Theosophists will naturally expect good reasons to be given for making the time-periods of the three completed Rounds about half what tradition makes them, and certainly the writer has no desire to challenge traditional interpretations unless they present insuperable difficulties. The orthodox view is set forth with lucidity by Miss E. W. Preston in a short book called *The Earth and Cycles*, in which she works closely with the time-cycles and revolutions as given by Prof. Arthur Holmes in *The Age of the Earth*. Miss Preston takes the traditional duration of one Chain Period of Seven Rounds as 4,320 m.y. and that of one Round to be 617 m.y. Starting from the traditional date of the origin of the earth accepted by Theosophists, viz B.Q. 2,000 m.y., and taking it as the opening date of the 1st Round she gives the dates of the beginnings of the 2nd, 3rd, and 4th Rounds, as B.Q. 1,250, 640, and 50 m.y., making quite reasonable adjustments to enable the initial date of the 3rd Round to fit in with that of the Killarnean Revolution and that of the 4th Round to fit in with that of the Alpine-Laramide Revolution. This is making the period of each Round equal to approximately 3½ Creation Days of 180 m.y. each. Now 4 Rounds have yet to be completed, commencing from B.Q. 50 or 60 m.y. which must on the foregoing lines occupy 4 times 617 m.y., that is 2,468 m.y. in all, or say 2,400 m.y. from the beginning of the Quaternary period which commenced on the 7th Sabbath Day at 2 p.m. of the Cosmic Day. In this case, according to the time-scale of Table P, the 7th Round will not expire till 3.20 a.m. of the next Cosmic Day. But what use is there for any Rounds at all during a Cosmic Night? The commencements of the Rounds should coincide with Major Revolutions, but even if we work to this by making each Round equal to two Creation Days and start the 1st Round in the 2nd Preparatory Day at 7.40 a.m. the 7th Round will not expire till 9.40 p.m. and the whole of it will fall in the early part of the Cosmic Night. It is evident that Miss Preston is reckoning on a 12-hour Day of 4,320 m.y. which is the traditional time-span of a "Day of Brahma." Mme. Blavatsky stated that the 4th Round started 300 m.y. ago, which would be at the beginning of the Carboniferous period and would include the whole of the Mesozoic Era. If we make the Creation Day 360 m.y. instead of 180 m.y. then it is impossible to work in with the time-scale of geological strata supplied by the radio-active rocks. If we continue with the method of starting the 1st Round on the 3rd Creation Day at 10.40 a.m. then the 7th Round will expire at 5.40 p.m. just 20 minutes (60 m.y.) before the end of the Cosmic Day.

The 7 Chains and the 7 Rounds have been called the Saturn, the Sun, the Moon, the Earth, the Jupiter, the Venus, and the Vulcan for reasons which have never been satisfactorily explained, and indeed cannot be until it is realised that by some mischance the 1st Chain and the 1st Round, as ordinarily described, constitute an amalgamation of 2 Chains and 2 Rounds. Let us confine our attention to Rounds alone for simplicity, since what applies to them applies also to the Saturn Chains. If the Rounds were named according to the order given in Table J, they would be called after Mercury, Venus, Mars, Minerva, and Jupiter, but after that one would have to revert to Venus and Mercury, in fact one really ought to turn back after the Earth Round to indicate that involution had given place to evolution. Now by no possible jugglery with symbolism can Saturn be associated with Mercury of (14) but he can and has been associated with Vulcan of (13) for when the Greeks and Egyptians correlated their deities for ritual and initiation purposes they worked up from Aphrodite and Hermes to Kronos whom they substituted for Ptah or Hephæstus.[1] Again it is said that the 2nd

[1] Here Mercury stands for the Atmic Sphere or World of Divine Spirit, and Saturn for the Nirvanic Sphere.

Basic Race obtained the archetypal senses of pineal sight (or feel) and hearing during the 1st Round but the former sense belongs to (13) *vide* Table M. Thirdly the 7th Round called Vulcan appears to by-pass Mercury in ascending from Venus, which is highly improbable. Hence the conclusion is inevitable that the so-called 1st Round is really a Double Round. The Rounds are virtually Life Waves of which the 1st was poured out during the 2nd Preparatory Day and misused in producing an abortive creation. The 2nd Life Wave was poured out on the 1st Creation Day to Produce the Shadow Race and the 3rd Life Wave on the 2nd Creation Day to produce the 1st Basic Race. We may perhaps correlate these three Rounds with invisible white planets. One can see one reason why Saturn was put into Vulcan's compartment, namely to have different names to distinguish between the involutionary and evolutionary Rounds of (13). Similarly one might introduce Uranus into the Mercury compartment (14) to distinguish the involutionary round from the evolutionary. For the same reason the Sun was introduced into the Venus compartment (15) to describe the involutionary Round and differentiate it from the evolutionary. The 3rd Round was called that of the Moon because Lunar influences were powerful during its passage. The Moon belongs to compartment (20) which is diagrammatically below (16). Similarly the 4th Round was called that of the Earth because its compartment (21) is diagrammatically below that of Minerva. What will be said further on concerning the Four Watches of Brahma confirms the belief that two Rounds have been amalgamated in the 1st for it is connected with (13) as being a Night of Brahma and the 3rd Round is connected with the Lunar Pitris as belonging to the Twilight of Brahma, but in between we must have rounds to correspond with the Dawn of Brahma (14) and the Day of Brahma (15).

There is a further complication about the Rounds which should be referred to at this juncture, because it affects the Seven Globes, A, B, C, D, E, F, and G, which are traversed in a round. These can only be numbered (14), (15), (16), (17), (16), (15), (14) in the case of the Saturn Chain because its own number is (14) and this fixes the number of the first globe. In the case of our present Cosmic Day whose number is (17), the numbers of the globes are (17), (18), (19), (20), (19), (18), and (17) which means that the 1st and the 7th globes are on the Lower Mental Sphere and the 4th or lowest is on the Lower Physical Sphere, which is the lowest plane reached in all the Planetary Chains.

The evolutionary history of the Seven Basic Races is shown on Table P. (i) and conforms to the organisation of the Eight Worlds of the Ovoid of Eternal Nature or World-egg and not to the 12 Spheres. At 4.50 p.m. the Crown Race which will summarise the preceding 7 Basic Races will enter into the Seventh Heaven, and the Great Day "Be with Us," that is with the Seven Flames or Planetary Logoi, will begin (1st Book of Dzyan. Stanza VII, 7). The Life History of a Basic Race, taking into account "invisible life waves" is about 80 m.y., and since these life waves started about B.Q. 50 m.y. in the case of the 5th Root Race its Life History will continue till A.Q. 30 m.y. It will continue for another

GEOLOGY AND THE GENESIS STORY OF CREATION

90 m.y. before the 6th Basic Race appears but just dragging out its existence without any new impulses energising it.

The Story of Genesis

Many scientists seem to go out of their way to stress the incompatibility of the account given in Genesis of the creation of the solar system, man, and animals with the findings of geologists. But most of the difficulties raised by them do not prove formidable upon examination. The work of the 1st Day is said to have been the creation of light, a diffused gentle luminosity emanated by the sun which may have been of the same character as the zodiacal light or the light of haloes. If science cannot prove that such a light was created at a remote epoch in the past it has no data whatever to enable it to prove that such a light was not created. The work of the 2nd Day was to arrange the ocean of cloudland, the atmosphere, the surface of the waters, and the earth in four layers with horizontal planes as boundaries, in accordance with the known law of gravity. Science has no adequate ground whatever for questioning the possibility of this creative act or connected series of acts. The work of the 3rd Day, performed towards the close of the Upper Pre-Cambrian period, was to raise an unspecified area of land from beneath the surface of the ocean, and it was at this time that the tremendous Charnian Revolution of the Old World and the Killarnean Revolution of the New took place, the ascertained results of which are known to every geologist, of which the chief were the raising of continents above sea-level. Thus geological science so far from denying the work of the 3rd Day confirms it. But according to Genesis plant life appeared later on in the 3rd Day while no mention is made of the existence of primitive forms of animal life, though on the other hand the fact of their existence, as proved by geology, is not denied and when the first mention is made of the appearance of animals on the 5th Day only relatively advanced types such as reptiles and pterosaurs are mentioned (winged fowl, not feathered fowl), leaving one to infer that the inferior types were already in existence. The fact that a specified kind of creative work was done on a specific Day does not exclude the possibility of other creative work having been performed on the same Day. The work of the 4th Day was to illuminate the sun, moon, and planets. The Hebrews had only one word for stars and planets and consequently one cannot reasonably say that Genesis i, 14-19 asserts the creation of the stars of the firmament on the 4th Day. As already mentioned, the reptiles, which include many monsters of the deep, appeared in the Permian period during the working part of the 5th Day, but on the other hand pterosaurs even of the primitive mesozoic type did not appear until the Triassic period which coincides with the early evening of the 6th Day. It is however quite legitimate to regard a new creative impetus having been given on the last third of one Creation Night-Day and working out its consequence during the first third of the next Creation Night-Day. The geological record, though it speaks unmistakably of the occurrence of four Major Revolutions in the Old and New Worlds, does not give one the impression that evolution proceeded by fits and starts, such as 60 m.y. of creative activity followed by 120 m.y. of quiescence and inactivity which is disproved by the minor revolutions. Again the specific work of certain Creation Days seems to have been anticipated, for small primitive mammals appeared in the Triassic period, though the large modern mammals with which we are familiar were created on the 6th Day in the Tertiary period. Man as we know him to-day as represented by the 5th root race appeared on earth during the latter part of the 6th Day. From this we may infer that Gen. i, 26-28 applies only to perfected man, complete in spirit, soul, and body.

The question may be asked here as to what may be expected to happen during the remaining three hours of the Cosmic Day following upon the completion of the 7th Day? The Scriptures are silent on the subject but the Puranas give an account of the creative work performed on the first six creative days in their own peculiar idiom and predict the nature of the work to be performed during four other days yet to come, that is from 3 p.m. to 6 p.m. of the Cosmic Day.

Theosophical Commentaries on Gen. I

A few theosophical and Rosicrucian commentaries have been published on the Creation Story of Gen. i, but their value is largely discounted by the fact that they fail to discriminate between the work performed on the six Creation Night-Days of 180 m.y. and the corresponding Cosmic Night-Days which are 24 times as lengthy, since each Creation Day is equal to one hour of a Cosmic Day. In two or three commentaries the work performed on the 4th Cosmic Day, namely that of illuminating the universes of stars, is described as if it had been performed on the 4th Creation Day, which was completed as regards its work about 400 m.y. ago instead of about 8,650 m.y. ago. Astronomers would be prepared to give the latter figure serious consideration in this connection whereas they would treat the former with derision. This estimate is based on the assumption that we are now nearing the end of the 6th Cosmic Creation Day, which is the 8th if we take into account the two Preparatory Cosmic Days. The Cosmic Days are arranged in groups of four watches, each group consisting of an Evening, Night, Dawn, and Day of Brahma. In view of the fact that the 1st Preparatory Day of the present series of Creation Days began at 6 a.m. it is reasonable to suppose that the 1st Preparatory Cosmic Day was a Dawn-watch of Brahma, whence it follows that the present 8th Cosmic Day is a Night-watch of Brahma. (8) and (17) are numbers associated with the perfecting of form and with the colour green which predominates in vegetation on the earth's surface. They are connected with civilisation, good taste, and humanitarian idealism as well as with Man, the Thinker, using his concrete mind. The two highest globes of the seven are situated in the region of concrete thoughts. (8) or twice (4) sets forth the objectivity of the 4 Elements.

In concluding the subject of Geology it is of interest to draw attention to the manifestation of the influence of centricity and foundational strength in the periods and strata of the central column III. The fundamental features and characteristics of the earth's crust as it exists to-day were determined by the Charnian and Killarnean Revolutions, the work of the 3rd Creation Day, which was extended and rounded off in the Cambrian period, in which the forces of (22) developed their architectural consequences in (21), to use the language of the Diagram. Towards the close of the Cambrian period many of the deposits were elevated to a very marked degree. We find no particular evidence of structural consolidation in the Carboniferous period but it was then that the true wealth of the earth was created in the form of solid, liquid, and gaseous fuels upon which the foundations of material civilisation rest far more than on gold, which man industriously digs out and extracts from one part of the earth in order to bury in another. Having effected this masterpiece of chemical transformation the Palæozoic Era passed away to give place to the intriguing but relatively fluidic Mesozoic Era. Permanent consolidation and the introduction of the modern world-order set in once more with Alpines and Cascadian Laramide Revolutions which to some extent repeated on the 6th Day the initial work of the 3rd. We may regard the Quaternary period as giving architectural finish to the structural changes accomplished in the Tertiary just as the Cambrian period finished off those of the 3rd Day. The Alpine Revolution created a home for the Alpine Race which is the central ethnological axis and pivot of the various branches of the human race.

THE GREAT PYRAMID

The bearing of the Great Pyramid upon Geology may not appear obvious at first sight but can easily be demonstrated. The passage from Tertiary Period to the Quaternary was of the nature of an evolutionary ascent from the Four to the Three, from the Cube to the Pyramid. The Quaternary period witnessed the operation of forces which gave the surface of the earth its existing architectural finish and it would seem that after the Adamic Race had lived on the earth for about 1,000 years or so the project for building the Great Pyramid as a memorial to Creation was set on foot. According to tradition the design of the Great Pyramid was given to Enoch by revelation and before he was removed from the earth in or about 3,021 B.C. he communicated it to others whom he charged to take the needful steps to put the project into effect. For reasons which have not been clear, however, the plan remained in abeyance for some time and the Pyramid was not completed until exactly 400 years later in 2,622 B.C. in the reign of the Pharaoh Khufu who died the same year. Only the Sethite Race could have produced architects capable of superintending such a gigantic work but Egypt was able to furnish numbers of efficient stonemasons and quarrymen and unlimited unskilled labour. It is said that no slave labour was employed but that all those who took part in the work of construction gave their services as an act of thankfulness to the Almighty. No modern scientist can offer any explanation as to how such an astounding structure came to be erected without Divine revelation and aid. Leaving out of account all mystical and prophetic interpretations of the design and dimensions, the amount of accurate information conveyed to the modern world by this building in regard to units of measurement and astronomical and geographical facts is bewildering in its variety. Mr. D. Davidson has written a monumental work on the subject and of recent years the Rev. Adam Rutherford has published several books on it which can be readily understood without much knowledge of mathematics, mensuration, or engineering.

SIXTH BRANCH-RACE OF FIFTH ROOT-RACE

It would seem rather early for any true Sixth Root-Race Egos to appear, since according to the time-scale adopted in this chapter they are not due for another 120 m.y. Theosophists teach that 5 Branch-races or Subraces of the 5th Root-Race have so far appeared of which the following is a list with the approximate dates of their advents:— Aryan, 75,000 B.C.; Arabian, 35,000 B.C.; Persian, 30,000 B.C.; Celtic, 20,000 B.C.; and Teutonic, 20,000 B.C. So it looks as if the 6th Subrace were long overdue whether we identify it with the Anglo-Saxons or not. Ethnologically the name of Anglo-Saxon is meaningless unless it is taken to denote an offshoot of the Teutonic subrace, but the origin of the most important of the racial ingredients in the British People is that of the Brits of Phœnicia, known to Hindus as the Barats in the "Mahabharata." Now these Barats were stated to be akin to the Kurus or Syrians whom the Hebrews recognised as descendants of Abraham's third wife, Keturah, whose second son was named Sur (Josephus. *Antiquities*). Hence the British or Building Race of Pyramid symbolism are racially of the Seed of Abraham, and therefore of Adamic stock through Shem and Noah. Theosophists have shown themselves strangely indifferent to the historical event of the appearance of the Family of Adam about 6,000 years ago, and treat the Book of Genesis as if it were totally unreliable in its ethnological statements and datings. Prof. Sayce was of opinion that the entire White Race was descended from Adam but leaving out of account all questions of colour there is no doubt that about 6,000 years ago a race appeared which in scientific knowledge was far ahead of any contemporary race. It is true that Enoch deplored the communication of most of this knowledge to mankind, as he said that it emanated from 200 Archangels (Beni-Elohim or Watchers) who descended to earth in the days of Jared and cohabited with certain Sethite women (between 3,548 and 3,386 B.C.). But whatever the source of the knowledge possessed by the Sethites, good came out of evil, for without it the Sethites could not have built the Great Pyramid. Archæologists have traced the origins of civilisation to Chinese Turkestan and, as Davidson has shown in his *Connected History of Early Egypt, Babylonia, and Central Asia* (Chart 23), a cross-section of the Tarim Basin looking west shows a most remarkable resemblance to the conceptions of the world by the Chaldeans and Egyptians as depicted diagrammatically by Maspero. This Basin was flooded out by the Deluge of 2,352 B.C. when the "Forty Cities of the Takla Makan" were destroyed. But the Sethites appear to have spread themselves over the chief centres of existing civilisation long before that, perhaps as early as 3,000 B.C., and according to some were the prototypes of the mysterious Kabiri who were worshipped in Samothrace for about three centuries B.C. The name Kabiri is supposed to be Phœnician and to mean, "Mighty Ones." According to Sanchoniathon the main Cainite line settled in Phœnicia.

The question then arises as to how we should regard the Shemites and other races sprung from Adam in regard to the preceding 5 Aryan Subraces. The first thing to realise is that race names are perpetuated independently of generation and persist over long periods of time like place names. The Aryan Root Race sprang from the Original Shemites who were the 5th subrace of the Atlantean Root-Race and Noah may well have named his eldest son after the Original Shem. It is unlikely that the languages of the Sethites differentiated until after the Deluge, at any rate the story of the scattering of the Builders of Babel is clear on that point, and therefore the Aryan languages spoken to-day represent the original speech of the sons of Japhet, but the descendants of these sons, of whom there were seven, may well have taken the name of Aryan through intermarrying with the pre-Adamite race of that name. So also the Cymri and Gaels who were descended from Gomer and known as the Gimirru to the Assyrians, may well have taken the name of Celt. Arabia is not mentioned by that name in the Bible and was certainly given to the tract now known by that name by the 2nd subrace of the 5th Root-Race. The Teutons were originally sons of Magog according to Swedish tradition and the latter may have taken the name from pre-Adamite Teutons of the 5th subrace. So also we may assume that the sons of Madai intermarried with Iranians of the 3rd subrace. It is common knowledge that the Muscovites are descended from Meshech and the Thracians from Tiras. Ion (*cp.* Ionians) is practically the same word as Javan. The Tubalites settled in Iberia, the modern Georgia, and from them came the Cossacks of the Steppes who conquered Siberia and from whom the Siberian Russians are largely sprung. Meshech and Tubal were in brief the ancestors of the Western and Eastern Slavs. According to the information given in *The Little Genesis*, concerning the division of the then-known world among the sons of Noah, Madai was allotted an area in Europe, probably the vast tract of ancient Lithuania, but a large section of the Madai migrated eastwards to Persia. Rama was apparently a Lithuanian priest who followed the latter and founded two great kingdoms in Persia and India. The Prussians, Poles and Western Russians include large ingredients of Lithuanian origin. The Adamic Race, the 6th Branch-race of the 5th Root-Race, foreshadows the 6th Root-Race of which it is the forerunner. Now it is generally agreed that the seat of the consciousness of the 6th Root-Race will be Buddhi, the 4th Heaven, and as such it will be intuitive. The Adamic Race, especially the Shemite branch, possesses a "heart-conscience" which produces a much more elevated moral sense than that possessed by the first five Branch-races of the 5th Root-Race, which reveals itself in its conceptions of Law, Ethics, and Religion. It is in terms of colour-psychology the Indigo-Purple-Violet Race. Buddhic consciousness confers supremacy in the sphere of the arts and in the intuitive perception of the inner meaning of the same. As already mentioned the representatives of the 1st half of the 7th Branch-race, which is of course Adamite, take naturally to the Iranian religious conceptions as formulated by Zarathustra but probably established in the first instance by Rama. The representatives of the 2nd half of the 7th Branch-race on the other hand are attracted by Esoteric Buddhism, Hinduism, Theosophy, and Rosicrucianism. The Christians of these two divisions of the 7th Branch-race are organised as "The White Knights" and the "Order of Melchizedek." Both claim that their orders have a remote origin, and are supervised by exalted Beings. They are in sympathy with each other. The second is however by far the most numerous and powerful.

CHAPTER XI

ANALYSIS OF STATIONARY ENGINES

See TABLE S

THE analogies furnished by the working parts of stationary engines are so fertile in their suggestiveness that a classification of them on a systematic basis is well worth making. There are two chief kinds of heat engines used to generate power, the steam-engine and the internal combustion engine, both as it were constructed symbolically round their respective fuels, coal and fire (19) and (18) and liquid and vapourised petrol and producer gas (20) and (16). Both require admixture of air (14) to enable them to develop their fuel-power to a maximum. The analysis will be carried out on the following lines:—(10) Controls. (11) Gauges. (12) Brake. (13) Flywheel and Governor. (14) Draught and Carburettor. (15) Cylinder, Piston, Valves. (16) Main Steam Pipe. Feed from Carburettor to Explosion Chamber. (17) Boiler. Explosion Chamber. (18) Furnace. Magneto Ignition. (19) Coal. Fuel Oil. (20) Petrol spirit. Alcohol. Producer gas. (21) Condenser. (22) Silencer.

(10) CONTROLS

The controls obviously belong to the governing compartment (10) together with the Brain and the Hand. Directive power flows from the brain to the hand or foot and is applied by one or the other to the lever, switch, or wheel which operates the control to be applied. Steering can be left out of account since we are confining our attention to stationary engines and in any case steering-gear is a chassis and not an engine control. Voluntary controls can be applied to operate brakes, forced draught, petrol supercharger, petrol mixture, feed of mixture to explosion chamber, steam-escape valve, ignition of furnace, mechanical stoking or fuel oil feeding, and magneto-ignition. Every machine is designed to effect some purpose and unless its action is designedly automatic requires operation by an intelligent individual who employs hands or feet or perhaps both in the process, so that we have come to speak of a mechanic as a hand. There is a saying that bad workmen quarrel with their tools and it is equally true that an inefficient driver or mechanic will sooner or later quarrel with his engine or machine however efficient it may be. Controls are themselves mechanical hands and feet which enable the driver to move parts quickly and easily which he could not reach or manipulate with his physical hands and feet. Controls are linked with the Power principle not only by the principle of Effectuation but also by the part played by the time factor in operating them, which becomes greatly increased in importance in locomotives, airplanes, and marine engines. A driver has often only a second or two given to him to decide what action he must take to avoid damage to his engine or injury to himself and perhaps others. In the case of mobile engines, that is to say those which drive movable structures, the time-factor comes into operation in routine movements as well.

(11) GAUGES AND INDICATORS

Gauges and indicators are the sense-organs of engines, confining the term to what are called entero-ceptors, that is those nerve terminals which give information about the internal state of the body. Those corresponding with extero-ceptors are only needed in the case of engines driving mobile structures, ships, aircraft, etc. In the former case, that is of stationary engines, gauges and indicators give the driver timely information of situations which may lead to accidents such as excessive head of steam in a boiler. The positive aspect of (11) is concerned with Direction and therefore with the operation of steering gear in the case of mobile machines. Mechanical sense organs for these latter include a great variety of gadgets, compasses, direction finders, altimeters, depth gauges, speedometers, cyclometers, sound detectors and many others.

(12) BRAKES

Brakes operate by a method which inevitably throws a strain on the engine, namely the employment of friction. Except in brake mechanisms friction is the bugbear of the engineer owing to the wear and tear which it produces in bearing surfaces and the heat which it generates. Friction is closely allied to cohesion and may be regarded as the resistance which matter offers to the transfer of energy of property. If bearing surfaces such as those of an axle drum and brake-shoe are brought into light contact, friction is set up between them, but if the contact be firm the axle drum coheres to the brake-shoe and the machine stops. Lever or wheel controls of brakes have to be made very strong to stand the stresses to which they are subjected. The force of gravity may be brought into service on occasions to assist in braking. The design of the muscular-osseous system of the body enables it to be used as a brake without generation of internal friction. The whole of an engine is in a sense a brake, especially the piston and cylinder, since if the power is cut off the friction of the bearing parts brings about a stoppage sooner or later, otherwise perpetual motion would be obtainable. The metaphysical implications of braking are numerous and are employed to denote the means by which imprudent actions may be halted or called off before they produce complications or disasters. The fat which protects the muscular-osseous framework finds its counterpart in springs and shock-absorbers provided to protect engine-frames, chassis, etc., from jars and jolts, or minimise the force with which they are administered.

(13) Flywheel—Governor

The flywheel of an engine, which is always provided in the case of stationary engines driving fixed plants and machinery, ensures steady running by absorbing variations in momentum due to fluctuations in load, controllable and uncontrollable, or alterations in the supply of power arising from the manipulation of controls or variations in combustions of fuel mixtures. A flywheel also assists the pistons of steam engines over dead points. The flywheel is made massive and heavy, the chief limiting factor being the difficulty of starting it revolving if it be made too large and ponderous. The flywheels of large stationary engines are always manhandled to facilitate starting. All large wheels in machinery driven by stationary engines act to some extent as flywheels. A racing engine can however impart a dangerous velocity to a flywheel if not checked in time, in which case the latter becomes a liability rather than an asset. The metaphysical uses of the flywheel are many and link up in several ways with those of the gyroscope, though the latter serves to preserve the verticality of an axis which would otherwise tend to be lost. But the conceptions of regulation and stabilisation are common to both, though the second is much more under the dominion of gravity. A flywheel is the simplest form of the automatic control, which may be developed so that it becomes a complicated device as in the case of an automatic stabiliser in an aeroplane. A governor is an automatic mechanical device provided for steam engines to enable the valve of the main steam pipe to control the flow of steam in accordance with the power requirements of a fluctuating load or varying pressures in the boiler. The governor is driven from the main crankshaft and operates by the agency of two balls which are fixed by hinged arms to a vertical spindle and fly apart centrifugally as the speed of the engine increases, lifting a collar which causes the valve of the m.s.p. to close. The reverse happens when the engine slows down. In some designs the governor controls the slide valve of the cylinder. A governor to be efficient must be strong yet sensitive and the setting and design of a governor determines the number of revolutions per minute for any given load and head of steam.

ANALYSIS OF STATIONARY ENGINES

(14) Draught—Natural and Forced

Air is a form of fuel owing to the free oxygen which it contains and as such its supply to the furnace of a steam boiler must be regulated, and special means may have to be provided to force the draught in emergencies. By controlling the draught the head of steam in the boiler can be regulated through the acceleration or retardation of the combustion of the fuel.

(14) Carburettor—Air Inlet—Supercharger

The air inlet which is part of the carburettor of an internal combustion engine can be set to any desired position by the driver or engineer and as easily altered. A device called a supercharger is used by racing motorists and airmen to enable them to move at greater speed than would be possible by operating the ordinary control or relying on the float. It works by forcing the petrol and air mixture more rapidly than the float would permit if left to work automatically. Air-draught symbolism is bound up with that of the respiratory mechanism of men and animals, which accelerates automatically when extra speed has to be put on in order to feed additional oxygen to the muscles.

(15) Cylinder—Piston—Valves

The cylinder and piston of a steam engine, internal combustion engine, or pump provide means by which steam or gas pressure is convertible into mechanical pressure. This can, if desired, be converted into rotary motion by a connecting rod geared to a crankshaft. The valve gear is such an integral part of a cylinder-piston mechanism that it cannot well be separated from it in theory. Without it no reciprocating motion could be secured in the case of a steam cylinder. In the case of the heart, which is a force pump driven by a powerful system of contracting muscles, the valves are part and parcel of the four chambers. Valves may act as maintainers of a one-way flow or as distributors of flow or as inhibitors of flow. Just as the entire balance of the blood-circulation depends upon the perfect adjustment and timing of the valves of the heart, so likewise does the efficient functioning of the piston-cylinder mechanism of a steam or internal combustion engine depend upon similar conditions being observed. We do not make much use of cylinder-piston symbolism because the heart with its valves and circulatory system usually provide us with more illuminating analogies. Consider for instance the innumerable uses to which the word circulation can be put, other than merely mechanical, of ocean currents, news, coinage, words, proverbs, and fashions. And in all cases forces are in operation which start and maintain the circulation whether they are obvious or not.

(15) Turbine—Water-wheel—Jet-propulsion

The turbine is another device of a simpler character designed to enable steam or water power to be readily converted into mechanical power. The principle on which the turbine works is directing steam from a pipe nozzle at high velocity and allowing it to impinge on blades or buckets arranged round the rim of a wheel geared to a revolving shaft. The blades are enclosed in a drum, casing, or jacket which is the counterpart of the cylinder of a steam engine. Compressed air or water may be substituted for steam. The turbine principle is likewise illustrated in windmills and water wheels. The turbine principle does not involve the introduction of reciprocating motion which has to be subsequently converted to rotary motion. Yet another means of power application is furnished by the jet propulsion principle which is essentially the same as that by which a rocket is projected. A simple modification of it was incorporated in the design of the squid many millions of years ago, which enables it to propel itself backwards by ejecting water from its mantle which it sucks in through its mouth.

(16) Main Steam Pipe—Throttle Valve

The main steam pipe is a very important element in a steam-producing plant whether the steam be used to provide power, which is usually the case, or for other purposes. It has to be made of tough metal or special alloy, since it has to stand up to the same high pressure as the boiler. It is often long and sinuous in shape as it may not be feasible to place the engine close to its boiler. When it supplies steam to a cylinder it is liable to jump like a fire hose if the steam becomes suddenly cut off at the cylinder end. The symbolism of the steam pipe covers all pipes, tubes, or hoses which convey power in the form of steam or compressed air to specified places at a distance from the source of supply. It comes under the general heading of distribution as illustrated in the lymphatics of the body which convey nutritive substances to the actual cells which feed on them. It stands for purposeful as opposed to haphazard distribution and includes, of course, the distribution of electricity by power mains. Sociologically it is seen in the distribution over the face of the earth of human beings to regions where they can be healthy and happy as opposed to mass deportations. The m.s.p. or any other long, sinuous, distributing tube links up with serpent symbolism, for (16) is the Reptile compartment in Zoology, and if it drives a rock-drill or concrete-drill makes contact with the symbolism of the serpent's tooth.

(16) Petrol Supply Pipe—Carburettor to Explosion Chamber

In the case of an internal combustion engine, which is designed so as to combine explosion chamber and cylinder in one, there can be no equivalent of the main steam pipe but the principle is seen in the pipe which conveys the explosive gas mixture to the chamber where it is ignited by the magneto, or as in the case of a heavy-oil engine by the heat set up through compression of gas by the piston.

(17) Boiler

The boiler is the most massive and obvious part of a stationary steam plant and governs the whole design and shape of a locomotive steam engine. The boiler illustrates the principle of form in a steam plant and in the case of a locomotive its lines are made as graceful as possible. The well-known fact that a boiler is liable to burst if the head of steam exceeds a safe limit and no safety-valve is provided gives rise to a variety of metaphors. The ex-planet whose correct name is Minerva may have broken up to form the minor planets and asteroids owing to an internal explosion and many disastrous earthquakes arise from a similar cause. When nations "burst their boilers" the result is manifested in revolutions, such as the French of 1793, when the entire political structure of a country may be disrupted. Human beings may burst their boilers by indulging in uncontrolled outbursts of fury and inflict actual physiological damage upon themselves. There are three elements in Force, magnitude (or potential), direction, and point of application and in the present case magnitude is seen in the boiler and the head of steam while the direction and point of application is illustrated by the m.s.p.

(17) Explosion Chamber

Explosion chambers are designed to withstand the development of pressures by gases which expand suddenly on ignition to many times their original volume, and what spells disaster to a steam boiler is all part of the day's work for them. The worst trouble that can happen to them is to crack unless made of abnormally poor metal.

(18) Furnace—Ignition

The furnace of a boiler is a receptacle which is designed to enable fuel to be burnt in contact with the boiler or collected boiler tubes without risk of fire spreading where it might be dangerous or involve wastage of heat. The boot or saddle-backed boiler which supplies hot water for domestic purposes is heated on precisely the same principle. The symbolism of the furnace is, however, not restricted to its use for heating water or ovens but covers the home fires generally which we seek to keep burning, and the house fires which we do not want to start burning, any more than we want to start forest or bush fires. Ara, the Burning Altar, a decanate of Sagittarius, is the focal point of all furnace symbolism, including the wrath of man, which may smoulder for long periods and then suddenly burst into flames of fiery indignation. The symbolism of the Brazen Altar of sacrifice is bound up with self-dedication and submission to have one's imperfections burnt out by appropriate discipline.

(18) Magneto-ignition

An internal combustion engine works by the ignition of an explosive gaseous mixture brought about by an electric spark, which is introduced into the explosive chamber by a sparking plug. The electricity is generated by a magneto which can be set to ignite the spark with clockwork regularity at the precise moments when the maximum results can be obtained from the explosions. The sparking links up with the general symbolism of electro-magnetic phenomena which in turn leads one to the domain of Jupiter Tonans and Jupiter Pluvius, two aspects of one Power.

(19) Non-explosive Fuels

Under (19) we may range all fuels of a non-explosive character which can be safely introduced into a furnace without suddenly releasing large quantities of heat energy. These fuels contain potential energy in a form which only permits of its being gradually converted into kinetic energy by the process of combustion. They are mostly coal, peat, wood, or heavy oil introduced into a furnace by piped burners. The first three can be made to smoulder so that the fires of a furnace can be damped down without being extinguished during times at which only a low head of steam is required. The psychological equivalent of these fuels is seen in the mentality which does not permit itself to be quickly aroused to wrath but when it does can be all the more dangerous because of the restraint which it had previously exercised. We all know the difference between the temperament of, say, the Irishman which can be roused to fury at a moment's notice and that of the Russian which is normally cold and calculating, Saturnine rather than Jupiterian, but which when provoked beyond endurance can shake itself as Samson did when he cast off his bonds and exact a terrible vengeance upon those who presumed upon its continued inertia.

(20) Explosive Fuels

The explosive fuels are either volatile liquids such as petrol, alcohol, and acetone, or gases such as producer gas and acetylene. They can only be used for power-production in chambers which are strong enough to resist the force of explosion. The corresponding element of an internal combustion engine is the pipe which leads from the tank or generating plant (if a gas) to the carburettor or equivalent device for mixing with air. The psychological temperament suggested by explosive fuel is neither fiery nor self-contained, and is not so calculating and patient as the Saturnine. It seldom behaves irrationally like the fiery but acts with Uranian suddenness when it judges that a suitable moment has arrived. Volatility here corresponds with awareness or perceptiveness.

(21) Condenser

After expanding steam has completed its allotted task of driving a piston head forwards or backwards and has passed out of the exhaust port it is essential that it should be cooled as rapidly as possible, unless it is passed into another cylinder to do more work at a lower pressure. The cooling is effected by passing the exhaust steam through a condenser, which is virtually the same as a cooler, since according to the laws of the thermodynamics the greater the fall of temperature, that is heat potential, between boiler and condenser, the greater is the amount of work which can be got out of the steam. Condensers are usually in communication with boilers in steam engines and return their contents to the boiler so that a regular circulation of steam and water is maintained. This is more important in locomotives which have to carry their water in a tank than in a stationary steam engine. Condensers are either air-cooled or water-cooled or both. Nothing is gained by cooling the exhaust gases of an internal combustion engine. It is however necessary to provide means of cooling the jackets of high-speed cylinders in the latter case to avoid unnecessary burning of lubricating oil and the resulting danger of the seizing of piston heads, in spite of the loss of power which results.

The psychological counterpart of the condenser is the cool-headed, realistic temperament which is suspicious of everything that is idealistic, enthusiastic, and highfalutin. People of this type act as dampers and when they make a cult of depreciating everything that is not obviously utilitarian are liable to be very exasperating, but it cannot be denied that they have their uses in this world of hard fact in which economic laws work out their appointed effects with scant regard for sentiment.

(22) Silencer

A silencer is a device fitted to the exhaust of internal combustion engines to deaden the noise made by the explosions. The same principle is utilised in the provision of silencers for rifles or pistols. (22) is the lower harmonic of the Flywheel of (13) which should always revolve noiselessly, since this is an indication that there is no vibration of any kind being set up which would strain the parts of the engine. Smooth running is almost synonymous with silent running.

(23) Whistle—Siren—Hooter

The transition from (4) to (5) or their harmonics is invariably from smoothness to vibration or from silence to noise. The draught of air into a furnace, especially when forced, always makes its presence known by a certain amount of noise and may even roar up a flue. When, however, it is desired to enable a steam engine to emit a warning sound of any kind, the obvious means to adopt is to utilise a jet of steam from the boiler or main steam pipe to actuate a whistle or hooter.

(24) Lubrication

The lubrication of all the bearing surfaces of a machine except the brakes is an important matter at all times, but it becomes especially urgent when forced draught or supercharging is resorted to in order to accelerate speed in a mobile machine. Above all other parts the bearing surfaces of the piston-rings and the cylinder must be kept well lubricated, since any seizing of these is attended with serious consequences. Lubrication of these parts also assists the action of air and water in keeping the temperature reasonably low. A good lubricant is composed of oily substances the molecules of which slide easily over one another and do not readily vaporise under the action of heat. In no department of chemical engineering has greater progress been made than in the production of efficient lubricants. Nothing shortens the life of an engine so quickly as improper functioning of lubrication unless it be weakness of springing in the case of an engine mounted on a chassis. Oil is life and health to machinery as it is to men and animals, whose joints are lubricated by a fluid, the synovial, which is perfect of its kind. (6) and its harmonics, the number of the Venusian qualities, is always concerned in some way with smoothness, ease, absence of friction, and adaptability.

(25) Mechanical Petrol Feed

Petrol normally flows to the carburettor from the storage tank by gravity, but any mechanical contrivance designed to assist this process in any way would come under the heading of (25).

(26) Safety Valves

All high-pressure boilers are fitted with safety valves to reduce to a minimum the risk of boiler explosions, which are capable of causing fearful havoc.

(27) Mechanical Stokers

The greater the draught in furnaces the more rapidly ashes accumulate and unless these are raked out regularly combustion does not take place as it ought to, and consequently in large furnaces it is often necessary to provide mechanical devices to remove ashes and sometimes to shovel coal.

Physiological Analogies

The structure and functioning of engines, chassis, and machinery provides many physiological and psychological analogies. One cannot enter into the subject of the latter without involving oneself in many complications but that of the former is comparatively simple. The Alimentary Canal is the equivalent of the furnace, for the digestive juices cook up the food introduced into it by chemical action, which includes active oxidisation. We use the word "stoke-up" as a slang expression, for eating and defecation is the physiological equivalent of raking out the ashes of a furnace. Both dung and potash (the ash from the pot) are valuable fertilizers. Digested food passes into the circulation in the form of chyle and when it reaches the liver serves to enable that organ to maintain its chemical potential and so promote the growth of the body to maturity and also repair its wastage. Finally chyme is then passed into the lymphatics from the blood where it is further worked up into lymph and distributed to the cells of the body, part being used to enable the heart to beat regularly and continuously. Draught is obviously the mechanical equivalent of respiration and the balancing action of the flywheel under varying loads, which is dynamic, finds its counterpart in the balancing action of the thyroid gland in maintaining the static proportions of the body according to their original design. The counterparts of the encephalic and peripheral nervous systems and of the muscular-osseous system have already been noted.

CHAPTER XII

ANALYSIS OF SPEECH SOUNDS

See TABLES T, U, V

THE complex sounds by which human beings communicate their ideas to one another are termed words, which are built up of simple sounds represented by letters of the alphabet. In order to classify these sounds according to the principles of the Philosophy of Analogy it is necessary first of all to analyse the component parts of the mechanism by which human speech is produced, that is to say the mouth, nasal cavities, throat, and windpipe.

We shall find that the vocal organs are analysable on the same general principles as the skeleton, though the external skeleton of lower animals should be selected for purposes of illustration, rather than the highly articulated skeleton of the vertebrates.

If we work between tiers IV and VII, we have the vaulted arch in compartment (12), represented in the case of the mouth by the hard palate. This is commonly called the roof of the mouth but its architectural counterpart is really a ceiling, for the nasal fossae are of the nature of attics. If we look at the Skeletal Table I we see that the equivalent of the roof of the body, excluding the head which is a tower, is the pair of shoulder-blades. The equivalent of the ceiling is the arm which can be multiplied as required. This becomes clear if we consider a tree whose lower branches serve as a ceiling to those who take shelter beneath it. The rows of pillars on either side of the central aisle of a Gothic cathedral with groins which mark the intersection of vaulting springing from the pillars resemble an avenue of mighty forest trees and were in fact originally intended to do so. But we cannot proceed far with the architectural analogy, for the jaws of the face resemble an inverted box since the lower jaws, being hinged to the skull, represent the lid. Thus the arched ceiling of the palate does not spring from side walls but from the sides of a box. Instead of walls we have curtains in the form of the cheeks.

The hard palate is a bony plate covered by the mucous membrane of the mouth, and is formed by the superior maxillary and palate bones. It extends backwards a little beyond the wisdom teeth and merges at the back into the soft palate, a flexible muscular layer covered with mucous membrane, which is prolonged in the centre to form the uvula and to the sides to form the palato-pharyngeal folds or curtains, known as the velum. The functions fulfilled by the soft palate in voice production and speech are extremely important. It decides whether vibrating air coming from the larynx shall pass through the nasal cavities or the mouth, or if split up, what proportionate amount shall pass through either channel. By opening or closing the curtains the resonating chamber formed by the upper part of the pharynx is enlarged or contracted with consequent modification of the vocal sounds. It is particularly important in regulating the intensity and timbre of vowel sounds, the lion's roar, which terrorises the other denizens of the forest, being a noise in the production of which the soft palate is intimately concerned. There is no other speech organ except the tongue which is so flexible and controllable as to shape. We may think of it as a curtained apartment the entrance and dimensions of which are controllable with great speed and delicacy, and as a double doorway, which we may picture to ourselves as two contiguous door-openings, either one of which may be closed by a single door hinged between them.

The proper diagrammatic position for the soft palate and its appurtenances is clearly compartment (10) as it is a continuation of the hard palate and constitutes the posterior portion of the roof of the mouth. Furthermore their functions of control and general complexity of tructure fit them for the dominant compartment.

Behind the soft palate we have the pharynx which communicates with the nasal cavities at the upper part and with the oesophagus at the lower. Pharynx means a cleft or bore and is allied in derivation with the Greek pharanx, a chasm. It is the large enclosure which we see when the mouth is opened wide. The middle portion of the pharynx is common to the two avenues by which air and food are conveyed from without to the interior of the body. The back portion of the throat is the posterior wall of the pharynx and is continuous with the back wall of the gullet or oesophagus. Like the palate it is chiefly muscular in structure and is loosely attached to the spinal column. It is carried upwards along the spinal column behind the soft palate until it reaches the base of the skull when it bends forward into a vaulted roof. The Eustachian tubes open into the pharynx slightly above the floor of the nasal cavities. They are cartilaginous tubes which convey air to the drum cavity of the middle ear. Between the Eustachian tubes there is a mass of glandular tissue, sometimes called the third tonsil, which when enlarged produces the condition known as adenoids. The muscles which close in the back and side of the pharynx and gullet are three in number and spread out fanwise along the back. The gullet or oesophagus is a tube about 9 inches long down which the food passes from the pharynx to the stomach. The tonsils are glands situated near the base of the tongue at the top of the gullet, shaped something like the blades of paddles (L. *tonsilis*, a small oar). They consist of lymphoid tissue and easily get inflamed and enlarged. The pharynx and gullet correspond generally with the cavities of the thorax and abdomen which are enclosed by the ribs and hips respectively, and are placed in compartments (14) and (18) in consequence.

Further down we have the epiglottis, a curved projection formed of cartilage which covers the entrance to the windpipe during the act of swallowing so as to prevent food from getting into the respiratory tracts.

It participates in the movement of the tongue and is attached to its base by a strong ligament. It is also attached by ligaments to the side of the throat. When drawn tight these ligaments have sharp edges and feel to the finger like a foreign body such as a fishbone. The gullet can be partly closed by the epiglottis when the latter is pressed back and this is done automatically in singing to give freer passage to air and assist in the production of certain vowel sounds. Below the epiglottis are situated the false vocal chords or ventricular bands, which are movable flaps situated above the true vocal chords which they protect. They assist in the formation of a small resonant cavity of variable size and shape which affects the vibration of air passing up through the windpipe and larynx. According to Sir Richard Paget and Dr. Russell they determine what is known as the voicing of consonants, producing the difference between sonants such as D and surds such as T. A surd is a damped or muted sonant. Hence we may think of the false vocal chords as acting like the mute of a stringed instrument or the pedals of a piano. They are also able to vibrate independently of the true vocal chords and to produce notes of definite pitch. Thus we have in the epiglottis the counterpart of the false palate and uvula both as regards shape and function, for the latter regulate the voicing of vowels, that is they determine whether they are to be aspirated or not. When we aspirate vowel sounds we damp them down and soften them. The false vocal chords are the counterpart of the palato-pharyngeal folds which are structural continuations of the soft palate. The proper place for the epiglottis and false vocal chords is in compartment (19), the lower harmonic of (10).

In architectural analysis the openings in the front wall of a house belong to Col. II and there we must place nose, mouth, and lips. It is clear that the nose belongs to the top compartment (11). The nose bears certain analogies with the finger (Table I) as in the case of the elephant in which it is prolonged into a trunk and provided with specially formed movable nostrils which enable it to pick up small objects as if with a thumb and forefinger. In many animals such as the ant-eater it constitutes a tactile organ which is used for investigation in lieu of paws and claws with the added advantage that it can smell. The upper mandible of a bird is a nose and upper lip in combination. The nose is a complex structure if we take into account the nasal fossae which form part of the skull and which act as resonators.

Next we have three features of the face, lips, teeth, and gums, to accommodate in the three compartments (15), (16), and (20).

The teeth belong to the analytical compartment (16) *vide* Table T. The teeth not the lips are the real doors of the mouth as they can be closed with a snap. The lips are of the nature of curtains unless combined with the gums to form beaks as in the case of birds. They play a very important part in securing clearness of articulation and decision of enunciation, as those find out who are so unfortunate as to be without teeth and mislay their dentures. The gums belong to the lower compartment and in many animals such as the Edentata are hardened so as to act as masticators. (16) is the martial compartment and carnivorous animals do much of their fighting with their teeth.

The gums hold the roots of the teeth firmly, and since the root is symbolically below the trunk or body we must place the gums in (20), although in the case of the upper teeth the gums are above the teeth. This leaves the lips, which are Venusian organs extensively used for kissing, in compartment (15). It is now the fashion to rouge them.

The tongue is the backbone of the mouth for purposes of articulation and like the backbone belongs to the central column III and is very flexible. Its tip belongs to compartment (13), its body to (17) and its root to (21). We may place the bed of the tongue in (22).

We are now in a position to classify all speech sounds. Vowels constitute the substance and body of speech and can be uttered continuously. They are collectively the voice, whereas consonants are modifications of vocal sounds. They are the airy material upon which the consonantal organs or tools work, cutting them up into sections, defining them with sharpness and clarity, and rendering trifling distinctions more readily perceived by the ear. They are as it were projected by the pharynx like arrows from a bow with the minimum of interference by the mechanisms which produce consonants. They contain the free energy of voice and speech, whereas consonants represent bound energy, i.e. attractive and cohesive forces which produce stoppage or frictional resistance. Consequently vowels belong to the ruling compartment (10).

Below the vowels we have the aspirates in compartment (14) which are formed by surding the vowels as with a soft pedal. Aspirates are produced by the action of breath on pure vocal sounds, otherwise of lung wind on throat wind.

SH and the soft French J belong to compartment (12) as they are formed by the tongue and the roof of the mouth or hard palate. They are the most distinctively palatal of all simple sounds and the Hebrews emphasised their importance by calling the letter Schin one of the three parent letters, the other two being Aleph, the aspirate of the soft palate and the nasal Mem. SH and the soft J will be referred to in future as Aspiro-palatals and will be located in (12), the compartment of the hard palate.

The Nasal consonants M and N, known as open consonants or semi-vowels, belong to (11), the compartment of the nose.

The lingual R is pronounced by allowing the tongue to vibrate against the hard palate so that a rolling sound is produced. The English produce a very strong roll by using the tip of the tongue to pronounce R and bending it backwards so as to permit of amplitude of vibration. The French produce the sound at the back of the hard palate and the Germans even further back. The tongue is treated as a flexible backbone or sapling stem whenever R is pronounced and we must locate it as said before in compartment (13) and the other lingual which is pronounced at the side of the mouth between the tongue and the cheek may be placed in the lower part of the same compartment.

Many peoples, e.g. the Chinese, who cannot produce R sounds substitute L sounds. The Dentals and Gutturals fall automatically into the teeth and throat compartments (16) and (18). The closed Labials P and B belong to the lip compartment (15). The Labio-dentals F and V are semi-vowels, as they admit of continuity in production like the nasal sounds in (11), and may be placed in the lower harmonic compartment (20). They might be called lisped labials for they can be produced by the tongue and gums in the absence of teeth. The tongue being sinuous and serpentine, especially in the snake itself, is specially adapted to pronounce sibilants, which are central supports of the consonant-system. In compartment (17) we have Sibilants used in conjunction with Dentals as in TS which is easily modified into TCH by aspiration. The ordinary S which can be pronounced by the tongue and gums without the necessary intervention of the teeth, that is by lisping, as in the case of small children and old people, may be placed in compartment (21), the lower harmonic of (12). The last consonant to be considered, the Naso-guttural NG, may be placed in compartment (19) below the Gutturals. There is a ringing sound about it which counteracts surding, and it is possible that the false vocal chords play a part in producing it. At any rate, it is produced below the true gutturals in the region of the windpipe orifice.

Examining some of the elementary sounds more closely, the Nasals, M and N, are formed by the passage of air through the nasal cavities, which gives them a nasal twang before they emerge. The lips assist in forming the sound M and the tongue and palate in forming the sound N. The vowel-like character of the consonant N is best appreciated by pronouncing it as the French do when it terminates a word such as *maman* or is conjoined to a final dental T or D or to a guttural G. It is practically impossible to force air through the nasal passages without it being affected by vibrations set up there.

N is a palato-nasal and is partly formed by the mechanism which produces D so that when people have colds they sound N like D. For a similar reason they sound M like B when the nasal passages are blocked. M is called a labio-nasal on that account. When the lips are closed and air is forced up from the windpipe it passes through the nasal fossae and the vibration produced gives rise to the sound M. The soft palate is concerned in producing both Nasals as it diverts the air current emerging from the windpipe into the fossae. If compartment (10) were not already occupied by H we might place N there as its close relative NG is in the lower harmonic (19). The extent to which English people forsake pure pronunciation and speak through their noses when they migrate to other parts of the world as colonists is a remarkable phenomenon and once the habit is acquired pure pronunciation through the mouth seems affected. The Cockney accent, as it is called, is rendered unmelodious by the same defect.

Both the lingual sounds belong to the category of semi-vowels, as they only partially obstruct the passage of air. The vowel character of R is well seen in English words in which it occupies a terminal position, when it is hardly pronounced at all, unless followed by another word commencing with a vowel. The French "*lle*" used terminally is eminently vowel-like.

In many foreign tongues R is pronounced by vibrating the back of the tongue or even the pharynx and some R's sound as if they were produced entirely by vibration of the gullet.

The dentals D and T and the gutturals G and K are fully stopped consonants which are produced at opposite ends of the mouth. Aspiration turns the surds T and K into partially stopped consonants since the sounds TH and CH (as in the German word "*ich*") can be produced continuously.

DZ and TS are well-known consonantal combinations which are represented by single letters in some languages, e.g. TS by the Hebrew *tsaddi*. When aspirated they become hardly distinguishable from the English sounds J and CH (as in judge and church). In English G is pronounced as J before certain vowels such as E.

KS is also a familiar combination and is represented by the single letter X in many languages. GZ is less common but is equally easily pronounced.

It will be seen from the above that D and T, J and CH, and G and K (hard G and hard C) form a closely affiliated group which is brought out by placing them in the same tier VI. J and CH are appropriately placed in compartment (17) between the other two pairs.

Table V contains an analysis of the vowel sounds. The principle of construction is to place the broad and sustained sounds in the lower tiers and the short and crisp sounds in the upper tiers on the general principle that low-pitched sounds are produced by slow vibrations and long waves and high-pitched sounds by rapid vibrations and short waves. As regards the columns, vowel sounds formed at the back of the mouth belong to column I, vowel sounds formed by protruding the lips belong to column II, and vowel sounds produced by making the lips circular belong to column III.

Commencing with the A's, there are four long A sounds and one short. A as in bane is akin to AY or AI and belongs to column I and compartment (19) which is a foundational number. A as in pawn is akin to AU or AW and belongs to column II and compartment (20). A as in bare and A as in balm belong to the central column as being neutral between I and U. Their numbers are (21) and (22), A as in bare being placed in (21) because it is more nearly related to A as in bane (19) than is A as in balm. We then proceed to build up the central column III by placing OU, OW, or AU as in sound in (17). AU is pronounced OW in German as in frau. Although we use two vowels to make this sound in English it is really elementary and is formed by making the mouth and lips as round as possible. Now (17) is the number of culture and civilisation, and capacity to pronounce a perfect OW is a test of cultured speech. Many people who have no trace of an uncultured accent in any other respect flatten their OW's to AOW's by importing the A's of (21) or (19). In Hertfordshire one sometimes hears

ANALYSIS OF SPEECH SOUNDS

OW pronounced A as in bane with no trace of the OW retained. The cockney converts OW into the A of balm (22) and says aht instead of out. The general ideas associated with (17) are rotundity, enclosure, stability, potential, protective structure, and bodily clothing, to take a few salient examples. These are exemplified in the words round about, (com)pound, redoubt, bound(ary), found(ation), ground, mound, mount, stout, tower, bower, house, town, power, gown, blouse, and clout. OW constitutes the lumbar vertebræ of the skeleton framework of the table of vowels and enters into the word Vowel itself. Long O as in pole and short O as in pot follow naturally in (13) and (12). It may be noted that (13) and its lower harmonic (22) are religious numbers and so we have O or OH as the priestly interjection prefacing prayer and AH as a prophetic interjection (Is. i. 4, 24). Long O conveys the notion of height since the letter is a vertical ellipse and might be called high O. It may be regarded as completing the backbone of the Table. In (8) we have OY or OI as in boy obtained by modification of OW as in pound (17). This is illustrated in the German word frau (pronounced frow) which appears in a modified form in fräulein (pronounced froylein). In (4) we have the English ER in which the R remains mute, a similar sound being made by after-dinner speakers when they find themselves bereft of words or ideas.

In column I we have the sound EE as in keep or initial Y in (18) and in column II the sound OO or long U as in hoot, otherwise the initial W, in (16). You is pronounced EEOO and We is pronounced OOEE. We can bring (16) in diagrammatic contact with (18) by curling the table round vertically to make a cylinder. Long I or high I (AY, AI, EI) as in pint and modified U as in the French tu and the Scottish fule (dialect) belong to columns I and II respectively, and therefore to (14) and (15). In numerology (5) and (14) are numbers which represent the I-consciousness which theosophists call ahamkara. Continuing upwards we have short A as in pat in (10) and medium U as in put in (11). In tier III we must place short I in (9) since we have OI in (8). In the lower harmonic (18) we have EE, a sound which is represented by I in some foreign languages, as in the French il. Similarly we must place short U as in but in (7) since (16), the lower harmonic of (7) contains long U or UU. Finally in tier II we have short E as in bet in (5). The sound EU or OEU as in the French words peu and œuvre belongs to (6) because the lips have to be pursed to produce it, which is not necessary in the case of ER or IR.

These 19 compartments provide accommodation for all the primary vowel sounds though of course there are many intermediate sounds in foreign languages and even in the dialects of the British Isles. For instance, the French il is intermediate between eel and ill.

It will be observed that the letters in tier IV of Tables U and V, AH or HA, M, and SH agree with the three Mother Letters of the Hebrew Alphabet, Aleph, Mem, and Schin to which the other letters were subordinate except Iod which was regarded as the source of all the letters.

We have pictured the basic ideas which collectively constitute knowledge and wisdom as so many radii passing from the exterior to the interior of the cylinder or cone of knowledge. In the process of constructing words, men work subconsciously along these radii, building up their conceptions by the association of appropriate elementary speech-sounds.

The difficulties presented by such a line of inquiry are admittedly formidable, as a little ingenuity would suffice to give a superficial verisimilitude to other tabular arrangements. But only that which is intrinsically watertight could hope to survive prolonged and microscopic examination.

The trouble is that even in any one language, word- and idea-building by means of sounds have reached a high degree of complexity, and even if one studies hypothetical roots, such as the Indo-Germanic given in Skeat's Etymological Dictionary, it is by no means easy to reach absolutely simple ideas. For instance "taste" may seem a simple idea and so may "touch," but I have shown in analysing the senses that there are three kinds of taste and four kinds of touch. Taste regarded as a purely discriminative sense, utilised in conjunction with smell for the purpose of discerning the essential nature of the object tasted, may be represented by a dental, but if associated with the idea of the act of swallowing it is represented by a guttural. If, on the other hand, the idea of relish, while food is being worked up to a bolus in the mouth, predominates, taste is represented by a sibilant, or the noise made by a slovenly eater enjoying thick soup. Since animals are seldom taught table manners they usually "swaffle," and a generic title for animals is "sus," the swaffler, as seen in ursus (bear), Pegasus, and of course sus, the swine.

The foregoing analysis does not by any means cover all there is to be said on the subject. In the major work the use of each letter in the composition of words is considered and reasons are given for showing that the arrangement as given in the Tables enables them to be correlated with the fundamental principles of each compartment as symbolised by the radii which intersect them at right angles.

There is, however, another line of argument by which the probability of the above arrangement being correct can be established and that is by studying the musical instruments which are associable with the basic consonantal sounds and classifying them accordingly.

MUSICAL INSTRUMENTS

See TABLE W.

GENERAL

The evolution of musical instruments has followed the general lines of that of consonantal speech sounds, each instrument emphasising one or other of these sounds.

Musical instruments are classifiable as either wind, string, or percussion, and these three kinds fall into columns I, II, and III, respectively. Wind instruments are distinguished by the fact that they emit continuous sounds, which can be sustained so long as either the natural expired breath of the body or the artificial wind obtained by bellows (i.e. artificial lungs) lasts out. They are capable of disposing of a large amount of sound energy, especially in the case of organs, in which modern artifices for the production of considerable quantities of wind-power have been brought to a high degree of perfection. Steam sirens, foghorns, and locomotive whistles carry sounds to considerable distances, and even a bugle or trumpet can be sounded so as to be audible for many miles if the direction of the wind be favourable.[1] There can be no doubt therefore that the proper column for wind instruments is the free energy column, in which the animal lungs are accommodated. (Table H.)

Wind instruments express the principle of passion in its widest application and stringed instruments that of emotional tension.

Stringed instruments, with the exception of those which are bowed, produce discontinuous sounds of comparatively small power, but are capable of effecting more refined and delicate combinations of sound than wind instruments. In comparing stringed instruments with an organ one must of course take an orchestra into consideration, as the latter consists of several wind instruments built into a single composite structure. It is generally conceded that the violin is supreme as an instrument of emotional expression, the poignancy of the music which can be obtained from it by an artist of the first rank being far in advance of anything which can be drawn out of any other instrument. The fact that it makes use of the element of complete continuity gives it a marked lead over non-bowed stringed instruments.

Percussion instruments exemplify the principles of forcefulness and desire. The call of a peal of sweet-toned church bells ringing over the country-side is wellnigh irresistible, and the conception of forcefulness is well brought out in the free arm strokes of a big-drummer in a military band. The attractive influence of drums is very strong when played rhythmically and soldiers instinctively follow the lead of a band which contains a large proportion of drums as if they were being pulled after it.

In tabulating the musical instruments the associated letter-sounds will be shown, together, as a rule, with the others of the same tier, which in the majority of cases enter into the names of the instruments. Thus in the case of Drum we have M as well as R utilised in spelling it. The Greek TyMpaNoN has no R but one M and two N's.

(10) THE HORN—VOWEL SOUND A (H)

The Horn is the acknowledged king of the wind instruments, for its sound has far more body than that of the Pipes and the Reeds. The metal-wind instruments consist of Trumpets, Cornets, Trombones, Bass Tubas, the French Horn and various Saxhorns. The Saxophone is a

[1] The Burists of Northern Asia use a horn 20 feet long which can be heard 20 miles away.

cross between a reed and a metal wind instrument. The Saxhorn family of brass instruments constitutes the foundation of modern military bands, its ancestor being the ram's horn.

The Hebrew straight trumpet of silver, the *Chatzotzerah*, was used mainly for sacred purposes. The metal-wind instruments have a double origin as regards form from straight metal tubes and curved animal horns. The Hebrew ram's horn cornet was called the "Keren" (Gk. *keras*, animal horn). Associated with this was the *Shophar* or *Shaum*, a long curved horn, used for arousing religious or political enthusiasm and patriotic ardour. It is translated by the Greek *keratinē*. All the Hebrew horns were used to awaken racial passions or religious fervour and are therefore fitly placed in Col. I, which is associated with patriotic ardour. In modern times we find that the military brass band has altogether unique powers in inciting men to action and enabling them to endure the fatigue of long marches. The trumpet and bugle calls used in action are invaluable for transmitting commands which require to be obeyed instantly. As the Apostle Paul said, "If the trumpet utter an uncertain sound, who shall prepare himself for the battle?" The sounds produced by metal-wind instruments resemble those made by animals, which have great carrying power owing to their having been reinforced by powerful vibrations of the soft palate, the roaring of lions and the lowing of cattle being examples. The word bugle is derived from the Latin *buculus*, the diminutive of *bos*, an ox. The words trumpet, trump, and trombone, etc., are derived from a root word *truba* (Latin form, *tuba*), which was designed to describe the mode of exit of the sound rather than imitate the sound itself.

Cornet is derived from the Latin *cornu*. Of all the names of horns the Hebrew word *Shophar* is the most descriptive of the sounds emitted by these instruments.

(14) Wood-wind Instruments—Flute or Pipe—Vowel I (Long)

The English words Pipe and Fife admirably describe the nature of the flute sound since the I represents the imitation of the feminine human voice and P and F the delivery ends. The flute, like the reed pipe, is one of the most ancient of instruments. It produces a sound which is more easily imitated by the human voice or lips than that of any other instrument, it being really a kind of whistle. The familiar penny-whistle is really a primitive variety of flute. The word (h)wistle, spelt whistle, contains H and L, two of the characteristic letters of tier V. The equivalent French word *siffler* contains the labio-dental F. The piccolo is a small flute with the notes pitched an octave higher than the ordinary flute. The flute is the acknowledged leader of the wood-wind instruments and boasts of the most extensive repertory of them all.

The associations of the pipe, like those of the reed, are definitely pastoral and the instrument falls appropriately enough into the Aries or Ram compartment. The flute produced a sound of a refined sexual order, according to the Greeks, and they connected it with the mating calls of birds. But its use by some of the ancients was decidedly lascivious and Plato banished it from his ideal republic on that account. Johannes Secundus called it the instrument of Venus and Aristonachus considered it to have power to excite the sex-passions. The Peruvians believed that it spoke an eloquent love language. (14) represents the male element in the Hermaphrodite couple. The Hebrew *Machol* was a popular instrument of the flute type used for holiday dances.

(18) THE REEDS—VOWEL EE

The reed family of wood-wind instruments contribute to the orchestra a sound which is described as wheezing when it emanates from the bagpipes. In the bassoon it is combined with a nasal intonation. Reeds have a reed or piece of thin wood in the mouthpiece which produces the characteristic chesty buzz or twang. The most important members of the reed family are the Oboe, the Bass Oboe or Bassoon, the Double-bass Oboe or Contra-bassoon, the Tenor Oboe or Cor Anglais, the Clarinet, and the Bass Clarinet. The frequent appearance of nasal sounds in the names of these instruments is noticeable. The suffix "soon" is derived from the Latin *sonus*, meaning sound. Whenever a music-hall artiste attempts to imitate a bassoon he does so by closing his lips and emitting sounds through his nose. The Hebrew *Mena'an'im*, translated cornet in the A.V. and pipe in the Septuagint, was probably a reed instrument, though some have concluded that the fact that the name was derived from a root meaning to vibrate indicated some instrument of the rattle family. The Chaldean *Sumphonyah* is rendered dulcimer in the A.V. but more correctly bagpipes in the R.V. margin. Bagpipes are reeds provided with what might be called an artificial lung to give continuity of sound. A very ancient reed instrument, in fact probably the prototype of all reeds, was that known as the pan-pipes. Some are of opinion that the Hebrew *chalil* was a reed but this is translated as *aulos* or flute in the Septuagint. The root means something pierced. The Greek *syrinx* was a shepherd's reed, or calamus. The bagpipes are famous in Scottish history as having inspired many deeds of military valour, interspersed with cattle-thieving and private murder. It is said to have been an English instrument before it reached Scotland, having been brought over by the Romans. Even angels have been depicted as skirling. It has a wonderful value as an incentive to marching, as an accompaniment to dancing, and for playing dirges and laments.

(19) ORGAN

The organ is the synthesis of all the wind instruments and of all the sounds which they express. We must place it in (19) and not (10) because its characteristic notes are the deep mysterious sounds which appear to emanate from the earth and which constitute an admirable representation in music of the passions resident in the subconscious region. The word passion is used here to describe all psychological forces of a profound and powerful character.

The modern organ is a combination of at least four separate organs, the great, the choir, the swell, and the pedal, to which are sometimes added an echo, a solo, and a bombarde, making a maximum of seven. Each organ consists of an assemblage of pipes controlled by speaking (or intensifying) stops, and these are subdivided into families carefully grouped to maintain tonal balance.

The great organ lays emphasis on the open and closed diapasons, which are the foundation stops of the whole instrument and give it its characteristic musical temperament as opposed to the eleven other kinds of instruments. From the diapasons we obtain the magnificent and impressive sounds which resemble peals of thunder. Diapason means "through all," the connection being with the Greek phrase *"diapason chordon sumphonia"* meaning "concord through all the notes." The word organ is connected with the Greek *ergon*, work, from which we get our word en-ergy. Each organ except the pedal is operated by a manual, indicating the important part played by the hands. These perform a secondary part in primitive wind instruments which they only serve to support. Hardly less important are the feet operating the deep bass notes which are heard as a sort of muffled rumbling.

Taking the component organs in detail and commencing with the Choir, the general practice in the nineteenth century was to design it for semi-solo purposes and equip it mainly with flute stops and dulcianas, but in the new organ installed in Liverpool Cathedral soft diapasons and reeds have been incorporated. The Swell organ depends mainly upon reed stops, such as hautboys, krummhorns, and cornopeans, but the Liverpool organ includes a family of geigens to balance up with a diapason tone, and salicionals and lieblichs to provide the flute constituents. The predominant tone of the Pedal organ is a heavy diapason or bass trumpet, but the modern tendency is to introduce flute and reed stops in addition. The Echo organ is designed to provide a sort of distance effect somewhat of the character of the Great, the Solo organ being intended to supplement the Choir. The Bombarde is designed to give a strong reed effect with tubas, but no modern organ is unbalanced, and the Liverpool organ evens up the tubas with a grand chorus of ten ranks.

A large modern organ is a stupendous example of structural genius operating in the domain of music, as these few details of the Liverpool organ will suffice to demonstrate. This instrument is the second largest in the world and comprises five manuals and 168 speaking stops. In addition there are 48 couplers and innumerable accessories, such as pistons and pedals, both adjustable and reversible. The cost of the instrument exceeded £35,000.

All small instruments of the bellows type, except the bagpipes, may be classed as small organs and are usually called by that name. Such are seraphines, harmoniums, and concertinas. They mostly suggest the "whEEze" of a person suffering from asthma when of a primitive construction.

ANALYSIS OF SPEECH SOUNDS

(11) THE HARP—M.N

It is by no means easy to draw a hard and fast distinction between instruments of the harp class and those of the lute class, any more than one can define the difference between the "plucking" or the "twanging" of a string by the finger. The distinction must be sought in size and portability, which imposes limitations on the manner in which both classes of instruments are played, and which, in the case of the former, permits of a pedal mechanism being utilised to effect mechanical changes.

The harp is an instrument of emotional and artistic suceptibility, and has been adopted by the Celtic race, both in Wales and Ireland, as the chief, one might almost say the sole, medium for expressing its musical genius and for accompanying the human voice. It is essentially a regal instrument, and in olden times harpists stood in high favour with kings. The fact that it is usually played in a sitting posture and calls for slow extension of the arms and restrained manipulation of the fingers, enables it to bring out to the full whatever grace and comeliness there may be in the person of the performer.

It is selected in the Book of the Revelation as the most appropriate symbol of the beauty and majesty of the heavenly worship, and there can be no doubt but that it occupied an important place in the ancient Druidic ceremonial, which was highly mystical. There is something celestial about the sweeping arpeggios which are easily played on the harp, and the sweetness and dignity of the tone is highly conducive to a spiritual frame of mind. The Chaldean *Sabbeka* (Greek *sa.Mbuke*, Eng. sackbut) was a true harp of large size which emitted full rich tones. The Phœnician *Nebel* was a large harp of 10 strings. The Egyptian harp, judging from a wall painting in a Theban tomb, was also a large instrument. The Hebrew *KiNNor* was a triangular lyre formed of two flat pieces of wood whose ends were united with eight or nine strings. It was held under the left arm and played with the fingers or plectrum. The Assyrian *Asor* was a small instrument. Both of these might be classified with the lute family. The harpsichord and spiNet occupy a position midway between the harp and the piano, since they embody the plucking principle as applied to the strings and the keyboard principle for mechanical operation.

(15) THE PIANOFORTE—B.P.

The essence of the pianoforte principle is the use of a hammer to excite vibrations in strings under high tension, in which respect it has affinities with the xylophone of the Bell class. The most ancient member of this family known to antiquarians is the dulcimer, the name of which means sweet song. It bears the same relationship to the pianoforte that the concertina does to the organ, for in both cases we have elaborate mechanical developments and adaptations of simple musical principles as exemplified in small portable instruments.

The fundamental haMMer basis of the piano is made plain by the words which we apply to unskilled piano-playing, such as "struMMing," "thumPing," and "Pounding." The piano is associated with the idea of manufacture and mass production in a manner that is impossible in the case of the organ, which always has had and always will have to be specially built, however widespread the demand of this instrument for cinemas may become. It may safely be said that 10,000 pianos are turned out for every one large organ built, and this fact alone enables the manufacture of pianos to be standardised in a manner that is impossible in the case of organs. The harmonium occupies a position midway between organs and pianos, being a wind instrument like the former and portable like the latter. The task which the organist has to perform is much more complex than that of the pianist, for he has to use his feet for the pedal organ and his hands for the organs operated by manuals, while at the same time he has to be ready to interrupt the even flow of his playing from moment to moment in order to operate stops, couplers, and kindred mechanical or electrical devices, without listeners being conscious of any break in continuity. An organist has to systematise his brain physiologically on the lines of a telephone exchange and literally grow the nerve fibres necessary to enable him to direct associated movements of hands and feet. The pianist, on the other hand, has a far simpler task before him in learning to master his instrument, and his main object is to acquire executive efficiency. It is true that recently the cinema organist has invaded the preserves of the church organist and plays music which no member of the old school would have dreamt of attempting, and in fact which he would have regarded as sheer desecration. But the pianist still holds his place as the supreme exponent of executive efficiency acquired by continuous repetition of similar groups of finger movements. And for this reason numbers of people who have not a note of real music in them are set to learn the piano when they are young, and in due course acquire among the uninitiated the reputation of being really good players.

The essence of the artistic rendering of pianoforte music lies in the exploiting of contrasts between loudness and softness, of quickness and slowness, of vigour and gentleness, of detachment and sympathy, so as to exhibit contrasts of light and shade, for the instrument which he plays is a musical word-painter and is more easily understood because as a rule it is used for solo-playing and under such conditions the audience are able to concentrate upon the performer's interpretation.

The pianoforte is provided with a loud and a soft pedal, the proper use of which add greatly to the effectiveness of its playing.

(16) THE LUTE—TH.—D.T.

The lute, the lyre, and the Greek zither (*kaithross, kithara*) all belong to the same class of instrument. The fact that they were all portable admitted of their being used by dancers or to set the rhythm in dances, especially those of a dignified and sacred character. From the Greek *kiThara* we get the modern ciThern, the Tyrolese ZiTher, and the guiTar. The manDoline and the banjo come under the same heading as the foregoing, while the Polynesian ukulele, being played in a sitting posture, has some affinity with the harp on this account. Some of these instruments were or are played with a plecTrum of a toothlike character, which gives a more Twanging sound than that obtained by the finger.

(20) BOWED STRINGS—VIOLIN—V.F.

The violin and its associates the viola, the 'cello, bass-viol, and the double-bass are distinguished sharply from other stringed instruments by the fact that the vibrations are excited by the friction of a horsehair bow. The sound obtained is therefore continuous like that of the labio-dentals V and F. This is exemplified in the initial letter of the word Violin and in the popular name Fiddle. At the same time brilliant and arresting effects may be obtained by using the bow with hammer effect in fast movements. The word Viol is derived from the Lat. *Vitulari* which in turn is probably derived from the sacrifice of a calf (Veal) in Roman ceremonials at public festivals. The violin is admirably adapted to interpret those weird and fantastic emotional turmoils which well up from the sub-conscious self and throw the autonomic system into convulsions. The Hungarian Gypsies are past masters in the art of working up not only themselves but their hearers into frenzies of excitement, in the course of which the latter empty their pockets into the hands of the performers. Not a few Hungarians have been of the opinion that the national stamina was being undermined by Tsigöne music. There is no other instrument which can touch the violin in the portrayal of the whole gamut of human emotions when played by a master-musician. It reaches up to heights of ecstatic joy one moment and touches the depths of despair the next. Boldness and fear, love and hate, harmony and discord, excitement and peacefulness lie within its strings and sound-board ready to be evoked by those who understand its temperament and possibilities.

It has been stated that great violinists develop nerve cells in their finger-tips, which contain grey matter similar in composition to that found in the brain. The hurdy-gurdy is like a primitive violin with a rosined wheel substituted for a bow.

The Italians of the Later Renaissance produced the most successful makers of violins that the world has so far seen, the names of Stradivarius, Guarnerius, and Amati being household words. Their success was mainly due to their having discovered a varnish which preserved its elasticity indefinitely.

(12) CASTANETS—S.SH.—(M.N.)

The Hebrews had an instrument called *Mena'an'im* derived from a root meaning to vibrate. It is translated *Sistra* in the Vulgate and is believed to have been a rattle consisting of an oval hoop with a handle, having cross-bars of metal rods, on which loose rings were threaded, and which jingled when shaken like the plates of a timbrel. The Spanish *castaneta* is a musical instrument of percussion in the form of two hollow shells of ivory or hard wood, which are bound together by a band fastening on the thumb and struck by manipulating the fingers to produce a clicking sound in keeping with the rhythm of the music. It is much used as an accompaniment to dances and guitar music. The name is derived from the Latin *castanea*—chestnut. The *Shalishim* of the Hebrews was another instrument of percussion similar to the *Men'an'im*, which was supposed to be a rattle, sistra, or triangle.

(13) THE DRUM—R.—(P.B.)

Nearly all words descriptive of instruments of the dRum category contain R's, such as tabRet, tambouR, tambouRine, and timbRel. DRum is derived from an Idg root *dhRan*, sound, and is connected with the Greek *threnos*, dirge and the Danish *dRone*, to RoaR. We instinctively describe the noise made by dRums as Rolling or Rattling. The word is used as a verb on account of its suggestion of forcefulness, which means to dRum out, expel, summon, or to worry people to buy what they do not want by persistent advertisement. A drum-head court-martial assembled during active service is a sinister assembly having powers of life and death over those arraigned before it. The dRum is in no way inferior to the hoRn in its powers of generating martial energy and assisting troops to march, and has the advantage in respect of producing rhythmic sounds in strict tempo. A considerable expenditure of muscular energy is required to play the big drum, especially when it has to be carried as well. Drums are capable of producing thundeRous sounds, like the deeper notes of an organ or the bass notes of the piano. All three instruments are exponents of the power and majesty of sound in their several ways.

No instrument can compare with the drum as a means of communicating information over long distances. Every village of importance in the bushveldt and forests of Central and South Africa has its signal drum, and Livingstone complained that no sooner had he left a kraal than the drum began to send messages to those ahead. The drummers do not use a Morse code but, as Fulahn explained in an article in Chambers's Journal, they imitate the sounds of the human voice, a male drum imitating low tones and a female drum high tones. When only one drum is used the hide stretched over the drum-head is tuned to give forth different tones when struck in different places. Log drums consisting of wooden cylinders are sometimes used in place of hide drums, and these also give forth different tones according to the spot where they are struck. The sound emitted by many of the big drums is like a gentle murmur when heard at a close distance and like a dull roar when heard ten miles away. The drum known as the talker mimics the syllabic speech spoken by many tribes, which consists of about 100 simple syllables arranged in different combinations. Skilled drummers use tuners of rubber, wax, rosin, which are fixed to the drum-heads, and rings, bells and thongs are placed inside. Drumsticks of different kinds of wood are used to get variations in sound and each kraal has its own call-sign. In addition messages are sent in a symbolic code which cannot be easily interpreted by white men. The efficiency with which these drums can transmit messages over long distances is shown by the fact that when Gordon was killed at Khartoum the news was known in the bazaars of Mombasa the next day, some 2,000 miles away. The outbreak of the Great War of 1914-18 was known in the kraals of Zululand before it was announced in Cape Town. Some tribes use horns as instruments of percussion to transmit news and others use whistles. Drum-horns have also been used to transmit love-greetings.

(17) CYMBALS—TS.CH.DZ.

The Hebrews had instruments of percussion called *MeTZilloth*, which are believed to have been cymbals of the nature of metal cups suspended from the bridles of horses (Zech. xiv, 20). Another and similar instrument was called *MeZilaim* and was probably shaped like a soup-plate and strapped to the hands. There was also the *TSilTSilim*, which is believed to have been conical and cuplike, with a thin edge, and which was played by bringing one down sharply upon the other.

(21) XYLOPHONE—HARMONICON—S.Z.—(F.V.PH.NG.)

The Xylophone may be taken as the representative of a class of instruments in which bands, strips, or cups of wood were shaped to emit notes of different pitch when struck by hammers. The principle of the Harmonicon consists in the production of musical sounds by hammering a series of thin plates of glass or metal graduated in a scale of notes. Both these instruments occupy a position midway between Cymbals and Bells.

(22)—BELLS—GONGS—L. (NG)

The bell is the largest and heaviest musical instrument made. The Tsar Kolokol at the Kremlin, Moscow, weighs 130 tons and that at Trotzkoi 171. A large bell of this nature represents a considerable item of wealth to the community possessing it, and a carillon of good bells costs a great deal of money. Like the organ and the piano modern peals of bells are designed so as to be capable of considerable mechanical control and to ring changes by means of an apparatus which can be managed by a single individual. Nearly all names for bells and instruments of percussion of the same class contain L's, e.g. crotaLo, cymbaL, cLog, (Celtic), squiLLa, Lebetes (funeral bell), noLa (small tower bell), cymbaLum (cloister bell), campaneLLa, noLuLa and cLepsydra. A cariLLon was originally a group of four bells. We speak of toLLing or peaLing bells, and the bell itself with its tongue and its cheek is not unlike the vocal apparatus by which human beings produce lingual sounds.

The bell is more intimately associated with the church and the monastery than any other musical instrument, being long anterior to the organ in point of time. As such it is bound up with the spiritual desires and aspirations of mankind, and when hung in a tower bids men look upwards to receive the Divine message which shall save their souls. Bells chime out to celebrate the advent into the world of important babies, heirs to crowns or large estates, they ring merrily when weddings are celebrated, and toll mournfully when the dead are laid to rest.

Instruments of percussion of the bell family are also used largely to convey warnings, and in the Middle Ages most towns possessed bells which notified citizens when any danger menaced them. At Ripon the curfew bell has been sounded continuously from one of the Minster towers for more than a thousand years. From the very nature of their manufacture and the materials of which they are composed bells are the most permanent of all musical instruments. The first bell in this country of which we have any record was hung in Wearmouth Abbey in 680. A peal was installed at Croyland Abbey in the tenth century. Dr. C. H. Moody writes of bells, "The development of bell-ringing is due to the vision and fervour of ecclesiastics in the Middle Ages," and it is a curious fact that ringing "in peal" is, with the exception of a few "rings" in America and the Dominions, peculiar to England. In the Low Countries, where every important belfry has from 20 to 65 bells, the latter number belonging to Antwerp Cathedral, the bells are either played mechanically, that is by means of a revolving drum, or by an expert carillonneur, who controls them by hands and feet in the same fashion as an organist controls his instrument. The usual number of bells in an English peal is from six to twelve. There is something inexpressibly soothing about bell tunes, and Victor Hugo, in spite of a sleepless night engendered by the carillon of Mechlin Cathedral, could scrawl on the window pane of his room a glowing tribute to the beauty of these old-world chimes. America and Canada vie with each other in cultivating bell-music on Belgian lines.

The passing bell was rung to scare away evil spirits from the departing soul. The signal for the massacre of St. Bartholomew was given on one of the bells of St. Germain l'Auxerrois, Paris. Ships' bells are used to chime the hours and many of them are highly prized. Valuable bells are often presented to warships by interested parties. Edgar Allan Poe revealed the genius of bells in a poem which will rank for all time as a masterpiece of the poet's art.

The function of the bell, and of its close relatives the glockenspiel, the portable carillon, the tubular bells, and the xylophone, is to emphasise the letter L of musical speech. The pure liquidity of tone which distinguishes the glockenspiel, for instance, is produced by the most exquisite adjustment of timbre. L is the great harmoniser among alphabetical sounds, and is reproduced musically by the elimination of all discordant overtones, so that a pure, ringing, translucent, and lambent tone floats into the air. In the same compartment we have the organised carillon, controllable by a keyboard, or the equivalent, and this compartment must house all bells which are too large for orchestral purposes, and whose proper habitation is a bell-tower.

Less interesting but more necessary forms of bells of to-day are doorbells, house-bells, office-bells, and telephone-bells. In fact the bell is the most vocal and informative of all musical instruments, and that which we could least afford to dispense with.

Perhaps the most important characteristic of the bell family, large and small, is the clearness of the message which its members address to the understanding. Many musical instruments speak to the intellect but few to the understanding. To take the humblest example, when a bell-hop hears the office bell ring he understands at once that his sixpenny detective novel has to be put forthwith in a safe hiding-place, while he presents himself with the least possible delay before the ringer. The message which wedding bells transmit to all the village swains is to pluck up courage and put their fortunes to the test. It is, however, derogatory to a bell of the L family to mention it in the same breath with one of the ING family.

The foregoing analysis of musical instruments provides the raw material for a scientific theory of orchestration. I have shown how extensive is the range of ideas affiliated to each letter of the alphabet, and the same ideas can be correlated to the letters of the musical alphabet. All tables of psychological import can be utilised to classify and define the effect produced by musical instruments in stimulating the passions, desires, and emotions in their various grades from the coarsest and most realistic to the most refined and ethereal. It is true that the letters of the alphabet can be used to construct words in a manner that is impossible to apply in the case of the timbres of musical instruments. Music has its own principles of architecture, and cannot be made to conform to the rules of etymology. But by developing the analogies between letter-ideas and sound-ideas a great deal could be done to make music more understandable. At the present time every kind of music has its message, but there is a lamentable want of unity among listeners in deciding as to what the message is, even in the case of descriptive programme compositions. A composer calls such a piece by some such title as say *Sunrise on the Ocean*, but if an audience heard the piece first without knowing the title, and each member was then invited to write down what he thought the composer intended to depict, one might safely predict that few would get as far as recognising the sunrise, much less the ocean. Perhaps this is an extreme case but the principle is clear, and that is that a great deal yet remains to be done in exploring the etymology of music, before its language can be interpreted. The language of the various instruments of an orchestra is ascertainable and definable, and should be lifted above argument and debate as regards its essential principles.

CHAPTER XIII

HANDBOOK OF PHYSIOLOGY, 1950
(*Extracts*)

See TABLES X, Y, Z

DURING the five years from 1945 to 1950 the attitude of physiologists towards the science of the body altered in many respects. Less attention was paid to meticulously detailed anatomical analysis and more towards reliance upon common-sense views to provide major premises for reasoning and argument. In consequence considerable progress was registered in regard to knowledge of the functions of the body and in particular to those of the organs of the encephalon. It was argued that if the brain be an engine of thought then it should conform to the principles governing all engines and thus it came about that the functions of the brain were appraised anew on these lines. It was obvious at the outset that the cerebral hemispheres corresponded to the controls of an engine, whether stationary or mobile, but there the analogy seemed to end. However, Control was duly accepted as the first and dominating function of the encephalon and then progress was gradually made on the following lines:

(2) THE ARCHEPALLIUM OR HIPPOCAMPI

It became an accepted practice in studying any organ to concentrate upon the behaviour of the particular animal or groups of animals in which such an organ was abnormally well-developed. Now the hippocampus is abnormally well-developed in certain reptiles and fishes in relation to other animals, especially in the turtle, and consequently this creature was selected for observation. In these animals the hippocampus is in no way the curiously shaped organ that it is in man but appears as a ganglionic lobe intervening between the corpora striata and olfactory bulbs. As the result of considering the habits of the turtle it became obvious that here was an animal which usually made its home on an island and which nevertheless swam out to sea for long distances out of sight of land without any fear of being unable to find its way back. Therefore the chances were ten to one that it had a very active sense of direction, since it could only lift its head a few inches above the level of the sea and even on calm days could not command much of a view. It then became clear that the odds were in favour of the hippocampus, which had no other known function, being a sense-organ of direction, especially in view of its situation in the forepart of the head and the fact that the olfactory bulbs are directive organs in all the higher animals, especially in dogs, who are used as trackers on that account. The only obvious method by which a directive sense-organ could act would be by being able to estimate the angle between its path and that of the magnetic meridians which it crossed and consequently intensive tests were carried out with young turtles in tanks with a view to ascertaining the manner in which they reacted to the lines of force of magnetic fields created by powerful electro-magnets. The results confirmed the hypothesis that the hippocampus was a sense-organ of direction and moreover one of extreme sensitiveness. The question then arose as to whether the hippocampi (major and minor) in man had any useful function and it was suggested that they served as amplifiers of other sense impressions in view of their being in communication with the thalamus (or thalami) where all information collected by exteroceptors and interoceptors are sorted out and integrated. Since bears have a good sense of direction and very keen perceptions permission was obtained from the Finnish Government to shoot some of its surplus bears and extract their hippocampi. These organs were then crushed and administered to selected subjects with the result that it was definitely established that they contained some substance, probably in the form of a hormone, which notably increased the acuteness of perceptiveness of the special sense-organs. Hence the hippocampi were classified from that time onwards as the gauges or indicators of the brain-engine, bearing the same relationship to the cerebral hemispheres that vivid imaginativeness does to considered judgment in the region of psychology.

(3) The Corpora Striata

Each of the two corpora striata consists of two nuclei, the caudate and the lenticular, and all four ganglionic masses lie on the motor tract of the crura cerebri which connects the hemispheres with the medulla. The motor nerves from the hemispheres do not however run straight through them but terminate in their substance from which new origins arise. It is evident therefore that these organs must have important functions to perform and since there can hardly fail to be a centre in the brain charged with the duty of forming habits of specific muscular co-ordinations and this centre must be motor and not sensory and must work in conjunction with the muscular sense, it is not surprising that many physiologists in the last century should have regarded the corpora striata as centres of co-ordinated automatic action for the voluntary muscles. This would involve their being reflex centres but for the fact that few sensory nerves can be traced as terminating in them. In the early stages of embryonic life they act as the floor of the nascent cerebral hemispheres. No human organisation can exist if the heads have to supervise so much routine work that they have no time to consider new developments, and it is irrational to suppose that the cerebral hemispheres which are organised as organs of progressive thinking should be unable to delegate routine muscular co-ordinations to some inferior centres. Modern research has definitely established the fact that the corpora striata control the rate of combustion of the muscle fuels, fat, oil, and glycogen (in the form of glucose). Too rapid combustion overheats the blood and when blood which is above the normal temperature reaches the corpora striata they retard the rate of combustion and this has the inevitable effect of putting the brake on muscular activity. Majendie affirmed that these organs excited backward movement, which might well be the case if they are of the nature of brakes, for human beings and animals normally move forward and at times have to exercise braking action to reduce their momentum to avoid accidents. He stated that if these organs were removed automatic movement proceeded in a forward direction without let or hindrance. It is evident that any brain centre charged with the functions of executing automatic co-ordinated movements of the muscles must be provided with a mechanism for checking them as required, for without them it would be difficult to perform rapid discontinuous movements. Thus it became generally accepted that just as the hippocampi furnished the gauges of the brain engine, perhaps the major gauges of exteroceptor sensations and the minor of interoceptor sensation, so the corpora striata were capable of being used as brakes to check muscular-osseous momenta. All motorists know that the mere cutting off of the fuel supply to the engine introduces a brake action due to internal friction of the moving parts of the machinery.

(4) The Pineal Gland—The Thalami—The Hypothalami

The Pineal Gland or Coronarium is a reddish-coloured organ about the size of a pea which is situated on the upper part of the junction of the two thalami, where they make contact with the Corpora Quadrigemina. It contains particles of lime salts which have received the name of brain sand though they contain no silicon. The gland is attached to the thalami by two peduncles. Rowntree, Clark, Steinberg, and Hanson injected pinealin into four successive generations of rats and described the third and fourth as precocious dwarfs, which confirmed the belief previously held that the pineal gland was a regulator of the rate of cell-metabolism with a tendency to retard the same rather than accelerate it. The effect of pinealin upon the tuartera lizard, in which the gland is well developed, is to make it the most sluggish animal in existence, for it seeks to conserve all its nerve energy for prolonging its existence rather than by frittering it away on unprofitable activities. It is said that a movement over a distance of one foot costs it a year of its life. Some physiologists regard the pineal gland as controlling the activities of all other glands in such a manner as to prevent them functioning too rapidly. The disease of the muscles known as muscular dystrophe is accompanied by calcification of the pineal gland. The Austrian neurologist Von Hochwart reported a case of a boy of five who suddenly began to develop rapidly in all respects and in a few months became like a boy of thirteen. His intellect became correspondingly precocious. But he soon exhausted his vital forces and a post-mortem examination revealed the existence of a tumour on the pineal gland, which may possibly have affected the adjoining corpora quadrigemina. It should be clear from the foregoing that we have in the pineal gland a third and most important element in our Brain Engine, that is a reliable flywheel which can only race under exceptional circumstances but which normally is rather more inclined to slow down from friction consequent upon the weight of the axle upon the bearings.

The pineal gland like a flywheel is an automatic control, and so also are the thalami and hypothalami. The thalami are the oldest organ of the encephalon with which consciousness may be definitely associated. Lesions in its substance have been proved to be concomitant with impairment of the auditory, visual, and tactile senses. All sensory impressions which reach the brain, whether from extero- or interoceptors, must first of all be congregated in the thalami, so that they are able to keep the brain fully informed regarding the internal state of the body and the effect upon it of passions, emotions, and desires. Berman says of the thalami in his book, *Glands regulating Personality*, 1928, p. 127, "It (the thalamus) seems to mediate the most primitive form of consciousness of emotion, an awareness of the condition of the viscera as they respond to the environment. When the thalamus is diseased, the individual may suffer attacks of forced laughing, crying, automatic screaming or shivering, disturbances of mimicry and emotional responses. In the human being the thalamus has specific connections with the various lobes of the brain which dominate the most complex phases of any behaviour." It seems clear that the pineal gland must derive all sensory impressions, which enable it to control the rate of metabolism, from the thalami (the two chambers of the thalamus) to which it is attached. The hypothalamus is known to control all automatic and instinctive body processes. It must therefore be a motor organ as well as a sensory organ and as such has something in common with the pineal gland, which may be said to be its father while the thalami are its mother. A flywheel is a motor organ in view of the fact that it is fixed to a rotating shaft driven by the piston and cylinder of the engine, but by itself it has no means of preventing an engine from racing and so gradually increasing its own momentum. To equip it with this means it is geared to a governor in the case of a steam engine which automatically throttles the steam in the main pipe by closing a valve and so cutting off the supply of power to the cylinder to some extent until equilibrium has been restored between it and the load. Thus we must think of the counterpart of the pineal gland, the thalami, and the hypothalami, as the flywheel and governor of a steam-engine.

(14) THE CORPORA QUADRIGEMINA

The Corpora Quadrigemina are four ganglionic bodies of small size which rest upon a transparent arched lamina forming the roof of the Aqueduct of Sylvius, a channel which conveys the fluid secretion of the chorioid gland to the fourth ventricle. The anterior pair are known as the nates. The physiologists who experimented with these glands in the early part of the last century were unanimous in believing that they were connected with the visual sense and called them the optic lobes in consequence. But experimenters in the present century regard them as relay stations for messages travelling from the ear to the cortex of the temporal lobe. However, the whole question of the function of these bodies came to be reviewed from a wider aspect as time progressed, taken in conjunction with the physiological peculiarities of the Rodents. It had been long recognised that of all animals the great apes had developed the faculties of control by the cerebral hemispheres to the highest pitch of efficiency. The Bears, in turn, were studied as affording examples of the highest development of the spinal-peripheral and autonomic nervous systems. The bears have very keen senses and being great wanderers have a well-developed sense of direction and locality. It was their nervousness and irritability which was the cause of the degrading sport of bear-baiting becoming so popular in this country because teasing the animals never failed to rouse them to paroxysms of fury. The study of the corpora striata naturally produced the best results when it was focused on massive and muscular animals such as the pachyderms, most of which, such as the elephant, the rhinoceros, and the tapir, are fond of charging with great speed yet are able to check themselves and come to a halt within remarkably short distances. The temper of the Ruminants, which is essentially phlegmatic, affords evidence of its belonging to the category of the metaphorical flywheel. Since many of them are used to draw vehicles and carry burdens, oxen, reindeer, llamas, and camels, they learn automatically how to equilibrate between the energy which they are able to put forth and the demands made upon it by man. The llama in particular flatly refuses to allow itself to be overworked or overloaded. Most of the ruminants are thyroid and parathyroid subjects. Erratic secretion of thyroxin has been proved to have a repercussive effect on the thalami, and the parathyroids which control the secretion of calcium salts cause calcification of the pineal gland when they work inefficiently. Following an appreciation of the foregoing facts physiologists concentrated upon the Rodents, especially hares and rabbits, in seeking to ascertain the true functions of the corpora quadrigemina. The whole question revolves round the functions of the respiratory system, which in turn is related to the auditory, for it is the former which produces the intelligible sounds perceptible by the ear. The rodents are on the whole small and poorly equipped for aggressive warfare and have to be very much on the *qui vive* to escape their numerous foes, both feathered and four-footed. Hares have very acute hearing, as is evident from the size and conformation of their ears. They have well-developed chests and lungs which enable them to run at high speed for long distances, and their reflexes are active, which enables them to start running on the slightest warning. Rabbits, rats, squirrels, marmots, and chinchillas have the same capacity. Brunton as the result of his experiments on birds affirmed that electrical stimulation of the corpora quadrigemina produced deeper respiration and so prolongation of the cardiac beats. Ferrier found that in rabbits a slight puncture of the organ caused the subject to start suddenly and bound away as if in fear. Electrical stimulation caused retraction of the ears and extension of the jaws. Many physiologists have stated their belief that the corpora quadrigemina assisted in co-ordinating muscular movements. The Rodents as a class are notoriously timid and for very good reasons, the hare being despised for lack of courage though the female will defend its young with energy. The capacity which the hare possesses of running under forced draught and Brunton's experiment on the effect of the corpora quadrigemina on respiration were regarded as giving the clue to the main purpose of these organs, which was to enable respiration to keep pace with the demands made upon it, especially in emergencies, and so to act as draught-fans do in the case of steam-engines and super-chargers do in the case of internal combustion engines. The connection of the organs with the sense of hearing would enable them to get ready for a quick move should any suspicious sound fall upon the ear. Hearing is associated with the sense of fear more than sight because if we can see an object we know the worst whereas if we can only hear a noise made by it the imagination at once gets busy to conjure up all sorts of catastrophic possibilities. This is especially the case at night when even hardened campaigners are liable to get jumpy and misinterpret noises. Birds are temperamentally not unlike rodents for they not only have abnormally acute hearing but are able to fly away at a second's notice. Their lung-power is prodigious, especially in the case of migrants, and their breasts are well developed in proportion to the rest of their bodies. The fact that the lark is able to sing loudly while soaring upwards is of itself a proof that it possesses exceptional lung development.

(15) THE PITUITARY GLAND

The pituitary gland lies at the base of the brain and is enclosed in a bony case called the Turkish saddle. It has two lobes, of which the front one, which is found in the higher animals, develops from the embryonic mouth cavity, while the rear one is found in animals as far down in the scale as echinoderms. The complete gland is no bigger than a pea yet it secrets far more hormones than any other gland and to a certain extent governs the activities of all other glands, except the pineal, and helps to maintain the balance between them. It is essentially an administrator and equilibrator and comes under (15), the number of Libra, the Scales. In the East the pituitary gland has always been connected with the heart and circulation and those in whom it is active are said to be intuitive, sympathetic, sociable, harmonious, artistic, and idealistic, in fact they conform to the astrological Libra type. Amphibians and fishes have a double set of hormones which enable them to change colour with rapidity for purposes of camouflage or to attract the opposite sex. Chameleons and dolphin fishes head the list of these colour specialists. No evidence of an experimental kind is available to show that the pituitary gland controls the heart's action but the hormone called pitressin constricts the arteries and maintains the tone of the capillaries, and it may well assist the heart's action. Since the gland is absolutely dependent upon the heart and the circulatory system to distribute its hormones it is profoundly interested in maintaining them both in working order. The pituitary assists in energy transform-ation, expenditure, and co-ordination, and insufficient secretion becomes apparent by incapacity to maintain continuous effort and liability to be easily fatigued. The heart needs plenty of energy, for it has to pump continuously day and night to maintain the circulation of the blood, working with perfect rhythm at a specified rate and expending the same amount of energy at all times in performing its normal functions.

It was the fact of the obvious analogies between the activities of the pituitary gland and of the heart and their undoubted physiological association which, when appreciated, led men to regard the gland as the heart of the encephalic system and as the piston, cylinder, and valves of the cerebral engine. For the heart is a true mechanical contrivance and acts like a pump in drawing a certain amount of liquid into a chamber of a certain volume and then contracting the walls of the chamber so that the contents are forced past a one-way valve. The pump effects the contraction of the volumetric capacity of the chamber by means of a movable piston head, but the result is the same.

(16) THE CEREBELLUM—LATERAL LOBES
(18) THE CEREBELLUM—MEDIAL LOBE
(17) THE PONS VAROLII

It has long been known that the cerebellum was a centre of balance but from the date of Gall all phrenologists, and of recent times an emnient physician, Dr. Bernard Hollander, have stoutly maintained that it is also associated with the sex-instinct and is a factory of sexual energy. The controversy still goes on and few text-books of physiology say anything about the functions of the organ except that it automatically maintains the balance of the body in standing, whether at rest or in motion. Dispassionate onlookers who weigh up the evidence mostly come to the conclusion that the lateral lobes are primarily concerned with equilibration and the medial lobe with the manufacture of sex-force or, if preferred, of energy which may be used for purposes of procreation but is by no means confined to them. Cerebellar energy in fact conforms generally to the kundalini or serpent-force of the Hindus, which can be so transmuted that it has little or no effect in producing sexual excitement. Consequently the possession of a large and heavy medial lobe by any individual or racial type affords no positive proof that the sexual propensity is abnormally active in either. A broad-viewed consideration of the problems involved, coupled with the realisation that the Pons Varolii formed a triad with the medial and lateral pair of lobes of the cerebellum, led physiologists to agree that, in tracing out the analogies between the functions of the brain and those of a steam engine, the medial lobe should be regarded as the furnace, the pons as the boiler, and the lateral lobes as the main steam pipe. It should be appreciated that by far the greater part of the energy of the brain comes from the food digested in the alimentary canal and further assimilated by the lymphatics and that this must of necessity pass upwards through the medulla to some part of the brain which is adapted to convert its energy content into a form capable of utilisation by the organs of the encephalon. One must not push the analogy with the steam engine too far, however, for in no sense is the pons interposed between the medial and lateral lobes of the cerebellum, but the principle holds good that somewhere in the brain there must be created a head of potential energy which enables it to be distributed in kinetic form and responds instantaneously to emergency calls. We may liken the medial lobe to a pump which draws water from a well and forces it upwards to a water-tower carrying a tank and thus creates a head for the mains distributing water to a district. Alternatively we may think of the medial lobe as an electric battery or dynamo which charges up accumulators to a given potential. This latter may well accord more closely with the anatomical facts, for it is easy to conceive of the pons being equipped with cells capable of acting as accumulators for motor nerve energy upon which the lateral lobes may draw either continuously or in emergencies. The distribution of energy by two lateral lobes strikes one as appropriate in the case of animal bodies which are bilaterally symmetrical. Whether or not the lateral lobes of the cerebellum control the balance of energy supplied to the vital organs of the body has not yet been proved but the chances are that it supplies working energy to the pituitary gland just as the main steam pipe leading from a boiler supplies steam to the cylinder as regulated by the slide valve. The pons is well placed for distributing energy to the lateral lobes for it is composed of commissural fibres which connect them together, hence its name of the Bridge. These are superficial but there are also deep fibres running to the crura or peduncles of the cerebrum and cerebellum. The posterior surface of the pons is composed of two nerve bundles ascending from the medulla and it contains a grey substance, the nuclei pontis, consisting of cells which are round, oval, or spindle-shaped, and these are so connected with nerve fibres as to form a complete network. It is the nuclei pontis which might conceivably be containers of potential energy especially as they form networks. Brown-Séquard held that the transmission of sensory impressions in the pons was chiefly effected in the central portion while the anterior portion was mainly instrumental in conducting impulses of the will to the muscles.

(19) THE MESENCEPHALON OR TUBER ANNULARE

Before dealing with the Mesencephalon (which should be distinguished from the Mesocephalon) we shall have to consider three modes of activity which dominate the entire nervous system, encephalic and peripheral alike. They are the Constrictive of Col. III, the Relaxative of Col. II, and the Alternating of Col. I. The first is characteristic of the behaviour of solid matter including frozen water, the second is characteristic of that of fluids, especially of air, and the third is characteristic of that of ether, which is the source of vibrations in which constriction and relaxation alternate. In the sphere of government Constriction is seen in severity and disciplinarianism and Relaxation in concessivism, yielding, and compromising. Governments are often faced with the problem as to whether to enforce authority and risk disturbances or allow it to lapse temporarily and risk leniency being taken advantage of. A salient instance of this dilemma is furnished by that which faced Rehoboam, the son of Solomon, when he ascended the throne of Judah and Israel. The people sent representatives to him to beg him to lighten the yoke which his father had imposed upon them, whereupon he consulted the elder statesmen who gave him what astrologers would call Aquarian advice and told him to speak peaceably to his subjects. Then he consulted his companions of his own age and they gave him Scorpionic advice to the effect that he should add to his father's burden and chastise his subjects with scorpions. Rehoboam oscillated between the two policies for a while like a true son of Leo who likes to deliberate before acting and then accepted the advice of his own boon companions with disastrous results. The natural mode of activity of the brain, that is the cerebral hemispheres, is deliberative or alternating, weighing up pros and cons and saying, "To be or not to be, that is the question." That of the directive organs, as represented to some extent by the executive, is necessarily tentative because it involves trying to peer into the future. That of the forceful organs, like the corpora striata, is constrictive, because they control the muscles which move the bones of the skeleton by contraction and at all times bind them together. The parathyroids, which as we have seen have a connection with the pineal gland, can cause severe muscular constriction under certain pathological conditions, and the very fact that the pineal gland restrains metabolism proves that its influence is constrictive. All distributive and circulatory systems are from their very nature relaxative in character and this applies especially to the lymphatics. The physiologists and anatomists of the early part of the last century attached considerable importance to ascertaining to which of the three pathological forms of the primary modes of activity any organ was predisposed, these forms being epileptic (Col. I), paralytic (Col. II), and tetanic (Col. III). Dr. Todd, who experimented with the corpora quadrigemina, assigned them definitely to the epileptic class which justifies their being placed in Col. I. If they control Respiration then clearly this function must be placed in the alternating class since it involves alternations between inspiration and expiration. Similarly if the central lobe or vermiform process of the cerebellum is asociated with the genital organs then its action is of the epileptic kind as exemplified in the act of parturition. Furthermore the peristaltic movements of the bowels, which when too strong produce griping, are of the alternating class. And so we come to the Tuber Annulare of (19) which Dr. Todd classed as unmistakably epileptic. This organ, which is also known as the Mesencephalon, is a projection or boss on the surface of the medulla which contains a considerable amount of vesicular matter. It is a complicated organ and Longet who experimented with it was confident that it was an independent centre of both motor and sensory activity and with Dr. Todd classed it as epileptic because electrical stimulation of it produced convulsive movements. Fort, in his *Physiologie Humaine*, quoted authorities who held that the Tuber was a centre for the control of automatic movements, both in standing and moving. This means in effect that it is a centre of control under the domination of the automatic or instinctive will, which can and does deliberate, but conceals its debates. The control exercised by this organ is easily distinguishable from that exercised by the lateral lobes of the cerebellum which is distributive and in a pathological form paralytic, for over-indulgence in alcohol produces the paralysis of the drunkard, which causes staggering in its early stages and coma in its later. Thus there appears to be little doubt that compartment (19) is the proper place for the mesencephalon, which is *ipso facto* then constituted the ruler of the Spinal-Peripheral system.

(20) THE 12 PAIRS OF CRANIAL NERVES

The 12 pairs of Cranial Nerves have their origins in the undersurface of the brain, some being motor, some sensory, and some mixed. Of these 10 pairs supply the head and 2 pairs the body. The last-named which are known as the 10th and 11th, the Vagus and Spinal Accessory, should be given the two lowest of the numbers, 11th and 12th, to be symbolically accurate. The 1st pair, the Olfactory, are purely sensory, and the 2nd pair, the Optic, are the nerves of sight. The 3rd, 4th, and 6th pairs move the eyeballs. The 5th Trigeminal pair are facial and supply motor impulses to the muscles of mastication. The 7th pair or Facial control the muscles of expression. The 8th pair are purely auditory and convey impressions relating to balance as well. The 9th pair or Glossopharyngeal control muscles of the tongue and convey gustatory impressions. The 10th pair or Vagi send branches to many vital organs of the body. The 11th pair or Spinal Accessory are concerned with voice production and general muscular effort and are chiefly motor. The 12th pair or Hypoglossal controls the muscles of the tongue. It will be observed that of the 12 pairs of cranial nerves no less than four are connected with the eyes, three being motor and one sensory. The 12 pairs of Cranial Nerves fall into the lower harmonic of the Archepallium and the sense of Direction. This organ may also, as we have seen, serve to amplify all sense impressions transmitted to the brain, especially those of special sensation, auditory, visual, olfactory, and gustatory. The cranial nerves, being eminently distributive in so far as their motor activities are concerned, must clearly be placed in Col. II. It is difficult to see any analogies between the cranial nerves and any constituent part of a steam engine. Symbolically (20) represents volatile fuels such as petrol and alcohol in relation to the coal, peat, and wood of (19) and the former are only used with internal combustion engines. The question then arises as to whether the cranial nerves may not be able to convey sensory energy to the brain in sufficient quantity to assist in raising the potential of energy stored in the Pons Varolii.

The parasympathetic nerves of the autonomic system which travel in the 3rd, 7th, 9th Cranial nerves must be included in compartment (20).

(21) THE MEDULLA OBLONGATA—THE OLIVARY BODIES

The Medulla Oblongata may be described as a bulbous terminal situated at the top of the spinal cord which connects it with the pons, the crura (peduncles) cerebelli, and the crura cerebri. It was classed by

Dr. Todd as a tetanic organ and belongs therefore to column III. Injury to it causes instant death and humane killers used by butchers are designed to send bullets straight into the medulla of animals which have to be slaughtered. The organ has an anterior and posterior medial fissure like the spinal cord. In spite of its relatively small size it contains innumerable reflex centres of primary importance in the maintenance of vital functions. In its substance are two or three centres which control respiration and others which govern closure of the eyelids, sneezing, coughing, sucking, salivary secretion, deglutition, vomiting, dilatation of the pupils, mimetic expression, acceleration and inhibition of the heart's action. It contains the chief vasomotor centre, a convulsive centre, co-ordinating centres for reflexes of the spinal cord, and a sweating centre. These are all independent of conscious volitional control but the medulla also contains voluntary masticatory and speech centres.

The Olivary Bodies may be regarded as the representatives of the autonomic system in the organisation of the medulla. They are embedded in its substance and send out processes to every important centre, being especially related to the sensory tract. Lockhart Clarke considered that the olivary bodies were not only centres for co-ordinating muscular movements expressive of passion, desire, or emotion, but that they contain motor centres through which movements are effected under the stimuli of sudden, violent, or peculiar impressions impinging on the special senses.

The part of a steam engine corresponding to the medulla is the condenser, the purpose of which is to reduce the temperature of the steam emitted from the cylinder to a minimum. According to one of the fundamental principles of thermodynamics the amount of work obtainable from an engine is proportional to the fall in temperature between the boiler and the condenser and on the same principle the amount of work obtainable from the cerebellum is determined by the fall of energy potential between the pons and the medulla. That some fall of potential must occur is inevitable but the medulla may well be so constituted that the fall is increased to a maximum. The action of a condenser as the name implies is bound to be constrictive.

(22) THE SPINAL CORD AND VERTEBRAL GANGLIA
(23) THE PULMONARY AND CARDIAC PLEXUSES
(24) THE MOTOR AND SENSORY SOMATIC NERVES

Continuing with the diagrammatic construction illustrative of the nervous system, it is obvious that the spinal cord with its two chains of sympathetic ganglia must be placed in the central column III. The pulmonary and cardiac sympathetic plexuses belong to the Respiratory compartment (23). In an analysis of the Circulatory System (14) accommodates the Pulmonary Circulation. This leaves (24) for the 31 pairs of motor and sensory spinal somatic nerves the first of which are under the control of the will, being cerebro-spinal and not sympathetic.

Dr. Todd found the spinal cord to be tetanic as well as the medulla. The nerves which control the lungs and heart, both of which function rhythmically, must obviously be rhythmic themselves. The distributive spinal nerves must be placed in the same column as the distributive cranial nerves, both of which are more prone to become paralytic than tetanic or rhythmic because they draw energy away from its source and often waste it. The tetanic nature of the spinal cord may be seen in the fact that it contains reflex centres which control coughing, sneezing, and hiccuping.

(25) THE SYMPATHETIC SYSTEM
  PREVERTEBRAL GANGLIA, SOLAR PLEXUS, ETC.
(26) THE PARASYMPATHETIC SYSTEM. FIBRES OF THE PNEUMOGASTRIC AND SPINAL ACCESSORY NERVES
(27) THE MESENTERIC AND HYPOGASTRIC PLEXUSES

The Sympathetic System consists primarily of two chains of sympathetic ganglia situated on either side of the spinal cord, three splanchnic nerves on either side, the prevertebral ganglia, and the abdominal plexuses of which the solar plexus is the chief. The Parasympathetic System in the body consists mainly of fibres which travel in the pneumogastric and spinal accessory nerves and which supply energy to the same organs served by the sympathetic system. The Pelvic and Sacral plexuses, which contain fibres from both the preceding systems, may be placed in compartment (27), this being the lower harmonic of (18) of Table H which contains the Alimentary and Generative systems. The sympathetic and parasympathetic systems balance each other and have complementary functions. The former comes into action when new situations have to be met which require the taking of special measures involving the supply of energy to various organs. These may entail constriction or dilatation but are always stimulative in character and are directed to secure increase of output from the organs which they serve. The latter comes into action when the bodily organs stimulated by the sympathetic system have to be restored to their normal condition. The whole organisation of the Autonomic system is incredibly complicated and it is impossible to represent it here with anything like an approach to detailed accuracy, but on the other hand it is important to indicate how it may be worked in with the general scheme as applied to the physiology of the peripheral nerves. The system of control is elaborate and works independently of the will, though on the other hand it is profoundly affected by emotional changes and states. One cannot say that either of the two major systems is predominantly constrictive or dilative in its action, but any severe disturbance of the sympathetic system tends to produce paralysis, since a blow delivered in the region of the solar plexus causes the phenomenon which we describe as being winded. Analogy suggests that the parasympathetic nerves are liable to become tetanic under abnormal conditions, but the statement cannot be proved. It is generally agreed that the autonomic system is the most ancient of the peripheral systems and that we share it with the less advanced forms of life. During sleep when all voluntary control is in abeyance the autonomic system ensures that the vital functions are carried on with the maximum efficiency.

All important organs of the body are supplied with both sympathetic and parasympathetic branches so that they are maintained in a state of healthy balance. The nervous energy of the sacral parasympathetic system is really a blend of the two forms of autonomic energy which produce a third. Normally this latter discharges and works by alternations of constrictive and relaxative stimuli which are governed by many kinds of body rhythms, but if it becomes unduly accumulated and is then suddenly discharged it may cause spasms and even convulsions of a highly dangerous character which are almost epileptic. The pelvic and sacral plexuses govern the movements of the alimentary canal, and the bladder, and also the functions of sex.

There is no intention of questioning the generally accepted teaching of physiologists that the sympathetic and parasympathetic balance each other, or should do so in the healthy subject, but rather that imbalance, when it occurs, produces disturbances which are either epileptic, paralytic, or tetanic. Epileptic imbalance, when it occurs, may be of four kinds according as it affects the cerebral, respiratory, alimentary, or reproductive systems. The nephritic system occupies a position between the respiratory and alimentary systems. All the brain rhythms of the body emanate from the cerebral hemispheres, though some may be modified by the corpora quadrigemina. They are mostly correlated with time-cycles of the solar system, which include lunar months and days. The cells of the body are renewed once in seven years. The period of gestation of the embryo is ten lunar months, and the interval between feminine periods is one lunar month. Night and day corresponds roughly with sleeping and waking states. Animals have usually annual mating seasons. Man's constitution demands one day's rest in seven, at the least, and longer working periods have been found to provide insufficient relaxation. There are of course brain rhythms in addition which are confined to the brain and are characteristic of different states of consciousness, and it is these that are disturbed in true epilepsy. Instead of the brain waves being generated rhythmically with regular accentuations their regularity is completely upset, the result being reflected in the pulsations generated by the medulla and spinal cord which affect the voluntary muscular system.

The development of the potentialities of rhythmic breathing is a science of the East. Prana or solar energy is drawn into the etheric body by combining breathing with mental concentration. In the form of Yoga known as Laya breathing is employed to control the kundalini, the basis of sex attraction. Many of the exercises are, however, dangerous for anyone to carry out without supervision by a skilled teacher. Lung rhythms involve regularity in expansion and contraction which under certain conditions may be transmuted into vibration. It has affinities with reciprocal motion. Expired air passing through the vocal cords is the primary agent in voice production and its associated vibrations.

The alimentary canal propels its contents and ultimately evacuates them by the travelling rhythmic contractions known as peristaltic movements, in which intensity or amplitude, wave length and rate of wave propagation are all concerned. The churning movements by which food is mixed up in the stomach also come under the heading of rhythmic though they involve no propagation, other than the contractile movement necessary to empty the stomach contents into the duodenum.

The womb expels the matured foetus by violent contractions which give rise to severe pains. The bladder also expels urine, usually by voluntary control but sometimes by involuntary spasms.

The possibilities of paralysis arise chiefly in the working of the distributive systems of the body, viz. the spinal-peripheral, the circulatory, and the lymphatic, and may supervene in consequence of interruption of nerve impulses or blockage of vessels and canals. The executive effectiveness of a motor nerve depends upon the inviolability of the chain of command. The strength of a chain is measured by its weakest link. The failure of a single neuron to transmit its message would render the activity of all the remaining neurons of the nerve fibre ineffective. Any permanent break in a motor nerve causes paralysis of the muscles or glands which it serves. The moral counterpart of reception and transmission of an impulse from above is obedience just as that of reception and transmission of a sense impression from below is truthfulness. A clot in an artery or arteriole induces the equivalent of paralysis in the organ which it serves, namely perishing from malnutrition. Similarly undue sluggishness of the lymphatics produce disease through paralysis of what is largely a drainage system.

The basis of tetanic imbalance is the disfunctioning of systems concerned in the accumulation of energy. The results sometimes resemble epileptic convulsions when large accumulations of energy, which should have been permitted to filter away gradually, suddenly break loose as in volcanic eruptions and earthquakes. The tetanic rigidity is the first stage of tetanic imbalance. It normally affects the muscular system in the form of cramp, brought about by the braking of the minute engines which collectively cause muscular contractions. Certain forms of parathyroidal disease produce cramp. We really need a fourth term to describe irregular glandular secretion, which is due to the raising of potential above normal and lowering it below normal so that the gland pours out too much or too little of its characteristic secretion. In column III we have the glandular syndrome of (13) and the hepatic system of (17) as in Table H.

THE GLANDULAR OR COLLOIDAL SYNDROME

The term syndrome as used here is intended to denote a group of related organs, though its usual technical meaning is a group of related symptoms. The existence of a special glandular syndrome began to be suspected as the result of classifying the physiological systems shown on Table H. There could be no doubt about the limitations of all the systems except the Thyroidal from the Encephalic to the Alimentary-Reproductive and the question then arose as to whether the Thyroid were not the chief of a glandular system of its own which constituted a syndrome. This possibility became a probability when the various physical forces concerned in the physiological systems came to be considered, for the Muscular-Osseous was clearly forceful and mechanistic; the Respiratory was primarily elastic in the popular sense of extensibility and not rigidity; the Circulatory was concerned with the equalisation of temperature; the Lymphatic made free use of solution, differences of osmotic tension, diffusion, and capillarity; the Liver was the laboratory for crystalloid chemistry; and the Reproductive if not also the Alimentary was largely concerned with the forces of electro-magnetism, not only as stimulating and regulating chemical reactions but as specialised in the form of animal magnetism. The only major physical form of energy omitted in this list is the colloidal and the thesis was then provisionally accepted that the Thyroid was the chief colloidal chemist of the body. All animal tissues are colloidal and organic, it is true, but glandular secretions are nearly all colloidal suspensions and the Glandular Syndrome specialised in these, especially in the all-important one of milk. Attention then became focused on the Ruminants, the chief of which, namely Cattle, had not only large and active thyroids but with some of the other ruminants were the sole members of the animal kingdom which supplied milk to mankind. The further question then arose as to whether the differentiation of the leading genera of the Ruminants did not proceed on the lines of the organs of the Glandular syndrome. The Oxen had without doubt the largest thyroids not only as compared with non-ruminant mammals but with the other genera of ruminants. Following out the same scheme the Antelopes, the nearest relatives of the cattle, should specialise in the parathyroids. This was not so easy to prove as less was known about the functions of the parathyroids, but the hyper-parathoidal temperament in human beings was known well enough and it was invariably nervous and intractable. Now not a single species of antelope has ever been domesticated, whereas most Deer are easily tamable and the reindeer are to the Lapps and Esquimaux in the far north what cattle are to the rest of mankind in temperate and tropical parts. The Deer are noted not only for the size, spread, and complex design of their antlers but for the extraordinary speed with which these are formed. The architectural mechanism of their production is not fully understood but it can only be effected by skin glands first and foremost whether hormones from the thyroid and parathyroids are utilised as well or not. The skin possesses certain glands which secrete internally a substance called dermosterol, deficiency of which causes rickets owing to incomplete absorption of lime and phosphorus salts. Those in whom the thyroid is too active and the parathyroids too sluggish are liable to the same disease. Now horn is not bone, it is an epithelial growth at the outset but bone tissue with lime and phosphorus is quickly formed in the horns as they develop. It is known that lipides and lipoids are active cell-builders and are mostly sterols, the chief being cholesterol and ergosterol, and these may well be products of skin-glands like dermosterol. It is known that cholesterol is freely secreted by the adrenals. The efficiency of the chorioid gland in goats is easily proved. Ever since the last war (1914-18) it has been known that shell shock was liable to affect the chorioid gland adversely and impair the value of its secretion, mainly because of its proximity to the thalami which receive all the shock-sensations in the first instance. Now shocks are part of the goat's ordinary life for he is very combative, has a thickened skull over the frontal sinus and possesses a pair of strong horns permanently fixed to his skull. Wild goats of the male sex engage in furious battles with each other during the rutting season and it is said that when they leap from heights they land by preference on the frontal sinus and base of the horns. The hurricane charge of an angry he-goat is well described in the Vision of the He-goat and the Ram in Dan. vii. The fact that a he-goat is not only equipped for charging but appears to enjoy it points unmistakably to his chorioid gland being above the average in respect of efficiency. The ceratous glands of the ears are designed to preserve the elasticity of the drum, and though we cannot prove that these glands secrete more freely in sheep than in other ruminants it is well known that their hearing is more acute and far more discriminative. No other ruminants will follow a man or pay any particular regard to his commands except draught-oxen and reindeer when spoken to from a short distance, whereas sheep will respond to calls and whistles from a long distance in the East where they are taught to do so. When Christ said "My sheep hear My voice and I know them and they follow Me, but a stranger will they not follow for they know not the voice of a stranger," He spoke from firsthand acquaintance with the facts. The vicuña or wild llama of the Andes has abnormally keen sight and the domestic species has large limpid eyes which are obviously well lubricated by lacrymeal glands. It is well known that the camel has very active mucous glands in its nasal organs and the upper part of its throat, otherwise the gritty particles of sand, which it cannot help drawing into its nostrils while journeying through the desert, especially during sandstorms, would produce inflammation of the nasal fossae. In plants sharp crystals embedded in the tissues are always surrounded by an envelope of mucin to prevent them causing damage. The milk of the giraffe is very rich and nutritious, a fact vouched for by Dr. Vevers of the Zoological Society in a letter to the writer.

There is plenty of evidence to show that all animals can be classified on the same lines by the simple process of comparing the secondary analyses of them with those of the fundamental physiological systems (Table H). There are of course many cases in which tabular correspondences cannot be proved from anatomical or physiological evidence for lack of experimental data. As regards Apes and Monkeys the chimpanzee (11) has the keenest senses of any of the genus. The orang-outang (12) is very muscular, perhaps as much so as the gorilla. The rare kerit or mountain ape (13), not yet seen by any European, is said by experienced native hunters to have a glowing pineal eye in its forehead. Monkeys (14) are noted for their lung-power and gibbons (15) must have strong hearts judging from their tireless gymnastic exercises. Baboons (16) are noted for their sense of balance and capacity for maintaining equilibrium which is much more necessary for rock-climbing monkeys than tree climbing, for the latter are able to grip branches with their hands and feet.

The pachyderms and pigs provide many verifiable correspondences. The elephant specialises in tendons and the muscular sense which registers their tensions, as do most dynamic and mobile animals. The hippopotamus specialises in ligaments as do most strong animals which are relatively immobile. It does not need strong bones because it is partly supported by the water in which it habitually lives. The rhinoceros, on the other hand, needs very strong bones, especially of the legs, to support its weight on land and enable it to indulge in shock tactics. The rock-rabbit or coney, like the Rodents generally, possesses much elastic cartilage and the tree-coney, which is perpetually wailing, enjoys lung-exercise which involves exercise of the cartilaginous ribs. The joints of the tapir are specially well lubricated for it loves to run round in circular forest tracks which it makes for itself, for hours at a time. The porcine tribe and the fatty tissues are certainly no strangers. Not much evidence can be obtained from the Rodents though most of the higher species have well-developed respiratory organs.

The association of the lion with the heart is psychological rather than physiological, as may be seen in Richard I's title of Cœur-de-lion. Lions when tamed as cubs show the most remarkable devotion to their masters. Regulus, one of the four Royal Stars, is called Cor Leonis. The spleen is the ruler of the Lymphatics and secretes a hormone which, since it admittedly stimulates the peristaltic action of the bowel, must also encourage the flow of lymph in the Lymphatics. The members of the Canine tribe are notoriously splenetic, though whether the hyæna, the ruler of the Dogs, is particularly so there is no evidence to show. The adrenals, the glands of fight and fright, correspond with the jackals who exhibit a strange combination of courage and cowardice. The whole Equine tribe is liverish and also sweats readily unlike the Dogs. Certainly the horse and even more so the ass are made to sweat in the service of mankind. Among the Mustelidæ, the otter corresponds to the stomach and is well known to be as voracious as the glutton, being able to clear a stream of all good fish in a surprisingly short space of time. Most of the Mustelidæ have scent glands situated near the anus which render them offensive to the nostrils of man. This applies specially to the skunk.

The main phyla of animals can be classified on the same basis. *See* Table Q.

General Summary and Conclusion

The purpose of an Organon, part of which is to check the prevailing trend in the West to segregate all branches of knowledge into watertight compartments, is lucidly set forth by P. D. Ouspensky in his *Tertium Organum* in the following passage: "We do not understand many things because we too easily and too arbitrarily specialise. Philosophy, religion, psychology, mathematics, the natural sciences, sociology, the history of culture, art—each has its own separate literature. There is no complete whole at all. Even the little bridges between these separate literatures are built very badly and unsuccessfully, while they are often altogether absent. And this formation of special literatures is the chief evil and the chief obstacle to the correct understanding of things. Each 'literature' elaborates its own terminology, its own language, which is incomprehensible to the students of other literatures, and does not coincide with other languages; by this it defines its own limits the more sharply, divides itself from others, and makes these limits impassable. But there are movements of thought which strive, not in words but in action, to fight this specialisation."[1] How far the attempt to prove that time is a fourth dimension of space, which is Ouspensky's speciality, is likely to achieve the object which he sets before him may be problematical, but the aim and purpose considered by themselves are admirable. The *Philosophy of Analogy and Symbolism* constitutes an attempt to provide at least a common language for the various branches of knowledge and to furnish a means by which they can be interpreted in terms of each other. But it can do little more than provide a *prima facie* case until the major natural sciences are subjected to primary, secondary, and even tertiary analyses. For instance, the Physiological Table H by itself does not add much to our knowledge of the classification of the organs of the body, but when each of the first nine compartments is further subdivided into nine on precisely the same principles as the first nine, then a definite scheme of classification begins to appear which presents many points of interest and suggests a number of possibilities which would not otherwise occur even to an expert. In the case of elaborate organs such as the eye or ear a further tertiary analysis can be made. Needless to say that it is the formal sciences which lend themselves most readily to refinements of analysis. Table Z shows the general scheme on which the various departments of knowledge are organisable, but no attempt can be made here to justify it as archetypal and it must simply be regarded as a convenient list until it can be discussed in detail and a secondary analysis of its 13 compartments made.

[1] 1937, p. 309.

TABLE A

The Twelve Fundamental Processes of Psychology

See Chapter III

II	III	I	Columns / Tiers	
			Colours	
(2)	(3)	(1)	Electrum.	I
(6)	(4)	(5)	Amber.	II
(7) (Law).	(8) (Philosophy. Ethics).	(9) (Religion).	Conscientious Mind. Purple.	III
(11) Directive Association.	(12) Constructive Association. Effort.	(10) Equilibrative Association.	Conative Mind. Blue.	IV
(15) Conception of Space.	(13) Conception of State. Memory.	(14) Conception of Time.	Subjective Mind. Green.	V
(16) Individualistic Construction. Agreement.	(17) Hedonistic Construction.	(18) Impulsive Construction. Impulse.	Objective Mind. Yellow.	VI
(20) Immediate Presentation.	(21) Realism. Negation.	(19) Unit Concept.	Instinctive Mind. Red.	VII
(24)	(22) (Subconscious Memory).	(23)	Preconscious Mind. Brown.	VIII
(25)	(26)	(27)	Subconscious Mind. Grey.	IX
(29)	(30)	(28)	Basic Mind. Black.	X

TABLE B

Analysis of Logic

See Chapter IV

II	III	I	Columns / Tiers
(2)	(3)	(1)	I
(6)	(4)	(5)	II
(7)	(8)	(9)	III
(11) Deduction. Theory.	(12) Induction. Super-generalisation.	(10) Proposition. Assertive and Hypothetical.	IV
(15) Synthetic Evidences. The Probable.	(13) Belief. The Certain.	(14) Logical Argument. The Possible.	V
(16) Explanatory Generalisation. Regulative.	(17) Explanatory Generalisation. Classificatory.	(18) Explanatory Generalisation. Teleological.	VI
(20) Empirical Generalisation. Qualitative.	(21) Empirical Generalisation. Quantitative.	(19) Empirical Generalisation. Quidditive.	VII
(24)	(22)	(23)	VIII
(25)	(26)	(27)	IX
(29)	(30)	(28)	X

TABLE C

ANALYSIS OF GRAMMATICAL PARTS OF SPEECH

See Chapter IV

II	III	I	Columns / Tiers
(2)	(3)	(1)	I
(6)	(4)	(5)	II
(7)	(8)	(9)	III
(11) Verbs.	(12) Nouns.	(10) Pronouns.	IV
(15) Adverbs of Adaptation.	(13) Adverbs of Fixation.	(14) Adverbs of Condition.	V
(16) Pronominal Adjective.	(17) Qualitative Adjectives.	(18) Quantitative Adjectives.	VI
(20) Interjections.	(21) Prepositions.	(19) Conjunctions.	VII
(24)	(22)	(23)	VIII
(25)	(26)	(27)	IX
(29)	(30)	(28)	X

TABLE D

The Twelve Fundamental Principles of Mysticism
See Chapter V

II	III	I	Columns / Tiers
(2)	(3)	(1)	I
(6)	(4)	(5)	II
(7)	(8)	(9)	III
(11) Involution.	(12) Evolution.	(10) Repetition.	IV
(15) Space-organisation.	(13) Karma.	(14) Time-cycles.	V
(16) Incarnation.	(17) Incorporation.	(18) Generation.	VI
(20) Conduct.	(21) Environment.	(19) Government.	VII
(24)	(22) Stabilisation.	(23)	VIII
(25)	(26)	(27)	IX
(29)	(30)	(28)	X

TABLE E

The Twelve Principles of Mystical Philosophy

See Chapter VI

II	III	I	Columns / Tiers
(2)	(3)	(1)	I
(6)	(4)	(5)	II
(7)	(8)	(9)	III
(11) Symbols.	(12) Configurations.	(10) Fiat.	IV
(15) Colours.	(13) Numbers.	(14) Sounds.	V
(16) Letters.	(17) Forms.	(18) Words.	VI
(20) Magical Acts.	(21) Sacraments. Charms.	(19) Mantras.	VII
(24)	(22)	(23)	VIII
(25)	(26)	(27)	IX
(29)	(30)	(28)	X

TABLE F
THEOSOPHICAL PLANES AND WORLDS
See Chapter VI

Note—There are 8 Worlds below the Great Boundary which are identical with the Theosophical Planes. These may be classified as 12 Spheres, (13) to (24). The four lower Astral Subplanes extend from (19) to (22). The World Ovoid consists of the 8 Worlds or 12 Spheres.

II	III	I	Columns / Tiers
(2)	(3)	(1)	I
(6)	(4)	(5)	II
(7)	(8)	(9)	III
(11) Lower Adi.	(12) Anupadaka. Great Boundary.	(10) Higher Adi.	IV
(15) Buddhi. World of Life Spirit. New Jerusalem.	(13) Upper Nirvana. World of Virgin Spirits. Still Eternity.	(14) Lower Nirvana. Atma. World of Divine Spirit. New Zion.	V
(16) Upper Mental. World of Abstract Thought. Mount Morish.	(17) Lower Mental. World of Concrete Thought. Mount Zion.	(18) Astral. Desire World. Paradise.	VI
(20) Lower Physical World. Gaseous and Liquid.	(21) Physical World Solid. Subphysical.	(19) Upper Physical World. Etheric.	VII
(24) Proserpinal World.	(22) Upper Plutonic World.	(23) Lower Plutonic World.	VIII
(25)	(26)	(27)	IX
(29)	(30)	(28)	X

TABLE G
HEAVENS AND HIERARCHIES
See Chapter VI

II	III	I	Columns / Tiers
(2)	(3)	(1)	I
(6)	(4)	(5)	II
(7)	(8)	(9)	III
(11) 8th. Elohim. Angels of Presence.	(12) 7th. Planetary Logoi. Angels of Presence.	(10) 9th. Powers or Fiery Lions.	IV
(15) 6th. Angels of Heat and Cold. Messengers of Fathers.	(13) 4th. Angels of Sanctuary. Sparks.	(14) 5th. Angels of Fire and Wind. Sacred Animals.	V
(16) 3rd. Angels of Four Seasons. Crocodile Spirits.	(17) 2nd. Angels of Snow and Frost. Race and Group Spirits.	(18) 1st. Angels of Thunder and Lightning. Astral Angels.	VI
(20) Moon. Sublunary. Moon Spirits.	(21) Earth. Nature Spirits.	(19) Sun. Subsolar. Sun Spirits.	VII
(24)	(22)	(23)	VIII
(25)	(26)	(27)	IX
(29)	(30)	(28)	X

TABLE H

Physiological Systems

See Chapter VI

II	III	I	Columns / Tiers
(2)	(3)	(1)	I
(6)	(4)	(5)	II
(7)	(8)	(9)	III
(11) Cerebro-Spinal. Autonomic.	(12) Muscular-Osseous. Fat.	(10) Cerebral. Cerebellar.	IV
(15) Cardiac-Thymic.	(13) Thyroidal-Mammary.	(14) Respiratory. Urinary.	V
(16) Lymphatic.	(17) Hepatic.	(18) Alimentary. Generative.	VI
(20) Skin. Papillary Layer.	(21) Skin. Epidermis.	(19) Skin. Corium.	VII
(24)	(22)	(23)	VIII
(25)	(26)	(27)	IX
(29)	(30)	(28)	X

TABLE I
Archetypal Pattern of Grand Man. Human Skeleton
See Chapter VI

II	III	I	Columns / Tiers
(2)	(3)	(1)	I
(6)	(4) Head.	(5)	II
(7) Collar-bone.	(8) Neck.	(9) Shoulder-blades.	III
(11) Fingers.	(12) Arms.	(10) Hands.	IV
(15) Breastbone.	(13) Upper Backbone. Dorsal Vertebrae.	(14) Ribs.	V
(16) Pelvic Spines. Ischium.	(17) Lower Backbone. Lumbar Vertebrae. Sacral Bone.	(18) Hips.	VI
(20) Toes.	(21) Legs.	(19) Feet.	VII
(24)	(22)	(23)	VIII
(25)	(26)	(27)	IX
(29)	(30)	(28)	X

TABLE J
Graeco-Latin Gods, Planets, and Zodiacal Signs
See Chapter VII

Note.—It follows inevitably from this Table that there should be considerable differences between the correspondences of signs and planets as indicated and the traditional correspondences accepted by astrologers.

II	III	I	Columns / Tiers
(2)	(3)	(1)	I
(6)	(4)	(5)	II
(7)	(8)	(9)	III
(11) Diana. Moon. Aquarius.	(12) Great Mother. Earth. Scorpio.	(10) Apollo. Sun. Leo.	IV
(15) Venus. Libra.	(13) Vulcan. Taurus.	(14) Mercury. Aries.	V
(16) Mars. Gemini.	(17) Minerva. Asteroids. Pisces.	(18) Jupiter. Sagittarius.	VI
(20) Uranus. Capricorn.	(21) Neptune-Ceres. Virgo.	(19) Saturn. Cancer.	VII
(24) Proserpina. Libra.	(22) Pluto. Taurus.	(23) Adonis. Aries.	VIII
(25)	(26)	(27)	IX
(29)	(30)	(28)	X

TABLE K

The Fifteen Branches of Mathematics

See Chapter VIII

II	III	I	Columns / Tiers
(2)	(3)	(1)	I
(6)	(4)	(5)	II
(7)	(8)	(9)	III
(11) Determinants. Symmetric Functions. Generating Functions.	(12) Infinitesimal Calculus.	(10) Theory of Groups.	IV
(15) Algebraic Forms. Transformations.	(13) Co-ordinate Frameworks.	(14) Expansion of Algebraic Series.	V
(16) Algebraic Equations.	(17) Algebraic Forms. Geometrical Figures.	(18) Logarithms.	VI
(20) Theory of Numbers.	(21) Partition of Numbers.	(19) Arithmetic.	VII
(24) Theory of Probabilities.	(22) Combinatorial Analysis.	(23) Progressions.	VIII
(25)	(26)	(27)	IX
(29)	(30)	(28)	X

TABLE L

Thirteen Arts

See Chapter IX

II	III	I	Columns / Tiers
(2)	(3)	(1)	I
(6)	(4)	(5)	II
(7)	(8)	(9)	III
(11) Drama.	(12) Architecture.	(10) Poetry.	IV
(15) Painting. Drawing.	(13) Mosaic.	(14) Music.	V
(16) Literature.	(17) Sculpture.	(18) Oratory.	VI
(20) Acting.	(21) Ceramics.	(19) Dancing.	VII
(24)	(22) Metal-working. Toreutics.	(23)	VIII
(25)	(26)	(27)	IX
(29)	(30)	(28)	X

TABLE M

The Physiological Senses of Man

See Chapter IX

II	III	I	Columns / Tiers
(2)	(3)	(1)	I
(6)	(4)	(5)	II
(7)	(8)	(9)	III
(11) Direction.	(12) Muscularity.	(10) Balance.	IV
(15) Sight.	(13) Pineal.	(14) Hearing.	V
(16) Smell.	(17) Taste.	(18) Avid Taste.	VI
(20) Contact.	(21) Tension.	(19) Sensitiveness.	VII
(24)	(22) Compression.	(23)	VIII
(25)	(26)	(27)	IX
(29)	(30)	(28)	X

TABLE N

GEOLOGICAL PERIODS AND STRATA. EVOLUTIONARY

See Chapter X

Cainozoic	Quaternary.
Mesozoic	Cretaceous to Permian.
Palæozoic	Carboniferous to Cambrian.
Proterozoic	Upper and Middle Pre-Cambrian.
Archæan. Eozoic	Lower Pre-Cambrian.

Numbers denote millions of years before the Quaternary Epoch.

II	III	I	Columns / Tiers	
(2)	(3)	(1)	Creation Days	I
(6)	(4)	(5)		II
(7)	(8)	(9)		III
(11)	(12) Quaternary zero date.	(10)	Seventh.	IV
(15) Jurassic. Triassic. 180	(13) Tertiary. 60	(14) Cretaceous. 120	Sixth.	V
(16) Permian. 240	(17) Carboniferous. 300	(18) Devonian. Silurian. 360	Fifth.	VI
(20) Upper Cambrian. 480	(21) Lower Cambrian. 540	(19) Ordovician. 420	Fourth.	VII
(24) Upper Pre-Cambrian. 720	(22) Upper Pre-Cambrian. 600	(23) Upper Pre-Cambrian. 660	Third.	VIII
(25) Upper Pre-Cambrian. 780	(26) Upper Pre-Cambrian. 840	(27) Upper Pre-Cambrian. 900	Second.	IX
(29) Middle Pre-Cambrian. 1,020	(30) Middle Pre-Cambrian. 1,080	(28) Middle Pre-Cambrian. 960	First.	X

TABLE O

The Major Geological Revolutions
See Chapter X
O.W. = Old World.
N.W. = New World.

II	III	I	Columns / Tiers
(2)	(3)	(1)	I
(6)	(4)	(5)	II
(7)	(8)	(9)	III
(11)	(12)	(10)	IV
(15) Nevada (minor). N.W.	(13) Alpine-Himalayan. O.W. Cascadian-Laramide. N.W.	(14)	V
(16) Hercynian. O.W. Appalachian-Ouachita. N.W.	(17)	(18) Acadian (minor). N.W.	VI
(20)	(21)	(19) Caledonian. O.W. Tacomic. N.W.	VII
(24)	(22) Charnian. O.W. Killarnean. N.W.	(23)	VIII
(25)	(26)	(27)	IX
(29)	(30)	(28)	X

TABLE P

Present Cosmic Day

See Chapter X

Two Preparatory Days and Seven Creation Days.

Note.—This Table is applicable in principle to the preceding Cosmic Days.

II	III	I	Columns / Tiers
(2)	(3) Cosmic Night-Day = 4,320 m.y. Creation Night-Day = 180 m.y.	(1)	I
(6)	(4)	(5)	II
(7)	(8) Awakening of Deity into Activity. 4.30 a.m. Formation of Pleroma and World-Egg of 8 Worlds. 4 a.m.	(9) Generation of Hierarchies. 5 a.m.	III
(11) 2nd Preparatory Day Abortive Creation of Monstrosities destroyed. 7 a.m.	(12) 1st Creation Day. Shadow Race. 8 a.m.	(10) 1st Preparatory Day. Earth Spirit asks for Inhabitants. 6 a.m.	IV
(15) 4th Creation Day. 3rd Basic Race. 2nd Round 11 a.m.	(13) 2nd Creation Day. 1st Basic Race. 9 a.m.	(14) 3rd Creation Day. 2nd Basic Race. 1st Round. 10 a.m.	V
(16) 5th Creation Day. 4th Basic Race. 3rd Round. 12 noon.	(17) 6th Creation Day. 5th Basic Race. 4th Round. 1 p.m.	(18) 7th Sabbath Day. 6th Basic Race. 5th Round. 2 p.m.	VI
(20) (9th Puranic Day). 7th Round. 4 p.m.	(21) (10th Puranic Day). 7th Round ends 5.40 p.m. 5 p.m.	(19) (8th Puranic Day). 7th Basic Race. 6th Round. 3 p.m.	VII
(24)	(22) Pralaya of Rest begins. Duration—7 Eternities of 270 m.y. each. 6 p.m.	(23)	VIII
(25)	(26)	(27)	IX
(29)	(30)	(28)	X

TABLE Q

Classification of Animals

See Chapter X

II	III	I	Columns / Tiers
(2)	(3)	(1)	I
(6)	(4)	(5)	II
(7)	(8)	(9)	III
(11) Lesser Land Mammals. Marsupials.	(12) Sea Mammals.	(10) Greater Land Mammals.	IV
(15) Dragons.	(13) Lesser Land Mammals. Edentata, etc.	(14) Birds.	V
(16) Reptiles.	(17) Amphibians.	(18) Fishes.	VI
(20) Cyclostomes. Bivalves. Cephalopods.	(21) Annelids. Echinoderms. Entozoa.	(19) Crustaceans. Insects. Arachnids.	VII
(24) Porozoa. Anthozoa. Infusoria.	(22) Brachiopods. Rotifera. Polyzoa.	(23) Chordata. Ctenophora. Medusae.	VIII
(25) Protozoa.	(26)	(27)	IX
(29)	(30)	(28)	X

TABLE R

Classification of Plants
(Abridged)

See Chapter X

II	III	I	Columns / Tiers
(2)	(3)	(1)	I
(6)	(4)	(5)	II
(7)	(8)	(9)	III
(11)	(12)	(10)	IV
(15) Angiosperms. Monocotyledons. Liliiflora.	(13) Angiosperms. Dicotyledons. Forest Trees, etc.	(14) Angiosperms. Monocotyledons. Grasses.	V
(16) Angiosperms. Monocotyledons. Palms.	(17) Gymnosperms. Dicotyledons. Coniferae.	(18) Gymnosperms. Dicotyledons. Screw-Pines.	VI
(20) Fungi. Sea-weeds. Lichens.	(21) Oscillating Algae. Diatoms. Mucous Bacteria.	(19) Cycads. Ferns. Mosses.	VII
(24)	(22) Bacteria Viruses.	(23)	VIII
(25)	(26)	(27)	IX
(29)	(30)	(28)	X

TABLE S

Analysis of Stationary Engines
Steam Engines (S.) and Internal Combustion Engines (I.C.)

See Chapter XI

II	III	I	Columns / Tiers
(2)	(3)	(1)	I
(6)	(4)	(5)	II
(7)	(8)	(9)	III
(11) Gauges and Indicators	(12) Brakes. Springs.	(10) Voluntary Controls.	IV
(15) Cylinder and Piston. Valves.	(13) Flywheel. Governor. (S.)	(14) Draught. Forced and Natural. (S.) Carburettor. (I.C.)	V
(16) Main Steam Pipe. Valve. (S.) Feed Pipe. Carburettor to Explosion Chamber. (I.C.)	(17) Boiler. (S.) Explosion Chamber. (I.C.)	(18) Furnace. Ignition. (S.) Magneto. Sparking-plug. (I.C.)	VI
(20) Explosive Fuels. Petrol. Producer Gas. (I.C.)	(21) Condenser. (S.) Coolers. (I.C.)	(19) Non-explosive Fuels. Coal. Wood. (S.)	VII
(24) Lubricating Mechanism.	(22) Silencer. (I.C.)	(23) Whistle. Hooter. (S.)	VIII
(25) Mechanical Petrol Feed. (I.C.)	(26) Safety Valve. (S.)	(27) Mechanical Stoker. (S.)	IX
(29)	(30) Frame. Bed.	(28)	X

TABLE T

PHILOLOGY. ANALYSIS OF SPEECH ORGANS

See Chapter XII

II	III	I	Columns / Tiers
(2)	(3)	(1)	I
(6)	(4)	(5)	II
(7)	(8)	(9)	III
(11) Nostrils. Nasal Fossae.	(12) Roof of Mouth. Hard Palate.	(10) Roof of Mouth. Soft Palate. Curtains. Uvula.	IV
(15) Lips.	(13) Tongue. Tip. (Cheeks).	(14) Pharynx. Eustachian Tubes. Third Tonsil.	V
(16) Teeth.	(17) Tongue. Body. (Cheeks).	(18) Gullet or Oesophagus. Tonsils.	VI
(20) Gums.	(21) Tongue. Back and Root. (Cheeks).	(19) Epiglottis. False Vocal Chords.	VII
(24) (Chin).	(22) (Bed of Tongue).	(23) (Larynx).	VIII
(25)	(26)	(27)	IX
(29)	(30)	(28)	X

TABLE U

Classification of Consonants

See Chapter XII

II	III	I	Columns / Tiers
(2)	(3)	(1)	I
(6)	(4)	(5)	II
(7)	(8)	(9)	III
(11) Nasals. M.N.	(12) Aspiro-Sibilants. ZH. SH.	(10) Mute Aspirates. H.	IV
(15) Labials. B.P. BH. PH.	(13) Palato-Lingual or Reverberant. R. RH. Lingual. L. LH.	(14) Sounded Aspirate. H.	V
(16) Dentals. D.T. DH. TH.	(17) Dental—Sibilants. DZ. TS.	(18) Gutturals. G.K. Hard C.	VI
(20) Labio-Dentals. V.F. VH. FH.	(21) Sibilants. Z.S. Soft C.	(19) Naso-Gutturals. NG. NK.	VII
(24)	(22)	(23)	VIII
(25)	(26)	(27)	IX
(29)	(30)	(28)	X

TABLE V
Classification of Vowels

Diphthong EU (or EW) as in new. (18 + 16)
Diphthong OU (or OW) as in pout. (13 + 15)
Diphthong OI (or OY) as in point. (17 + 18)

See Chapter XII

II	III	I	Columns / Tiers
(2)	(3)	(1)	I
(6) Short EU or OEU, as in French un peu or œuvre.	(4) Short E as in her.	(5) Short E as in bet.	II
(7) Short U as in but.	(8) OY, OI as in boy, modified OW or AU.	(9) Short I as in bit.	III
(11) Medium U as in put.	(12) Short O as in pot.	(10) Short A as in pat.	IV
(15) Modified U as in French tu.	(13) Long O as in pole.	(14) Long I (AY, AI, EI) as in pint.	V
(16) Long U, OO as in pool. Initial W.	(17) Round OW, OU, AU as in pound.	(18) Long E, EE, IE, as in feet. Initial Y.	VI
(20) Long A, AU, AW as in pawn.	(21) Long A, EA as in bare.	(19) Long A, AY as in bane.	VII
(24)	(22) Long A, AH as in balm.	(23)	VIII
(25)	(26)	(27)	IX
(29)	(30)	(28)	X

TABLE W

Classification of Musical Instruments

See Chapter XII

II	III	I	Columns / Tiers
(2)	(3)	(1)	I
(6)	(4)	(5)	II
(7)	(8)	(9)	III
(11) Harp.	(12) Castanets. Sistra.	(10) Metal-wind Class. Animal Horns.	IV
(15) Pianoforte.	(13) Drum.	(14) Wood-wind Class.	V
(16) Lute Class.	(17) Cymbals.	(18) Reed Class.	VI
(20) Viol Class.	(21) Xylophone Class.	(19) Organs.	VII
(24)	(22) Bell Class.	(23)	VIII
(25)	(26)	(27)	IX
(29)	(30)	(28)	X

TABLE X

Classification of the Organs of the Encephalic and Spinal Systems
See Chapter XIII

Relaxative Influence.	Constrictive Influence.	Alternating Influence.	
II	III	I	Columns / Tiers
(2)	(3)	(1)	I
(6)	(4)	(5)	II
(7)	(8)	(9)	III
(11) Archepallium or Hippocampi. Major and Minor.	(12) Corpora Striata. Caudate and Lenticular.	(10) Cerebral Hemispheres. Corpus Callosum.	IV
(15) Pituitary Gland. Anterior and Posterior.	(13) Pineal Gland. Thalami. Hypothalami.	(14) Corpora Quadrigemina. Aqueduct of Sylvius.	V
(16) Cerebellum. Lateral Lobes.	(17) Crura Cerebri. Pons Varolii. Crura Cerebelli or Restiform Bodies.	(18) Cerebellum. Media Lobe or Vermiform Process.	VI
(20) 12 Pairs of Cranial Nerves. 10 Cranial 2 Somatic.	(21) Medulla Oblongata. Olivary Bodies.	(19) Mesencephalon or Tuber Annulare.	VII
(24) Spinal Nerves. 31 Pairs. Motor and Sensory.	(22) Spinal Cord. Motor and Sensory Tracts. Sympathetic System. Vertebral Ganglia.	(23) Sympathetic System. Cardiac and Pulmonary Plexuses. Parasympathetic Nerves from Vagus.	VIII
(25) Sympathetic System. Vertebral Chains. Splanchnic Nerves. Prevertebral Ganglia. Solar Plexus, etc.	(26) Parasympathetic System. Fibres travelling in Pneumogastric and Spinal Accessory Cranial Nerves.	(27) Sympathetic and Parasympathetic Nerves. Mesenteric and Hypogastric Plexuses.	IX
(29)	(30)	(28)	X

TABLE Y

CORRESPONDENCE BETWEEN THE RUMINANTS AND THE GLANDS OF THE THYROID SYSTEM

See Chapter XIII

II	III	I	Columns / Tiers
(2)	(3)	(1)	I
(6)	(4)	(5)	II
(7)	(8)	(9)	III
(11) Antelope. Parathyroids.	(12) Deer. Skin Glands. Internal Secretion.	(10) Ox. Thyroid.	IV
(15) Llama. Lacrymeal.	(13) Goat. Chorioid.	(14) Sheep. Ceratous.	V
(16) Camel. Diffusive Mucous.	(17) Giraffe.	(18) Okapi. Horny Mucous.	VI
(20)	(21)	(19)	VII
(24)	(22)	(23)	VIII
(25)	(26)	(27)	IX
(29)	(30)	(28)	X

TABLE Z
FRAMEWORK TABLE
SCHEME OF BRANCHES OF KNOWLEDGE
See Chapter XIII

II	III	I	Columns / Tiers
(2)	(3)	(1)	I
(6)	(4)	(5)	II
(7)	(8)	(9)	III
(11) Mystical Philosophy.	(12) Theosophy.	(10) Cosmogenesis. Anthropogenesis.	IV
(15) Aesthetic Art.	(13) Organised Religion.	(14) Philosophy.	V
(16) Mechanised Art.	(17) Formal Sciences.	(18) Biological Sciences.	VI
(20) Terrestrial Sciences.	(21) Applied Sciences.	(19) Astronomical Science.	VII
(24)	(22) Geology.	(23)	VIII
(25)	(26)	(27)	IX
(29)	(30)	(28)	X

THE END